The Inner Touch

The Inner Touch
Archaeology of a Sensation

Daniel Heller-Roazen

ZONE BOOKS · NEW YORK

2007

ZONE BOOKS
1226 Prospect Ave.
Brooklyn, NY 11218

Page 12: Illustration by Maximilian Liebenwein from E. T. A.
Hoffmann, *Lebensansichten des Katers Murr* (Zürich:
Amalthea, 1923).

Page 100: D'Arcy Wenworth Thomson, *A Glossary of Greek
Fishes* (London: Oxford University Press, 1947).

Printed in the United States of America.

Distributed by The MIT Press,
Cambridge, Massachusetts, and London, England

Library of Congress Cataloging-in-Publication Data

Heller-Roazen, Daniel.
    The inner touch : archaeology of a sensation / Daniel
Heller-Roazen.
        p. cm.
    Includes bibliographical references (p.   ) and index.
    ISBN 978-1-890951-76-4
        1. Sense (Philosophy) 2. Perception (Philosophy)
3. Senses and sensation. I. Title.
    B105.S45H45 2007
    152.1–dc22

                                            2006051057

Paul Roazen (1936–2005) *in memoriam*

In the absence of "absence of grief"

Contents

hoi Stōikoi tēnde tēn koinēn aisthēsin entos haphēn prosagoreousi,
kath' hēn kai hēmōn autōn antilambanometha.

The Stoics believe the common sense to be an inner touch by
which we perceive ourselves.

(Aëtius, *Placita* 4.8.7)

CHAPTER ONE

Murriana

A Preface to the Work, in which Hegel and
E.T.A. Hoffmann's writing Cat, Murr, consider the Relations
between Sensation and Consciousness

It is night, but a cat is awake and, if we take him at his word, he has never been more alert. Alone in the dark, the principal if not sole narrator of E.T.A. Hoffmann's *Opinions of Murr the Cat* finds himself overcome by the most powerful of sentiments: "feelings of existence" (*Gefühle des Daseins*), as he boldly calls them at the start of the record of his life and thoughts. "There is something so beautiful," the cat exclaims, "so magnificent, so sublime about life!" He recalls the hero of Goethe's *Egmont*, who sought to summon the "sweet familiarity of existence" while preparing, in a "painful instant," to bid farewell to life. But the cat, unlike the tragic personage, is very much alive and well, fully immersed in "that sweet familiarity" in the moment he names it, and he seems quite unable ever to imagine leaving it behind. All around him, the cat senses "the spiritual power, the unknown force, or however one wishes to call the principle that holds sway over us, which," he adds, "has in some way implanted in me the aforementioned familiarity, without my ever having consented to it." His sensibility has raised him to a "high point" seldom, if ever, attained by poets. Moved by the force of his feelings and the agility of his four legs, he has easily "leaped" — or rather, as he corrects himself, "climbed" — up and over the rooftops of the city in which he lives, the better to gaze at it in its nocturnal splendor. His prose betrays the unmistakable tone of an animal delighted with the position to which his natural abilities have brought him: "Over me lies the vaulted, starry sky; the full moon shines its sparkling rays, and roofs and towers stand, in fiery silver brilliance, all around me!"[1]

What does Murr feel as he remains perched at night high above the city? Despite his initial allusions to the famous outburst of "that Dutch hero in the tragedy," the cat seems unwilling to concede that any human being could grasp the full force of his existential sentiments. It is certain that Murr harbors doubts as to the capacities of the two-footed species in general, and that he by no means accepts as self-evident humans' right to rule over the other animals with whom they share the earth. "Is that upright walker on two feet something so great," Murr asks, with noticeable disdain, "that the species called humanity may claim mastery over us all, when we move about with so much more security and poise on our own four feet?" The cat, however, is no ingénue, and he is well aware that human beings have justified their claim to superiority in spite of their relatively feeble limbs. "I know," Murr continues, "that they make a great deal of something that is supposed to sit in their heads, which they call reason." Nevertheless, Murr remains skeptical: "I am not altogether sure of what exactly they mean by that," he comments. "But this much is certain: if I am correct in concluding from certain discourses of my master and patron that reason is nothing other than the capacity to act with consciousness, and not to play any dumb tricks, then I would not change places with any human being."[2]

Murr gives little indication of doubting the existence of that thing "that is supposed to sit" in the heads of humans, "which they call reason." And, from his own experience, he seems quite capable of recognizing the telltale signs of its central organ, consciousness. But the cat nonetheless suggests that the much-lauded faculty may be less important than many have claimed and that, in any case, its presence in the realm of human thought and action is a matter not of nature but of habit. "I absolutely believe," the cat explains, "that one only gets used to consciousness" (daß man sich das Bewußtsein nur angewöhnt). The situation is quite different with that which is common to all the animals, human and inhuman, which the cat experiences as a joy in itself: life. "One comes through life and to life," Murr declares, in programmatic terms, "without ever knowing how. At least that is how it was with me. And from what I hear, it is the same with human beings. Not one of them ever knows the how and the where of his birth from his own experience; they only know of it through tradition, which, it should be added, is often far from reliable."[3]

To the speaking cat, consciousness, therefore, is a thing of modest worth, a derivative being at best. But it is difficult to ascertain exactly where Murr himself stands with respect to the faculty he has often observed in those around him. Does he regard its presence among human beings as useful, albeit inessential? As unnecessary? As pernicious? Has Murr, one might wonder, ever entertained the possibility of acquiring it himself? It is certainly possible that in his eyes, as in those of many of his readers, consciousness lies beyond the province of animal nature. It is also conceivable, however, that the cat deems the faculty of reason accessible to the feline race. Perhaps he would grant that, if they so desired or so required, all the animals could cultivate consciousness, at least as successfully as human beings. This appears to have been the position on the issue represented by Kafka's Rotpeter, for example, who explained in his "Report to an Academy" exactly how he had passed, in captivity and in training, from ape to man: "I learned, gentlemen. One learns, alas, when one must; one learns when one wants a way out; one learns ruthlessly" (*Und ich lernte, meine Herren. Ach, man lernt, wenn man muß; man lernt, wenn man einen Ausweg will; man lernt rücksichtslos*).[4] The question, in any case, would most likely have struck the cat as academic. Hoffmann's feline narrator never knows the hardships of Kafka's incarcerated ape, desperately in search of any "way out" of his servitude, and the cat never appears to have felt compelled to acquire the habits of the rational animal. Nor does he seem ever to have been tempted to "get used" to consciousness for any reasons of his own. Murr shows every sign of being content to abandon himself fully to the sensation of life and its "sweet familiarity."

The cat himself, however, makes few claims for his sentiments and, perhaps on account of his distrust of consciousness, declines to compare them in detail to those of human beings. But Murr's feelings may well have more to do with human perceptions than he explicitly indicates, and it is possible that they even allow him to accede to a region of being sought more than once by "that upright walker on two feet." It is remarkable that the conditions in which the cat senses "something so beautiful, so sublime, so magnificent about life" are exactly those by which one of his better-known contemporaries, Georg Wilhelm Friedrich Hegel, once defined the principles from which the philosophy of nature and spirit must begin. Fifteen years before the publication of *Opinions of Murr the Cat*, Hegel sought to characterize the "simplicity without division" that, he argued, precedes and enables every complex activity of "subjective spirit." He did so by describing a state that he himself qualified as essentially "terrifying" (*furchtbar*) but that seems close to the one so blithely embraced by the cat. In his 1805–1806 Jena lecture course, Hegel explained that in its origin, the "pure Self" is nothing other than "an empty night," which is utterly "*conscious-less*, that is, without being, as an object, presented to representation."[5] And in his essay *The Difference Between Fichte's and Schelling's System of Philosophy*, the young philosopher charged the same image with the task of depicting something still more fundamental, which one might well consider the very principle of principles. "The Absolute," Hegel wrote in that seminal work, "is night, and light is younger than it." It is "the Nothing, the first, from which all being and the multiplicity of the finite emerged."[6]

The reflections of Hoffmann's cat are perhaps best considered in light of this "empty night." It is not difficult to see that, poised above the towers and roofs of his city, Murr confronts a principle that could be called "absolute," an indistinct and insuperable force to which he considers himself consigned, like every other living thing, "without ever having consented to it," and which he calls, with seeming philosophical naïveté, by an old and familiar name: "life." Not that the feline creature succeeds in knowing that which Hegel had described as by definition "*conscious-less*, that is, without being, as an object, presented to representation." At night, at least, Murr knows nothing; in the apparent absence of representation and cogitation, the dark night of the cat remains, by definition, utterly "conscious-less." The cat perceives "the principle that holds sway over us" not by the organ of reason "that is supposed to sit in the heads" of men but by an irreducibly animal faculty, namely, sensation, or, as Murr puts it, "feeling." He appears to need nothing else: one could say that for the cat, as for Faust, "feeling is everything" (*Gefühl ist alles*). For it is by sensing that Murr finds himself delivered over to that simplest and most universal dimension of all things, which is itself no thing: existence (*Dasein*).

Who is Murr the cat, and how are we to understand the "feelings of existence" with which he begins the testament of his thoughts and deeds? It is certainly possible to read the "opinions" of the reflective cat as the expressions of a decidedly human fantasy of natural simplicity, the anthropomorphic fiction of an animal ease unencumbered by the layers of consciousness and self-consciousness that were no doubt all too familiar to the well-read public of Hoffmann's volume. And this is indeed what Meister Abraham, Murr's benevolent patron, seems to suggest in the terms by which he introduces the cat toward the beginning of the book. Pointing out "Murr the cat, as I have named him," to his friend Kreisler, Abraham declares unambiguously, "This is the most reserved, most courteous, indeed the most amusing animal of his kind which one can find, who is lacking only in higher education" (*dem es nur noch an der höheren Bildung fehlt*).[7]

In this sense, the cat may be less an animal of extraordinary capacities than a human being devoid of the superior faculties of the mind, who, in the technical terms of jurisprudence invoked by Abraham, cannot be considered his own man from the point of view of the law, *homo sui juris*.[8] But it is not difficult to see that Hoffmann's cat is just as much a figure for that most advanced of literary personages, the author, and the opening section of the *Opinions of the Murr the Cat* can be said to furnish the reader with

a portrait of the artist as a kitten. Not only is Murr said to be particularly susceptible to "those soft reveries, those dreamy ponder-
ings, sleepwalking trances" that are widely considered hallmarks
of the moments in which one is visited by "the ideas of genius."[9]
By the time we first meet him, the cat has also already written
several books of different genres, the most important of which he
enumerates in the order he wrote them, "lest the world squab-
ble," he explains, "over the succession of my eternal works": a
novel, *Thought and Inkling, or Cat and Dog*; a political treatise, *On
Mousetraps and Their Influence on the Mind and Activity of Catdom*;
and a tragedy, *Kawdallor, King of Rats*.[10]

But the cat's literary activities extend still further, for Murr is
also the author of the very pages that record his many "opinions."
To be sure, E.T.A. Hoffmann, the "editor" of the volume, informs
the reader in the preface to *Opinions of Murr the Cat* that the
bound book is only in part the creation of its ostensibly feline
protagonist. The editor concedes that the cat certainly wrote the
pages of the work in which he speaks in his own name. But Murr
had nothing to do, we learn, with the others interspersed
between them, which are devoted to the life of the mad musician
Kreisler, whose "eccentric, wild, and playful" appearances in the
volume would inspire Schumann's great Opus 16 piano fantasies,
the *Kreisleriana*, barely twenty years later.[11] "Careful research and
inquiry" led the editor to conclude that the passages about the
musician stemmed from a printed book "containing the biography of Kapellmeister Kreisler," which most likely lay in the home
of Murr and his master. While writing, the somewhat distracted
feline author must have periodically and harmlessly shredded its
pages, "in part for padding, in part for blotting"; later, he must
have unwittingly included them in his own manuscript.[12] With
some embarrassment, the editor reports that these "foreign inter-
polations" (*fremde Einschiebsel*) were noticed too late in the print-
ing of the book to be deleted. The most that could be done was to
mark them in the body of the text by editorial abbreviations (*S.S.*
for "Spoiled Sheets," *M.C.O.* for "Murr Carries On"), to ensure
that the readers would not take them for anything other than

what they truly were. (Hence the full title of the published work, a testament to the probity of its editor: *Opinions of Murr the Cat, With A Fragmentary Biography of Kapellmeister Johannes Kreisler in Haphazard Spoiled Sheets.*)

Who is to say, however, what the cat himself really wrote? It is difficult to avoid the impression that the editor may have underestimated his author, for the apparently self-sufficient "biography" of Kreisler turns out to be an account of his good friend, Meister Abraham, and so inevitably also to contain at its center the portrait of that "most reserved, most courteous, indeed ... most amusing animal of his kind" who elsewhere speaks in his own name. One can hardly suppress the suspicion that the duplicity of the work could be something of a feline ruse. In the end, the opinions of the cat and the tale of the musician might well be two sides of a single creation; they could be two movements, so to speak, of one *Murriana*.

At once cat and artist, shredder and author, Murr, whoever and whatever he may have been, remains a witness to an experience that the "upright walker on two feet" has rarely perceived with such clarity. It is the experience of the one sense shared by all the individual senses and felt, however faintly and however intermittently, in all sensation: the sense of sensing, by which we find ourselves, like the existential cat of the empty night, consigned, before or beyond consciousness, to the omnipresent "life ... through which and to which" all animals come, "without ever knowing how." Few living beings can boast faculties as keen as those of the cat in the dark, and it may be that few could match the sensitivity of the nocturnal Murr, driven more than once by that "unnamable feeling" (*unnenbares Gefühl*) to a state of utter senselessness: "That singular feeling, woven of pleasure and displeasure, stunned my senses — overwhelmed me — cannot possibly resist — I ate the herring!"[13]

CHAPTER TWO

The Aesthetic Animal

Of the ancient Philosophers, Aristotle most especially, who, like the
Cat, spoke much of Sensation, little of Consciousness

Like the cat, the ancients spoke little of consciousness and a great
deal of sensing. Classical Greek sources contain several expressions designating an activity of moral introspection close to the
one we now identify with "conscience," the most prominent of
them being *suneidēsis* and *sunnoia* (as well as the corresponding
reflexive verbal constructions, in which conjugated forms could
be accompanied by dative personal pronouns).[1] But it is significant that the vocabularies of both Greek and Latin admit of no
single term that corresponds with any exactitude to our "consciousness," if one takes the modern word, in its current and
well-established sense, as the name for the cognitive faculty by
which we represent our thoughts to ourselves.[2] Not that the various phenomena we associate today with consciousness were
unknown in Antiquity. Classical literature can hardly be said to be
lacking in characters who express a clear awareness of both themselves and their actions, and it has never been denied that the
ancient philosophers, in particular, furnished the history of
thought with many of the most far-reaching accounts of the
nature of reflexivity in the tradition. But it is remarkable that the
classical authors who discussed the nature of awareness and self-
awareness were not especially inclined to speak in terms of
knowledge — or ignorance, for that matter — and they seem to
have done without any general conviction that the phenomena in
question were particularly cognitive in nature. In this respect,

21

their terminology differed fundamentally from that of their modern successors, who came, in large part, to view awareness and self-awareness as forms of cognition: as a "knowing with" in those languages, such as English and the members of the Romance family, that draw on the Latin *conscientia*, or as a form of "that which has been made known" (*Bewußtsein*), to cite the German expression that has been the standard term in the language since Christian Freiherr von Wolff employed it in the early eighteenth century as an equivalent of the Cartesian *cogitatio*.[3] For better or for worse, the ancient philosophers who wrote of awareness and self-awareness tended to employ a set of expressions linked semantically and etymologically to the name of a capacity that, in distinction to reason, has often been viewed as one of the lower faculties of the soul and that, more often than not, has been considered a characteristic as much of animal as of human nature. For they spoke of perception and, more simply still, of what they called sensation.

It is well known that in Greek philosophical works the term *aisthēsis* carries the meanings of "sensation," "perception," and also "feeling," a fact that considerably complicates the interpretation of ancient sources on the abilities of living beings.[4] Plato, Aristotle, the Epicureans, the Stoics, and the Neoplatonists, among others, all discussed forms of *aisthēsis* in their works, but few, if any, of their modern readers would be so rash as to render their many expressions by a single set of corresponding modern terms. The question whether "perception," with its suggestion of activity, should be preferred to "sensation," with its implication of passivity, remains difficult to decide in principle. But it is only part of the problem. The truth is that *aisthēsis* was by no means a technical term in the Greek language, and it could be employed in a range of meanings a good deal wider than the historian of philosophy might wish to admit, which extend well into the terrain of the often-elusive power of awareness that would later be said to be that of consciousness. Thucydides, for instance, employed the term in a sense that seems to have as little to do with perception as it does with sensation; "intellectual discernment" has been proposed as a better English equivalent in this case.[5] Even in Greek psychological writings, the meaning of the term was fluid, and it could stray very far from the field of human perception. At times, it was even employed to mark the affections of the inanimate, in punctual opposition to the animate: a fifth-century treatise in the Hippocratic corpus, for example, has the verb *aisthanesthai* characterize the effects of the wind on lifeless things.[6]

It has been suggested for a number of good reasons that the psychological meaning of *aisthēsis* was something of an Attic invention, unknown to the Ionic authors and the early Greek thinkers but familiar to Plato and Aristotle and generally accepted by those who wrote in the wake of the Socratic school.[7] The diction of Plato's dialogues, however, indicates that even in Athens the meaning of the word could waver considerably. It is instructive, in this regard, to consider the *Theaetetus*, which contains what is perhaps the most programmatic discussion of the term in the Platonic corpus. Here Socrates and his interlocutors, in search of a definition of knowledge (*epistēmē*), briefly consider the possibility that it might be ultimately reducible to *aisthēsis*.[8] Most translators of the dialogue have rendered the term in this setting by "perception," "sensation," or a reasoned mix, such as "sense perception." But it is clear that more than sense data in any modern sense is at issue in the dialogue, for the *dramatis personae* who discuss the term show no signs of doubting that the field of *aisthēsis* can easily embrace affective, as well as perceptual, phenomena. By "senses" (*aisthēseis*), Socrates explains, one means not only "sight, hearing, smell, the sense of the cold and the hot," but also "pleasure and pain, desire and fear; and there are a great many more, of which many have names and of which an infinite number have none at all."[9] The *Timaeus* suggests that an *aisthēsis* can be grasped as any one of the "affections" (*pathēmata*) of the body, and several other Platonic dialogues, such as the *Phaedo* and the *Republic*, find Socrates and his interlocutors using the verb *aisthanesthai* in this sense, for various cases of awareness linked to physical states.[10] But even then, one scholar has written, "it would be rash to assume that the verb means sense-perception . . . for in these cases it is used almost interchangeably with *dokein* and *dox-asthein*, 'to seem' and 'to believe.'"[11] At other points, the Platonic field of application of the term could be still wider: in a passage of the *Apology*, it is suggested that death may be nothing other than the simple absence of all *aisthēsis*.[12] "Obviously," a classicist has written, commenting on these various passages, by Plato's time "*aisthēsis* had become a weasel word. Almost everything that affects a living being could be subsumed under it."[13]

The works Aristotle dedicated to the nature and structure of living beings are, in large part, monuments to the "weasel word" and to the many possibilities it afforded for considering animal experience. A glance at the contents of the treatise on the soul traditionally known as the *De anima* and the nine brief works on animal psychology and biology collected as the *Parva naturalia* suffices to indicate the extent to which Aristotle's doctrine of the soul can be said to constitute, above all, a doctrine of *aisthēsis*. The *De anima* begins with a double introduction, the first of which is historical in nature and occupies the entirety of Book Alpha and the second of which, methodological in intent, fills the first four chapters of Book Beta. Starting with the fifth section of Book Beta, Aristotle turns to the expository dimension of the treatise, which consists in an account of the logically distinct powers whose union defines the soul, the principle of life. In a dense single chapter, the Philosopher discusses the power of nutrition (*threptikon*) by which living beings sustain themselves; in three more, he treats the combined faculties of movement (*kinētikon kata topon*) and desire (*orektikon*); and in the five that soon follow, he presents an account of the structure of thinking (*dianoētikon*).[14]

The place of the sensitive faculty (*aisthētikon*) in the order of the *De anima* is quite different. At the center of his treatise, Aristotle devotes no fewer than ten chapters to sensation; if, following the medieval commentators, one classifies the chapter on the imaginative faculty (*phantastikon*) among those devoted to the senses, their number rises to eleven.[15] As Charles H. Kahn has written, "In terms of fullness of treatment, there can be no doubt:

Aristotle's work on the Soul is primarily a treatise on Sensation."[16] It is supplemented, moreover, by the first four treatises of the *Parva naturalia*, which devote further attention still to the various powers of sense, clarifying and at times completing the doctrines advanced in the larger work on the soul. They are the writings known to the tradition as the *De sensu et sensibilibus*, the *De memoria et reminiscentia*, the *De somno et vigilia*, and the *De insomniis*.

The "faculties" discussed by Aristotle in his works on psychology are stratified in form, and they extend from the most elementary power of nutrition, which is shared by all living beings, to the higher faculties founded upon it, from motion and desire to that most special of capacities, thought, which is said to be the exclusive province of man. On the scale of increasing vital complexity and diversification, a threshold separates those beings with a nutritive faculty, but no more, from those living things with more able souls. It is *aisthēsis*. Plant life, as Aristotle presents it, consists entirely in the power of nutrition (*threptikon*), which includes at once conservation, growth, reproduction, and decline. But animals also possess the power of perception, which grants them access to the many still higher faculties denied the purely vegetative soul. "Sensation" (*aisthēsis*), Aristotle thus writes, "is not necessary in all living things," yet animals, by definition, could not subsist in its absence.[17] The fact bears witness to the equivocation in the basic expression of life, the ambiguity by which "living," as the Philosopher explained, with a characteristic turn of phrase, "is said in many ways" (*pleonakhōs de tou zēn legomenou*).[18] While it is through the principle of nutrition alone that life can be said to "belong to living beings" in general, it is through the principle of sensation that animals as such can be said to be.[19]

Aristotle defines sensation in the *De anima*, using terms that recur in his other works and those of his successors, as "a kind of being moved upon and acted upon [or 'being affected']" (*hē d' aisthēsis en tōi kineisthai te kai paskhein sumbainei*).[20] The terminology he developed for discussing the phenomenon was complex, and it allowed him to distinguish, in principle if not always in fact, between four structurally distinct dimensions, which, in the act of sensation, invariably combine: the perceptual faculty that senses, which Aristotle calls *aisthētikon*; the sensing organ, that is, the part of the body capable of perception, which he calls *aisthētērion*; that which can be sensed, which he generally designates by the term *aisthēton*; and the actual event of sensation, whose sole name is *aisthēsis*.[21]

In Book Beta of the *De anima*, Aristotle teaches that there are five senses (*aisthēseis*): sight, hearing, smell, taste, and touch. To each, he argues, there correspond a proper object (*idion*), a characteristic medium (*metaxu*), and a particular organ (*aisthētērion*). Take, for instance, the sense of sight. Its object is the visible. Its medium is the element Aristotle calls "the transparent" (*diaphanēs*), whose activity is light and whose potentiality is darkness; it is the element in which the visible may emerge.[22] The organ of sight, finally, can be located in the eyes. Sensation, Aristotle continues, constitutes "a kind of mean" (*ti mesotētos*), for it receives the sensible, with the aid of its organ, at a certain point on a continuum between two opposed qualities.[23] The visible object that is seen by the eyes, for example, falls invariably between the extremes of the bright and the dark. So, too, Aristotle reasons, the audible that is heard by the ears sounds, in the air, between the quiet and the loud, and, to take an example from still another sense, the gustable that is tasted in water and in the air, by the tongue and by the nose, can be situated between the extremes of the bitter and the sweet.[24] The sensible object, its medium, and the organ of its apprehension thus constitute formally distinct elements of sensation, which combine, in the event of actual *aisthēsis*, to form a single experience: one always encounters the visible in the transparent medium of light at some point between the extremes of the bright and the dark, and one always senses the audible by means of the ears as it rings, loudly or quietly, in the medium of the air.

To this point the doctrine of sensation proposed in the *De anima* seems without complications and, in principle, applicable to each of the five senses. But the exposition soon grows a good deal less pellucid, and the analogies among the forms of sense

26

appear increasingly uncertain. The difficulties become most intractable with the sense Aristotle presents as the most elementary of the forms of sensible affection, which he treats, for felicity of exposition, last among the senses.[25] "Touch," Aristotle argues, "is the primary sensation that belongs to all animals" (*aisthēseōs de prōton huparkhei pasin haphē*).[26] Sensible life comes into being with the presence of the power of touch and inevitably ends, with perfect symmetry, in its absence.[27] A difference of hierarchy thus separates the tactile faculty from the other senses: the existence of one founds that of the remaining four.[28] But touch seems distinguished still further, on grounds that trouble the sense in which it can be called, in the terms of the *De anima*, a sense at all.

Aristotle clearly established that to each sense there correspond a medium, a sensible object, and an organ. But in this case, the elements of perception seem difficult, if not impossible, to identify. In what sense can touch admit of a medium? Contact would seem immediate by definition. Aristotle argues that it is not so: in fact, he maintains, an interval always separates that which touches from that which is touched, and it alone allows for the possibility of sensation. Consider two bodies that meet in water. Since their edges are not dry, Aristotle reasons, those things that touch "must have water between them, with which their extremities are full."[29] The contact of bodies in air is no different: they too, if they are dry, cannot fail to be separated, no matter how close they may seem, by a layer of air. Whence, then, the impression that the sense of touch, in distinction to that of sight, for instance, knows no distance? "We surely sense all things," Aristotle insists, "through a medium."[30] Only in contact, unlike vision, hearing, and smell, the sensible remains too close, and we cannot perceive the distance that divides us from it; and so, as he twice writes, the interval inevitably "escapes our notice" (*lanthanei*).[31] The proximity of contact comes from this distance, which is no less decisive for being undetectable by sense. It is in the imperceptible space between that which touches and that which is touched that one body can be felt, no matter how closely, to be different from another.

Like the other senses, touch therefore implies a medium, albeit one that vanishes from perception, by definition, in the act of sensation. But what of the organ of this sense? An obvious answer would be flesh (*sarx*), but in the Aristotelian doctrine of *aisthēsis* the outer layers of the animal body have another role to play. "Just as air and water are to sight, hearing, and smell," the philosopher reasons, "so flesh and the tongue are to the corresponding sense-organ of each." Flesh thus constitutes the medium of touch and cannot, for this reason, be its organ. The deduction is irreproachable in its logic. But to illustrate the argument, Aristotle also furnishes a proof. When there is direct contact between the sensible object and the sense organ, no sensation can occur: when something white is placed on the eye, for example, nothing at all can be seen, and, one imagines, when something of a particular odor is set immediately against sensitive membrane of the nose, nothing can be smelled.[32] Were flesh an organ, it would be of such a nature; the superposition of the tactile upon it would inhibit all sensation. But, of course, the opposite is the case. Touch occurs precisely there where the flesh comes into contact with the tangible, separated from it by the subtlest of membranes, which can barely be perceived as such.

Aristotle, to be sure, concedes that flesh possesses a distinctive feature among the media of sensation. This is, simply, that it cannot be separated from the sensing body itself. Unlike air and water, which can be said to "act upon us" in sight and hearing, in touch flesh cannot be said to exert itself on us, as if we were clearly distinct from it. We sense the tangible, Aristotle writes, not "through" a medium but "simultaneously with the medium" (*oukh hupo tou metaxu all' hama tōi metaxu*), for in this case the medium is not distinct from our own bodily form.[33] The quandary nonetheless remains. As a medium, flesh can be no organ. Aristotle concludes that the part responsible for touch must be "internal" (*entos*), but he says no more. One suspects that the enigmatic claim remains at least in part a concession to the demands of doctrine, which stipulate that every sense functions by means of an organ, no less than a medium and a proper sensible object. "The organ of touch is internal," Aristotle writes, "For then the same thing will hold of touch as holds for the other senses."[34]

The question of the tangible proves at least as intractable. Vision, hearing, smell, and taste can all be defined and distinguished from one another, to differing degrees, by their corresponding sensible qualities.[35] The visible that is the object of sight can be told apart from the audible, for instance, with relative ease: seeing, one can perceive no sound, and by hearing one can hardly be said to sense a color. But with the tactile faculty nothing is so simple. A first problem concerns the structure of touch itself, by which it seems receptive to sensible qualities of the most varied sorts. Aristotle has established that to every sense corresponds a single set of opposed sensible qualities: to sight, for instance, the bright and the dark; to hearing, the loud and the soft; to taste, the bitter and the sweet. But "in the object of touch, there are many pairs of opposites: hot and cold, dry and wet, rough and smooth, and so on for the rest."[36] In the *De generatione et corruptione*, the Philosopher extends the list still further: the sensible contraries perceived by touch also include, we learn, the heavy and the light, the hard and the soft, the viscous and the brittle, and the thick and the thin.[37] How to extract, from such diversity, a single differential trait by which to identify the nature of the tangible? Aristotle offers no answer. "The one thing that is the subject of touch, as sound is for hearing," he writes, simply and in conclusion to the discussion of the question, "is not clear."[38]

The most fundamental of the forms of sensation, touch therefore remains, in more than one sense, the most elusive as well. Before the tactile faculty, the criteria developed by Aristotle for the identification of the distinct forms of sensation seem to lose their force, leading unavoidably, in their faltering, to a conclusion nowhere explicitly drawn in the *De anima* itself: one must infer that despite the classic count, touch cannot easily be numbered among any set of five. Not only before but also after the completion of the chapters devoted by the *De anima* to the nature of *aisthēsis*, "it remains a question," in the words of the Philosopher, "whether touch is many or one."[39] Apparently the first of the set of sensitive faculties, the tactile power seems to shelter within it the possibility of all the others that follow it in the development and progressive differentiation of the powers of the sensitive soul. For to the extent that all five senses operate in a medium and so by means of contact, "they all," as Aristotle writes in the last chapter of the *De anima*, "sense by touch" (*haphēi aisthanetai*).[40]

One can understand, therefore, how the Philosopher could explain in passing that by the term "sensible" he meant simply "tactile,"[41] and how, for him, "tangible qualities" were ultimately equivalent to "the qualities of the body as a body" (*diaphorai tou sōmatos hēi sōma*).[42] With touch, the Aristotelian analysis of perceptual awareness arrives at its most elementary term, but also its limit, the point at which the forms and structures of sensation reach their shared source in a principle as universal, and as indistinct, as that of animal life itself. In the ancient theory, which accorded no particular privileges to consciousness or its absence, the principle held equally for all those beings for whom to live, simply put, was to perceive. The sensitive soul in the classical doctrine encountered nothing if not by contact, and the terrain of the tactile body remained everywhere as wide, and as varied, as that of *aisthēsis* itself. Where, in such a world, to set the bounds beyond which touch cannot venture, the limits at which sense grows dull, obliged to relinquish its rights to the more subtle powers, desire and movement, imagination, memory, and intellection? In the age of the domination of the knowing being, the question is a pressing one, but it appears not to have occurred to the ancient philosopher. Thoughtful or thoughtless, conscious or not, the life of the animal, in his eyes, remained a matter of tact before all else.

CHAPTER THREE

The Primary Power

Containing Aristotle's Doctrine of the common Sense,
the master Faculty by which Animals sense that they are sensing

The treatment of touch in the *De anima* announces a transition. The last chapter in the exposition of the doctrine of the five senses, the discussion of the nature of contact leads to the end of an important section of the work, which, in the modern editions of the classical text, assumes a decisive form no reader could mistake: soon after the completion of the analysis of touch, the second book of the treatise comes to a close, clearing the way for the discussion of the more differentiated faculties of the soul in the third and final part of the work. One can certainly accept the justice of this textual partition and minimize the ties that bind the analyses of sight, hearing, smell, taste, and touch to the considerations that immediately follow them, which unequivocally abandon the problem of the identification of the five senses. But the next three chapters nevertheless continue resolutely along the path of those that precede them, and at no point can they be said to leave the terrain of *aisthēsis*. They turn, with increasing force and precision, to more complex powers of sensation, starting with a dense discussion of a question first raised by the consideration of touch: that of a perceptual power that, extending throughout the body of the living animal, cannot be reduced to the activity of any one sense. For this reason, a number of modern editors of the *De anima* have observed that although they are separated from those of Book Beta by a book division, these chapters have as much to do with the discussion that precedes them as with that which follows them.[1] It was clearly for this reason, too, that the classical Arabic editors of the Aristotelian text decided, with a resolve at once philosophical and philological, simply to append all three sections to the end of Book Beta.[2]

Aristotle begins his considerations by formulating a difficulty in need of clarification. There are no more senses (*aisthēseis*), he maintains, beyond the five already discussed, yet on their own the numbered faculties cannot account for the full range of sensuous experience. The Philosopher opens the discussion by considering a perceptual phenomenon to which he has already alluded once before, the "common sensible qualities" (*koina aisthēta*): motion, rest, figure, magnitude, number, and unity.[3] When, for example, one perceives that something is moving, or at rest, or square, or large, or three, or one, by means of what sense does one do so? Aristotle makes it clear that such sensible qualities cannot be said to impress themselves upon the soul through any one of the forms of sensation he has already discussed. As he has defined them in the preceding chapters, the five senses remain exclusively bound to their various proper objects, from the visible to the tactile, whatever its nature. They cannot be said to apprehend any qualities other than their own, if not "incidentally" and "by accident" (*kata sumbebēkos*), as when one sees that "this white thing," a visible object of its own, happens to be the son of Darius or Cleon.[4] But the Philosopher is equally unwilling to concede that the common qualities are the objects of a sixth sense, independently apprehended and subsequently joined to the sensible objects of one or all of the five senses. For the common sensible quality, as he has already declared, is "sensible by itself" or "absolutely" (*kath'auto*), and it belongs to its nature to be perceptible, in one act, by more than a single sense.[5] The movement of a body, for instance, can be sensed immediately, by touch or by sight, and from this elementary apprehension one may in turn derive that of the other common sensible qualities, magnitude (*megethos*), figure (*skhēma*), and rest (*stasis*) being all, in differing ways, modifications of movement.[6]

The problem is inescapable. The common sensible qualities

cannot be referred to the activity of the five senses, at least as they have been defined to this point; nor can they be attributed, for that matter, to a sixth sense, specially suited to their apprehension. Aristotle offers no immediate solution to this difficulty. He proceeds, instead, to consider another form of sensation that exceeds the bounds of the five senses as he has presented them. It is the experience of complex sensation, in which one perceives, in a single moment, a number of sensible qualities of different types. Each sense, the Philosopher has by now well established, "discerns differences in its sensible object" (*krinei tas tou hupokeimenou aisthētou diaphoras*): by definition, sight, as he has explained, distinguishes the bright from the dark, as taste tells the sweet from the bitter.[7] But the faculty of sense also does more, for which the doctrine of the five senses cannot easily account. "We also distinguish the bright and the sweet," Aristotle continues, "and we compare all objects perceived by each other, and it is by some principle that we sense their differences."[8] Unlike many of his modern counterparts, Aristotle will not hold that as a form of "discernment" (*krinein*) such perception belongs to a field of judgment distinct from sense.[9] To him, the apprehension of complex sensible qualities is still very much a matter of *aisthēsis*, albeit of a kind whose nature remains unclear. "It must evidently be by some sense," he comments, "that we perceive the difference, for they are objects of sense."[10]

The limitations of the theory of the five forms of perception proposed to this point now come fully to light. The sense of sight can clearly distinguish between the bright and the dark, as the sense of taste can tell the sweet from the bitter. But how, in the terms afforded by the second book of the *De anima*, can one explain the sense that something is bright and also sweet, or, alternately, the perception that something is bright but not sweet? The particular sense can perceive the difference that defines its own proper object, but it can do no more; the apprehension of the conjunction and disjunction of sensible qualities lies beyond it. After maintaining that there are no more than five senses, Aristotle would seem obliged, for the explanation of the phenomena that he himself has adduced, to posit a further power among the capacities of the sensitive soul: a faculty that coordinates, unifies, and distinguishes the five senses, while coinciding, at the same time, with none.

In the *De anima*, however, the Philosopher takes no such step. He further complicates the problem, raising the question of yet another form of sense, as irreducible to the functions of sight, hearing, smell, taste, and touch as the perception of the common sensible and the complex sensation. To the modern eye, it is perhaps the most striking of the phenomena attributed by the classical philosopher to the realm of *aisthēsis*. It is the sense of sensing, the mere feeling that something at all is felt. Aristotle observes that the activity of a such a sense cannot easily be explained: "Since we sense that we are seeing and hearing [*epei d' aisthano-metha hoti horōmen kai akouomen*], it must either be by sight that one senses that one is seeing or by another [sense]. But in that case there will be the same [sense] for sight and color, which is the object of sight. So that either there will be two [senses] for the same thing or [the sense] itself will be of itself."[11] By what power can one account for the "sense that we are seeing and hearing," which Aristotle takes to be self-evident? On the surface, both the answers suggested by the Philosopher in this passage lead to perplexity. If it is by the sense of sight that we perceive that we are seeing, he reasons, then the sense of sight must be said to have not one but two objects: the proper sensible quality of vision will be not only the visible, as he has until now maintained, but also the mere fact of vision, and it will be necessary to reject the doctrine developed in the preceding sections of the treatise, according to which to every particular sense there corresponds a particular quality, grasped by means of an organ in a medium at a point between two extremes. But if, instead, it is by a sense other than sight that we perceive that we are seeing, the problem still cannot be said to be solved. It seems, if anything, more pressing. For what will one say of this second sense: does it, too, perceive that it perceives the fact of vision?

To answer in the affirmative would be to open the door to an endless regress, in which to every sense there would correspond another, responsible for sensing the fact of its sensing. The visible would be sensed by sight, and, to this degree, the analysis of sensation proposed by Aristotle would still hold, but the activity of sight would then be sensed by a second sense, and the activity of the second sense, in turn, would be sensed by that of a third, in a vertiginous multiplication of senses to which no limit could be set. Aristotle chooses to end the series before it has begun. He opts for the second solution he proposed, no matter how troubling to his account of the proper objects of the senses. Considering the possible solutions to the perplexity, he reaches his decision: "Either the process will go to infinity," he writes, "or there will be some sense that is [the sense] of itself [*ē eis apeiron eisin ē autē tis estai hautēs*]."[12] Rejecting the infinite regress implied by the idea of a sense turned toward a sensing distinct from itself, Aristotle thus admits, despite the analysis he has already given, that the senses perceive something other than their characteristic sensible objects; he grants that sight, for instance, receives something other than the visible and that hearing, in the same way, perceives something other than the audible. *Sensu stricto* then, no sense can be considered the sense of its sensible object alone. It must also be "of itself" (*autē hautēs*), receptive, in other words, to the second degree. Capable of perceiving that which lies outside it, every sense must, at the same time, be capable of being affected by its own pure power to do so.

The discussion of the matter in the *De anima* is brief, and, on its own, the theory of sensation as it is developed in the treatise remains insufficient fully to resolve the difficulties it provokes. How exactly, one wonders, can a sense be said to be "of itself," and how does this perception of perceiving relate to the perception of the proper sensible established by Aristotle in the preceding sections of the work? If one reads the *De anima* together with the lesser treatises in the *Parva naturalia*, however, the elements of an answer to the question soon emerge. In an enigmatic turn of phrase in the *De anima* on which commentators, both ancient and modern, have often dwelled, Aristotle invokes a "common" faculty of sensation to explain the perception of rest, movement, figure, number, and size: "We grasp the common sensible qualities," he writes, in a single, pregnant sentence, "by means of [a] common sensation [or a 'common sense']" (*tōn de koinōn ēdē aisthēsin koinēn*).[13] The short treatises on natural history develop the claim for such a faculty, extending the field of its application to include the two other forms of sensation that, in the treatise on the soul, appear to lie beyond the distinct activities of the five senses.

The final chapter of the *De sensu et sensibilibus* contains an extended discussion of the problem of complex sensation, which poses the question raised by the *De anima* in unmistakable terms: How is it possible, Aristotle once again asks, to perceive the sweet and the white at once?[14] Taste can perceive the sweet, and vision, the bright. But the sensation of the "sweet and white" is originally unitary, and it cannot be explained with reference to two distinct acts of perception, of which it would constitute a combination. The truth, we learn, is that the phenomenon of complex sensation implies the existence of a single faculty: a "total sense" (*aisthētikon pantōn*), which perceives, combining and comparing, everything that is apprehended by the five senses.[15]

In terms close to those of both the *De anima* and the *De sensu*, the *De somno et vigilia*, by contrast, returns to the problem of the sensation of sensing. With reference to each sense, Aristotle now explains, one must distinguish a "proper function" (*ti idion*) from a "common function" (*ti koinon*) that invariably accompanies it. Only then will one be able to explain how it is that when one sees, for example, one perceives that one perceives by sight, and when one hears, one senses, at the same time, that one senses by hearing; only then, moreover, can one coherently account for the irreducible unity of complex sensation. Aristotle writes:

> With regard to every sense, there exist a proper function and a common function. For sight, for example, the proper function is seeing; for hearing, it is hearing; and so it is for all the other senses. There is a common faculty that accompanies all the senses, by which one senses that one is seeing and that one is hearing. For it is certainly

not by sight that one sees that one is seeing, and it is not thanks to taste, nor is it thanks to sight, nor thanks to the two [together] that one discerns, and that one can discern, that sweet tastes are different from bright colors. It is, rather, thanks to a certain part of the soul that is common to the sense organs [*aisthēterion*], since then sensation is unitary and the dominant sense organ is unitary.[16]

Here Aristotle expands the powers of the "shared" or "common sensation" (*koinē aisthēsis*) mentioned in the *De anima*, whose activity in the more extended treatise had seemed restricted to the apprehension of common sensible qualities. Complex sensation and the sense of sensing, too, are now said to number among the capacities of a single common dimension of sensation. Together, they form the functions of a "dominant sense organ" (*kurion aisthētērion*), which, we read a few lines later, "remains for the most part simultaneous with touch" (*d' hama tōi haptikō malisth' huparkhei*).[17]

On the surface, the differences between the accounts of sensation proposed in the *De anima* and the various treatises of the *Parva naturalia* seem undeniable, if not irreconcilable. Modern scholars have interpreted them in various ways. Many, if not most, have sought to resolve them with recourse to hypotheses of dating. For some, the *De anima* must have been composed after the shorter treatises; for others, the lesser works represent the final stage in the elaboration of the doctrine of *aisthēsis* initially proposed in the large work on the soul.[18] It is not clear, however, that a historical ordering of Aristotle's works can settle differences of doctrine more decisively than philosophical interpretation. A chronology may be more or less well founded, but it is still conjecture, felicitous or not, and, in any case, one can treat the corpus as a whole. This appears to have been the path followed, in large part, by the thinkers of the ancient and medieval tradition. They took the various Aristotelian discussions of common sensation as the starting points for far-reaching theories of a faculty that, in the idioms of Greek, Arabic, Hebrew, and Latin philosophical reflection, they consistently called the "common sense" (*koinē aisthēsis*, *al-h(hiss al-mushtarak*, (*hush* or *da'at meshutaf*, and *sensus communis*), despite the fact that the Philosopher himself had employed a similar term no more than three times.[19]

Even if one takes the *De anima* and the treatises of the *Parva naturalia* as elements in the exposition of a single doctrine, however, one must admit that the remarks on the common faculty of sensation are elliptical and often difficult to interpret. One wonders, at the very least, about the reasons for the multiplication of terms, from the "common sense" of the *De anima* to the "total sense" of the *De sensu*, the "master sense" of the *De somno*, and the "primary sense" (*prōton aisthētikon*) invoked in the *De memoria*, apparently as a synonym of the "common sense" (*koinē aisthēsis*). One may ask, too, about the striking association in the *De somno* of the "dominant sense organ" with the sense of touch, which was to lead some commentators to conclusions nowhere explicitly drawn in the work of the Stagirite himself, such as when Michael of Ephesus observed that "if one must tell the truth, touch and the common sense are one [*haphē kai koinē aisthēsis tauton estin*]."[20]

It is as if the common power resisted being given a single title, as if its every appellation were, in the end, a kind of catachresis, an improper name for a power that could not be lent a single term and easily represented as one among others in the animal soul. Modern scholars have not failed to be drawn to the elusive power, and not only because of the enigmatic and shifting role it plays in Aristotle's psychological writings. As the faculty of the soul by which "we sense that we are seeing and [that we are] hearing," Aristotle's "common sense" seems to resemble less a form of sensation according to any ordinary meaning than the form of cognition so prized by the philosophers of modernity, thanks to which thinking beings, in distinction to all other things, can be said to be aware of themselves. Could the "common sense" of the Stagirite, some have wondered, be a name for consciousness?

It has been noted more than once that Aristotle, a child of his times, seems to have lacked any exact equivalent for the modern term. At times, the fact has been presented simply as a matter of linguistic means, as when Charles H. Kahn remarked that "the

Greek of Aristotle's day has no term which really corresponds to the modern usage of 'consciousnesses,' for the process or condition of awareness as such," or when Richard Sorabji observed that "Aristotle has no word corresponding to 'mental act,' or to Descartes' *cogitatio* (consciousness)," or when, finally, Deborah K.W. Modrak noted that "Aristotle has no general term for consciousness."[21] At other times, however, it has been suggested that the lacuna may well have been of consequence for the notions developed by the ancient thinker. Henry J. Blumenthal has thus written that "Aristotle himself had no formal concept of consciousness, and it is by no means clear that he had the idea at all."[22] Some, going further, have even found in the absence of the concept the reason for the characteristic debilities of Aristotle's doctrine of mind. D.W. Hamlyn, one of the classical philosopher's modern editors, cast Aristotle's account of shared sensation as an attempt to seek "something like the notion of a unity of consciousness or Kant's synthetic unity of apperception," with the significant caveat that the Stagirite, in contrast to his successor from Königsberg, did "not have the concept of consciousness."[23] In Hamlyn's eyes, the consequences of the omission were grave. Inevitably, we learn, Aristotle's "dealings with the mind-body problem were perfunctory"; "concepts like consciousness do not figure in his conceptual scheme at all"; an intelligent modern reader finds himself consequently obliged to decry "an almost total neglect of any problem arising from psycho-physical dualism and the facts of consciousness."[24]

More sympathetic readers have wished to bring Aristotle close to the terms of modern philosophy, and they have not hesitated to liken the Peripatetic common sense to the modern cognitive faculty. "The central faculty," Kahn wrote, "obviously exercises many of the functions we now refer to as 'consciousness.'"[25] L.A. Kosman similarly remarked that the *De anima*'s discussion of the "sense of sensing" constituted "an account of what appears to be a mode ... of self-consciousness."[26] In an article pointedly titled "An Aristotelian Theory of Consciousness?" Modrak went further. Considering, as she wrote, which of the "psychological faculties described by Aristotle are such that consciousness could be ascribed to the possessor of the faculty," she judged the shared sense to be the "most likely candidate" for the position. Although she acknowledged that the Greek philosopher did not "seem very interested in the nature of consciousness in general," she nevertheless reached a conclusion that was no less bold for the unsparing judgment it passed on the thought of Aristotle himself: "His conception of a central sense is such that it could be used to give a rudimentary but relatively satisfactory account of consciousness."[27]

It is difficult to avoid the impression that, as compelling as they may be in their own terms, such studies labor under the weight of an unstated supposition that cannot but obscure the ideas they ostensibly aim to elucidate: the supposition, namely, that the classical philosopher's concepts acquire their ultimate meaning when they are viewed as "candidates" applying, with varying degrees of success, for positions already well occupied by modern philosophical notions. It can hardly be considered a surprising finding that, when held against the measuring stick of consciousnesses, the Aristotelian common sense seems, if "relatively satisfactory," "rudimentary" at best. Pursuing an inverse line of argument may prove more fruitful. It may be that the significance of the primary sensation of the classical philosopher lies not in its proximity to the modern notion of consciousness but in its removal from it. For the distance from which the ancient theory reaches us today shelters a question all the more pressing for its apparent untimeliness. What if the activities of awareness and self-awareness attributed to the modern faculty were forms not of cognition but rather, as Aristotle maintained, of sensation? What if consciousness, in short, were a variety of tact and contact in the literal sense, "an inner touch," as the Stoics are reported to have said of the "common sense," "by which we perceive ourselves"?[28] Reading the psychological works of Aristotle and his classical and medieval commentators, one can hardly avoid this question, which points, beneath the conceptual edifice familiar to us today, to the uncertain terrain over which the concept of consciousness was long ago erected. There are good reasons to excavate. The "thinking thing" of modernity conceals a past still to be uncovered, in which the relations between cogitation and perception, thought and feeling, were not what they became, and in which sensation, the primary power of the tactile being, held the keys to the life of all beasts, no less the two-legged one who would raise himself above those around him.

Chapter Four

The Circle and the Point

A Likeness of the Philosopher and his Pupils, which links the foregoing common Sense to Time and to Language too

Aristotle clearly meant the concept of the common sense to provide answers to several of the more delicate questions in his doctrine of the soul, and this it certainly did. But it raised still more, and in the centuries following the dissemination of the Peripatetic teachings, the ancient and medieval commentators were inevitably left with difficulties to which no simple solutions could be found. First, there was the problem of the relations that were to obtain between the various activities said to be carried out by the master sense. How exactly could such diverse phenomena as common and accidental sensible qualities, complex sensations, and the sense of sensing all be said to be the objects of a single faculty of perception? Could an order, perhaps a hierarchy, of functions, from the most elementary to the most refined, be discerned among them? Such questions bore on the structural unity of the primary power in Aristotelian psychology; they involved the sense in which the common sense could be said, with any precision, to be "a" sense at all. But there were also other questions, which were at least as worrisome and which, as long as they remained unresolved, continued to cast doubt on the very existence of the master faculty elliptically but repeatedly invoked by the Philosopher. These queries, by contrast, involved the sense in which the common sense could be said to be a "sense" in any clear meaning of the term. It was Aristotle, after all, who had maintained in the opening sentence of what would become Book

Gamma of the *De anima* "that there is no sense other than the five, and by these I mean sight, hearing, smell, taste, and touch," and it was also he who had sought to demonstrate this thesis beyond all doubt.[1] It was not possible for the common sense, for this reason, to be considered a sixth in the set of the sensible powers. But it could also not be reduced to one of the five, being by definition simultaneous with the activity of perception in all its forms. The central faculty might well be "master" among the senses, but it had, in short, no set place among them, and it proved all the more difficult to situate among the sensitive abilities for being by nature present at every point in the life of the animal.

There were few pertinent remarks on the subject to be found in the works of the ancient philosopher himself, and it did not help matters that on the surface, at least, they appeared to be divergent — if not simply contradictory — in intent. At times, Aristotle clearly suggested that the master sense differed not only in function but also in essence from the five senses between which it mediated and whose activity, as a whole, it could be said to apprehend. Hence the dictum of the *De somno et vigilia*, which seemed to establish the independence of the common sense from the multiple proper *aisthēseis* in no uncertain terms. "It is certainly not by sight that one senses that one is seeing," the Stagirite had written in that treatise, attributing the sense of sensing to a single perceptual faculty responsible, in addition, for the perception of common sensible qualities and complex sensations.[2] But the *De anima* contained a statement that was at least as unequivocal and that seemed, by contrast, to deny that the perception of perceiving could be assigned to any sense other than the five. Raising the question of whether it is by sight or by some other sense that "we sense that we are seeing," Aristotle had offered the following answer, before moving on to a different topic: "It is to the first of these powers that we must attribute this sensing."[3] The contradiction is flagrant, and the ancient followers of the Stagirite had no choice but to make sense of it in one way or another. This difficulty still confronts the modern interpreter: depending on the Aristotelian treatise to which one turns, one may surmise that the master power constitutes a faculty separate from the forms of perception or, alternatively, indistinct from them, being said at times to be irreducible, and at other times to be identical, to the five.

The *locus classicus* for the examination of the problem can be found in the latter half of the second chapter of the *De anima* traditionally taken to expound the doctrine of the central sense. Having discussed the question of the "sense by which we sense that we are seeing and [sense that we are] hearing," Aristotle turns to the problem of complex sensation: the single perception, to take the classic example, of "the white and the sweet." That neither sight nor taste alone can furnish a principle for such a sensation would seem by now clear, the first being limited to discriminating between the bright and the dark, the second being merely capable of telling the sweet from the bitter. As Aristotle has defined them to this point, the senses, taken individually, could not allow for the single apprehension of heterogeneous sensible qualities. But the Philosopher also excludes the possibility that the phenomenon in question can be explained as an act carried out by several senses at once. He adduces the reason by directly addressing the reader of his tract. "Otherwise," he writes, "while I perceived one thing and you perceived another, it would still be evident that they differed. It is necessary that one [faculty] says that they are different [*dei te to hen legein hoti heteron*]; for sweet is different from white."[4] The unity of the complex perception thus implies a single perceptual faculty, which, when asserting that which it discerns, invariably "speaks" (*legei*), as Aristotle writes, in a single voice. The final chapter of the *De sensu*, which treats the problem of complex sensation at some length, reaches a similar conclusion, albeit without reference to the discord of speaking parties. In order for the white and the sweet to be the object of a single sensation, we read there, "it is necessary that there be some unity in the soul, by which it senses everything."[5]

It is by no means clear, however, how a single faculty could be posited, in the terms of the treatise, within the powers of the soul.

At first glance, the very existence of a total sense would seem to imply a logical and physical impossibility: that "one thing," as Aristotle indicates, "be moved simultaneously in opposite directions." Here, too, the example of the sweet and the white suffices for the purposes of illustration. "If something is sweet," the Philosopher recalls, "it moves sensation or thought in one way; but the bitter moves it in the opposite way; and the white moves it quite differently."[6] That which simultaneously perceives multiple sensible qualities would seem necessarily drawn, by its passive power, in several directions at once, defined by traits incompatible with one another.

Aristotle proposes an explanation. The perceptive power could be unitary in nature, both temporally and spatially, but still multiple in function. "It is indeed in one way that which is divisible that perceives divided qualities," the Philosopher reasons, "yet in another way it is this *qua* indivisible; it is divisible in being but indivisible in place and number [*tōi einai gar diareton, topōi de kai arithmōi adiaireton*]."[7] But this cannot be, and to claim as much is to mistake the difference between potentiality and actuality that everywhere determines Peripatetic metaphysics. One thing can certainly be said to be two opposite things potentially and can be termed in this sense divisible. But in act it can be only one or the other, and so irreparably divided. It is not possible for a thing to be simultaneously dark and bright; for the same reason, a single faculty cannot be capable of being affected at once, in actuality, by two opposed sensible qualities.

Now Aristotle offers a second and definitive explanation, for whose exposition he resorts to the simplest of geometrical figures: the point (*stigmē*). "It is like what some call a point," he explains,

> which is [both indivisible] and divisible in so far as it is [considered] one or two. Insofar as it is indivisible, that which discerns, therefore, is one and discerns at one time; but insofar as it is divisible, it is no longer one, since it simultaneously uses the same point twice [*dis tōi autōi khrētai sēmēiōi hama*]. Insofar, then, as it uses the boundary-

point twice it discerns two separate things in a way separately; but insofar as it uses it as one it discerns one thing and at one time [*ēi men oun dis khrētai tōi perati, duo krinei kai kekhōrismenos estin hōs kekhōrismenōi. hēi d' heni, hen kai hama*].[8]

The unity of sensation, therefore, is that of the point: at once indivisible and divisible, unitary and multiple, according to the various possible forms of its apprehension. If it is taken on its own, it is necessarily one. But as that which marks a boundary (*peras*), it must be two: the double sign of a *terminus ad quem* and a *terminus a quo*, the end of one segment and the inception of another.

Aristotle did not comment further on the sense of the simile, and it remained to later readers a perplexing figure in his psychological corpus, whose elements and doctrinal content could both be questioned in numerous ways. How, for example, did the image of the point in the treatise help to contribute a new account of the perceptual power that differed fundamentally from the one earlier proposed and expressly rejected? One in essence but counted twice, the geometrical figure could clearly recall the hypothesis according to which the sensitive soul was unitary in nature yet multiple in function, which Aristotle, for reasons of principle, would not admit. And how was one to understand the figure of the doubled, single point itself — was it an emblem of the sensitive soul, as the words by which it was introduced suggested, or was it instead a cipher of a thing distinct from the sensitive faculties, of which they merely made "use," as the passage later also implied? The simile resisted interpretation, even as it remained of obvious import for the exposition of the doctrine of the animal soul.

That the ancient followers of Aristotle found themselves drawn to the enigmatic point is clear from the works of Alexander of Aphrodisias, the most prominent of the ancient Aristotelians, known to his successors, such as Simplicius and Philoponus, as the commentator on the Philosopher par excellence.[9] Alexander alluded to Aristotle's invocation of the geometrical figure in several of works, and he even went so far as to devote one of his minor exegetical writings to its interpretation. It constituted the ninth section of the third book of his much-read *Quaestiones*, or *School Puzzles and Solutions on Nature* (*Phusikai skholikai aporiai kai luseis*), designated by the rubrics of the manuscripts that transmit the work by an exact, if prolix, title: "Explanation of a Passage from the Third [Book of the] *De anima*, in which Aristotle Shows that There Is Something with which We Sense Everything Simultaneously."[10] Alexander began his *quaestio* with a reconstruction of the problem of complex sensation in the *De anima* and a summary of the first, insufficient explanation proposed by the Stagirite to account for it. The commentator then considered the second solution offered by the Philosopher. "This passage is expressed very obscurely and very concisely" (*ētis lexis sphodra asaphōs kai brakheōs eirēmenē*), he noted.[11]

> But what it means is like this. It requires that that by which living creatures have sensation of things that can be sensed should be such that it can simultaneously be one and many, in the way that a point, too, [is simultaneously one and many,] when it is taken as the terminus of many lines. For the straight (lines) drawn from the circumference of a circle to the centre all have the centre of the circle as their terminus, a single point; and this point, being one, is also in a way many, when it is taken as the terminus of each of the lines drawn from it. For if sensation is something like this, [then] in so far as it is one and indivisible, what judges will be one, though it simultaneously judges what is at the termini of the lines, since all the termini are together and are a single thing. But in so far as it is taken as the terminus of this [line], and then this, and it is taken as many times as [there are] straight [lines], [in this respect] it is many. And in this respect, again, in so far as there are many termini and [they belong] to different lines, the things that are judged will be many and separated and different; and in a way what discerns will be separated in the way in which the centre was in a way many, and each of these [things that discern] discerns the affection on its own particular line. But in so far as what is [formed] from them all is one and undifferentiated and in every way the same, what discerns will itself be one thing and will discern [the different aspects] simultaneously.[12]

Here the commentator does not restrict himself to clarifying the recondite expressions of his teacher, for he transforms them. From the Aristotelian point, which marked a limit, he draws not one but countless lines, which extend in differing directions toward a circumference that mirrors, in its regularity, the fixity of its center. It was a figure that Alexander, turning from commentator to philosopher, did not hesitate elsewhere to invoke as his own. In his own *De anima*, he explained, without any explicit reference to his master, that the "common sense" (*koinē aisthēsis*) was "in one respect a unity, but distinguishable into a plurality when considered from another point of view," just as the radii of a circle "are indeed many when taken at the circumference but come together in unity as they approach the center."[13]

The figure was to have a long life in the history of philosophy. More than a century after Alexander composed his works, his explanation of the Aristotelian simile appeared in the *Paraphrase* of the *De anima* by the influential fourth-century scholiast of Constantinople, Themistius; with its translation into Arabic by Ḥunayn ibn Isḥāq in the ninth century and into Latin by William of Moerbeke in the thirteenth, the circle and the point came to count as stable elements in the exposition of medieval psychologies.[14] Among the thinkers of the Arabic language, Avicenna and Averroës referred to the figure regularly, and their assiduous students, the doctors of the Latin universities of Europe, in turn availed themselves of it systematically in their own commentaries and works *de potentiis animae*.[15] But Alexander's gloss also had an afterlife outside the Aristotelian traditions of Antiquity and the Middle Ages in the strict sense, for it recurred in the fourth *Ennead*, in a capital passage in which Plotinus considered the unity of the soul in sensation. "How can one say that sensible impressions [*aisthēmatōn elthontōn*] differ," the Neoplatonist asked, "if, together, they do not reach the same thing?" The answer was clear: "It will be necessary that this thing be like a center, and the sensations from all parts find their end in it, like the radii that return from the circumference of a circle; for such is the perceiving being, which is truly one" (*toiouton to antilambanomenon einai, hen on ontōs*).[16]

From Aristotle to the commentators and from the ancient exegetes to the philosophers of the Middle Ages, the two geometrical figures remain the double emblems of a shared power of sensation, passive in its reception of sensible qualities and active in its total unification and "discernment": divisible and undivided, "not one," as Alexander had written, "and one at once."[17] But in every case, the problem of the structural unity of *aisthēsis* also remained, and for those who considered the classical doctrines with acuity, as for those who continue to do so today, the question of the element in which the senses find their unity could not be avoided. By what principle can the many lines of sense be said to converge, all leading back, like radii, to a single point?

Twentieth-century scholars suggested answers one might well have anticipated from those versed in the dominant doctrines of modern philosophy. Some recalled that the problem broached by the traditional psychologists, that of "the unity of the senses," could not be explained adequately without positing "the notion of a person with a unity of consciousness," although, they must of course immediately also admit, "it is not clear" that Aristotle himself aware was of that fact.[18] Others, opting for an explanation no less tributary of modern thought, presented the problem as that of "the synthetic act of knowledge."[19]

It is certainly true that in the Aristotelian discussion of complex perception, the faculty of thought, if not knowledge, at one point appears. The treatise on the soul contains an indication that a solution to the difficulty of complex sensation would involve the nature of intellection: the faculty that asserts that the white differs from the sweet, the Philosopher writes, "thinks even as it perceives" (*houtō kai noei kai aisthanetai*).[20] But this is an act of thinking simultaneous with sensing and apparently inextricable from it, not an act of cognition capable of founding the functions of perception. And it is worth recalling that the *De anima* itself leaves no doubt as to the terrain in which it carries out its investigation into the unity of sensation, which is neither that of thought nor that of representation, and still less that of the "notion of a person." After having considered the proper sensible qualities in much of Book Beta, the common sensible qualities in the first chapter of Book Gamma, and both the sensation of sensing and the sensation of diverse sensible qualities in its second, the Philosopher concludes with a statement that leaves no doubt as to his understanding of the section of the treatise that has now reached its end: "So much," he writes, in summary, "by way of the principle according which animals can be said to be capable of sensation [*to zōion aisthētikon einai*]."[21]

If one examines the classical work attentively, it is possible to identify a principle at the root of the unity of the senses. This principle is, however, neither knowledge nor thought but the concept of time and, more precisely, the determination of the element of time as the strictly indivisible moment in which sensation comes to pass. By definition, *aisthēsis*, we learn, occurs "now," and, if it is to remain itself in the coincidence of its multiplicity and unity, it can do so at no other time. Aristotle insists that, in sensation, "the 'when' is not accidental" (*ou kata sumbebēkos to hote*):

> That it is not possible [for the various senses to discern] at different times is clear from the following. For just as it is the same [principle] which asserts that the good and the bad are different, so also when it asserts that the one and the other are different, the "when" is not accidental. I mean [accidental] as, for example, when I now say that they are different, but not that they are different now. But it asserts both now and [it asserts] that they are different now [*all' houtō legei, kai nun, kai hoti nun*]; all at the same time, therefore [*hama ara*]. It is thus an undivided [principle] [that discerns] in an undivided time [*hōste akhōriston kai en akhōristōi khronōi*].[22]

The passage is difficult, and the decision of many modern editors to follow Ingram Bywater in placing a good part of it in parentheses can lead one to consider it of minor importance in the development of Aristotle's argument.[23] But it is, in truth, capital, and its excision from the main body of the text, even in part, obscures a decisive moment in the exposition of the doctrine of the treatise.

It is at this point that Aristotle lays bare a principle that remains merely implicit elsewhere in his account of the soul, although it profoundly determines the entire doctrine of *aisthēsis*. This is the principle that all sensation occurs in time and, more precisely, at one time in particular — namely, "now." We learn here that the perception that "the white differs from the sweet" remains bound by definition to the present moment in two ways. As an active "discrimination" (*krinein*) registered in propositional form, the sensation occurs now, just as every actual assertion, in the event of its utterance, takes place at a certain moment. But it also occurs now in the sense that that of which it constitutes a discernment — the reception of the sensation itself — invariably occurs in the present. The first "now" ("as when I now say they are different") Aristotle terms "accidental" (*kata sumbebēkos*); it pertains to the form of any assertion as such, which, to occur in act, must by definition take place at a certain moment. But the second "now" ("that they are different now") is essential to sensation, and one may therefore say, in the characteristic diction of the philosopher, that it pertains to all *aisthēsis* "absolutely" and "by itself" (*kath'auto*). This "now" is the sole element in which the different sensible qualities perceived by the soul may meet. A present coextensive with perception as such, it is the time indicated, in its barest form, in the "and" of "the white *and* the sweet," or "the dark *and* the sour." It is that in which, or at which, the various qualities perceived can be said to "differ," and one could hardly overestimate its importance in the theory of sensation proposed in the *De anima* and the *Parva naturalia*.

That which founds the unity and difference of the forms of perception can thus be understood to be no more, and no less, than that being which can be defined by its undivided presence alone: the "now." It is perhaps in this sense that we are to understand the enigmatic geometrical figure invoked in the treatise on the soul, which strikingly recalls a famous graphic sign that appears elsewhere in the Aristotelian corpus: the "point" (*stigmē*) of Book Delta of the *Physics*. In the treatise on time that fills the first chapters of that work, Aristotle defines "the now" (*to nun*) as the ultimate element of time (*khronos*), and he characterizes it, in terms that recur throughout the history of philosophy, as both a "point" (*stigmē*) and a "limit" (*horos*), conceivable in relation to both the line (*grammē*) of temporal succession and the circle (*sphaira*) of eternity.[24] The "point" of the *De anima*, which can be one or two by virtue of its position as a "boundary" or "limit" (*peras*), can be understood to mark the same undivided and yet divisible temporal unit. It indicates the position at which the many senses meet, drawn back, as divisible lines, to their undivided center: the time of the now. Such a reading allows one to comprehend the good reasons for which the *De memoria et reminiscentia*, in a different setting, ascribes the perception of time to a faculty that is in fact an "affection" (*pathos*) of the central sense, namely, the imagination.[25] The commanding force of the master perceptual faculty may lie in this simplest and most primary of activities, by which the many forms of perception in turn grow possible: the sensation of the form of time.

Aristotle suggests that such perception involves, however, still a further power, which seems less one of sensation than of indication and, for this reason, language. This is a "faculty" nowhere explicitly discussed in the Peripatetic psychological works, although its presence can be clearly detected at several points, not least in the treatise on the soul. It is remarkable that the common power, as the *De anima* presents it in these lines, does not only perceive. It also speaks, and that a good number of times. Of two sensible qualities, the shared sense, we read, "asserts [or "says," *legei*] that the one and the other are different," and "it asserts [or "says," *legei*] both now and [it asserts or says] that they are different now."[26] Themistius's *Paraphrase* finds the faculty even more loquacious. Here the central sense

> does not perceive the whiteness at one time and the coldness at another, but [both] at one and the same time. And it says that one of them is distinct at exactly the same time [it says that] the other is too. I mean that the [time] when [this happens] is not accidental. For example, I could here and now say that Plato the philosopher has arrived in Sicily, but I am [just] saying it now, but not that [it is] also

[happening] right now. But the [sense] that distinguishes between white and cold also says that [distinction] at the time, and says at the time that [it is] also [true] at the time. It therefore [says both] at the same time, so that not only is it itself a single thing, but it is [so] at a single time too.

Each of the "discernments" of the central sense now wears an unmistakably linguistic guise. But no matter their number, the utterances of the power all appear to share a common form. Uttered "at one and the same time," they all refer to the undivided instant of sensation: the "one and the same time" (*en khronōi heni*), in the words of the commentator, a time at once registered and retained, for the duration of the sensation, by the unified faculty of perception.

Aristotle does not explore the nature of the power that, in sensation, speaks "at one and the same time." As that which marks the present moment without which sensation would not be itself in the *De anima*, it is ostensibly meant to indicate the present that is, so to speak, simultaneous with sensation. But the function of the speaking faculty is, in truth, more complex than it seems at first glance, since it introduces into the presence of *aisthēsis* a duration that is not reducible to it: that in which the present of perception comes to pass. Aristotle, to be sure, establishes beyond all doubt that to posit such a thing as perception, one must always also posit a "now," in whose undivided presence the multiple aspects of sensation can form a unity. But with such a proposition, the account of perception cannot be complete. For in what terms will one grasp the appearance of the "now" itself? If it is received by a faculty, it must be apprehended in a certain time; if it is "said" by anything in the soul, registered, recorded, and retained, it must necessarily be so at a certain moment. The undivided "now" of sensation, in short, must rest upon a duration with which it does not altogether coincide; the present moment must conceal, within itself, the passing of another, immeasurable by its own standard.

This is a duration that remains unnamed in the *De anima* and its commentaries but not unmarked. One can find its imprint in all the utterances of the sensitive faculty, which repeat, in every act of perception, that sensation occurs "at one and the same time." For to be made, this statement, which establishes the presence of the present instant, must itself take a certain time. A "certain time," but not time itself, insofar as its concept, for the classical philosopher and his commentators alike, could be reduced to that of the undivided present; a "certain time," but none that could be strictly "now," insofar as the "now" constitutes the result of the process of "saying now" in the soul and cannot, therefore, for its part determine it. It is another time; to the degree to which time cannot admit of varieties of itself, it may well be something other than any time at all.[27] The classical treatise suggests that without coinciding with it, such a "time," if it is one, may still persist together with the instant of sensation and so, too, with everything, simple and complex, that occurs within its bounds. Irreducible to the present moment and to the perception carried out in it, such a "time" may, in this way, still accompany it, "all at the same time" (*hama ara*). In the circle and the line, after all, there may be the single point, but in them both one may also glimpse the movement of a further power, more common still: that of their tracing.

CHAPTER FIVE

Sentio Ergo Sum

*In which Aristotle and the ancient Commentators explain why
Beasts, so long as they live, cannot fail to notice that they exist*

Compared with the *De anima*, Aristotle's *De sensu et sensibilibus* is a work of modest ambition, which aims to do no more than explain the nature of the various sense organs and the multiple sensible qualities to which they are suited. But there are points where the lesser treatise follows paths that stray far from the argumentative course of the larger work, leading to regions otherwise unvisited by the ancient Philosopher. Here the entire classical doctrine of the soul acquires a new shape. An example can be found in the concluding chapter of the brief treatise. Dwelling at some length on the problem of the simultaneous perception of various sensible qualities, Aristotle pauses for a long paragraph to consider a troubling possibility raised nowhere in the *De anima*, whose consequences, if admitted, would be of great import. It is the possibility that the principle in which sensation finds its unity might be ultimately an illusion, the result of an inadequate perception at best. The large treatise insisted, for several reasons, on the absolutely unitary temporal form of sensation: it taught that, no matter how complex its constituents, *aisthēsis* must occur in a single instant. But in the brief tract, the Philosopher shows himself willing to entertain a doubt. What if the "now" of perception, he wonders, were in truth a fiction? The present of perception could be an impression created in the sensitive soul by the passage of different times too quick, or too slow, to be sensed in their real diversity.[1]

The possibility Aristotle now contemplates is that of an "imperceptible time" (*khronos anaisthētos*), a duration that remains undetectable by the faculties of the sensing animal. It is clear that the existence of such an interval, if granted, would threaten the unity of perception established by the Peripatetic works on the soul. Consider, as an example, the perception of something by both sight and hearing. In the terms afforded by the Aristotelian doctrine, it would seem a straightforward case of complex sensation. But if one admits the possibility of a time that eludes perception, one can hardly continue to defer to such an impression. It could always be that one apprehension had occurred well before the other, the two sensations being, despite the animal's own perceptions, not simultaneous at all. One would be obliged to say not that "one sees and hears something at once" but, as Aristotle writes, "that one believes oneself to hear and to see something at the same time, because the times escape us [*hoti hoi metaxu khronoi lanthanousin*]."[2] In fact, one would see, and, later or before, one would in addition hear. And so it would be with every complex sensation. The "now" of perception, in each case, would be explicable as the sign of the animal's limited perceptual means. Far from constituting the unitary and unifying principle of the sensitive faculties, as Aristotle had strenuously argued, it would be but a mistaken impression, the result of the operation of powers unable fully to grasp the occurrences they registered.

One need not involve several faculties of perception, however, to grasp the full force of the difficulty raised by the *De sensu*. Were one to accept the existence of an imperceptible time, the theory proposed by Aristotle for each individual sense would demand revision. Take the perception, by audition, of a chord. In the terms of the Aristotelian doctrine, the sense of harmony would seem clear evidence for the necessity of a present coextensive with sensation. As Aristotle's student Theophrastus of Eresus would later insist in polemic against the Pythagoreans, to be perceptible as such, the notes sensed in chords must reach the hearing faculty all at once. "The high note cannot differ from the low by its speed," Theophrastus is reported to have reasoned, faithful to his master, "since if it did, it would reach the ears before the low note, and all accord [*sumphōnia*] would be impossible; for if there is an accord, it is because the sounds have an equal speed."[3] But it is evident that once one posits an imperceptible moment, the argument no longer holds. One can then assert that certain pitches do reach the ears before others, although they may well be perceived, on account of the somewhat insensible senses, as simultaneous with each other.

Aristotle's position on the subject remains unwavering. He refuses to admit the existence of an imperceptible time in sensation and, to exclude its presence once and for all in the theory of the soul, renders explicit a principle of sensation with which it cannot in any sense be reconciled. Although its implications extend far beyond the immediate subject matter of the brief treatise on perception, the thesis can be found nowhere outside the *De sensu et sensibilibus*, where it appears in a startlingly abbreviated form. "If someone senses himself or something else in a continuous time," the Philosopher writes, with deceptive ease, "then it is impossible for him not to notice that he exists" (*ei gar hote autos hautou tis asithanetai ē allou en sunekhei khronōi, mē endekhetai tote lanthanein hoti estin*).[4] It is a simple matter to demonstrate that this principle and the hypothesis of an insensible time cannot both be maintained, and Aristotle proceeds to do so immediately. He suggests an experiment to make the contrast clear. Consider, first, the continuous sensation evoked in the principle, "in which it is impossible for him not to notice that he exists." Then, imagine an imperceptible moment within it. What will be sensed? There are two possible answers to the question. There can continue to be perception in the Aristotelian sense: "One will continue to exist, one will see and perceive as a result," and the insensible moment, which would necessarily interrupt perception, will be impossible.[5] Or the imperceptible moment may remain. Then there will be a time in which one does not perceive and in which it eludes one's notice that one exists; and then the principle formulated will no longer hold. If one accepts the thesis on sensation proposed by

59

Aristotle, the conclusion, therefore, is clear: "It is evident that there is no time that is imperceptible."[6]

The demonstration raises fewer questions than does the principle by which it is conducted, for which Aristotle himself, strangely, offers no justification. It may have seemed to him merely a consequence of the theory of perception he developed elsewhere in his multiple works. But the truth is that the refutation of the hypothesis of imperceptible time in the *De sensu* reveals an aspect of the Peripatetic doctrine that would not have been easily anticipated. It is clear that the newly formulated principle does not merely state, in the terms of the *De anima*, that sensation occurs in the present; it also does not simply add to that classic proposition the thesis according to which the time of perception, in its structural continuity, cannot admit of a lapse undetectable by the sensing faculties. Aristotle now says more. He indicates that the act of *aisthēsis* reveals to the sensing being a thing far more fundamental than any perceptual quality, organ, or medium: the bare fact, namely, "that he exists" (*hoti estin*).

The assertion has rarely been considered in all its implications. What does it mean, after all, for the sensing creature to be, by definition, unable "not to notice that he exists"? The twentieth-century scholars who remarked on the passage in the *De sensu* did not fail to be struck by its resemblance to that most famous of proofs in modern philosophy, which aims to show that the cogitating being, by nature, cannot doubt his own existence: the Cartesian "I think, therefore I am." In a brief article published in 1942–1943, Émile Bréhier thus went so far as to dub the Aristotelian passage, with few words of explanation, "an archaic form of the '*Cogito ergo sum*.'"[7] Rodolfo Mondolfo elaborated on the claim only a few years later in the pages of the same journal. In a paper significantly titled "The Unity of the Subject in Aristotle's Epistemology," he cited the text of the *De sensu*, offering of it the following paraphrase and interpretation:

> In other words, whether one senses oneself or something else, one still senses oneself; one is conscious of existing (*sentio ergo sum*). But

if one admits the existence of insensible intervals, one admits that, since one does not sense them, one does not sense oneself existing in them, such that the consciousness of existing would have to be interrupted and discontinuous. Aristotle, on the contrary, believes that in the subject, self-consciousness or consciousness of one's own existence is always present and continuous.[8]

Wishing to elucidate the structure of the "archaic" argument, the scholar here began by admitting the distance that separates the modern thinker's demonstration from the classical philosopher's proof. Whereas the Cartesian *cogito ergo sum* derives being from cogitation, the Aristotelian formulation links existence to sensation, in a chain more aptly transcribed, for this reason, as "I sense, therefore I am" (*sentio ergo sum*). Eager to bring Aristotle close to Descartes in a more substantial form, however, the modern historian of philosophy then took a further step. From the classical claim that a sensing being cannot "not notice that he exists," he drew another conclusion, whose diction betrays a wish to complete and rectify the formulations of the antiquated master: "In the subject, self-consciousness or consciousness of one's own existence is always present and continuous."

This commentary did little justice to the original. Not only did the scholar, without any explicit admission of the fact, refer the predicate of continuity, which had been originally bound to the time of sensation, to the sensing being himself, whom he now declared to possess an awareness of his existence that is "always present and continuous." Ostensibly to explain the terms of the ancient treatise, the historian also introduced into the gloss three expressions hardly to be found in the Aristotelian text: "the subject," "self-consciousness," and "consciousness." The terms bestowed upon the ancient argument a meaning it could not have had, distorting it beyond repair. It is significant that the argument of the *De sensu*, for its part, proceeds along a different path. It lends no single name to that which can be deduced, by necessity, from the act of *aisthēsis*, and it nowhere passes from the sensation "of something or oneself in a continuous time" to the position of any substance, be it one capable of representation, self-representation, or knowledge. The proposition of the classical tract is infinitely more discrete. Perception, it argues, unavoidably implies a fact of being: that the sensing animal exists.

The modern paraphrase, however, does not err only in its will to make of existence a certain "subject." It also mistakes the nature of its apprehension by the perceiving being, and for a simple reason: because it understands "consciousness" as simply equivalent to the psychological condition by which something "cannot not be noticed." A moment of reflection, however, suffices to grasp that the two states are by nature quite distinct. It is certainly true that for something not to be able to escape one can imply, at times, that one is aware of it in cognition and in recognition, that one represents it to oneself with clarity and precision. But it can also be much more, and less: to retain, to recall, to imagine, to discern, however obscurely and however distantly, something one may never know as such. It can also be, in short, to sense something, in all the meanings given by the ancient thinker to the term.

The brief tract suggests that existence, for the classical philosopher, is precisely such a "thing," one that cannot escape sensing beings in the uninterrupted time in which they continue to subsist. It was to become a principle of the Peripatetic doctrine in Antiquity. "Everyone, when perceiving," Alexander would thus explain in his commentary on the *De sensu*, "perceives jointly that he exists and perceives" (*pas gar hote aisthanetai, heautou ontos te kai aisthanomenou sunaisthanetai*).[9] "Perceives," not knows: existence seems never to have struck these ancient thinkers, so far from many of their successors, as the object of an especially rational mind. They suggest that it can be summoned to thought and so, too, left to wander from it. But the fact of being in any case remains: unforgettable in thinking and its absence, it can be felt as long as sensation lasts. Here lies perhaps the ultimate consequence of the theory of the "common sense" invoked throughout the Aristotelian psychological corpus, which comes finally to light, almost in passing, in the refutation of the hypothesis of imperceptible time in this minor treatise. That all *aisthēsis* is "of itself," that perceiving remains turned toward the perceptible and also toward the activity of perception itself, means simply this: in all sensation, simple or complex, sharp or dull, the animal feels, in ways too varied to be submitted to the form of consciousness, that it lives. It senses, and therefore it is: a touching thing whose powers never cease to skim, however lightly, the fragile surface of its being.

Chapter Six

Sleep

Containing a Discussion of Aristotle's Account of the insuperable Law which dictates that sentient Beings, if they are ever to be awake, must rest

Animals feel, from birth to death. But the perceptive powers of every creature admit of degrees, and just as there are moments when the senses rise, for one reason or another, to points of particular precision, there are also times when they grow increasingly dull, as the living being, receding into itself, enters a state of relative indifference to the world around it. This fact struck Aristotle as of prime importance. He understood it to be the consequence of a fundamental principle in natural psychology and physiology: the insuperable law that dictates that sentient beings, if they are ever to be awake, must rest. "If there exists a living being capable of sensation," the Philosopher thus explained in categorical terms in the opening chapter of the *De somno et vigilia*, "then it is not possible that it neither sleeps nor wakes."[1] Nor is it possible, he added, that only one of the twin states pertains to the life of a sentient being, and that "one species of animal," for instance, "always sleeps, or that another is incessantly awake."[2] In the world of beasts, the two conditions imply each other, and every execution of the powers of perception leads, by necessity, to a period of corresponding powerlessness. "Among all animals," Aristotle argued, in programmatic terms, "where an organ is exercised naturally, whenever the time in which it can exert its functions is exceeded, it is necessary for it to be powerless [*anangkē adunatein*], for example, for the eyes to cease to see and the same for the hand and every other organ that fulfils some function."[3]

According to the classical philosopher, intermittency is for this reason inescapable in sensation: sooner or later, all *aisthēsis* must lapse, and this on account of its very operation. Discussing the nature of faculty of intellection in Book Gamma of his great treatise on the soul, the Stagirite could allude to the problem of the "cause for [our] not always thinking," and he could even dub the dilemma, which touched upon the obscure root of human incomprehension, a difficulty particularly "in need of examination" (*episkepteon*).[4] But a similar question could not possibly be posed in the realm of perception, for there inactivity remains the natural complement to all activity. By definition, animals, in time, grow tired; and so they must pause to rest their sensing organs, if only for a while.

"Sleep" is the name traditionally given to this rest. It plays an important role in the Peripatetic doctrine of the soul, where it constitutes the necessary, if temporary, suspension (*dialusis*) of sensation to which no animal can be immune: an "affection" (*pathos*) of the perceiving power, in which a period of inactivity inevitably comes to follow on the heels of activity, as the otherwise sensitive being withdraws into a state of mere self-conservation and organic growth close in form to that of the nutritive life of plants. According to the classical theory, it is at once a physiological and a psychological process. The *De somno* presents the matter in the most lucid of terms. "Sensation," the Philosopher explains in that work, "is the proper characteristic neither of the body nor of the soul," being, in actuality, "a kind of movement of the soul by the intermediary of the body" (*kinēsis tis dia tou sōmatos tēs psukhēs*).[5] Its inactivity, for this reason, cannot be attributed to the matter or the animating form of life with any exclusivity. The "privation [*sterēsis*] of waking" must, like all varieties of *aisthēsis*, involve *sōma* and *psukhē* both.[6]

At certain points, the Peripatetic account of rest, to be sure, seems less than complete, and the ancient and medieval commentators of the Stagirite found themselves in some disagreement over a number of the more technical aspects of the theory. A particularly thorny set of problems involved the extent to which the dormant state could be linked to particular regions and faculties of the living body elsewhere identified in the Aristotelian psychological works. The Philosopher himself had clearly associated the beginning and end of sleep to variations in the temperature of the animal body, but he had failed to specify exactly how waking and its absence could be explained with reference to the heating and cooling of the principle of sensation, which, he taught, lies "in the central area between the head and the lower stomach."[7] Was the onset of sleep due to the cooling of the heart, as, for example, Sophonias and Theodoros Metochites had argued, or was it to be explained simply with reference to the movement of heat through the body after eating, as Georgios Pachumeres had instead maintained?[8] Could the state of sleep, many also wondered, be referred in its inception and perhaps even its total duration to a particular organ of the sensing body? Gershom ben Solomon of Arles held that the drowsiness of the animal had its origins in a modification of the sense of touch that subsequently extended itself to the sensitive faculties as a whole.[9] The proposition recalled a claim made by Michael of Ephesus in his *In Parva naturalia commentaria*, the oldest such exposition to have survived. There, the Byzantine commentator stated in forceful terms that "sleep is an affection of the sense of touch and of no other [*ho hupnos tēs haphēs esti pathos kai oudemias allēs*]."[10]

Aristotle himself, of course, had nowhere written anything quite so unequivocal. But one can understand the good reasons that prompted the eleventh-century scholar to argue as he did. At several points, the Philosopher recalls that sleep cannot be grasped as the affection of any single organ of perception: otherwise, "the animal, sensing with one organ and not sensing with the other, would perceive this condition, which is impossible."[11] To fall asleep is to grow insensible not to one but to all the forms of perception, and all at once. For this reason, if one is to account with any rigor for the privation of waking, as for its presence, one cannot remain at the level of the individual senses, their organs, and their proper objects; one must take into consideration the structure of the perceptive power as a whole. Then sleep and waking may show themselves for what they truly are: affections of that single, "common faculty which accompanies all the senses, by which one senses that one is seeing and that one is hearing," and which "remains for the most part simultaneous with touch."[12] "When the powerlessness [adunamia] of using the senses does not reside in a particular sense and does not have any particular cause," the Philosopher explains, "but rather affects the sense that functions to perceive everything, and when this principle finds itself reduced to powerlessness, all the organs of sensation also must be powerless to sense."[13] It is a matter of principle, which involves the natural hierarchy of the soul: "When some modification is undergone by the sense that is master over all the other senses, and to which the [individual] senses all lead, necessarily the others all undergo it too; whereas, if one or two [of the individual senses] is powerless, it is not necessary for it [the master sense] to be powerless."[14]

Even in the impotence of the master, however, a certain order holds. Several passages of the *Parva naturalia* suggest that, for the classical philosopher, the slumbering animal remains, in some way, a sensitive being. Distinguishing between the powerlessness of the forms of perception and the affection of the primary perceptual principle itself, Aristotle observes that it would be an error to take sleep for a state in which the individual senses were simply incapacitated, utterly deprived of their characteristic activities. "It is clear from a number of facts," the Philosopher observes, "that sleep consists neither in the fact that senses do not act and are not used, nor in not having the power to sense [mē dunasthai aisthanetai]." These more drastic qualities, we learn, characterize the states of unconsciousness (leipopsukhia) brought on by madness, illness, and injury to the nerves.[15] Sleeping beings, by contrast, still remain capable of aisthēsis; their capacity to awaken is the proof. And even while asleep, they may continue in some way to perceive, albeit naturally not as when awake.

Aristotle dwells at greater length on the sensing power of the dormant animal in the *De insomniis*, which immediately follows the *De somno et vigilia* in the traditional classification of the treatises of the *Parva naturalia*. There, he explains that certain effects of sensation never cease to exert themselves on animals: there are minor "movements caused by perceptions," we read, "which, whether they come from outside or from inside the body, continue to be produced not only in waking but also in the affection that is called sleep." By day, "when sensation and thinking cooperate," these tiny affections of the sensing body are hardly noticed and therefore "vanish," the Stagirite writes, "like a small flame before a large one, like minor ills and pleasures before stronger ills and pleasures." But at night, in the absence of waking, nothing inhibits the little affections from persisting in the soul and making their way to the root (*arkhē*) of sensation, where they can at last be felt. At one level, at least, perception, therefore, does not cease. "Just as small eddies form in rivers," Aristotle writes, discussing the minor affections that surface in sleep, "so every movement of sensation takes place continuously."[16]

Certain sensations also remain with sleeping beings from the time in which they woke. The reason, Aristotle teaches, is simple: a sensation can always outlast the instant in which it is registered. "Sensible things produce sensation in us according to each sense organ," the Philosopher explains, "and the impression that is engendered by them exists in the organs, not only when the sensations are actual [*energousōn tōn aisthēseōn*], but also when they have disappeared."[17] Long after the sensible thing has departed and after the sensing organ has ceased to sense it, a sensible quality may therefore persist, "for an affection," we learn, "is also in the organs that have ceased to sense, and in the depths as well as in the surface" of the body.[18] The temporal structure of such a sensation can be compared to the movement of an object thrown in space, which continues "even when the mover has ceased to touch it."[19] Aristotle recalls, as an illustration, what happens "when one passes from the sun to darkness": vision is momentarily impaired because "the movement caused in the eyes by the sun still subsists," even though the sensible quality that produced it is now gone, and even though the eyes, strictly speaking, no longer see anything at all.[20]

Combined with the tiny sensations that affect the dormant animal, these remnants of the waking state form the elements of those elusive and transient appearances that are called dreams, which show themselves to the sleeper and to no one else. Their place in the Peripatetic doctrine of sensation is difficult to determine with precision. Aristotle leaves no doubt that, as the effects of the absence of waking, they cannot be considered sensations in any narrow sense. But his statements on the subject are varied in form and suggest more than a single claim. At the start of the *De insomniis*, the Philosopher states, in an apodictic tone, that *aisthē-sis* cannot be the faculty responsible for the perception of dreams. As he recalls with some haste, rest marks the suspension of the forms of perception, and "in sleep we sense nothing." But the apparently unequivocal formulation bears witness to a certain difficulty, since it continues to invoke the very power it would seem in principle to exclude: "It is clear that it is not by sensation," Aristotle writes, with paradoxical simplicity, "that we sense the dream" (*ouk ara ge tēi aisthēsei to enupnion aisthanometha*). The next page of the treatise returns to the problem and proposes a more qualified solution: "That affection which we call the dream," we read, "is not of the faculty of opinion [*doxazontos*], nor of thinking [*dianoomenou*], nor of sensation purely [*aisthoumenou haplōs*]."[21] The *De somno* contains a somewhat different answer, which goes even further in attributing the dream to the field of perception: "In a certain way," we read in that work, "the dream is a sensation" (literally, "a sensible thing": *to gar enupnion estin aisthēma tropon tina*).[22]

It is certainly possible that these statements flatly contradict one another, being no more than the telltale signs of a continued hesitation and uncertainty on Aristotle's part as to the exact place of dreams among the multiple affections of the soul. But the various claims may also be read together as the components of a single theory, which admits of more than a single level of perceptual activity. The Philosopher clearly teaches that in the oblivion that marks the dreaming state, the perceptions felt in waking by nature cease. But a further dimension of sensation, one may infer, persists in the suspension that is sleep. This is a dimension of *aisthēsis* that is clearly irreducible to consciousness, since it outlasts it, being still effective in the depths of slumber. It seems a dimension of *aisthēsis* that is undeniably distinct, too, from the unconsciousness of fainting and disease, in which the sensitive faculty no longer operates at all. Beyond, or before, both the presence and the absence of waking, it seems, there is something in the soul that does not cease to sense. Aristotle appears to have held that it continues also to speak. When one sleeps and when one dreams, the Philosopher once remarked, "there is something in the soul that says that the appearance is a dream" (*ti legei en tēi psukhē hoti enupnion to phainomenon*).[23] He went no further, but his words suffice. "Something" in the soul speaks (*ti legei*), but not someone, the only "one" worthy of the name being fast asleep, by definition, at the moment of its speaking. Something speaks, somewhere "in" the soul, to say simply "the appearance is a dream" (*enupnion to phaianomenon*) — and so to summon the animal, however softly, to begin to wake.

CHAPTER SEVEN

Awakening

A short Chapter, in which Proust, Valéry, and Benjamin say
much about the Disturbances at the End of Sleep

Nous veillons dormans, et veillans dormons.
— Montaigne*

Sleep ends in waking, as the animal, having conserved itself in rest, at last regains its senses. That an awakening can be more than a little discombobulating has been noted often, and, even when it does not find one transformed into a "monstrous vermin" of immense proportions, like Kafka's unluckily incapacitated traveling salesman, the event can still be an experience of considerable disorientation. The opening pages of *In Search of Lost Time* contain an exemplary discussion of the phenomenon:

> A sleeping man holds in a circle around him the sequence of the hours, the order of the years and worlds. He consults them instinctively as he wakes, and in a second he reads the point on the earth that he occupies and the time that has elapsed before his waking. But their ranks can be mixed up; they can broken. If toward morning, after a bout of insomnia, sleep overcomes him as he is reading, in a position quite different from the one in which he usually sleeps, his raised arm alone is enough to stop the sun and make it retreat; and, in the first minute of his waking, he will no longer know what time it is and he will think he has only just gone to bed. If he dozes off in

* *Oeuvres complètes*, p. 581.

73

a position still more displaced and divergent, after dinner sitting in an armchair, for instance, the confusion among the disordered worlds will be complete: the magic armchair will send him traveling at top speed through time and space, and, at the moment of opening his eyelids, he will believe he went to bed several months earlier in another country. But it was enough if, in my own bed, my sleep was deep and allowed my mind to relax entirely; then it would let go of the map of the place where I had fallen asleep and, when I woke in the middle of the night, since I did not know where I was, I did not even understand in the first moment who I was. I had only, in its original simplicity, the feeling of existence as it may quiver in the depths of an animal. I was more destitute than a cave dweller; but then the memory — not yet of the place where I was, but of several of those where I had lived and where I might have been — would come to me, like help to pull me from the abyss in which I would not have been able to escape on my own; and in a second, I passed through centuries of civilization, and the image confusedly glimpsed of oil lamps, then of wing-collar shirts, gradually recomposed the original features of my self.[1]

As Proust's chronically bedridden narrator presents it, sleep sub-tracts the sleeper from the most elementary conditions of sense, "sending" him, while still "sitting in his armchair," "at top speed through time and space." If, once fully awake, he has regained "the original features" of his self, it is only because they have been "gradually recomposed" in the time following the waking mo-ment itself (and this, it should be added, by a thing with which he himself does not altogether coincide: "the memory" that "comes to pull" him from the "abyss" from which he would "not have been able to escape" on his own). In the instant of waking, little is clear: "When I woke in the middle of the night," the narrator recalls, "since I did not know where I was, I did not even under-stand in the first moment who I was." The awakening itself brought with it no more than a mere sensation of being, and not even of a human being at that: "I had only, in its original simplicity," the narrator comments, "the feeling of existence as it may quiver in the depths of an animal" (*J'avais seulement dans sa simplicité pre-mière, le sentiment de l'existence comme il peut frémir au fond d'un animal*).[2]

Paul Valéry, if one takes him at his word, found nothing in the world more exciting. "There is no more stimulating phenomenon for me than awakening," he recorded in an elliptical entry in one of the volumes of his *Cahiers* dating from the last years of his life. "Nothing *tends* to give a more extraordinary idea of... *everything*, than this auto-genesis — This beginning of what was — which also has its beginning = *That which is*, — and this is nothing but shock, stupor, contrast."[3] Not unlike the novelist, the poet and thinker placed the startling event at the origin of the progressive recom-position of the self that defines the waking state. "What is being awake?" we read in another compressed text from the *Cahiers*. "It is *re-covering* [*c'est de* re-trouver]. This RE essential notation."[4] It was a point he stressed often from the 1920s on: "Waking means — re-covering"; "The capital fact of memory consists in recover-ing oneself in waking, recovering one's own body and oneself"; "Finding one's footing again [*reprendre pied*] — returning."[5] In the event of awakening, the observations lead us to believe, the move-ment of literal "re-turn" designated by the reduplicative prefix is key: "Re-covering | Re-cognizing | This *re* is capital."[6] Else-where, Valéry went so far as to suggest that all of psychology could be found inscribed, *in nuce*, within it: "The great affair of the function *psi*," he remarked, "is re-cognizing, *reconstituting*, of which the capital [function] is *REcognizing ONESELF, pulling ONESELF together AGAIN.*"[7]

It is all the more important, for this reason, precisely to under-stand the structure of the recovery that defines the moment of awakening. What exactly does it mean, after all, to "pull oneself together again"? The structural condition of such a movement, like that of any "return" worthy of the name, is the irreparable loss of that which is to be recovered — in this case, the fabric of "oneself." The reason is quite simple: to retrieve something, it must already be long gone. Otherwise there can be continuation, perseverance, and prolongation — but no reconstitution, no recovery, and no memory, at least as Valéry understood it. "Memory" (*mémoire*), he once wrote, "is the gift of the return to the same, or of the same. Its great affair is not the past, but the re-present. This is why it returns from the 'past' and never *climbs back up* to it" (*la mémoire est le don du retour au même ou du même. Ce n'est donc pas le passé, sa grande affaire — c'est le re-présent. C'est pourquoi elle revient du 'passé' et ne le remonte jamais*).[8] If it leads to the recovery of a self, waking does so, therefore, not by "climbing up" to it through the continuity of a past still present but by returning to it, or, more precisely, by allowing it to return, after the interruption that is sleep and following the utter astonishment in which its end is sensed.

This is why Valéry could write both "Waking means — recovering" and "I always wake up surprised."[9] Awakening can be termed an "autogenesis," in that it leads to the emergence of a self. But it is not autarkic and cannot found itself, since it departs from an event that is by definition irreducible to any self: the "shock, stupor, contrast" that mark the end of sleep. The poet-philosopher was acutely aware of the complex structure of the event that so excited him, and in his view it demanded a revision of the classical grammar of the act: "One should not say *I* wake," he commented in his *Cahiers*, "but There is waking — for the *I* is the result, the end, the ultimate Q.E.D. of the congruence — superimposition of what one finds on what one must have been expecting to find" (*Il ne faut pas dire: Je m'éveille — mais Il y a éveil — car le JE est le résultat, la fin, le c.q.f.d. final de la congruence — superposition de ce que l'on trouve à ce que l'on devait s'attendre à trouver*).[10] It is not difficult to grasp the reasons for the altered expression Valéry proposed. According to his account, the self comes to be in awakening; for this reason, it cannot be said, for its part, to occasion it. "One should not say *I* wake — but There is waking" means that the "I" emerges, as "the result, the end, the ultimate Q.E.D." of a process with which it does not altogether coincide. It means that a sensitive being comes to its senses, in other words, outside itself, woken up before it could ever be said to wake.

Walter Benjamin, who was drawn not only to the phenomenology of waking but also to its exploration in the works of Proust and Valéry, once observed that "it is an implicit presupposition of psychoanalysis that the contrary opposition of sleep and waking has no validity for the empirical forms of human consciousness; it allows, instead, for an infinite variety of concrete states of consciousness, which are conditioned by all possible centers, through all conceivable degrees of being awake."[11] In place of the two apparently opposed "empirical forms of human consciousnesses," sleep and waking, that principle sets "an infinite variety of concrete states of consciousness" (*einer unendlichen Varitetät konkreter Bewußtseinszustände*), which are determined by purely intensive "degrees" (*Gradstufen*) of wakefulness and oblivion. Such degrees, if one admits them, extend to both states traditionally placed in "contrary opposition." The waking condition, one will assert, contains its own degree of drowsiness: in moments of apparent alertness, the laws of the resting psyche can still hold. And, in turn, where night and day grow indistinct, oblivion, too, may harbor an unexpected probity. "The coming awakening," Benjamin wrote, "stands in the Troy of the dream like the wooden horse of the Greeks."[12] One creature stealthily crouched within the dormant imagination of another, the beast would announce a possibility hidden in all slumber. It would mark the secret chance sealed even in the deepest sleep: the chance to awaken and, in the sensation of the mere fact of sensing, to recover and retrieve, "in a second," "the feeling of existence as it may quiver in the depths of an animal."

Chapter Eight

Company

The ancient Concept of Sunaisthēsis, *the Faculty by which Animals feel when they feel and feel, no less, when they do not*

Between a work and its commentary, there is always an interval. It may consist of a historical removal, the temporal distance that separates a written thing from one that later seeks to explain it. But the interval need not be merely chronological in nature. Its presence can also be detected in the blanker regions of a single page: the typographical spaces that divide a major text from the lesser ones that, beneath or beside it, aim to clarify its argument. The border is, in any case, decisive. It belongs to the essence of the commentary to come into being at the outermost edges of a work and to move in the areas that at once surround and do not coincide with it. This fact follows from the nature of the form and can be easily ascertained. If an explanation were without relation to that which it aimed to explain, it would obviously be none at all; but if, by contrast, it were truly a part of that which it aimed to clarify, it would be equally impossible to distinguish it as such. A commentary always moves in the narrow regions that wind around the work upon which it bears, following and tracing its contours, and no matter how distant or how close to its text it may seem, an exposition never seeks either to leap beyond it or to venture within it. As its classical name indicates with a clarity that leaves little room for comment, the *commentum* stays at every point "with" that upon which it comments. In the realm of texts, it is an eternal accompanist, a permanent resident of the shifting space of being "with" (*cum*). It lives nowhere if not in company:

79

were it ever forced to be, so to speak, without its "with," it would not be at all.

For the greater part of its history, philosophy has been a practice of commentary, and it has conceived its most brilliant inventions at the edges of the corpus it has continued to accompany. Late Antiquity and the Middle Ages are perhaps the most illustrious cases, periods of the proliferation of glosses, expositions, and paraphrases (to say nothing of annotated editions and indexes) of all kinds. It is a truism that the thinkers of these epochs regularly departed from the theses of the tradition and, more precisely, from those stated *in littera* by the one who was for them the Philosopher par excellence. But such a claim means little as long as it leaves unspecified the role played by the encounter with "tradition" in such a setting. The commentators of late Antiquity, the *falāsifa* and *filosofim* of classical Arabic culture, and the doctors of the Latin Middle Ages may well all have conjoined their inquiries, in differing ways, to those of the authorities of Antiquity. The fact remains: more than once, they received from the classics something other than what had been transmitted to them. It followed from the nature of their craft. Glossators and their kind are incessantly in search of the animating element in their textual objects that bears no name: the dimension in them that, remaining unsaid, demands in time to be exposed. Thinkers trained as readers, the philosophers of the tradition were no exception. They knew how to find the secret source of incompletion sealed in every work of thought, and they knew, too, how to draw from it the matter of their art.

Consider that most far-reaching of ancient philosophical inventions: the concept of the perception of the fact of perception, the "sense," as Aristotle wrote in the *De anima*, "that we are seeing and hearing." The Philosopher himself invoked it more than once. He found himself obliged, for reasons of method, to raise the question of the faculty of the soul to which one might attribute its activity; and if one considers all his treatises together, one must conclude that on the surface, at least, he proposed more than a single answer to that question. At no point, however, did

Aristotle dwell at length on the nature of the "sensation of sens-ing" as a particular variety of *aisthēsis*, distinct or indistinct from others of its kind, or even in its own varieties, and nowhere did he dedicate more attention to it than in the *De anima*, where his dis-cussion of the matter fills less than a single page. The sensation of sensing is nowhere treated in any systematic fashion in the classic treatises, which assign to it no technical designation; strictly speaking, its concept, one must conclude, is not Aristotle's own. It is, by contrast, Aristotelian. For it was not the master but his pupils who, in the centuries following the dissemination of the Peripatetic doctrine, made of the perception of perceiving a full-fledged philosophical concept. And it was they who gave to it a single name: *sunaisthēsis*.

The distant origin of the modern "synaesthesia," the Greek term was no neologism when the thinkers of late Antiquity be-stowed upon it a technical sense in the doctrine of the soul. In the classical varieties of the language, admittedly, the noun ap-pears to have constituted something of a rare expression; but it is not without significance that the verb from which it was drawn, *sunaisthanesthai*, can be found in two passages of Aristotle's own treatises. Formed by the addition of the prefix "with" (*sun-*) to the verb "to sense" or "to perceive" (*aisthanesthai*), the expres-sion in all likelihood designated a "feeling in common," a per-ception shared by more than one. It is telling that the Stagirite invoked it in his analysis of friendship in the *Eudemian* as well as the *Nicomachean Ethics*.[1] At this point in the development of the Greek language, the term applied to the communal life of many, and its meaning lay far from the one that would later be attrib-uted to it by the commentators.

One of the earliest indications of a shift in the sense of the expression can be found in the medical literature that flourished after the beginning of the Christian era. It has been noted that Galen, for instance, employs *sunaisthēsis* to designate a sensation "in common," not in that it is shared by many but in that it reaches a single body all at once, while consisting, in effect, of multiple physiological affections: the physician can characterize pain, for example, as being "felt simultaneously with the perception of the seething of the blood" (*meta sphugmou sunaisthēseōs*).[2] In other medical authors of the period, such as Aretaeus, one finds the nominal and verbal forms of the expression used in a much more general sense: here the word appears to designate the acts of "detection," "registration," and "realization" of any sensation.[3] The word in this broad meaning soon left the terrain of medicine and entered common usage, and it was not long before authors as diverse as Philo Judaeus and Sextus Empiricus could invoke it to refer to the process of "noticing" or "remarking" upon a felt fact.[4]

Sometime close to the beginning of the third century AD, Alexander of Aphrodisias devoted one of his *Quaestiones* to *sunaisthēsis*, which he defined in an acceptation at once wider than that of the Hellenistic physicians and a good deal more precise than that of many of the writers of the time. His point of departure was the dictum of the third book of the Aristotelian *De anima*: "Since we sense that we are seeing and hearing, necessarily it is either by sight that [one] senses that one sees, or by another sense."[5] The remark with which he opened his discussion of the classical proposition already contained the new term, by which the commentator named an act to which the Philosopher himself had given no name. One must understand, Alexander began by explaining, that in this sentence Aristotle "enquires how *sunaisthēsis* comes about for us when we sense certain things, and by what [it comes about] [*zētei, pōs hē sunaisthēsis hēmin ginetai, epeidan aisthanōmetha tinōn, kai tini*]."[6] The commentator went on to assert the universality of the phenomenon: "For to everyone who senses something," he made clear, "there comes about, in addition to the apprehension of the thing that he is sensing, also a certain *sunaisthēsis* of [the fact] that he is sensing" (*panti gar aisthanomenōi tinos pros tēi antilēpsei toutou ou aisthanetai, ginetai sunaisthēsis tis kai tou hoti aisthanetai*).[7] It was a variation on the claim he advanced in the commentary on the *De sensu et sensibilibus*, where he wrote that "everyone, when perceiving," possesses a *sunaisthēsis* that "he exists and perceives."[8] In the *quaestio* on the

De anima, Alexander went to the greatest of lengths to insist on the importance of this fact, which pertained by nature "to everything that has sensation." "The *sunaisthēsis* of sensing," the exegete explained in his conclusion, "comes about in sensation's simultaneously sensing both the thing sensed and its own proper ability in relation to the thing sensed. And for this reason it follows necessarily, for everything that has sensation, that it also has *sunaisthēsis* of its own sensing; it follows, for the sensation that senses some one of the outside things sensed, that it simultaneously also senses itself."[9]

Reading the classical *quaestio* today, it is difficult to avoid the impression that it bears on a structure of the soul close in form to much better-known varieties of awareness named long after it. In the guise of annotating an obscure principle in the Aristotelian doctrine of sensation, the Hellenistic commentator could be said to have offered an unmistakable, if compressed, account of what would one day be called self-consciousness: one might even infer that *sunaisthēsis* is its oldest name. But everything depends on the translation of the ancient term, and on this question contemporary classical scholars, for better or for worse, do not concur. Many, to be sure, make no mention of a philosophical or even philological question, but their practice as editors and translators betrays the difficulty of the problem. In contemporary discussions of Alexander, Simplicius, Damascius, Philoponus, and Priscian, one very often finds the Greek expression rendered by "consciousness" and "self-consciousness."[10] Yet other choices have also been made. In his English version of Alexander's *Quaestiones*, Robert W. Sharples consistently translates the term as "self-awareness," and in his edition of Alexander's commentary on the *De sensu*, Alan Towey opts for another expression, further still from the modern idiom: "joint perception."[11]

The rendition is literal but exact. It is significant that, in distinction to almost all the modern equivalents proposed for it, the Greek term *sunaisthēsis* contains no reference to a "self," and, in contrast to many of the contemporary scholars, Alexander at no point raises the question of an awareness of a subjective state (let

alone one of cognition, as is implied by the invocation in this setting of "consciousness," if one takes the modern philosophical
term in its standard sense). In his gloss, the commentator finds in
the letter of his teacher not an inquiry into the nature of "self-
sensation" or "self-awareness," as the English translation has it,
but what one might term "*with*-sensation," and "how it comes
about for us."[12] Alexander shows little interest in the reflection of
perception upon itself, and there is no clear sign that he believed
Aristotle, for his part, to have meditated on such a subject in the
De anima. The commentator's *quaestio* defines a movement of the
soul that involves the coincidence not of the self with itself but of
an event and its potentiality to occur: the soul's sensation of a
"sensible thing" and its "ability in relation to the thing sensed."
This is an activity in the life of the animal that lies beyond, or
before, the awareness of a single and a double self alike: a structural "perceiving-with," by which the perception of perceptual
qualities would be, at every moment, necessarily "joined" to
another perception, with which it did not altogether coincide.
This would be the natural accompaniment to the execution of
every act of sensation. Constantly with it, without being completely one with it, it would tap out the measures, so to speak, of
the time in which something was sensed at all.

 Sunaisthēsis remained a technical term in ancient philosophy
long after Alexander of Aphrodisias. It played a notable role in the
thought of Plotinus, who knew the Aristotelian commentators
well and discussed Alexander's exegeses, in particular, in the sem-
inars he held in Rome in the middle of the third century.[13] In
time, the works of the early commentator thus became the regular objects of study and even commentary, and later thinkers
came to draw from Alexander's concept consequences that its
maker appears never to have considered. It is already possible to
detect the signs of an alteration of the notion of *sunaisthēsis* in the
first systematic exposition of the Aristotelian treatise on the soul
to have survived from Antiquity, the *Paraphrasis* on the *De anima*
completed by Themistius in the mid-fourth century. Themistius
commented on the Aristotelian work in meticulous detail, and,

when he came to discuss the sense of sensing considered by the Philosopher in Book Gamma, he naturally invoked the concept defined by Alexander for the act. To infer that the commentator of Constantinople limited himself to retracing the exegetical steps of his predecessor, however, would be profoundly to mistake the nature of his art. If one examines the text of the *Paraphrasis* carefully, it seems that Themistius took from the tradition a thing he was the first to find in it, and his reflections lead one to believe that he may well have received from those who went before him a concept that was never transmitted to him as such.

Themistius recalls and rephrases Aristotle's discussion of the sense by which "we sense that we are seeing and hearing" with precision, and at no point in his explanation of the perception of perceiving does he invoke any term other than the one employed for the experience by the Philosopher himself: *aisthēsis*. This fact alone marks a departure from Alexander, but it is less significant than the one that soon follows. Having established that it cannot be by a sense other than sight that one perceives that one is seeing, Themistius turns to the successive principle advanced by the Philosopher. This thesis follows ineluctably from the impossibility of there being a distinct sense from sight, responsible for sensing its operation. We learn that sight needs no faculty beyond itself to sense its own seeing because it already does so on its own, accomplishing a double task: it perceives the sensible and it perceives the event of its own perception. For this reason, "it is clear," Aristotle had written, "that sensing by sight is not a single thing" (*oukh hen to tēi opsei aisthanesthai*). And as an illustration of the thesis, he had adduced a further fact: "When we do not see," he wrote, "it is by sight that we discern darkness from light" (*gar hotan mē horōmen, tēi opsei krinomen kai to skotos kai to phōs*).[14]

Although the Philosopher himself did not address it at any length, the phenomenon to which he alluded raised at least as many questions as it answered. In what way, after all, can one discern obscurity by the faculty of vision and see, in the full meaning of the term, the dark? None would doubt that a sense can be affected by the presence of its proper quality: as it is commonly understood, perception is nothing else. But in what way could the senses be said to apprehend a mere privation and to be receptive not to the presence but to the absence of their characteristic qualities? Themistius finds the solution to the difficulty in the concept of *sunaisthēsis.* "Indeed, when we do not see," he writes, paraphrasing the Stagirite, "<as well as when we see>, we 'discern [objects] by sight,' and we not only perceive light but also jointly perceive darkness [*skotous sunaisthanometha*], yet not in exactly the same way."[15] There is, in other words, a perception of the absence of perception. But it is not so much a "sensing" (*aisthēsis*) in the narrow sense as a "sensing-with" (*sunaisthēsis*), by which the sensitive faculty, finding itself in the lack of all positive qualities, "jointly perceives" its purely privative state. Themistius leaves no doubt that in psychology, such a sensation of the absence of sensation is every bit as important as the sensation of its presence. He defines the two as the symmetrical acts of a single faculty, which apprehends, in each case, a bare fact of perception: "We perceive that we are not seeing," he writes, "by the very same sense by which we also perceive that we are seeing."[16]

Methodically retracing the path of the Aristotelian treatise, Themistius immediately moves on from this passage and its problems, and, faithful to the book on which he comments, he goes no further in the analysis of the sense of sensing and its absence. That was to be the achievement of a later scholar. Of the last generation of the Greek commentators of Antiquity, Priscian of Lydia lived a good three centuries after the author of the *Quaestiones* and some hundred years after Themistius. He was a distinguished representative of that moment of late Antiquity in which the interpretation of the Peripatetic teachings could no longer be distinguished from the elaboration of Neoplatonic doctrine. Little is known of his life, but he is said to have played an active role in the Academy of Athens until 529, when Justinian decreed that the pagan center of learning be definitively closed. Accepting an invitation from a monarch more benevolently disposed to his profession than was the Christian emperor, Priscian then journeyed, together with his two illustrious colleagues, Damascius and Simplicius, to the court of the Persian king Khosrow. Today only one of Priscian's works survives in its totality: a *metaphrasis* of a lost treatise on psychology by Aristotle's early successor, Theophrastus. It offers a brief but far-reaching exposition of the problem of the sensation of sensing, which at once recalls and refashions the invention of the Aristotelian exegetes.

Turning to the question of *sunaisthēsis* in the final paragraphs of his *Metaphrasis*, Priscian introduces Theophrastus's argument by explaining that "it proceeds along the same lines as Aristotle" (*kata ta auta tōi Aristotelei diatithēsi ton logon*).[17] One would be at a loss, however, to find any exact textual source, in either the *De anima* or the *Parva naturalia*, for the bulk of the discussion that then follows; it is unmistakably Neoplatonic in its terminology, and it is difficult to imagine that it could have been altogether contained in the lost work of the Stagirite's first student. The commentator begins, to be sure, by recalling a basic principle in the Aristotelian doctrine of the forms of perception: in the commentator's condensed terms, that "the opposites are of the same [sense]" (*tēs gar autēs tanantia*).[18] He then concludes that the faculty that senses the "activity" (*energeia*) of perception must, by that token, sense its "inactivity" (*argia*) too. Priscian explains that the simultaneously unitary and multiple faculty of the "common sense" (*koinē aisthēsis*) alone could be responsible for such acts:

> Following this, about how we sense that we sense, he <Theophrastus> sets out his argument on the same lines as Aristotle, wanting the common sense to be that which has this extra distinction [*boulomenos eina tēn epikrinousan*], since it perceives jointly both the activity of each <sense> and its inactivity [*tēs energeieas sunaisthanomenēn hekastēs kai tēs argias*]. For the opposites are of the same <sense>. But the common sense is neither the same as the particular ones nor entirely different. For it is by way of the synthesis of all <the senses> and their concentration into an undivided one [*sunairesin kai tēn eis hen ameriston apokoruphōsin*]. Hence in a way each <sense> senses jointly that it perceives [*sunaisthēsetai hoti aisthanetai*], not as having been divided off but as joined together in

87

the one [*sunēptai tēi miai*]. For it belongs to a power already separate from bodies to revert into itself and know itself, and each is more corporeal in so far as it has been divided up, and it goes up more to what is apart by means of its indivisible unity with the others. For in fact this indivisible unity [*ameristos henōsin*] is appropriate to the forms which are apart from bodies. But if, as he himself well claims, it belongs to the same <sense> to discern opposites, and for this reason of <its own> inactivity also, on the one hand even each <sense> will grasp what is separate in a way from its own organs — for <otherwise> sight would not have perceived that the sense-organ's not being affected was darkness, for it <sight> appears to be active even when <that> is not affected — and, on the other, to a greater extent the common <sense>, which is aware also of the inactivity of the senses themselves. Hence, the common <sense>, but not each <individual one>, will jointly sense itself and its own activity: and if of its activity, then also of its inactivity: and if of its inactivity, it would at the same time be, as sensing-with, inactive and active at once [*dio kai hē koinē all'oukh hekastē heautēs sunaisthēsetai kai tēs oikeias energeias. ei men gar tēs energeias, kai tēs argias. ei de tēs argias, hama te an argoiē kai energoiē hōs sunaisthanomenē*].[19]

"Neither the same as the particular ones nor entirely different" from them, the common sense is that in accordance with which the individual senses "revert into" their indivisible and original principle. Where they are corporeal, it is incorporeal; where they are separated, it is undivided; where they are by definition multiple, it is by essence unitary. The central sense is that power in the soul which "jointly perceives itself" (*heautēs sunaisthēsetai*), not as a "self" but as a faculty in which the multiple activities of the senses, all felt at once, reach their "indivisible unity." Priscian presents it as the constant companion to sensuous life, which by nature cannot cease. As the commentator observes, whenever the senses are active, the common sense, sensing their operation, also remains active; and when, by contrast, the senses fall into inactivity, it senses, too, their rest, "as sensing-with, inactive and active at once" (*hama te an argoiē kai energoiē hōs sunaisthanomenē*).

This common sense is at once more and less than those that went before it and bore its classic name. The principle of the presence of perception as of its absence, it is that by which living beings feel that they feel and feel, no less, that they do not. When the various perceptual powers of the living being would seem to end, when all the organs of perception find themselves consigned, like the eyes in darkness, to the privation of those qualities to whose apprehension they are suited, an element in the sensing power does not end: an *aisthēsis*, Priscian teaches, continues in anaesthesia. Sensation, in this way, outlasts its own activity. At the limit, there remains an absence of feeling that is felt, and "with" nothing at all, a perception of a kind persists. To this extent, the accompanying faculty defined by this last commentator on the commentators is absolute. It will not be deterred by the vanishing of that which it would escort. An accompanist to the end, it stays "with," without any being with which it could be said to be. Like a marginal note that exposes the blankness of the page that is its element, the common power may reveal its nature most fully then. It joins the animal, disjoined from all things sensible, to that which is no thing and which, never far from the edges of its senses, keeps it constant company: its life.

CHAPTER NINE

Historia Animalium

Containing a Remark or two on the Definition of human animal Nature, from Aristotle to Simplicius

The belief in the natural distinction of man among living creatures is a well-established one, and its origins can be traced without much difficulty to the inception of scientific and philosophical reflection in the classical world. But the idea that man is an animal no different from the others is at least as ancient, and it may well be even older. It suffices to recall the setting in which Aristotle proposed his famous definition of man as the "rational animal" (or, more precisely, the "living being possessing language," *zōon logon ekhōn*, which, in the passage from Greek to Latin philosophical terminology, later acquired its classic form of *animal rationale*). In time, this dictum came to be canonical, and today the full force of its influence on the history of inquiries into the nature of animal life can seem almost immeasurable. When he formulated this claim, however, Aristotle left no doubt that it came in clear contrast to those advanced by a great number of his pre-Socratic predecessors, who accepted no such partition between man and the other beasts. If we are to believe the accounts of them offered in the *Metaphysics* and the *De anima*, not only Homer but also Empedocles, Parmenides, and Democritus all failed to offer any systematic account of the differing powers possessed by living things. When they came to discuss the various faculties of the animal soul, the early thinkers did not distinguish clearly, therefore, between sensation and perception (*aisthēsis*), on the one hand, and reason and intelligence (*nous* and *phronēsis*), on the other.[1]

Aristotle recounts that Anaxagoras, in particular, taught that intellect (*nous*) was the cause of order and the good and, moreover, that it was identical with the soul (*psukhē*). All animals, the pre-Socratic thinker could then maintain, possess the same faculty of intelligence (*phronēsis*). Surely Anaxagoras, like those after him, knew well that its forms among living things can differ; while commenting critically on his views, Aristotle granted that his predecessor would probably never have denied that the faculty of thought could not be attributed to them all "in the same way" (*homoiōs*). The thinker could simply have held that such differences were not of nature but of degree. The ability itself could in any case be one, common to all animals, as Aristotle wrote, "large or small, superior or inferior" (*kai megalois kai mikrois, kai timiois kai atimoterois*).[2]

Setting a clear boundary between human and inhuman beings, the classical definition of man as a rational animal clearly aimed, among other things, to dispel this undifferentiated dimension of all animal life. It may have largely succeeded. But the truth is that in the history of thought, the positing of a distinction between man and animal has been followed, not only preceded, by its absence, and even when human nature and animal nature have been most strenuously distinguished, a region in which they cannot be told apart has continued to recur. The reason is one of necessity, and it can be found in the logical operation that lies at the root of the specification of what one might term, with a somewhat cumbersome phrase, "human animal nature." Since man is, among other things, himself an animal, the procedure by which one determines his proper quality must separate him not only from the other living beings but also from himself. Even as it distances him from the animals around him, the defining operation must distinguish man, in other words, from the nonman within him, separating the element in him that participates in human nature from the element that partakes of a nature common to all beasts.[3]

Consider, as an example, the specification of man as a rational animal. From the living, feeling, speaking being that is man, one abstracts a quality to be termed "human" with propriety: the possession of reason (however one may then wish to define the faculty). As conclusive as it may seem, such an operation invariably produces a remainder, which cannot be attributed with any exclusivity to either human or inhuman beings. It is, quite simply, the element that is left over in human beings once one has withdrawn from them what is particularly human: everything in man, for example, that remains after, or before, the life of reason, everything in him that cannot be said to owe its existence to the activity of thought. This is an element that persists in human nature without altogether coinciding with it. By definition, it cannot be said to be strictly human, since it remains distinct from the activity judged proper to man. To the degree to which it can, however, still be found in human beings, it also cannot be said with any exactitude to be inhuman. One could call it the inhuman aspect of humanity or, alternately, the human aspect of inhumanity, but such appellations are needlessly complex and disguise a more elementary fact. The remaining element testifies to a dimension of the living being in which the distinction between the human and the inhuman simply has no pertinence: a region common, by definition, to all animal life.

In the idiom of classical philosophy, the name of this shared region is "sensation" (*aisthēsis*). One may view the development of the theory of the soul from the pre-Socratics to Plato and to Aristotle, in large part, as the history of its conception. The early Greek thinkers must have differed in their terminology, but from the reports contained in later sources it appears that a number of them agreed on the necessity of ascribing a single power to all animals. For many, it was intelligence. Aëtius reports that Parmenides, Empedocles, and Democritus all took the principle of "thought" (*nous*) to be indistinguishable from that of the "soul" (*psychē*) and so ascribed an intellectual power to all animate beings.[4] Diogenes Laertius attributes a similar doctrine to Diogenes of Apollonia: by virtue of being alive, every animal, he claimed, possesses thought in addition to sensation.[5] There are traces of such a position in Plato's dialogues. A passage in the

Laws, for example, suggests that intellection (*nous*) and perception (*aisthēsis*) together ensure the subsistence of all living things;[6] other works, such as the *Timaeus*, the *Republic*, and the *Statesman*, find Socrates and his interlocutors entertaining the possibility that animals could be no less rational than men (a famous case is the dog in the *Republic*, whose powers of recognition are said to bespeak a "love of knowledge" close in nature to that of the philosopher).[7] In the *Theaetetus*, however, Socrates seems to take a further step. Discussing the relative competencies of men (*anthrōpoi*) and beasts (*thēria*), he argues that both can "perceive [*aisthanesthai*] certain things straight away on being born, namely, those impressions [*pathēmata*] that reach the soul from the body." But only those capable of hard-won education (*paideia*) and experience can aspire to "reflections [*analogismata*] about these as regards being and utility."[8]

Many scholars have taken this claim as an anticipation of the philosophical decision that Aristotle would soon make in his many works on living things: to grant beasts sensation (*aisthēsis*) but deny them "reason" (*logos*), "reasoning" (*logismos*), thought (*dianoia*), intellect (*nous*), and belief (*doxa*).[9] The proposition was of immense consequence, and, at certain points, the Stagirite could seem to retreat before the strictures it imposed. Instances of apparent hesitation have been found in the *Nicomachean Ethics*, but the most famous cases are contained in the zoological works.[10] It was no accident that in that monument to ancient vegetarianism that is the compendious treatise *On Abstinence from Killing Animals*, Porphyry could draw a host of examples from Aristotle's *Historia animalium*, even though the disciple of Plotinus argued at length against the dominant doctrines of the Peripatetic school. On the surface, Aristotle himself had provided numerous illustrations of what he considered the courage, good temper, technical skill, and even intelligence (*phronēsis*) of beasts in Books Eta and Theta.[11] It suffices to recall the discussion of the swallow building its nest with meticulous precision, the crane flying upward to achieve an exact and comprehensive view of the region beneath it, or the cuckoo ingeniously disposing of its young ones, lucidly

94

aware of that regrettable but inescapable fact: that it is a coward and cannot hope to provide lasting shelter for them.[12]

Considered in isolation, such examples can be misleading. They are best understood, as Richard Sorabji has written, "in the context of the programmatic warnings at the beginning of each of these books ..., punctuated by further warnings: it is only *as if* the dolphins calculate (*hōsper analogisamenoi*) how big a breath they need before diving."[13] Whenever Aristotle considered the question of the relative capacities of the human and inhuman animals in his more purely philosophical works, his conclusions left little room for doubt. A *scala naturae*, he taught, unites all animate things in a single continuum of increasing differentiation and progressive complication, in which each higher power contains, as its first conditions, those that lie beneath it. The ladder begins with the purely nutritive faculty of plants (*threptikon*). It culminates with the contemplative faculty (*theōrētikē dunamis*) of man, which, as the Philosopher commented in a famous passage of the *De anima*, seems so different a power as almost to belong "to another type of soul ... separable, like the eternal from the corruptible."[14] Between the two extremes of nourishment and thought lies the common terrain of animal life: perception. At times, Aristotle described it as consisting of several faculties, which include imagination (*phantasia*), desire (*orexis*), pain (*lupē*), pleasure (*hēdonē*), appetite (*epithumia*), and sensation (*aisthēsis*).[15] At others, he proposed a more economical analysis and suggested that all such activities could be subsumed under the twin powers of desire and perception.[16] Finally, at points of the greatest concision, he could reduce them all to the primary power, whose presence alone separates beasts from plants: the "principle of sensation, through which animals as such can be said to be."[17]

The proposition may seem severe. But the restriction of animal life to the sphere of sensation means little as long as its exact contours of Aristotelian *aisthēsis* are not made clear. The classical faculty is not to be confused with the passive reception of sense data for which many modern thinkers would later take the power of the same name. A perceptive soul, as Aristotle understood it, remains capable of apprehending not only the perceptual qualities of the five senses but also the common sensible properties, such as shape and number, which are bound, as modifications of movement, to the perception of time. For him, the activity of sensing, moreover, is by definition also one of judgment: it "discerns" (*krinein*) each sensible quality in its proper spectrum, and it discriminates between sensible qualities of different kinds, telling the properties of the sight, for example, from those of taste. A further fact brings the sensitive animals of the Peripatetic system startlingly closer to the self-conscious beings of modern thought. Since every sense, in the Peripatetic doctrine, is "of itself," receptive not only to the sensible quality but also to its own apprehension of it, one must conclude that in perceiving (*aisthanesthai*), animals, for Aristotle, "jointly perceive" (*sunaisthanesthai*) that they do so: beasts, by definition, feel when they feel (and feel, too, when they do not).

On this question, the author of the *De anima*, to be sure, was laconic. The treatise on the soul does not specify the exact nature of the "we" who "sense that we are seeing and hearing." A question, therefore, inevitably remains: who are "we" — animals like, or unlike, the others? Aristotle does not expressly affirm that the perception of the act of perception must be attributed to all the living beings that perceive. But he never denies it, and nowhere does he suggest, if not with the invocation of this "we" who sense, that the distinction between man and the other beasts must be granted any particular pertinence at this point. A gap in the argument cannot be excluded in principle. Yet it is difficult to imagine why, in the concluding portion of his analysis of the "principle through which animals as such can be said to be," the Philosopher would suddenly have restricted himself, without remarking on the fact, to the study of the two-legged beast to the exclusion of all others.

The classical commentary tradition suggests that, for one reason or another, Aristotle and his early exegetes did not consider the question at any length. It is significant that it is only in the final period of the ancient expositions of the *De anima* that one begins to find explicit debates on the subject of whether the sense of sensing constitutes a faculty proper to the human or, alternately, the merely animal soul. Such discussions may be taken as signs of the growing influence exerted by Neoplatonic doctrine on the interpretation of Aristotle. Plotinus had distinguished formally between sensation (*aisthēsis*), as a relation to an externality, and "awareness" (literally, "joint sensation," *sunaisthēsis*), as an internal relation of the sensing being to itself. "We have an awareness of ourselves," he had therefore written in the fourth *Ennead*, "but not sensation, which is always of something else" (*hēmeis hēmōn sunaisthanometha doteon, aisthēsin de aei heterou ousan ou deteon*).[18] Indications of such a teaching are clearly detectable in the exposition of the *De anima* traditionally ascribed to the sixth-century Christian Neoplatonist Philoponus, which may also have been the work of the later lecturer of Alexandria and Byzantium, Stephanus. When he considers the question of the sense by which "we sense that we are seeing and hearing," this commentator objects to the positions of the Philosopher and his expositor from Aphrodisias and takes great care to explain that it would be an error to ascribe the sense of sensing to the irrational soul.

In itself, this claim was not an absolute novelty at that time. As the commentator himself noted, Plutarch of Athens, the early fifth-century teacher of Syrianus and Proclus, had already held that "it is the function of the rational soul to know the activities of the senses."[19] In his commentary, however, Philoponus (or Pseudo-Philoponus) distinguishes himself equally from Plutarch, who concluded that the perception of perceiving was, in truth, the work of "opinion" (*doxa*).[20] "More recent exponents," the bold exegete writes, "neither tremble at Alexander's frown nor pay heed to Plutarch but, pushing Aristotle himself aside, have devised a novel interpretation: they say that it belongs to the attentive part [*tou prosektikou merous*] of the rational soul to lay hold of the activities of the senses."[21] Later commentators could similarly "push aside" the teaching of Aristotle's treatise, even when they did not invoke such forceful terms. But they appear to have done so consciously, and when they did insist that the perception of perceiving be restricted to human beings, they often remarked upon it, implying unmistakably, albeit delicately, that they knew their view was not shared by the earlier Aristotelians. Simplicius, who belonged to the last generation of the ancient commentators, thus explained in his exposition of the *De anima* that "the fact of sensing that we sense seems to me [*moi dokei*] to be the proper of man."[22] He said no more about the status of his claim. But as Ilsetraut Hadot has observed, the intrusion of the first-person pronoun into the otherwise neutral voice of the exegesis is telling in itself. It implies that on this matter, "Simplicius speaks here only in his own name."[23]

The history of the classical reception of the *De anima* clearly indicates that, by late Antiquity, many wished to attribute to the reason of men a faculty that Aristotle and his classical disciples had assigned to the perceptual powers of animal nature without distinction. On this question, at least, posterity in large part followed not Aristotle and Alexander but Philoponus and Simplicius, and we remain the successors to those successors of the early Christian era. The principle stated so unambiguously by the early commentator according to which "everything that has sensation . . . also has a joint sensing of its own sensing" boasts few partisans today.[24] Much more familiar is the position first voiced in somewhat timorous terms by the sixth-century thinker, which attributes to human beings alone the feeling that they feel. This fact pertains to the afterlife of the notion created by Aristotle and his pupils, but it also reveals a good deal more. It bears witness to a transformation in the conception of animal nature no less decisive for having been achieved over the course of centuries and in movements difficult to date with great precision. The sense of sensing was perhaps the most brilliant of the faculties of sensation identified by the classical philosophers and consigned, with the waning of Antiquity, to the vicissitudes of the shifting relations between living beings that then followed. But it was not the only one of its kind. Other powers played a role in the passage that brought the possessor of reason, in time, to claim for himself the elements of a nature once conceived in common. Just as the thinking beast could be separated in more ways than one from those around it, so there was more than a single region in which its merely sensing life could rejoin the shared history of all animals, "large or small, superior or inferior."

CHAPTER TEN

Appropriation

A long Chapter, containing an important Notion, as well
as the Doctrines of Chrysippus concerning a small Mussel and
a Crab, smaller still

"If there had been no Chrysippus," many in Antiquity were wont
to say, "there would have been no Portico."[1] One can certainly
understand the justice of this classic claim. Officially, of course,
the thinker of the second century BC was not the founder of the
philosophical school that, named after the Greek term designating its characteristic archway, came to be known as the Stoa. That
honor was accorded Zeno of Kition, who was the teacher of
Chrysippus's teacher, Cleanthes. But it was concerning the third
founding figure of classical Stoicism that "the majority" are said to
have concurred when they famously judged that "if there were to
be dialectic among the gods, it could only be that of Chrysippus."[2]
It was he who could be said to have most fully defined the three
branches of the Stoic system: logic, physics, and ethics. By all
accounts, he was also the most prolific of the ancient thinkers.
In the chapter of the *Lives of Eminent Philosophers* dedicated to
Chrysippus, Diogenes Laertius remarked that "in industry," the
third great Stoic "surpassed everyone, as the list of his writings
shows; for there are more than seven hundred and five of them."[3]
It is one of the regrettable facts of the classical tradition that not
one of them has survived. To learn anything of their contents
today, one must to turn to the later Greek and Latin authors who,
for reasons more or less polemical, chose to quote and paraphrase
them in part.

It seems that the early Stoic philosopher was fascinated by crustaceans and, in particular, by two lesser-known varieties of their kind: the pinna (*pinnē*) and the pinna-guard (*pinnotērēs* or *pinnophulax*). According to Plutarch, Chrysippus "spilled a great deal of ink" over both of them; with more than a little acrimony and, one presumes, a good deal of exaggeration, Plutarch once commented that the Stoic had clearly decided to reserve for them "a fixed place" in each of his many books, "whether ethical or physical."[4] Chrysippus, it should be noted, was not the first to mention the two small creatures. Before him, Aristotle had referred to both species, albeit in passing, in the classic treatment of shellfish in Book Epsilon of the *Historia animalium*.[5] For one reason or another, however, posterity smiled on the Stoic, not the Peripatetic, crustaceans. In time, Cicero, Philo, and Athenaeus, in addition to Plutarch, all came to discuss the Chrysippean account of them in different settings.[6] Nonetheless, there are signs that the pinna and the pinna-guard remained less than absolutely familiar to the laity of Antiquity, for several of the classical authors who discussed them took considerable care to explain, if only for the sake of their untrained audience, exactly what they were.

Modern students of classical thought may turn for clarification on such matters to the authoritative guide to classical sea creatures published in 1947 by D'Arcy Wentworth Thompson, *A Glossary of Greek Fishes*. This indispensable compendium contains an entry of considerable length on the pinna, identifying the creature, with an accompanying zoological illustration, as "a bivalve shellfish common in the Mediterranean, rare so far north as Britain." "The animal," we learn, "is famous for growing a *byssus* or tuft of silky fibres, as the common mussel does, but much longer and finer; this is the *pinninothrix mallos* of Constant. *De Them.* i 12, the *lana penna*, or *lana pesce*, of the fishermen in Southern Italy. It was spun and woven into a costly fabric resembling silk, and this industry lingers on in Taranto and Cagliari." After a brief survey of the various textiles that could (and still can) be made from the byssus, the author returns on the next page to the animal itself, as well as it to its famous guard.

"The Pinna," we then learn, "grows straight up out of the mud, anchored by its byssus, and is also celebrated for the little crab which acts as its watchman, or 'Pinna-guard' (*pinnotērēs, pinnophulax*)." A little later in the *Glossary*, those Greek terms, too, receive an entry of their own, which defines them as the double names of a single beast: "the so-called Pinna-guard, a little crab which makes its home within the Pinna's shell, and acts as sentinel."[7]

The ancient sources on the sea creatures are less well documented, but, if one excepts certain differences of terminology and taxonomy, they largely concur. Book Three of the *Deipnosophistai* contains the most elaborate discussion of the Stoic theory of the pinna and its guard. "Chrysippus of Soli," Athenaeus explains,

> states that the pinna [*pinnē*] and the pinna-guard [*pinnotērēs*] collaborate with each other in virtue of the good and enjoyment, since they could not subsist individually. The pinna is therefore an oyster [*ostreon estin*], while the pinna-guard is a small crayfish [*karkinos mikros*]. Opening its shell, the pinna remains immobile, looking out for whatever little fish might enter. The pinna-guard informs it whenever anything enters by biting it, as if making a sign [*hōsper sēmainōn*]; and once bitten, the pinna closes. It is thus that the pinna and the pinna-guard together eat whatever remains imprisoned on the inside.[8]

This account of the doctrine can be said to conform to those offered by Cicero and Plutarch (even if the latter adds that the sentinel is situated not inside but outside the pinna, "guarding the door of the shell and sitting in front [of it]").[9] The end of the collaboration is in each case the same and, for the pinna and its guard, at least, it is undeniably felicitous. "Two little beasts so different from one another thus procure their food in common" (*sic dissimillimis bestiolis communiter cibus quaeritur*), Cicero observes; and, in the somewhat less pacific terms afforded by Plutarch, "together they devour the prey that has entered the trap."[10]

The tale of the shellfish was striking and, as the ancients themselves clearly saw, it raised several questions to which answers could not easily be found. Convinced of what he elsewhere termed the "repugnancies of the Stoics," Plutarch, for one, could not accept it. In his extended dialogue on the intelligence of animals, *Whether Land or Sea Animals Are Cleverer* (known more succinctly to the Latin tradition as the *De sollertia animalium*), he naturally did not fail to mention the Stoic doctrine. But he left no doubt that the distinction accorded these two sea creatures among all others could rest on no scientific grounds. It is difficult not to discern the voice of the author in the words of Phaidimus, the dialogue's eloquent spokesman for the fish: "Chrysippus," he explains curtly, "has obviously not investigated the sponge-guard [*spongotēran*]; otherwise he could hardly have left it out."[11] By contrast, Cicero, who appears to have accepted the Stoic analysis, found it to be in itself still incomplete. An important question still remained. For how, he wondered, did the unlikely pair ever come to meet? "Here is a subject of much amazement [*admirandum*]," he remarked. "Did these little beasts come to associate with one another following an encounter of some sort, or did nature associate them from birth?"[12]

There was also a question of principle, which involved the description that Chrysippus had so famously offered of the creatures complicit in their hunt for fish. How could one explain, in the terms of the Stoic school, the seeming cleverness and sociality of the two crustaceans? As A.A. Long has observed, "No philosophers have emphasized more strongly than the Stoics that rationality is *the* determinant of human life, and that it marks men off sharply from all other animals."[13] The thinkers of the Portico held gods and human beings to be by nature *logoi*. All other things, inanimate and animate like, were for them irreparably *alogoi*, deprived of the divine element of speech present in the higher works of man. "I cannot help you more," wrote Seneca, explaining the doctrines of his school to Lucilius, "than if I indicate that good which corresponds to your nature and if I separate you from the mute animals, setting you at the level of a god."[14] Cicero

expressed the same tenet when he maintained that "it is important, for every investigation into duty, always to be aware how far
the nature of humanity lies from that of the other animals."[15]
Whereas the Platonic dialogues contained a number of differing
views on animal intelligence and the Aristotelian corpus, taken as
a whole, could be read as suggesting more than a single account of
the presence of thought and cunning among living things, for the
Stoics there could be no doubt: as far as reason was concerned,
they maintained, a gulf divided speaking beasts from all those
around them.[16] Chrysippus and his school consistently attributed
to the inhuman animals two faculties alone: impulse (*hormē*) and
sensation (*aisthēsis* or, in certain cases, what was for them its
lesser variety, *phantasia*, a faculty of "presentation" devoid of the
function of assent [*sunkatathesis, adsensio*] they took to characterize sensation or perception in the full sense of the terms).[17]

Even as they denied beasts reason with unprecedented deci-
siveness, however, the Stoics attributed to animal nature a power
that none before them had identified as such, whose limits in the
life of living things cannot easily be set. It was a thing the classical
philosophers of the Portico called *oikeiōsis*. Its concept was to
number among the most far-reaching and influential creations of
ancient philosophy, and in the school of Chrysippus it played a
role whose importance can hardly be overestimated. This fact has
not gone unnoticed by modern historians of classical thought.
Max Pohlenz once characterized the notion as "the starting point
and, as it were, firm ground of Stoic ethics," and S.G. Pembroke
argued that its importance well exceeded any particular branch of
the ancient system: "If there had been no *oikeiōsis*," he wrote simply and pointedly, "there would have been no Stoa."[18] In modern
works on classical thought, "the Greek term," as Gisela Striker
has observed, "is usually not translated, but transliterated; not
because it is untranslatable, but because any translation would
seem to be intolerably clumsy."[19] Thanks to a handful of philological studies, however, one may nonetheless reconstruct, with considerable exactitude, its formation and its meaning.

Oikeiōsis is a verbal noun, closely related to the adjective oikeion, which derives from the Greek term for "house": oikos, the same lexical element that survives in the first half of our "economy" and whose Indo-European root has long been thought to have given rise to the Latin vicus, "village," as well as to the characteristic English ending of place names, "-wick."[20] In the Greek language, the adjective oikeion designated the quality of being "of the same household or family" and signified, by extension, "that which belongs to (or is a member of) the household or oikia in question."[21] It could be opposed, in this sense, to the standard term in the language for "what belongs to someone else or is in a wider sense alien to oneself," allotrios.[22] The opposition between the two expressions played a notable role in classical Greek thought. Scholars have observed that in Book One of The Republic, for example, Thrasymachus invokes the "oikeios good" (oikeion agathon), in opposition to the "allotrios good" (allotrion agathon), as "the good which belongs most intimately to oneself because it is rooted in one's very nature, and so is opposed to the good which is not so rooted."[23] The adjective oikeios was closely related to the verb oikeioun, which occurs as early as Herodotus and can also be found in Thucydides, where it has been thought to mean "'to claim as one's own,' i.e., to claim as belonging to oneself."[24] The same verb appears often in works of the fifth and fourth centuries, where its sense is clearly transitive. Accompanied by a direct object (tina or ti), it indicates the act by which one "claims ownership" and "appropriates," and, when the objects in question are people, "wins over someone to one's side."[25]

Such actions have little do with the philosophical term coined by the thinkers of the Portico. Their oikeiōsis "is never used in the active sense of appropriation," deriving from a verb of the middle or passive voice: oikeiousthai, construed not with an accusative but with a dative or a preposition (tini or pros tina), employed to designate the process by which one thing "becomes proper" and "related" to another.[26] Herwig Görgemanns has called attention to the fact that in Stoic works the verb, despite its passive meaning, is never accompanied by the mention of any agent in the usual sense (one does not find it, for example, tied to the construction *hupo tinos*, "by what" or "by whom").[27] The reason for the fact can be simply stated, and it touches on the essence of the Stoic notion. In this act of becoming related, the "someone" or "something" to which one grows familiar can hardly be distinguished from the subject as such, for the *oikeiōsis* of the Portico signifies the process by which a living being comes to be appropriate to its own nature.

Hence the striking reflexive form so often employed by the Stoics: *oikeiousthai pros heauton*. The expression has been rendered by several English forms; the two most commonly proposed are "to be well disposed toward oneself" and the more sentimental, although grammatically exact, "to become endeared toward oneself."[28] The literal sense of the expression is quite clear, albeit difficult to render elegantly in English. The Stoic formulation designates the movement by which one "becomes related to (or toward) oneself," that is, by which a living being comes to be appropriated to itself. As such, the expression belongs to the set of those grammatical forms that followed in the wake of the Delphic injunction to "know yourself" (*gnōthi seauton*) and that flourished in the classical Greek period: from Antiphon's "to rule oneself" (*hauton kratein*) to Xenophon's "to care for onself" (*epimeleisthai hautou*) and "enslavers of oneself" (*andrapodizesthai heautōn*), Democritus's "to be ashamed of onself" (*heauton aiskhunesthai* and *aidesisthai*), Gorgias's "to betray oneself" (*prodidonai heauton*), and, above all, Sophocles's and Euripides's "to be a friend to oneself" (*heauton philein*), which was to play such an important role in Book Theta of Aristotle's *Nicomachean Ethics* in the slightly revised form of *philautia*.[29]

Discussing the Stoics in the seventh book of his *Lives*, Diogenes Laertius offered the following summary of their theory of *oikeiōsis*:

They say that the first impulse that an animal has is to preserve itself, because nature makes it proper to itself from the outset [*oikeiousēs auto tēs phuseōs ap' arkhēs*], as Chrysippus says in the first book of his work *On Ends*. He says that the first thing that belongs [*prōton oikeion*] is its own constitution [*sustasin*] and its awareness [literally, its "sensing-with," *sunaisthēsis*] of it.[30] For it would not have been reasonable for nature to assign the animal itself to another [literally, to "expropriate it," *allotriōsai*], nor when she had made it, that she should either assign it to another [*allotriōsai*] or not make it proper [*oikeiōsai*]. Accordingly, it remains to say that when she had constituted the animal she made it become proper to itself [*oikeiōsai pros heauto*]. For it is in this way that harmful things are thrust away and proper things [*ta oikeia*] are permitted to approach.[31]

Here the biographer leaves no doubt as to the important role played by appropriation in the Stoic account of animal nature. For the thinkers of the Portico, *oikeiōsis* constitutes nothing less than the principle of that "first impulse" common to all living things, without which no natural thing could last: self-preservation. Animals keep "harmful things" far from them and allow "proper things" to approach them, Chrysippus must have explained, because "from the outset" (*ap' arkhēs*) they find themselves assigned to themselves, because they are "made proper," and because, in a sense Diogenes himself does not define, they possess an "awareness" (*sunaisthēsis*) of their innate "constitution" (*suntasis*).

Book Three of Cicero's *De finibus* seems to contain a sketch of the same doctrine, transposed, with the teachings of all the ancient schools, from the first idiom of classical philosophy into its second. Cato, the spokesman of the Stoa in the work, explains:

> It is the view of those whose system I adopt that, as soon as it is born (for this is the point from which one should begin) an animal is conciliated to itself and it is commended to preserve itself and to love its own constitution and the things that tend to preserve that constitution, while it is alienated from destruction and things that seem to bring about destruction [*simulatque natum sit animal (hinc enim est ordiendum) ipsum sibi conciliari et commendari ad se conservandum et ad suum statum eaque quae conservantia sunt eius status diligenda, alienari autem ab interitu iisque rebus quae interitum videantur afferre*]. That this is the case they prove by the fact that children seek wholesome things and reject their opposites before pleasure or pain has touched

them. This would not happen unless they loved their own constitution and feared destruction. And it would be impossible for them to seek anything unless they had a sense of themselves [*nisi sensum haberent sui*] and for this reason loved themselves.[32]

Where Diogenes had spoken of the process by which nature makes all living things "appropriate to themselves," Cicero's personage invokes the movement by which every animal finds itself "conciliated to itself and . . . commended to preserve itself" (*ipsum sibi conciliari et commendari ad se conservandum*). The terms evidently differ in translation. But the doctrine remains unitary, and for this reason some have supposed the Latin summary to flow "from the same ultimate source as the passage in Diogenes Laertius," most likely "the work of Chrysippus cited by Diogenes."[33]

The passages constitute two invaluable records of a principle famously defined by the Stoics, in distinction to the rules traditionally said to be "by nature" (*kata phusin*), as "that which is first by nature" (*ta prōta kata phusin*): that most basic law, which remits every animal, "from the outset" (*ap' arkhēs*) and "as soon as it is born" (*simulatque natum*), to continue to live in conserving itself.[34] The principle applies no less to the rational than to the irrational animals, and according to the Stoics, its force, which manifests itself most clearly in early youth, extends throughout the life of every beast. The thinkers of the Portico taught that, by necessity, the living being approaches the things around it as things that might help or harm it, discovering the world in which it lives in inclining toward what might maintain it and in retreating, at the same time, from what might destroy it. Its relation to what is not itself, in other words, cannot be separated from its relation to the principle of its own conservation; at every point, its perception of the world around it remains determined by its indispensable "awareness" (*sunaisthēsis, sensus*) of its own "constitution" (*suntasis, constitutio*).

What is the nature of this "awareness"? Modern scholars have rarely hesitated to identify it with forms of representation and self-representation defined long after the end of the classical period, in the course of debates that often had little, if anything, to do with any nature other than that of the thinking being. The paraphrase offered by Striker of the argument contained in Book Zeta of the *Lives* is, in this sense, telling: "It is not reasonable to suppose that nature, after having created an animal, should not have provided it with the means of self-preservation; so she must have made it well-disposed towards itself, which implies that it has both consciousness of its own constitution and an instinct for those things beneficial or harmful to it."[35] Setting aside the question of the pertinence of the concept of "creation" to any analysis of classical thought, one may well wonder: may one legitimately attribute to the Stoics the thesis according to which all animals possess "consciousness," in addition to instinct? That modern term, to be sure, regularly appears in contemporary translations of the ancient authors, and the scholar's invocation, although questionable, cannot be taken as exceptional.[36] Some go even further: in Harris Rackham's classic translation of the *De finibus*, one thus finds Cato explaining, with a startling turn of phrase, that animals could not avoid the noxious and seek out the beneficent "unless they possessed self-consciousness."[37]

It is sometimes difficult to know exactly what modern scholars mean by the terms "consciousness" and "self-consciousness." But if they mean a power of thought or reason, as a reader familiar with philosophical terminology might well infer, it is certain that on this matter, at least, their views differ fundamentally from those of the ancients on whom they aim to comment. That the Stoic *oikeiōsis* is irreducible to reason is beyond all doubt: were it not, it could not be common to every "living being" by definition, as the thinkers of the Portico, according to all reports, never tired of repeating.[38] There is little indication, moreover, that it is to be understood as a fact of impulse in any standard sense. If anything, the appropriation of an animal to itself lies closer, as Pembroke has suggested, to the more fundamental "project" (*epibolē*) of the ancient school: an "impulse prior to impulse" (*hormēn pro hormēs*), which precedes and conditions all particular acts of self-conservation.[39]

The question, however, remains one of modest importance,

for it bears on a matter resolved long ago in unambiguous terms by the Stoics and their early commentators. The philosophers of Antiquity possessed a name for the faculty by which all animals apprehend their own nature, and it was not impulse. It was, instead, the one invoked by Cicero's Stoic. "It would be impossible," explains Cato, speaking of animals, "for them to seek anything unless they had a *sense* of themselves [*nisi sensum haberent sui*]." His usage was, by all appearances, orthodox both in his time and well after it. It suffices to recall Plutarch's definition of *oikeiōsis* as "the sensation of what is proper and its apprehension" (*hē gar oikeiōsis aisthēsis eoike tou oikeiou kai antilēpsis einai*).[40] Porphyry stressed the same point when, in Book Three of the *De abstinentia*, he dwelled on the concept as it was understood by the "disciples of Zeno": "All appropriation [*oikeiōsis*]," he wrote, "has its principle in sensation" (*oikeiōseōs pasēs ... arkhē to aisthanesthai*).[41]

Seneca's 121st letter to Lucilius contains a discussion of the matter that is of capital importance. "We asked ourselves," Seneca writes, referring to conversations carried out over some time, "whether all animals have a sense of their constitution" (*an esset omnibus animalibus constitutionis suae sensus*). The philosopher's answer to the question is unequivocally affirmative. "That it is so," Seneca explains, "is shown by the fact that their movements are apt and adjusted, as if they were learned; there is no part that does not possess great agility." Just as the artisan knows how to use his tools and the portraitist, to distinguish among the colors he has set before him, as he moves quickly and easily, with his hands and his eyes, between the wax and the easel, so the beast excels in its natural arts and, "with the same rapidity," exercises its inborn skills.[42] Among human beings, to be sure, such ease may be the fruit of training, while among beasts it springs from nature. But the principle is the same: "None tires in moving its joints; none hesitates in its own capacities" (*nemo aegre molitur artus suos, nemo in usu sui haesitat*). It is always so: beasts come into the world with all their "knowledge" (*scientia*), invariably born, as Seneca writes, already learned (*instituta nascuntur*).[43]

An objection can be raised, and Seneca is quick to cite it. The agility of living things could be the expression of no more than a fear of injury: "Animals move their limbs in the right way," one might maintain, "because if they moved them otherwise, they would feel pain." Were it so, however, the movements of beasts could hardly be called expert. Actions dictated by necessity are by nature "cautious" (*tarda*); the spontaneous alone are agile. Seneca, however, adduces more particular proof that no beast acts exclusively from fear of pain. Experience teaches that "animals," he recalls, "tend toward natural movements, even when they cause them pain."[44] Consider the small child impelled to stand upright, even though "he falls every time, and stands up again crying every time until, through suffering, he succeeds in carrying out his natural movements." Or observe, instead, animals "of hard backs." It may happen that, despite itself, a tortoise comes to be sadly overturned. It will do almost anything, Seneca recalls, to escape that miserable condition: contort itself, stretch out its legs as far as they may go, lean over, as best it can, to one side — all to reposition itself as it must. "The tortoise," the philosopher maintains, "feels no torment when it lies supine. But it is nevertheless agitated [*inquieta*], and it wants to regain its natural position; and it will not cease until it stands again on its feet."[45]

The phenomenon, as the Roman writer sees it, points to a single fact: "All animals possess a sense of their constitution."[46] This was a fundamental principle of the Stoic system, and in his letter to Lucilius, Seneca takes considerable care to ensure that it not be misunderstood. He considers the reply it would most likely provoke. "Constitution" (*constitutio*), as his adversaries would well know, is a technical term for the thinkers of the Portico, the Latin equivalent of a Greek expression (*sustasis*) that in classical Stoicism designates "the fundamental element of the soul in the relation that it assumes with respect to the body" (*principale animi quodam modo se habens erga corpus*).[47] "How," the philosopher imagines others replying, "can an infant understand such a complex and subtle concept, which you yourselves barely manage to explain? Every animal would have to be born a master in dialectics to understand this definition, which is obscure to most learned men."[48] Seneca concedes that the objection would be just had he truly claimed that children and animals "understand [*intelligitur*] the definition of constitution" — but he had not. The infant, he explains at greater length, does not know what a constitution is, but he does know his own (*infans ille quid sit constitution non novit, constitutionem suam novit*). "Knows" (*novit*), in such cases, ought not to mislead: when applied to all animals, rational and irrational alike, the expression is in truth shorthand for "senses." The beast does not know what it is to be itself. But ignorance poses no limit to the power of sensation: an animal does not know what it is to be animal, but still it feels itself to be one (*quid sit animal nescit, animal esse se sentit*).[49]

It was no more than the restatement of the classic Stoic claim, as old as the lost treatise *On Ends* Chrysippus is said to have written: the claim, namely, that living things, by sensation, come to be appropriated to themselves, that, in Seneca's words, "the animal conciliates itself first of all to itself [*primum sibi ipsum conciliatur animal*]."[50] Such a "conciliation" and "adaptation" of the self to itself, as Seneca makes clear, is not of the order of an event; it is, rather, a movement, to be continually achieved anew throughout all animal life. It is a matter of the attention shown to the self by itself, to whose cultivation Seneca's Stoic colleagues Epictetus and Marcus Aurelius would most famously also turn in their explorations of the "care of the self" (*heautou epimelesthai*).[51] Seneca, for his part, does not hesitate to invoke the practice in a letter devoted to the relation of every animal, rational and irrational, to itself. Nor does he show any reluctance to speak for all beasts in speaking for himself. "I wish for pleasure," Seneca writes. "For whom? For myself; and so I care for myself [*Pro quo? Pro me; ergo mei curam ago*]. I flee from pain. For whom? For myself; and so I care for myself. If I do everything to care for myself, the care of myself is before everything [*Si omnia propter curam mei facio, ante omnia est mei cura*]."[52]

The conclusion to which this reasoning ineluctably leads must be heard in its full force. It implies a striking consequence that has not always been distinctly perceived as such, no doubt because it is by nature alien to much that presents itself in terms of the "culture of the self." That "the care of myself is before everything" means, among other things, that the care in question "is before" that thing that is "the self." Seneca's statements on the subject must be taken literally. It is of great significance that the Roman philosopher nowhere agues that the animal simply senses itself: had he done so, one might well have inferred that the first of all things sensible was the self. The thesis he consistently advances is the one proposition that seems, by all accounts, to have also been that of Chrysippus: the living being, he repeats, senses before all else its "constitution." If it adapts itself to itself in caring for itself, it does so because of this primary sensation alone, which refers not to itself but to its nature.

The distinction may seem subtle, but it is, in truth, of prime importance, as the thinkers of Antiquity well knew. A text of uncertain authorship contained in the *De anima liber cum mantissa* attributed to Alexander of Aphrodisias most clearly illustrates the point. The pertinent passage consists of two sentences, the first of which attributes a doctrine to some Stoics, "but not all of them": the belief, namely, that "that which the animal senses as the first thing that belongs [*to prōton oikeion*] is nothing other than itself." The second sentence continues: "Others, instead, seeking to give a more elegant and precise definition, say that from the moment of birth we are appropriated to our constitution and to that which preserves it [*phasin pros tēn sustasin kai tērēsin ōikeiōsthai euthus genomenous hēmas tēn hēmōn autōn*]."[53]

The contrast between the two statements could not be more clear. It sets a formulation of some imprecision against the principle repeatedly espoused by Seneca and the masters of the Stoic school.[54] The "more elegant and precise definition" posits, at the heart of every living being, a difference without which it could not come to be itself: the difference between the self and its constitution, that "most proper thing" to which the animal, in relating itself to the world about it, comes by nature to be appropriated. Not the self but that to which the self perceives itself to be assigned and to which it must always adapt itself, the "constitution" is that element within the animal with which it never altogether coincides, to which, from birth, it continues to "conciliate" and "commend" itself. It is that for which every living thing, to be and to preserve itself, must "care," that which each being, rational or not, incessantly senses and never knows. One may call it the nature that the tortoise, overturned, aims in pain or pleasure to regain. But its names are many, at least as numerous as those of the creatures of the land and sea. It is that within each animal which is not the animal itself and, in not being it, allows it "from the outset" to come to be. A crustacean sentinel in constant motion between the outside and the inside of the self's mobile shell, it is the little crab that guards the oyster and that, from time to time, bites lightly, to alert it to the fact that the little fish are there.

CHAPTER ELEVEN

Elements of Ethics

A Treatise by Hierocles the Stoic, who sought to prove
beyond all Doubt that "Beasts perceive themselves continuously"

Toward the end of 1901, Ludwig Borchardt, archaeologist and smuggler, purchased a papyrus in Cairo. It measured some thirty centimeters in height and, tightly rolled, could well have been more than three times that in length. When he bought it, Borchardt was told it came from "the remains of an old house in Eschmunen," the ancient site of Hermopolis Magna, the fabled capital of Upper Egypt.[1] This information he naturally could not confirm. But it must have been immediately apparent to his trained eye that the thin *volumen* was of considerable antiquity, whatever its provenance, and one fact was beyond all doubt: the brown papyrus, "dark-brown at points," was everywhere covered with Greek letters, even if they were not equally legible and the outer layers of the roll were damaged, some beyond repair. Borchardt lost little time in bringing the ancient object back with him to Berlin, where he entrusted it to the safekeeping of the paleographers of the state museums. Then it was not long before the Egyptian papyrus came to be deciphered and transcribed with care. It turned out that "PBerol inv. 9789," as the roll has been called ever since, contained not one but two works of importance, printed in similar script with common abbreviations, although clearly executed by different hands. Once the papyrus was unrolled in Prussia, its disposition was unmistakable: the text of the recto could be seen to start at the precise point where, on the other side, that of the verso ended, concluding, with perfect symmetry, where the text of the verso in turn began.[2]

The work transcribed on the recto of the papyrus represents the third section of Didymus's commentary on Demosthenes's *Philippics*. It was published in 1904 as the first volume of the *Berliner Klassikertexte*, whose tomes would continue to appear in Berlin until 1939.[3] The edition of the work transcribed on the verso took longer to be printed, perhaps because the scholar to whom it had been assigned, Hans von Arnim, was at the time already preparing a work of great proportions: the three-volume set that was to be the first modern scholarly collection of all the ancient works relating the doctrines of the Portico, the *Stoicorum veterum fragmenta*, published in Leipzig in 1903.[4] When the verso of the papyrus finally appeared in 1906, it was published as the fourth of the *Berliner Klassikertexte*.[5] It revealed to the world the sole surviving work of a later disciple of Chrysippus, who had been excluded, on account of the tardiness with which his works were known and edited, from the compendious collection of Stoic sources published in the immediately preceding years: one Hierocles, who most likely lived in the latter half of the second century of the common era, the contemporary of Epictetus and Marcus Aurelius. Von Arnim identified him as the same "Hierocles the Stoic, holy and serious man" (*Hierocles Stoicus, vir sanctus et gravis*) said by Aulus Gellius to have been criticized by a Platonist of the second century, Gaius Calvenus Taurus.[6] Others have concurred, taking him to have been also the homonymous author of "philosophical things" (*philosophoumena*) mentioned by the Byzantine encyclopedic *Suidas*, as well as the unnamed source of fifteen Stoic fragments to be found in Stobaeus.[7] The papyrus itself, however, says nothing of the life of its author. The clear cursive script of its first column limits itself to designating him as Hierocles, even as it offers of his work a lapidary single title: *Elements of Ethics* (*ēthik[ē] stoikheiōsis*).[8]

It would be a grave error, however, to expect to find in the ancient work any extended account of that sublime moral agent, man. This *elementa moralia* opens with a statement that leaves no

doubt as to its central subject, and it is not a human one. Hierocles's terms are those of the masters of the Portico, and they are
audible from the clear *incipit* of the work to the point, in the
ninth column, where the damaged papyrus grows obscure and
soon illegible. "I consider the best principle for the elements of
ethics," the philosopher writes, "to be the discourse on the first
thing that belongs to the animal [or: the first thing that belongs
to the living being, *to prōton oikeion tōi zōōi*]."[9] With equal fidelity
to Stoic teachings, he later defines the "animal," in distinction to
the "nonanimal," by the possession of two faculties: "sensation"
(*aisthēsis*) and "impulse" (*hormē*). "Of these," Hierocles continues, "impulse is not necessary for now, but a discourse on sensation seems in every way opportune." The reason is that *aisthēsis*
constitutes the sole power by which the animal, adapting itself to
itself, comes to be appropriated to its nature. A "discourse on the
first thing that belongs to the animal" must, for this reason, take
the form of a "discourse on sensation"; as Hierocles presents it, a
philosopher wishing to offer a rigorous exposition of the principles of ethics has no choice but to begin with an account of the
nature of animal perception. "Sensation contributes to the knowledge of the first thing that belongs," Hierocles writes, "and it is
precisely that discourse which we have said constitutes the best
principle for the elements of ethics."[10]

The reader soon learns, however, that a primer in ethics must
begin not so much with perception, in the usual meaning of the
term, as with "self-perception," the faculty by which the animal
senses that which is its own. The expressions employed by the
ancient philosopher for this power are several, as numerous as
the Stoic terms for the perceptual act. They consist, for the most
part, of the addition of a reflexive pronoun to the verbs and verbal
nouns of sensation employed by the thinkers of the Portico:
heautou aisthanesthai, *heatou sunaisthēsis*, and *heautou antilēpsis* are all variations on a single theme.[11] The central place of the
phenomenon in the work, in any case, can hardly be doubted:
of twelve columns, several of which are difficult to read at all,
more than five, as Brad Inwood has observed, are devoted to the

perception that an animal possesses of itself.[12] The fact points to a central proposition in the philosophy of the Stoa, which was never formulated more fully than in the *Elements* of Hierocles. It is the thesis according to which perception involves self-perception, all sensation of external things implying, by definition, the simultaneous sensation of the sensing animal itself.[13]

Hierocles presents it as a universal fact among living beings, whose necessity can be demonstrated in decisive terms. "Generally," he explains, "the sensation of an external thing cannot be accomplished without the sensation of oneself."[14] Consider, for example, the sensation of the white and the sweet: "Together with the perception of the white, for example, we have the perception of ourselves as whitened. And together with the perception of the sweet, we have the perception of ourselves as sweetened. And together with that of the hot, of ourselves as heated; and so it is with all other cases of this kind."[15] S.G. Pembroke has observed that this reasoning turns a classic Skeptical "argument upside down."[16] The philosophers of the Cyrenaic school had famously maintained that the perception of external sensible qualities could not be taken as firm evidence of external things themselves. From the sense of white and sweet, for instance, all that could be inferred with certainty is that the sensing being alone experienced such sensations.[17] "Nothing," as Montaigne would later write, in summary, could then be said to be "perceptible by outside" (*par le dehors*). The only thing that could be sensed would be that which "touched us by the inner touch" (*qui nous touchoit par l'interne attouchement*).[18]

Hierocles, for his part, shows little interest in the epistemological problem to which this Skeptic argument responded. The Stoic seems not to doubt that perceptions point to corresponding qualities beyond the powers of the perceiving animal. If he recalls that the sensation of the white and the sweet implies that the sensing faculty is itself whitened and sweetened, he does so not to contest the possibility of perception in its common sense, as did the Cyrenaic thinkers, but to demonstrate that in all sensation the animal simultaneously senses itself, always "touched," in Montaigne's terms, at once by that which is "perceptible by the out-side" and by an "inner touch." Hence the syllogism with which Hierocles concludes his discussion of the subject, which the Stoic, for one, takes to be both "beautiful and irrefutable" (*kalēn kai anantilekton*): if one admits that the animal perceives something external to it from the moment it is born, and if one understands that the "perception of something other is conjoined [*sum-pephuken*] to the perception of oneself," one must accept, as a consequence, that "animals have a perception of themselves from the outset."[19]

One might well accept such a chain of reasoning in large part, yet still raise against it a simple query of some import: are there not times in the lives of sensing beings, one might wonder, when perception ceases? It is a problem Hierocles considers at some length in the fourth and fifth columns of his *Elements*. With the rhetorical and logical skill of one trained in the exposition of arguments, he seeks not to dismiss the idea of a cessation of sensa-tion but to entertain it briefly and then to refute it incontrovert-ibly. Willing to consider the possibility that there "is a moment in which the animal is completely deprived of self-perception," he maintains that this moment would be most likely (*pithanos*) sleep: the dormant state, after all, would seem nothing if not the condi-tion in which the animal retreats into the most impassive insensi-bility. But it is not so. "Even then," Hierocles asserts, "we see — although in a way that most cannot easily follow — that in fact the animal has a perception of itself."[20]

A glance at dormant bodies suffices to prove the point.[21] If a cover falls away from an area of our body while we sleep in winter months, "we pull up the blankets to repair the parts that have grown cold," even when we lie in the deepest slumber. If we have hurt ourselves when awake, we avoid putting undue pressure on the wounded regions of our bodies when asleep, "employing, as it were, the attention of the waking state." If we have made an appointment the day before and must rise when it is dark, "we wake at the set time." And the dispositions of waking beings, moreover, are clearly visible even in the dormant state: the drunkard sleeps with his bottle in his hand, the miser with his purse, Herakles, according to the tragic poets, "with his club."[22] All this is true not only "for us," Hierocles continues, "but also for the other animals."[23] But time presses, and the philosopher offers no more examples. Those mentioned suffice, he remarks, with some appreciation of his argument, "to constitute a very convincing proof of the fact that we have a sensation of ourselves even in sleep."[24] Since sleep would be the one "moment in which the animal is completely deprived of self-perception," and since sleep, as the various cases of dormant beings show, is not such a moment, Hierocles concludes that there can be none at all. In its logical structure, the proof is unusual.[25] But its function in the Stoic work is clear: it serves to illustrate the fundamental proposition of the *Elements*, which stipulates that from birth, living beings sense themselves without interruption.

To such formal demonstrations, Hierocles adds a host of evidence drawn from the natural history of animals. His examples repeatedly suggest, in classic Stoic fashion, that self-perception constitutes an apprehension less of a particular "self," be it psychological or somatic, than of a nature proper to the living being, to which it must incessantly adapt itself. The animal illustrations begin at the inception of the *Elements*, as the Stoic sets out to show the fundamental error of those who believe the sensitive faculty to have been given "for the perception of external things and not also for the perception of oneself."[26] "One must understand," Hierocles writes, "that in the first place, animals have a perception of their specific parts."[27] Here the later Stoic reaffirmed a principle that Seneca had once taught Lucilius: animals must "sense that through which they sense other things" (*necesse est enim id sentient per quod alia quoque sentient*).[28] But Hierocles illustrates the claim more fully than did his Roman predecessor. Creatures of the air, he observes, perceive the appropriateness of their wings to flight, even as those of the land sense "their proper parts, both the fact that they have them and that for which they have them." In this, too, human beings are no exception to the rule of animals: as the thinker notes, "we ourselves sense our eyes and our ears and the rest." When we desire to see, after all, we turn, like all other beasts, to that which draws our attention not with our ears but with our eyes. When we choose to walk, we have the sense to do so not on our hands but on our legs, and, the philosopher also observes, when we wish to take and to give, by contrast, we immediately perceive that that we are to do so with our hands, not our legs.[29]

As a "second proof," Hierocles cites the perception that every animal clearly possesses of the relative strengths of its parts in combat and defense. Von Arnim, who had little sympathy for the author of the *Elements*, took this to be but a specification of the first proof adduced by the later Stoic, which aimed to show that beasts sensed the aptness of their limbs for that to which they were suited.[30] But the second argument "involves an important new point," as Inwood has noted, as it makes clear that "such behavior presupposes the perception of others" in addition to self-perception.[31] Each animal, Hierocles observes, has a disposition toward a certain type of weapon. The discussion of the subject in the treatise is extensive, if not exhaustive. "Some animals, in effect, are fortified by hooves; others, by teeth; others, by tusks; others, by prickles; still others, by poison, and they use these arms for defense in the fight against other animals." Take, for instance, the variety of asp that Hierocles and his contemporaries called "ptiades" (*ptuados*), a serpentine creature "not unworthy of being mentioned." "This beast so exceeds others in dangerousness," Hierocles comments, "that, without biting, it casts its poison like a dart against whichever animal it wishes," and "when it is irritated against another animal, it may spit its poison out even from a distance, without any need to bite."[32] In all such cases, the "self-sensation" of the Stoic consists of a good deal more than an isolated perception of oneself. To the degree to which they grasp their natures with respect to those of the animals around them, the creatures of the Hellenistic bestiary perceive themselves in perceiving natures alien to their own and, in apprehending themselves, they sense themselves in relation to what they are not.

The author of the *Elements* also provides a third type of evidence to demonstrate the Stoic doctrine that all living things perceive themselves. By nature, animals, we learn, sense that on account of which they are weak: they perceive their own vulnerabilities, for otherwise they could hardly survive. Their behavior leaves no doubt. Why does the bull, when attacked, stand with its horns turned toward the one who threatens it, if not to guard the body it perceives to be otherwise defenseless? Consider the tortoise: "When it has the perception of an attack, it shelters its head and legs under its shell," which is hard and so "less susceptible to attack." The snail, too, Hierocles observes, "does more or less the same thing when it senses danger." And the bear "seems not to be unaware of the vulnerability of its head: this is why, when it is hit by clubs and other things that could injure that part, it places its paws in front of it so that they will bear the brunt of the blows." Or take, instead, the toad: when chased to a point at which it must leap across a pit to save itself, this animal senses, with unerring exactitude, when the distance is too great for it to jump. In leaping, "it is surpassed by no other animal of its size," and none has a more precise perception of the extent of a given spatial interval. But when it "has no faith in its capacity to jump to the other side," it perceives that it must "throw itself down into the pit, however it may go" — although not without blowing itself up as much as it can and tucking in its legs and its head, to lessen the damage it senses that it will inevitably incur.[33]

The deer may be the most striking member of this company. If one believes Hierocles, it senses not only that which it naturally lacks but also that which, in its body, exceeds good measure. "Let us concede," the Stoic writes, "that there is a disproportion [anisōs ekhein] between its legs and its antlers."[34] The antlers, he observes, may be "extraordinarily large and marvelous to see," but the legs are swift, light, "and difficult easily to dismiss." The deer itself feels it all, and, according to the philosopher, it does not cease to do so. "It has faith [pisteuei] in its legs, and if it must rise to extreme speed or make a great leap, it does not despair of them [apegnōken autōn]." Of the antlers, the animal, by contrast, "has a low opinion" [kategnōken]: they are outlandishly large, and "precisely for this reason," we learn, "they make life difficult both in general and when it is necessary to flee quickly." Hence the practice to which the animal invariably turns to moderate their periodic unwieldness. "Aware of their disproportionate growth, whenever it finds itself near crags and sharp rocks, it charges against them from afar, to break its antlers," and this, the philosopher adds, "not with moderate force, but with all its strength, until it has removed its excessive parts."[35]

The fabulous aspects of this demonstration are beyond all doubt, and modern scholars have remarked on them more than once with varying degrees of critical severity.[36] Commenting on the despairing deer in particular, the most recent editors of the *Elements* have observed that "whoever reads this passage out of context would be led to believe that it derived from a popular collection of animal *mirabilia* instead of a treatise on ethics."[37] But Hierocles's catalogue of beasts consigned to the sensation of their own debilities belongs exactly where it is. It is profoundly philosophical in purport, and it reveals a dimension in the concept of self-perception all too often overlooked. The creatures who crowd the columns of this Egyptian papyrus are united in their uninterrupted sense both of the world about them and of themselves, and it is this perception alone that allows them to accede to that "first thing that belongs" to each, to which they are assigned from birth. But one should make no mistake: their incessant "self-perceptions" are of no selves in any accepted sense. In sleep and waking, the beasts of Hierocles's *elementa moralia* perceive their parts, their limbs, their weapons, and all the many means that nature assigned to them. But this is but a portion of what they sense. Touched "by without and by within," they perceive, too, that which they do not possess, and, time and time again, their sensitive faculties remit them to a constitution no less their own for being one with which they cannot altogether coincide: a disproportion within their just proportions, an impropriety in that which is most proper to them, without which they would be unable to adapt themselves to themselves and without which all care would be inevitably in vain. This is why their despair in their own powers is no less natural than their faith in them, and why, with the lucidity of beasts who unfailingly feel themselves, they "are not unaware" that to conserve themselves they must at times "remove [their] excessive parts," "not with moderate force, but with all [their] strength." That, too, belongs to the life of the animal, for whom to live is to sense, and to sense the noncoincidence that makes the self; that, too, is an element of ethics.

CHAPTER TWELVE

The Hound and the Hare

Being the shortest Chapter in the Book

Sextus Empiricus relates in his *Outlines of Pyrrhonism* that "Chrysippus showed particular interest in irrational animals."[1] A dog, by all accounts, numbered among them. If one believes Sextus, who does not conceal his antagonism toward the chief of his "chief opponents," the Stoics, Chrysippus taught that when a hound, running fast in pursuit of a hare, happens upon a fork in the road, he does not hesitate. "After sniffing at two roads by which the quarry did not pass," Sextus writes, in summary, "he rushes off at once by the third, without pausing to sniff."[2] The sequence may appear natural enough. Sextus, however, reports that to the great logician of Antiquity, the occurrence seemed incontrovertible evidence that the dog was intimately familiar with the form of a propositional deduction that Chrysippus himself, as it happened, had been one of the first to identify with precision: the fifth complex disjunctive syllogism.[3] "For the old writer declared," explains Sextus, "that the dog implicitly reasons thus: the creature went either by this road, or by that, or by the other. But it did not go by this road or by that. Therefore it went by the other."[4]

There are reasons to doubt the accuracy of Sextus's account. Although it is consistent with the summary of Chrysippean doctrine contained in the work of another of the Stoic's later adversaries, Plutarch (whose words on the subject were in turn incorporated into Book Three of Porphyry's *De abstinentia*), it can hardly be reconciled with the reports of the early master to be found in two other classical sources, Aelian's *De natura animalium* and Philo's *De animalibus*.[5] When they refer to the deliberating dog, these two authors make no mention of a fork, and they suggest in unequivocal terms that Chrysippus spoke of not three roads but two, in the middle of which there lay a ditch into which the hare could easily have hopped. In Philo's dialogue on animal nature, which refers to the happenings twice, Alexander recounts that since the dog could perceive "no trace at all" either to the right or to the left, "without further sniffing he leaped into the ditch and continued on his way in all haste."[6]

Scholarly evidence has led at least one modern authority on the Stoic school, Max Pohlenz, to side with Philo and Aelian and dismiss the veracity of the fabled fork.[7] But the literary tradition, for better or for worse, seems largely to have stood by the opponents of the Portico. When Montaigne discussed Chrysippus in his *Apology for Raymond Sebond*, he recalled how the great Stoic, "although in all other matters as contemptuous a judge of animal behavior as any other philosopher," had shown considerable sympathy for "the movements of the dog who found himself at the crossroads of three paths." The essayist, to be sure, seems not to have been completely convinced that the animal, as the ancients had all agreed, was "in pursuit of the prey that fled from him." He did not exclude this possibility in principle, but he appears to have found it more likely that the dog had been "in search of his master, whom he had lost." Hence his reasoning, as Montaigne reports it: "I have followed my master all the way to this crossroads by his scent. He must necessarily have taken one of these paths; he did not take this one, or that; therefore he must indubitably have taken this other one."[8]

At least one other version of the ancient occurrence, however, has also been proposed. More minimal than either of the two ancient variants of the tale, it knows neither fork nor ditch: two paths alone remain, and a dog must decide between them. This is the account cited in the discussion of the question "whether dogs can make syllogismes" conducted before King James I at the University of Cambridge. The scholars of the early seventeenth century settled the matter by judging that "an Enthimeme is a lawful and real *Syllogisme*, but Dogs can make them." The grounds for their decision were furnished by the ancient anecdote, reduced to its barest form. As we read in Samuel Clarke's summary of the debate, it was Preston who concluded the discussion, citing the classic case: "He instanced in a Hound who had the major Proposition in his mind, namely: *The Hare is gone either this or that way*; smels out the minor with his Nose; namely, *She is not gon that way*, and follows the Conclusion, *Ergo this way with open mouth*."[9]

Without exception, all the writers who discuss the dog have concurred, however, in surmising that the appearance of canine logic once witnessed by Chrysippus was in truth no more than that: an appearance. Plutarch, who devoted a famous work to the intelligence of animals, thus had little patience for the supposition of a syllogistic hound. "A dog," he wrote, "has no need for such a testimonial, which is both false and fraudulent; for it is perception itself, by means of track and spoor, which indicates the way the creature fled; a dog does not bother with disjunctive and copulative propositions."[10] Philo was of the same opinion, and a good deal sterner with those who would differ with him. Having heard Alexander invoke the celebrated dog in the course of his defense of the reason of brutes, he enjoins his nephew in the final pages of the dialogue to "reject the argument of those who think dogs follow scents by making use of the fifth mode of the syllogism," as a delusion of "people with no sense for philosophy," who are "more accustomed to appearance and sophistry than to the discipline necessary for the inquiry into the truth."[11] Like Plutarch and Porphyry, Montaigne, for his part, was willing to grant animals much, but from a hound's habits, he remarked curtly in the *Apology*, one ought not to conclude that he had been schooled in the textbooks of dialectics by Georges de Trébizonde.[12] Preston drew the distinction with delicacy and concision: "Dogs might have *sagacity*," he stated, "but not *sapience*, in things especially of Prey, and that did not concern their Belly, [they] might be *nasutili*, but not *logici*; had much in their Mouthes, little in their Minds."[13]

The truth of that claim can hardly be denied. To grasp it in its full force, however, one must apply it to the state of the mythic hound as he runs in fast pursuit of the unseen hare. That dog, like all others of its kind, may have "little in its Mind." But as he chases his prey and pauses to "smel" her "out," he has even less than "little" in his mouth. Then he "has," strictly speaking, nothing at all, if not his bare capacity to smell, which persists undaunted in the absence of all scents. The fact may seem negligible. But the truth is that its importance cannot be overestimated. All those who recall the movements of the Stoic dog are more than willing to admit it, even if they seem, at times, to set it soon aside. It is the "perception" (*aisthēsis*) that, for Plutarch, "affords only the minor premise," the sensation of "no trace at all" invoked by Philo and Montaigne, the matter of the "minor" that the dog, in Preston's terms, "smels out with his Nose," and which the scholar knows to name: *She is not gon that way.* It is a sensation well worth pondering. A perception without qualities, it remains a sense, if only of the mere fact that the animal, at the crossroads or before the ditch, still senses. It affects the dog, even though it itself, the absence of all marks, is nothing and cannot but consign him to the limits of those powers that are his own. To the sage animal, if not to the sapient, it is enough. *Nasutilus* but not *logicus*, the Stoic hound perceives what he must do: without pausing again to sniff, "he rushes off at once."

CHAPTER THIRTEEN

Life Science

In which Augustine of Hippo invents the inner Sense, with some Help from Aristotle and the Stoics, among Others

To lead a life is not always to know it. Ovid famously remarked on that fact in the poem he composed in memory of the fateful night he was finally obliged, by Julius Caesar's command, to leave his native Rome. At once hastened by the coming dawn and slowed by the stupor that overcame him in the face of exile, he found himself, as he later recalled, like one struck by Jupiter, destined to "live and be ignorant of his own life" (*vivit et est vitae nescius ipse suae*).[1] For the poet himself, the condition was as extreme as it was dire. But the state of "not knowing" he invoked in the *Tristia* may be less exceptional than is sometimes thought, extending to the ordinary as well as the extraordinary moments of human life.

The philosophers of Antiquity cannot be said to have overlooked the unthinking condition in which the purportedly rational animal tends to find itself. But most classical accounts of the subject seem cursory when compared to the extended investigations into self-loss carried out in different settings by the writer of late Antiquity whose thought has traditionally been taken to inaugurate the inception of medieval philosophy as a whole: Augustine of Hippo. From the *Soliloquies*, composed less than a year after his conversion to Christianity in 386, to the many memorable analyses of self-deception and self-betrayal in the *Confessions* and the phenomenologies of self-awareness that fill the *De trinitate* and the *City of God* from his last years, Augustine continued to explore a single field: that of the life in the midst of which the thinking being discovers itself without any clear knowledge, and in which the alternately confused and lucid speaking animal strives, with varying degrees of felicity, to regain a clear awareness of itself.

The most penetrating of the Augustinian treatments of the lives known and unknown to the beings who lead them can be found in the *De libero arbitrio*. Completed in the final years of the fourth century, this work offers what is perhaps the fullest presentation of the faculties that the North African thinker took to be common to all animals and those that, by contrast, he understood to constitute the proper powers of human beings alone.[2] In the second book of this work, Augustine aims, with his friend Evodius, to establish that freedom of the will was "rightly given to man." This can be done, however, only once three more fundamental metaphysical questions have been resolved: whether the free will "is to be included among good things," whether "all good things, as good," derive from God and whether and in what sense, finally, "it is manifest that God exists." It is with the last and most fundamental of the questions that Augustine begins — but not without a detour that brings him to consider an even simpler matter still. "To begin with the most manifest of all things [*de manifestissimis*]," he states in didactic terms to Evodius, "I ask you first of all whether you yourself exist [*utrum tu ipse sis*]."[3]

Augustine immediately furnishes the answer to his own query. "Do you fear that you may deceive yourself in this discussion?" he asks. He answers: "But if you did not exist, you could not even deceive yourself."[4] From the possibility of error, one may thus derive the certainty of being: such is the demonstration offered by the philosopher for the existence of his interlocutor. It is an exemplary illustration of a principle repeatedly formulated by Augustine: *Si fallor, sum*, "If I may be mistaken, I must exist."[5] Evodius, for his part, seems persuaded. But the proof is but the beginning of a longer deduction, which seeks to define not one but three terms. After existence, the first to follow is life: "Since, therefore, it is clear to you that you exist," the philosopher continues, "and this would not be so if you did not live, it is also clear that you live." Here Augustine seems to pause: "Do you not understand," he asks Evodius, "that these two things are absolutely true?" Evodius, as always, complies: "I understand [*intelligo*] them absolutely."[6] It is a good answer, for it provides Augustine with a term beyond mere life, even as life (*vivere*), for its part, had stood above existence (*esse*): understanding (*intelligere*).

Now Augustine and Evodius have established the fundamental elements of a doctrine of all things. Together, "these three things, being, life, and understanding [*essere, vivere, intelligere*]" form the levels of a single hierarchical and stratified order, in which each higher term includes the one or ones beneath it. First on the ladder of creation is the state of things like the stone and the corpse, which exist but neither live nor understand. Then there is the condition of the animal (*pecus*), which lives and so also exists, even if it cannot be said to understand. And, at the highest level of creation, there are those like Augustine and Evodius, who understand and, by necessity, therefore also exist and live at once.[7] "We may therefore say," Augustine remarks, in conclusion, "that of the three [categories], two are lacking to the corpse, one is lacking to the animal, and none to man."[8]

For the philosopher and his friend, it clearly follows that "the preeminent [*praestantius*] of the three is the one that man has together with the other two, that is, understanding, in which being and life are included."[9] But neither Augustine nor Evodius shows any sign of wishing to consider the nature of the highest of all activities without a preliminary discussion of the power it seems to supersede, namely, life. Without lingering to consider the sense of that simplest and most universal dimension of all things, "being," they proceed to investigate the faculties that form the constituent powers of all animate beings. These are, of course, the senses. In barely a page, Augustine and Evodius recall the terms of a doctrine of perception that must have been canonical by the fourth century of the Christian era. To each of the five senses, according to this teaching, there corresponds a characteristic organ, as well as a proper object, apprehended among the world of "corporeal things" (*corporalia*) in which the animal lives.

Just as sight lays hold of the visible quality that is "color" by means of the eyes, so the sense of hearing functions, by the ears, to grasp the audible object that is "sound" (*sonus*), and so, too, the sense of smell (*olfactum*) perceives odor (*odor*), the gustative faculty receives "taste" (*sapor*), and touch, finally, embraces "the soft and the hard, the smooth and the coarse, and many others of this kind."[10]

As Augustine and Evodius define them, the perceptive powers of the animal, however, extend still further. The teacher recalls that there is also a sense by which living beings apprehend "the forms of bodies, be they large, small, square, round and similar." It is a faculty that cannot be reduced to any one of the five senses, for it can be exercised by them all — as much by sight, the philosopher indicates, to clarify matters, as by touch.[11] The animal, moreover, possesses a perception of this very fact: it can somehow discern "that which is proper to each sense and that which they all have in common," distinguishing between proper and shared sensible qualities.[12] This apprehension, too, cannot be due to any one particular form of sensation; to the degree that it involves the comparison of the sensible faculties taken individually, it must operate at a level above or beyond each among them.

There is, moreover, yet another perceptual power. It, too, is common to each of the five forms of sensation and so coincident with none: namely, the faculty which "not only senses those things that come from the five corporeal senses but also senses the senses themselves."[13] To Evodius, who seems at first not to grasp such a dimension of perception, Augustine proposes an obvious example, drawn from the field of sight. "I believe you will admit," the philosopher explains, "that color is one thing, that seeing color is another, and that there is still another: even when it is not there, having the sense with which, were it there, one could see it" (*aliud colorem esse et aliud colorem videre et item aliud, etiam cum color non subest, habere sensum quo videre posset si subesset*).[14] It is a perception of the existence of the perceptual faculty, which persists both in the presence and in the absence of sensible qualities.

To the reader familiar with the conceptual vocabulary of classical psychology, it is evident that Augustine alludes with these words to a sensitive power defined in classic terms by Aristotle and his ancient exegetes: the "common sense" (*koinē aisthēsis*) by which the animal perceives shared sensible qualities, the conjunction and disjunction of perceptual traits, and, finally, the very occurrence of its own sensitive abilities. It would be a grave error, however, to conclude that the *De libero arbitrio* simply restates an Aristotelian doctrine established long before it. For the Augustinian dialogue fuses the shared faculty of the Peripatetic school with an animal power conceived by the Stoic movement: the capacity by which every animal, as Chrysippus and his disciples taught, senses its own constitution, as that to which it is from birth appropriate.

In the *De libero arbitrio*, Augustine makes of the faculty of perception proposed by the Aristotelians and the principle of animal sensation defined by the Stoics two aspects of a single power common to all things animate. The faculty that "not only senses the things that derive from the five senses but also senses the senses themselves," we learn, is in truth the power that simultaneously allows every living being to survive and sustain itself. "In fact," Augustine explains, "the animal would not react, either desiring something or removing itself from something, if it did not perceive that it perceived; and this not to know such an object (such an activity being proper to reason), but only because it must react to stimulus; and this it certainly does not sense with any of the five senses."[15] The expressions by which Augustine recasts the activities of the common sense are no less those by which he recalls the orthodox terms of the Portico, developed to demonstrate that every beast senses itself before all else. "The animal," Augustine states, "would not be able to open its eyes and turn them toward what it wanted to see if it did not perceive that it is not seeing because its eyes are closed, or because they are not turned toward what it wants to see." The beast succeeds in approaching that which is suited to its nature and, at the same time, in avoiding that which would do it harm, because it not only perceives such things but also perceives, at the same time, when it does so and when it does not. "If the animal perceives when it does not see," Augustine reasons, "it is necessary that it also perceive when it does see. Indeed, if it sees what it desires, it does not remove its gaze, whereas it continues to move its eyes if it does not see it. And this movement indicates that it perceives both [seeing and not-seeing, *indicat se utrumque sentire*]."[16]

Augustine gives to this primary perceptual power a single name, which would resound throughout the medieval and the modern epochs. By all appearances, he did so, moreover, without the shadow of a doubt. Speaking of the higher sensitive faculty common to all animal souls, the philosopher declares to his friend Evodius: "I know what it is, and, without hesitation, I call it the *inner sense* [or 'the more inner sense': *agnosco istuc quidquid est, et eum interiorem sensum appellare non dubito*]."[17]

It is difficult not to speculate on the provenance of the technical term so surely introduced by Augustine.[18] It has been said that the expression seems "synonymous with Aristotle's 'common sense,'" but it is evident that Aristotle, for his part, possessed no such locution.[19] Nevertheless, the idea that the common sense might be an "inner" one could be reconciled with the Peripatetic doctrine on textual grounds. Was it not the Philosopher himself who tied the "master faculty" to the sense of touch in the *De somno et vigilia*, and was it not also he who suggested, in an enigmatic passage of the *De anima*, that "the organ of touch is internal"?[20] The more immediate source of the Latin usage, however, would most likely have been the lexicon of the Portico, on which Augustine tended so frequently to draw. It is to be noted not simply that the Stoics maintained that the sensation of "external things" could not be accomplished without a "self-sensation" that one might well consider, by contrast, "inner."[21] One may also recall the definition said to have been offered by disciples of Chrysippus for the "common sense": "An inner touch by which we perceive ourselves" (*entos haphēn ... kath' hēn kai hēmōn autōn antilambanometha*).[22] Yet such hypotheses, philologically admissible as they may be, do not restrict the originality of Augustine's invention, which is both terminological and conceptual. The faculty he designates as "the internal sense" responds to a necessity all the more inescapable for being presented, perhaps for the first time, in terms inextricably Aristotelian and Stoic. For him, it is by the "inner sense" that beasts inevitably "perceive that they live [*sentiunt vivere*]," and that, more simply stated, all "life," to last, "perceives itself" (*vita etiam se ipsam sentit*)."[23]

Such formulations must be taken literally. The inner sense allows every animal to "perceive" the life it leads, but this power can do no more. As a faculty of perception, such a sensation therefore remains by nature distinct from the exercise of reason that Augustine was among the first to define and to extol: "knowledge [or 'science'] of life" (*scientia vitae*). In the first book of the *De libero arbitrio*, Augustine takes great care to ensure that his interlocutor not mistake the gulf that separates the two activities, one of which pertains to life as such, the other of which involves the qualified life of understanding. "Can you," the philosopher asks his friend, "discern that living [*vivere*] is one thing, and knowing that one lives is another [*aliud nosse se vivere*]"? Evodius seems to accept the distinction, but still he raises a doubt. "I know that no one knows that he lives, if he does not live," Evodius answers. "But I do not know whether everything that lives knows that it lives" (*scio quidem neminem se nosse vivere nisi viventem, sed utrum omnis vivens nouerit se vivere ignoro*).[24] It is a clear call for further instruction. The philosopher therefore sets out to demonstrate indubitably that human beings alone possess not merely sensation but also knowledge (*scientia*) of that thing which is their life.

"I wish," Augustine begins, "that you would not only believe but know [*scires*] that animals lack reason." The thesis can easily be demonstrated. It suffices to consider a single fact: the speaking being alone, among all living things, subjugates the other animals around it, such that they "become, through habit and training, the instruments of human will." Since the human beast is clearly "inferior to many in strength and other physical capacities," and since, while in possession of the same faculties common to all animals, man nevertheless succeeds in dominating all the others, this must be by a power to which he alone may lay claim. Augustine takes it to be something "which is no trifle and is not nothing." It is that which furnishes humankind with the force "on account of which we," as the thinker proudly states, "are better than they" (*eis meliores simus*). "What better name could one give it," he asks, with a rhetorical flourish, "than reason, or intelligence [*ratio, vel intelligentia*]"? It is a definition of reason that has rarely been equaled in its frankness. "Intelligence," we learn, removes man from the realm of the other beasts by affording him that higher faculty which is domination: an *animus subiugandi* by which he can make inhuman animals the docile servants of his will, despite whatever physical forces they may muster in their own defense. "We," in short, "are better than they," because "we" enslave, as "they," devoid of intelligence, cannot. "And now you know," Augustine finally tells Evodius, with some satisfaction, "that of which you said you were unaware, namely, that not everything that lives knows that it lives, even if those who know that they live necessarily live."[25]

One may still wonder, however, exactly how the science of life accessible to man alone differs in nature from the sensation of sensation common to all beasts. Naturally, Augustine himself insists repeatedly on the importance of separating the intellect of man from the perceptual powers of animals, even as he stresses that animate life, in turn, must be strictly distinguished from the inanimate state of mere existence. This much is a matter of principle: the metaphysical hierarchy established in the dialogue rests on the tripartite articulation of "being, living, and understanding" (*essere vivere intelligere*), without which its conceptual distinctions would not hold. But if one examines the work closely, it appears that Augustine's statements are more equivocal than they might seem at first glance. When the philosopher characterizes the nature of science, his terms suggest that intellection may be less distinct from sensation than he himself elsewhere leads Evodius to believe. "Knowledge" (*scire, scientia*) in the full sense of the term, he explains, can be defined as "perception by reason" (*id*

quod scire dicimus nihil esse aliud quam ratione habere perceptum).[26]
It is a provocative claim, for it cannot but imply that science, a
"perception" (*perceptum*) of a sort, may be of the same nature as
apprehension in sensation.

The integrity of the "knowledge of life," however, can be
questioned on more serious grounds. At least once, Augustine
suggests that the opposition between life and science cannot altogether hold, and for a simple reason: because, as he explains to
Evodius, among human beings "intellection" (*intelligere*) is itself a
kind of life. "What does it mean to understand," he asks Evodius,
"if not to live more clearly and perfectly in the life of the mind?
For this reason, if I am not mistaken, you have preferred to life
not something else, but a kind of better life" (*Intellegere autem
quid est nisi ipsa luce mentis inlustrius perfectiusque vivere? Quare tu
mihi, nisi fallor, non vitae aliud aliquid, sed cuidam uitae meliorem
vitam praeposuisti*).[27]

The passage demands close attention. After Augustine establishes that understanding can be separated from life as life can be
distinguished from mere being, he suggests that the "science of
life," although knowledge in the full sense, "is not something
other than life" (*non vitae aliud aliquid*). These propositions point
to a logical difficulty of which it is not always evident that Augustine himself was fully cognizant. Without indicating it as such, the
author of the *De libero arbitrio* has formulated a dilemma in the
original sense: a conjunction of two distinct and conflicting *lem-
mata* that must, and yet cannot, both be maintained. On the one
hand, science, to be itself, cannot coincide with the life of which
it is to be the knowledge: by nature preferable to bare animal
existence, science must embrace that existence as the higher term
contains and supersedes the lower. On the other hand, science,
we learn, "is not something other than life"; it is, more precisely,
"a kind of better life."

A reader sympathetic to the express aims of the dialogue might
wish to stress the first thesis, setting aside the animal existence
Augustine described with care in favor of the higher life that is
knowledge. One could then admit that although the philosopher

himself defined "life" unequivocally as "animal or sensitive life in the beginning," when speaking of the "better life" he must have meant a higher thing that far transcended the life of the beast, a "more luminous life," as one contemporary scholar has argued, "an intellectual and spiritual life" blessedly removed from all animal existence.[28] Such an interpretation may seem at times condoned by the ancient philosopher, but it cannot truly resolve the quandary unmistakably raised by his text. The positing of two distinct and analogous lives within the speaking being would fracture the thinking animal at its core, dividing it to a point at which it could hardly be said to be one. There would be a higher life and a lower life, even as in man there are both understanding and sensation, and the more "science" advanced, the more it would efface and exclude the existence it constantly presupposed, producing in its stead a better, beatific life of thought. One should make no mistake as to the consequence that would follow from such a vital laceration: the rational animal would then be an enslaving animal who, before all else, enslaved himself.

A more pressing objection, however, can be raised against such an interpretation. If one makes of the life of "science" truly "a more luminous life," a life far beyond the life of the animal, one purifies it of the very thing of which it was to be knowledge: namely, sensitive existence, which the beast feels but does not know. A "science of life" in which life remains "intellectual and spiritual life" alone could be many things: knowledge turned upon itself, its reason, its spirit, its innate intelligence, a practice of cognition that takes itself as its sole object. But of the life Augustine defined — the life of the sensing animal — this "science" would know nothing. Such a "knowledge" would be not the comprehension of animal life but its willful forgetting; it would be its wishful substitution by another.

The alternative is to hold fast to the second proposition formulated by Augustine. One would then remain true to the principle according to which the knowledge of life "is not something other than life," following it wherever it may lead. Such a path of thought surely begins within the dialogue on the freedom of the will, but before long it must point beyond it. For if the science of life is truly "not something other than life," then rational animals remain, despite their best wishes, animals to the very end. No matter how much they think, they continue to live; understanding in "perceiving," they incessantly find themselves consigned to a dimension of existence common to subjugating and subjugated beasts alike. At least two of the positions in the threefold hierarchy of being must then waver: comprehension can no longer be opposed to perception, even as it grows increasingly difficult to distinguish with any rigor between "the knowledge that one lives" and the "inner sense" by which all animate life must perceive itself, its faculties, and the nature that, always accompanying it, is its own. To the bishop who assured himself in reasoned conversation that his existence was in essence "better" than those of the others submitted to his will, this would have been a possibility far from edifying. Perhaps this is why, having raised it, he chose not to ponder it; perhaps this is why, alluding to it, he resolved with his friend not to think upon it. On one level, at least, it may matter little. There are signs that the philosopher, unknowingly, may still have sensed it. Like one struck by a pagan god, he too may have lived more, or less, than he willed.

CHAPTER FOURTEEN

The Unnamed King

In which Greek passes into Arabic, and the master Sense makes
an unexpected Appearance in a Book by al-Fārābī

Augustine of Hippo died August 28, 430. By that time, the once-indomitable Roman Empire had suffered more than a single loss. In 406, the Vandals had invaded Gaul; in 415, the Visigoths had arrived in Spain; by the final years of the bishop's life, the Vandals had moved from the Iberian peninsula into a region near where Augustine himself had been born, the expanse of land in North Africa known to the ancients as Numidia. These were all important events in the political landscape of the Mediterranean region. But they were to seem discrete in scope and short-lived in effect compared to the transformations that were wrought upon the erstwhile territories of the Roman and Byzantine empires little more than two centuries later. Then the armies came from the Arabian peninsula, and they conquered vast regions of the southern and eastern shores of the Mediterranean in the name of a new religion revealed to a prophet from the tribe of Quraysh. By 732, one century after Muhammad's death, the territory conquered by the Arab armies was immense: much of North Africa, Egypt, the Levant, Western Asia, and Persia all now formed a new unity. The lands briefly subjugated a thousand years before by Alexander the Great had become the provinces of a single empire, ruled and administered in accordance with the legal and religious principles of Islam.

The fact was of inestimable importance for the ancient traditions of learning, for in time the new *pax islamica* brought about a movement of textual transmission and translation that has rarely been equaled in the history of civilizations. It has been stated, without exaggeration, that in the four centuries after the first Arab invasions, "almost *all* non-literary and non-historical secular Greek books that were available throughout the Eastern Byzantine Empire and the Near East were translated into Arabic."[1] Philosophical books were naturally among them. Today many aspects of the passage from Greek to Arabic thought remain obscure; the early practice of replacing Greek originals with Arabic renditions, in particular, continues to pose difficulties for a precise reconstruction of the various steps taken in the practice of translation. But it is clear that by the ninth century, the philosophers of the Arabic language were not few but many. Favored by the 'Abbasid dynasty in Baghdad for numerous reasons, both intellectual and political, they refined their science in delving into the works of their ancient predecessors both systematically and deeply.[2] This fact, of course, has long been known, but its consequences have not always been fully drawn.[3] As Dimitri Gutas has recently recalled, "the study of post-classical Greek secular writings can hardly proceed without the evidence in Arabic," and as far as the history of philosophy is concerned, one may argue that Arabic, not Latin, is "the second classical language."[4] If the science of Antiquity can be said to have known an "afterlife" in the centuries after the fall of Rome, it was in the lands of Islam; if the practice once named *philosophia* outlived the classical Greek language, it was, before all else, in the activity the Arabs long ago named *falsafa*.[5]

It would be a great error, however, to suppose that the Arabic "art of arts" (*sina'at as-sina'a*) was but a repetition of the Greek.[6] The translation was, inevitably, a transformation too. One may take the development of psychology as illustration of this point. It cannot be doubted that the works on the nature of the soul by the *falāsifa* owe much to their Greek precursors and, in particular, to the Peripatetic tradition of Antiquity, especially Aristotle's *De anima* and the so-called *Parva naturalia*, which were translated into Arabic by the early tenth century, if not sooner, and the exegetical corpus of the ancient Greek Aristotelian commentators, which also circulated widely in the Arab world.[7] But when one compares the classical Arabic psychology to the Greek, it is apparent that the later works contain elements extrinsic to the old. On more than a single point, philosophy seems to have retained its vitality no less in its "afterlife" than in its life.

Like the philosophers and physicians of antiquity, the classical Arabic thinkers understood the soul, principle of life, to consist of various powers, diversified by function and by part and ordered as the elements of a stratified and systematic whole. Chief among them, for the animal, was sensation. Students of Aristotle, the scholars of the Arabic tradition well knew that it is by perception that the beast can be distinguished from the plant. They could not fail to be familiar, too, with the five varieties of its kind identified by the psychological and medical knowledge of Antiquity: sight, hearing, smell, taste, and touch. But the thinkers of classical Islam did not end their enumerations of the senses there. They recognized a further set of perceptual powers, which none before them, if textual evidence may be trusted, had ever conceived as such. It is not exactly clear when or how the philosophers and physicians of Arabic culture came to identify these faculties as a class, but the sources that survive suggest that even the oldest thinkers in the tradition were already acquainted with them. To distinguish them from the five forms of perception known long before, these thinkers named them the "internal senses" (ḥawās bāṭina, ḥushim panimim).[8]

The classical Arabic and Hebrew treatises on the nature of the soul contain numerous classifications of these senses. But for the purposes of economy, the various taxonomies can be reduced, as Harry Austryn Wolfson demonstrated, to two sets. According to the first, represented by such figures as Ḥunayn ibn Isḥāq, al-Rāzī, Isaac Israeli, and Pseudo-Bahya, the internal senses consist of imagination (khayāl), cognition (fakr), and memory (dhikr); according to the second, proposed by Ibn Gabirol, Abraham Ibn ʿEzra, and Moses Maimonides, they are imagination, thinking, and "comprehension" (as in Ibn Gabirol and Maimonides, who employ the term *fahm*) or "wisdom" (as in Ibn 'Ezra, who uses *ḥikma*).[9] To the degree to which the internal senses consist of perceptual powers of the soul reminiscent of those discussed by Aristotle after the five proper senses in the *De anima*, they present obvious analogies with the "inner" faculties known to the early Christian tradition: the "more internal sense" (*sensus interior*) defined by Augustine in the *De libero arbitrio*, above all, but also the "sense of the brain" (*sensus cerebri*) invoked by Gregory the Great, which "presides within" (*intrinsecus praesidet*) and accomplishes many of the functions that were assigned by the Philosopher to the common sense. But these are analogies only, since there is no indication that the works of the Latin Church Fathers were ever known in the Arab world.[10]

It is remarkable that the early Arabic and Hebrew classifications of the internal senses omit any explicit reference to the Aristotelian sense to which Augustine and Gregory alluded in their invocations of an "internal sense" and a "sense of the brain," and which the Stoics, too, are said to have had in mind when they formulated the idea of an "inner touch by which we perceive ourselves." Despite the important role it played in the conception of the internal senses in late Greek and Latin thought, the Peripatetic "common sense" seems to have been excluded from the earliest systematic accounts of the inner powers in Arabo-Islamic thought. It is as if the first philosophers of the tradition held the "master sense" of the Aristotelian tradition to be no more a higher perceptual power than a lower one, as if, to their eyes, the shared faculty of sensation were not, in short, one sense among others, be it "internal" or "external."

One of the earliest surviving discussions of the common sense in the Arabic tradition confirms such an impression. It is the brief consideration accorded the faculty in the *Book of Elements* (*Kitāb al-Usṭuqsāt*) of the tenth-century Egyptian philosopher and physician Isaac ben Solomon Israeli. Often held to be the first of the Jewish philosophers of the Middle Ages, Isaac Israeli wrote in Arabic, like the other major figures of medieval Jewish thought.

But his works were translated into Hebrew and into Latin, and in the centuries after his death they circulated in Christian Europe as well as the Islamic world. In *the Book of Elements*, which survives only in fragmentary form in Hebrew and Latin translations, the original Arabic having been lost, Isaac devoted several pages to the psychological conditions of prophecy. Reconstructing the teaching of "the Ancients" on the nature of sleep and dreams, he could not fail to consider that faculty of which sleep and waking, in the classic doctrine, were both "affections." "The common sense," he wrote, "is intermediate between the corporeal sense of sight and the imaginative faculty, which resides in the anterior ventricle of the brain and is called *fantasia*."[11] Hence its designation, Isaac related, as "common": "It is for this reason that it is called 'common sense,' for it receives from a corporeal sense, i.e., that of sight, the corporeal aspects of things and transmits them to the spiritual sense mentioned before, i.e. the imaginative faculty."[12] The definition is striking. It situates the common sense at the limit between the twin sections of the bipartite soul: the corporeal and the incorporeal, the external and the internal, the sensible and the intellectual. The Aristotelian faculty can then be said to be "common" in a new sense: not because, as in the works of the tradition, its power can be attributed to each of the senses, but because it differs from them all, as the medium can be distinguished from that which it mediates. The common power of the Egyptian thinker constitutes a sense of the threshold between all the senses, a sense of the lines at which each fades into the next and the lower powers of the soul border on the higher.

If one turns to the surviving works of Isaac's great Arabo-Persian contemporary Abū Naṣr al-Fārābī, the position of the common sense seems no less exceptional. The "second master" (*al-muʿallim al-thānī*) after Aristotle, al-Fārābī bequeathed two classifications of the internal senses to the tradition. The first can be found in the *Enumeration of the Sciences*; it consists of a description as well as an enumeration. The second, contained in one of the lesser works, contains only an enumeration.[13] Both classifications fail altogether to mention the common sense. Given the importance of the faculty in the Aristotelian tradition, the omission is perplexing. It cannot but provoke a simple query: what becomes of the "dominant sense faculty," one might well ask, in the thought of the second master?

The twentieth chapter of *The Book of the Views of the Inhabitants of the Virtuous City* furnishes the elements of an answer. This section of the treatise is dedicated to the parts and powers of the human soul, which appear in the allegorical garb of personages of varying rank and function. After describing the nutritive faculty as composed of a "main power and others that are servants and nursemaids," al-Fārābī turns to the sensitive faculty. "The sensitive faculty is also composed of a main power (*ra'īs*) and nursemaids (*riwāḍa'*)," he explains:

> The latter are the five senses known to everyone, and they are located in the eyes, the ears, and the rest. Each of the five senses perceives the sensible that is proper to it. The main power is the one in which all the perceptions of the five senses are gathered together, the five senses being like its reporters. It is as if the five senses were all its advisers, each responsible for a different kind of information from one of the regions of the kingdom. The main power is like the king at whose court the advisers gather the news from all the regions of the kingdom.[14]

Al-Fārābī invokes a trope of Platonic origin, common to innumerable works of ancient psychology and medicine. The order of the soul appears as that of a political unity, albeit not the *polis* but the Arab *politeia* that was the "kingdom" (*mamlaka*). Behind the masks of its characteristic personages, it is not difficult to see the faculties of the Aristotelian tradition, newly clad in the official attire of Arabo-Islamic administrative functions. Just as to every sense, according to the Philosopher and his exegetes, there corresponds a particular object, to each of the five "advisers" there belongs a single region; just as the individual senses, in the account of the Stagirite, are said to receive their sensible objects by means of special organ, at a given position in the spectrum that defines its appearance, so each of al-Fārābī's "advisers" must relay to the single capital news drawn from his own terrain.

The striking invention of the Arabic philosopher consists in the elevation of the one faculty now said to rule as "king" (*malik*) over each of the parts of the sensitive soul. The royal personage is no less unmistakable in this chapter for remaining unidentified as such. For there can be no doubt: the unnamed king of the philosophical parable occupies the sovereign offices of the "master sense faculty" (*kurion aisthētērion*) to which classical Aristotelian doctrine assigned powers of perception beyond, or before, those of each of the five forms of sense. *The Virtuous City* represents a moment of major importance in the transmission and transformation of its concept. Here the classical capacity is no longer said to be merely "shared" among the faculties of perception; nor is it characterized as "intermediary" in the order of the soul. It is neither external nor internal but capital, the "main power" with respect to which the proper senses are but "nursemaids." Even as it is the ruler who establishes the law that divides and unifies the territories of a single kingdom, so it is the common sense, in the psychological fable, that secures the order of the powers of the sensible soul, allotting to each its terrain as well as the responsibility of drawing from it the "kind of information" proper to it. It follows that the disappearance of the shared faculty would inevitably bring about the demise of the entire regime of sensation. In the absence of the king, after all, there can be no kingdom, and without this "ruler" and his court, the second master suggests, the animal soul would not be one.

CHAPTER FIFTEEN

Psychology of the 449th Night

A short Chapter, in which a costly Slave discourses before a
Caliph concerning the Powers contained in the Brain

Among the many tales told by Queen Shahrazad to her murderous husband, King Shahryar, more than a few involved slave-girls of exceptional intelligence. To be sure, the heroines of these tales were a variegated class. Many made no particular pretensions to knowledge: the abilities nature had furnished them sufficed, as they invariably proved, to allow them to escape even the most intractable of situations, outwitting the masters who would judge them. Others, however, possessed learning of considerable proportions, which they could also deploy with unfailing skill. Tawaddud, the heroine of the tale of the 449th night, was one of this company. She suffered the misfortune of numbering among the possessions of a spendthrift Baghdadi, who, having all but squandered his estate, resolved at last to remedy the impecuniousness he had brought upon himself by selling her at an exorbitant price to Hārūn al-Rashīd. A man of means, the caliph declared himself willing to pay the amount that had been asked. But he was no impulsive buyer, and one fact remained to be verified before the transaction could come to pass. Tawaddud was said to be as erudite as she was beautiful, and before spending no less than ten thousand dinars to acquire her, the caliph demanded to know if it were truly so. Therefore, he assembled the experts at his court and commanded them to ascertain how far her learning stretched. First came a commentator of the Qur'ān, who put to her a series of questions concerning the exegesis of the Holy Book. These she answered without fail. Then came a physician, who examined, among other things, her familiarity with the brain. On this subject, too, her performance could not be faulted. When asked how many ventricles lay in the human head, she unhesitatingly furnished him with the correct response: "Three, which contain five faculties, styled the intrinsic senses, to wit, the common sense (al-(ḥiss al-mushtarak), imagination (al-khayāl), the thinking faculty (al-mutaṣarrifa), perception (al-wāhima), and memory (al-ḥāfiẓa)."[1]

One must wonder at Tawaddud's answer. Hārūn al-Rashīd ruled from 786 to 809, and at that time the massive Greco-Arabic translation movement that would last a good two centuries was in its earliest stages. No physician or philosopher of that time appears to have offered any enumeration of the internal senses of such systematic shape. When the first philosophers in the Arabic tradition did seek to classify these powers, they proposed a threefold account that, although variable in its details, could be understood to reproduce a Hellenistic distinction, possibly of Aristotelian origin, between "imagination" (phantastikon), "cogitation" (dianoētikon), and "memory" (mnēmoneutikon). To these three faculties, al-Fārābī would later add a fourth: "estimation" (wahm), a sense that would play a prominent role in the psychology of the Latin Schoolmen, to whom it would be known as aestimatio.[2] But the slavegirl's answer began with a faculty omitted by the "second master" from his lists: the common sense. In its five terms, Tawaddud's enumeration revealed her perfect familiarity with the classification of the internal senses proposed by Avicenna, the great Persian philosopher who — with a temporal distortion typical of medieval literature, Arabic and European — lived in the early eleventh century. Although the caliph could not have known it, Tawaddud's answer clearly showed that she numbered among the many readers of the most philosophical of the Avicennian treatises. In this, she resembled that thirteenth-century doctor of the universities of Christian Europe, Thomas Aquinas, who in the first part of the Summa theologiae likewise related, giving credit to his source, that

"in his book on the soul, Avicenna posits five inner sensitive powers, namely, common sense, imagination, the imaginative faculty,
estimation, and memory [*sensum communem, phantasiam, imagina-
tivam, aestimativam, et memorativam*]."[3]

Avicenna had, in fact, offered several classifications of the internal senses, which alternately reproduced the two taxonomies
of the tradition and exceeded their scope. In the medical treatise
known to the Latin West as *The Canon of Medicine*, at one point,
he adopted a threefold taxonomy; at another, he suggested that
the inner senses were four instead. It was in the philosophical
masterpiece of his maturity, the *Kitāb al-shifā'*, as well as its abridg-
ment in the *Kitāb al-Najāt*, that he proposed the psychological
teachings recalled by Tawaddud, distinguishing a total of five
internal senses (which, it should be added, could also rise to seven,
depending on the principles by which one counted them).[4] Each
of these enumerations revised the classical Arabic doctrines of the
internal senses on at least one point. From the *Canon* to the great
"book on the soul" to which Thomas alluded, Avicenna began the
set with the common sense.

The "book on the soul" was the treatise on psychology of the
Shifā', which, translated from Arabic into Latin in Toledo during
the second half of the twelfth century, came to be known to the
Christian West as the *Liber de anima* or *Sextus de naturalibus*. It
already contained a summary enumeration of the internal senses
in the fifth chapter of its first book, which began with the faculty
of "fantasy, which is common sense" (*bantāsīa, wa' l-ḥiss al-
mushtarak, fantasia, quae est sensus communis*).[5] But the work proposed a systematic account of the faculty only in the first chapter
of Book Four, which considered all the internal powers of the soul
as a whole. Avicenna began his discussion with the common
sense, and from the opening of the chapter he made it clear, with
a characteristic gesture, that he believed at least some of his predecessors to have greatly misunderstood the true nature of the
power. Against those who had invoked the faculty to explain common sensible qualities alone, he argued, in programmatic terms,
that "common sense, on the contrary, is the faculty that receives

all sensible things."[6] His proof was pellucid: were it not so, no animal, man or beast, could ever link a sensible object of one type to that of another. Were common sense not the sense of all things sensed, after eating something sweet, we would never know how to connect what we had tasted with something we could see, and after hearing the song of a certain man, we would not be able to recognize by vision the man who sang it. "The life of beasts," too, the philosopher commented, would then be harsh: had they no common sense, animals would not know to tie the sight of a wooden stick to the sense of pain, nor could they sense from a certain smell that they were close to the object of a certain taste.

Avicenna thus significantly extended the range and significance of the common sense, even as he inscribed it, for posterity, as the most elementary term in the hierarchical ascent of the inner faculties of the soul. At times, to be sure, it seems that the Persian philosopher sought to limit the functions once attributed to it. Although he invariably maintained that the shared faculty apprehended common sensible qualities and complex sensations, at times he denied that it could grasp the activity of the senses themselves.[7] But he always argued that its role in the animal soul was more fundamental than others before him had maintained. There was a simple reason for his audacious claim: he believed the common sense to be no less than the "center of all the senses" (*markaz al-ḥiwās, centrum omnium sensuum*). For him, the shared faculty was the single power enabling the animal to be affected by the five forms of sensation that it could distinguish with precision.

It was perhaps in the *Shifā'* that Avicenna went furthest in insisting on the importance of the central sense. Drawing on the classic figure of the circle and the point, Avicenna cast the inner power not only as the foundation of all the senses but also as their center, the point from which they all "emanated," engendered in the shared procession from a primary power.[8] The terms of the Persian philosopher's final characterization of the sense in his *Liber de anima* are memorable not least for the distance they mark with respect to the source of the doctrine in the Aristotelian treatise on the soul. Tawaddud herself, to be sure, did not cite them.

Perhaps it was because they were too obvious; perhaps it was because she hesitated, in all modesty, to cite them from a book she could not have read. In the centuries after Avicenna, they were to return, as echoes, to be glossed and amplified throughout the many idioms of medieval thought. "This power which is called the common sense," Avicenna wrote, "is the center from which the senses ramify, and to which they return, like rays, and it, in truth, is that which senses" (فهذ القوة هى التى تسمى الحس المشترك وهى مركز الحواس ومنها تتشعب الشعب وليها تؤدى الحواس وهى بالحقيقة التى تحس ; *Et haec virtus est quae vocatur sensus communis, que est centrum omnium sensuum et a qua derivantur rami et cui reddunt sensu, et ipsa est vere quae sentit*).[9]

Chapter Sixteen

The Fountain and the Source

Another short Chapter, considering the Fortunes of the
Arabic Doctrines among the Schoolmen and Others of their Age

Like Tawaddud, the European scholars of the late Middle Ages knew Avicenna well. By the time Albertus Magnus composed his commentary on Aristotle's *De anima* in the middle of the thirteenth century, the doctrine advanced in the work known to the West as the *Sextus de naturalibus* was one with which no philosopher could fail to reckon. The works of such figures as Jean de la Rochelle, Alexander of Hales, and Roger Kilwardby, to say nothing of the various anonymous *Questiones in tres libros De anima* published during the last century, all bear witness to the depth and extent of the engagement of the thirteenth-century Schoolmen with the works of *Avicenna Latinus*.[1] But the thirteenth-century students of Aristotle benefited also from that monument of philosophical exegesis that is Averroës's *Long commentary* on the Aristotelian treatise, which was translated sometime between 1220 and 1235 by Michael Scot (and which today survives in that form alone).[2] It is clear that the argument of Albertus's treatise on the *De anima* could not have been possible without either contribution to philosophical psychology. The master of Cologne continually departs, expressly and thoroughly, from a close reading of both Avicenna and Averroës, and he builds on the propositions of both *falāsifa* in offering an account of the nature of sensation that was in many respects unprecedented.

Albertus dedicates the fourth treatise of his commentary on the "second" book of the *De anima* to the nature of common

sense. His method is that of the systematic and progressive interpretation of the Aristotelian text *ad litteram* practiced in the universities of the time, which he distributes in twelve chapters
ordered by argument. Unlike Avicenna's, his exposition of the
theory of common sense therefore proceeds by means of the regular authoritative citation and exposition of the doctrine of the
Stagirite. Recalling the setting of the original discussion of the
"shared sense," Albertus explains that this faculty alone apprehends the five complex sensible qualities (*motus, status, figura,
magnitudo, numerus et unum*); that it alone allows for the composi-
tion and division of phenomena received by different forms of
sense perception; and that it alone, finally, permits us to "sense
that we are seeing and hearing" (*sentimus nos videre et audire*).[3] His
conclusion unites in one stroke the doctrine of the Aristotelian
text and the account of the foundation and source of the sensitive
faculties proposed by Avicenna in the *Sextus de naturalibus*. "We
say," Albertus writes, in the eleventh chapter of the treatise, "that
the common sense is the root of all the individual senses; it is the
form from which sense flows into all the proper senses" (*Dicimus
sensum comunem esse principium omnium sensuum particularium et
esse formam, a qua est influentia sensus in omnibus propriis sensibus*).[4]

The next and final chapter of the treatise abandons the form of
the commentary altogether. It is marked by the twentieth-century
editors of Albertus's *Opera omnia* as a "digression," but its argument, though novel, follows logically from the discussion of the
common sense until this point.[5] Here Albertus, deepening his
analysis of the status of the faculty as a single power that exercises
itself in each of the five senses, reflects on the nature of its unity.
He concludes that the common sense can be defined as a "universal" form, not, to be sure, in the sense of the predicable, but in the
sense that it is "a cause that formally preconceives that which
emanates from it, just as the architectural plan preconceives the
form of the house" (*est universalis non ut praedicabile, sed sicut
causa formaliter praehabens ea quae oriuntur ex ipsa, sicut architec-
tonica praehabet formam domus*).[6] The "universality" of the common sense thus consists in its specific causal relation to the

individual senses: "preconception" (*praehabitio*). As Alain de Libera has shown, Albertus turns with this term to a concept of medieval Neoplatonism to elucidate the nature of the Aristotelian faculty. *Praehabitio* hearkens back to Pseudo-Dionysius the Areopagite, who employs the Greek term *proekhein* in *De divinis nominibus*, as well as to Eustathius of Nicaea, who characterizes the Good as that which "preconceives" everything in itself, being at once *superhabens* and *praehabens* with respect to that which proceeds from it.[7]

The claim may startle the contemporary Aristotelian. But to the reader familiar with Avicenna, it appears as a rigorous development of the thesis in the *Sextus de naturalibus* according to which the five senses "emanate" from the common sense as the rays of a circle derive from its center. The shared capacity now shows itself to be the single power by which the entire sensorial faculty, with its many branches, comes into being. It is the *primum sentiens*, which, in its formal universality, already contains the proper senses according to the mode of the Neoplatonic "preconception." Hence the new definition of the common sense:

> the first sensing not in virtue of time, but in virtue of nature, that in which the entire sensitive capacity is originally founded — that is the common sense, which is the origin of the individual senses, since the proper senses are derived from it, and since it cannot be constituted *e converso* from them, nor can anything of its being come from them (*primum sentiens non quidem tempore, sed natura, hoc est in quo primitus salvatur tota virtus sensitive, est sensus communis, qui est origo sensuum propriorum ita, quo ab ipso derivantur sensu proprii, ita quod non e converso constituitur ab eis nec aliquid sui esse habet ab eis*).[8]

The master sense of the tradition comes close, at this point, to ceasing to be "a" sense at all. Unlike the other senses, the "shared faculty," as Albertus now defines it, constitutes not a distinct form of receptivity but the one power in which "the entire sensitive capacity is originally founded" (*primitus salvatur totat virtus sensitive*). If, adopting a term of the medieval doctors, one gives the name *medium* to the spectrum in which the individual sense perceives its object, then one must conclude, like the editors of Albertus's *Opera omnia*, that the common sense is the "medium of media," or, to employ the abstract noun of the medieval philosophers themselves, that the common sense constitutes the "mediality of all sensible things" (*medietas omnium sensibilium*).[9] It is the ultimate element of perception: the dimension in which, and from which, all sensation comes into being, preserving itself as long as it lasts.

This was largely the form in which the shared faculty of sensation passed, with the rest of Scholastic learning, from Latin into the first languages of modern Europe. One may recall Meister Eckhart's attempt, a generation after Albertus, to present the concept to those to whom he preached, as he explained that "the teachers say there is one power that sees by means of the eye and there is another, that is aware that it sees" (*daz in ander kraft ist, dâ von daz ouge sihet, und ein ander kraft, dâ ez bekennet, daz es sihet*).[10] But before long, an unknown author trained in the teachings of the medieval universities dwelled at greater length on the faculty that Albertus and the Arab thinkers had defined. The treatise known as *Li ars d'amour, de vertu et de boneurté*, a work once attributed to Jean le Bel, later assigned to Jean d'Arckel, and more recently thought to have been written by neither author, contains an exemplary sketch of the psychological concept. This work explains:

> The common sense is a power that embraces all proper things that affect the proper senses. And the particular and single senses, which are external, descend from the common sense, which is internal. It is like the various rays of a circle, which move from the middle of the circle toward all the parts of the circle. And thus the semblances of things that are sensed by the individual senses are brought to the common sense; this is how the common sense judges the properties of the individual senses, variously distinguishing among the different things by means of the senses that are sensed, just as we distinguish between white and sweet, for instance, in milk. We thus say that the

common sense is the fountain and the source of all the individual senses, to which all sensible movement is brought back, as to its ultimate end. This faculty possesses a [particular] object insofar as it is a sense, and it possesses a [particular object] insofar as it is common. Insofar as it is a sense, it receives from things a semblance without matter and without the presence of any material form. Insofar as it is common, it has two activities. One is the judgment on the sensed thing, by which we are aware that we are sensing, as when we judge that we are seeing and hearing by means of another sense. The second activity is to compare the different things that are sensed, and to imagine. Thus we say: this is sweet and this is even sweeter, this milk is white and it is sweet. And this is why all the aspects of sensed things are brought back to the common sense by each individual sense. Some locate this capacity in the back of the brain, where the nerves of the five senses meet; others place it in the heart, since it is the fountain and the source of life.[11]

Each of the functions that define the shared faculty of the soul appears here in an exemplary abbreviated form. The author has read not only Aristotle but also those who followed him and who, in the languages of Arabic and Latin culture, sought to comment on his works. The French writer defines common sense as an internal power (*en dedans*) that animates the external senses (*de dehors*) just as the "rays of a circle . . . move from the middle of the circle toward all the parts of the circle"; he or she specifies that it is by means of this faculty that it is possible to judge "the properties of the individual senses, variously distinguishing among the different things by means of the senses that are sensed," and to be "aware that we are sensing" (*ke nous connissons ke nous sommes sentant*). The vernacular *Ars*, however, is no simple summary of the Greek, Arabic, and Latin treatises that precede it. It also finds its own expression for the primary perceptual power: "the fountain and the source of all the individual senses, to which all sensible movement is brought back, as to its ultimate end" (*li fontaine et li sourgons de tous les sens singulars, ouquel tot li movement sensible sunt rapporté, si comme en fin derraine*). But it is, in truth, a double fountain and source. The common sense is not only "the fountain and the source of all the individual senses" but also, as we read at the end of the passage, "the fountain and the source of life" (*fontaine et racine de vie*). Perhaps this is because, for the sensitive animals that we are, to live is to be aware that we feel, and because, as Thomas wrote, at once glossing Aristotle and paraphrasing Augustine, "it is by the common sense that we perceive that we are living" (*sensu enim communi percipimus nos vivere*).[12]

CHAPTER SEVENTEEN

Perception Everywhere

A long Chapter, on Descartes, Bacon, and most especially
Campanella, who held the World to be a large sensing Animal

The early modern age was, among other things, a time of many senses. First there were the perceptions of external qualities defined by the doctors of the medieval schools, with which the authors of the sixteenth and seventeenth centuries were naturally familiar: the so-called five external senses enumerated by Aristotle and his commentators in their classic sequence, "sight, hearing, smell, taste, and touch."[1] Most followed Philoponus and Augustine in holding these to be common to every sensitive creature, but some recalled that the lives of beasts can also be complete without them all. The proof, they would note, lies with the hedgehog: according to Aristotle, at least, that animal manages perfectly without any sense of smell, just as whales and moles, as Pliny the Elder famously reported, live full lives while being completely blind.[2] But it was, in any case, accepted by all that the perceptual powers of the animal did not end with the external senses one chose to admit, for there were also those higher perceptions identified by the medieval tradition as "internal." By the sixteenth century, several perspectives, both medieval and modern, were already well established on the thorny question of their count. There had been those who based their enumerations of the inward powers on the number of ventricles in the brain, which some had taken to be two and others three. There had been those who, by contrast, refused on medical grounds to identify the inner senses with any regions of the brain, suggesting that they were in any case three ("imagination, thought, and memory"), as Galen had long before maintained. There were those who believed them to be four, as Thomas and, after him, Cajetan and Sylvester of Ferrara taught.[3] And, finally, there were many who, following Avicenna and his Latin pupils, took the "inner wits" to be five: the common sense (*sensus communis*), the imaginative power (*vis imaginativa*), estimation (*aestimatio*), imagination (*phantasia*), and memory (*memoria*). This was a doctrine shared by such diverse figures as al-Ghazālī, Albertus Magnus, and William Shakespeare, who in his 141st sonnet invoked a passion that his "five senses" as well as his "five wits" could not fully fathom.[4]

These were, in large part, inherited senses. There were newer ones to come, which in time would transform the theory of perception forever. But in this age, the old and the new were close contemporaries, and the years that witnessed the emergence of novel accounts of sensation were also those in which the ancient doctrines continued as before to be transmitted. In *The Anatomy of Melancholy* of 1621, for instance, one finds an account of the vital powers that is largely still that of the medieval doctors. After defining the vegetative power, Robert Burton turns to the power of perception, remarking that "the sensible faculty . . . is as far beyond the other in dignity as a beast is preferred to a plant, having those vegetal powers included in it."[5] That proposition is purely Aristotelian. Among living things, it stipulates, one may distinguish those that nourish themselves from those that in addition perceive; one may define the first as plants, and the second, whether rational or irrational, will then be beasts. Intellection, according to the same doctrine, marks a still higher level of activity, which separates man from animals, even as sensing beings can be separated, on account of their perceptions, from the merely vegetative.

Within a few years, the classical doctrine of sensation was to be famously contested by the thinker who has been regarded, more often than any other, as ushering in the modern age in philosophy. Starting with the *Regulae ad directionem ingenii*, which are thought to have been composed before 1628, Descartes asserted that the indubitable foundation of all knowledge could lie nowhere other than in the representative activity of the rational being, which he called, with a term at once old and new, *cogitatio*, "thought."[6] He would later explain that such a "cogitation" could not be opposed to perception as the "intellection" of the medieval doctors had been distinguished, at least in principle, from "sensation." The reason was that perception, for Descartes, was in every sense an act of the representing, conscious, and thinking "I"; for him, every human sensation was, in other words, an act of cogitation. "By the term 'thought' [*cogitationis nomine*]," the philosopher would thus explain in the first of his *Principia philosophiae*, "I understand everything which we are conscious of as happening within us, insofar as we have consciousness of it [*omnia, quae nobis consciis in nobis fiunt, quaetenus eorum in nobis conscientia est*]."[7] In the second set of *Replies* he was even more explicit. Speaking of the expression *cogitatio*, he declared: "I use this term to include everything that is within us in such a way that we are immediately conscious of it. Thus all the operations of the will, the intellect, the imagination, and the senses are thoughts" (*Cogitationis nomine complector illud omnes, quod sic in nobis est, ut ejus immediate conscii summus. Ita omnes voluntatis, intellectus, imaginationis et sensuum operationes sunt cogitationes*).[8]

The Cartesian definition of cogitation could not but transform the nature of sensation as it had been traditionally understood. In the classical and medieval traditions, perception had been the power shared by all beasts, no less the thinking than the unthinking ones among them; by definition, animals, for Aristotle and his successors, had all met in the terrain of the activity once called *aisthēsis*. Descartes's definition of the conscious mind erected an insurmountable barrier in this field. Once the sensation proper to human beings was understood as a *modus cogitandi* like every other, it could by nature have nothing to do with the multiple operations performed in the world of beasts. These had furnished countless classical and medieval thinkers with clear evidence of the sensitive powers common to the rational and irrational animals. To

Descartes, by contrast, the movements of the inhuman animals bore witness to a mechanical nature from which consciousness was by definition absent: that of divinely crafted but utterly mindless automatons, "machine-animals," as the philosopher of consciousness would repeatedly insist.[9]

It was a new perspective, from which each of the elements of the classical theory of perception was in time reconsidered, the idea of the sensitive soul no less than the theory of the individual senses. Some of the older terms could be retained; others, by contrast, were soon set aside. Among those to which the Cartesian theory could not be kind was the first of the inner senses, which in the medieval accounts of animal life had tied the lower to the higher powers of the sensitive soul. Burton still recognized its classic place, assigning it its old functions. In "Of the Inward Senses," he identified it as "the common sense," "the judge or moderator of all the rest, by whom we discern all differences of objects." "For by mine eye," he explained, "I do not know that I see or by mine ear that I hear, but by my common sense, which judgeth of sounds and colours: they are but the organs to bring the species to be censured; so that all their objects are his, and all their offices are his."[10]

As "the judge and moderator" of all the senses, which not only distinguished among all perceptions but also perceived the fact of perception ("that I see" and "that I hear"), the common sense had accomplished in medieval psychology a function close to that of Cartesian "thought." One might even suggest that it was the ancient perceptual power which furnished the logical model for the cogitating faculty that, in the modern age, would be attributed to the conscious "I."[11] But the differences between the two powers are quite clear. The classic faculty was sensory, not cognitive, and as a power of perception it belonged to a terrain in which animal awareness and human consciousness could not clearly be told apart. This was a region whose existence Descartes would not admit, and the medieval "common sense," for this reason, could find no stable place in the Cartesian theory of perception.

As historians of philosophy have amply demonstrated, however, Descartes did not reject the doctrine of the medieval *scholae* overnight. The fate of what he called "the common sense, which they grant even animals" is but one among many examples.[12] Scholars have observed that although the Cartesian doctrine of the inner senses "varies slightly" from work to work, Descartes "always showed a certain distance toward the expression *common sense*."[13] In the twelfth *regula* and in the *Dioptrics*, he referred to it as a term employed by the authors of the tradition (we read, in the first of these works, "*ad aliam quondam corporis partem, quae vocatur sensus communis*," and, in the second, "cette faculté qu'ils appellent le sens commun").[14] *The World* and the *Description of the Human Body* still present a traditional account of three inner senses (*Sens commun, l'Imagination*, and *Mémoire*), and a letter of uncertain date also contains a passing reference to the old faculty.[15] But in the *Second Meditation*, from 1640, Descartes casts the common sense as but a name for the "imaginative power" (*sensu conmuni, ut vocant, id est potentia imaginatrice*).[16] And by 1649, the sense has disappeared entirely from the account of the sensitive abilities: *The Passions of the Soul* makes no mention of the faculty in its discussion of sensation.[17] In his treatises, finally, Descartes nowhere invokes the medieval power. At times he employs the expression "common sense," but in these cases, as several scholars have indicated, it is to signify the Latin rhetorical ideal of "good sense" and "sound judgment" (*le bon sens*), which, since Roman times, had also been designated with the term *sensus communis*.[18] After Descartes, this usage was to prove in large part the dominant one. Starting with the seventeenth century, the expression "common sense" progressively lost its technical value as the designation of a power of perception, acquiring the acceptation it still holds today.[19]

There is little doubt that the Cartesian was among the most influential of the early modern theories of sensation, but it would be an unfortunate oversight to take it to have been alone in its kind. In the years during which Descartes aimed to found all knowledge, physical and metaphysical, on the activity of the thinking "I," the development of another current of thought was already well under way. With respect to the teachings of the medieval schools, this was a philosophical movement at least as innovative as the Cartesian. But it pursued a line of inquiry that was altogether its own, and in its account of perception, at least, it proceeded along a path of thought that can be understood to be in some sense the inverse of that of Descartes. It did not aim to separate the conscious "I" from the world around it, as cogitating being can be opposed to extended being; on the contrary, it sought to demonstrate that all intellection remains subject, by nature, to the principles that rule the purely material world. And it did not partition the realm of beasts, as did Descartes, dividing those beings who possessed the faculty of reason from those who lacked it. For it made of animal sensation, in its many varieties, the fundamental principle of all things.

This was the path taken by Descartes's slightly older and less well-known Calabrian contemporary, Tommaso Campanella, who developed his doctrine of nature in the wake of the influential sixteenth-century philosopher and scientist Bernardino Telesio. If one turns to Campanella's *De sensu rerum et magia*, which dates from 1589–1590 but was not published in Latin until 1620, one finds an account of perception that is as irreducible to the teachings of the medieval schools as it is to doctrine that Descartes would soon develop in distinction to it. Campanella unambiguously rejects the classical account of the "common sense" as a distinct faculty responsible for the discernment of sensible qualities of different types.[20] He does so clearly, moreover, and for a reason of principle. Faithful to Telesio's philosophy of nature, Campanella substitutes for the psychology of the schools a materialist theory according to which there is but a single animating substance in all things: "spirit" (*spiritus*), which, in animals, flows through the diverse parts of the body and, in interaction with their variously soft and resilient portions, produces the many varieties of perception.[21] Hence the superfluity of a common sense, which in the traditional doctrine of the soul had united the many operations of the perceptual faculty in a single principle. There is no need to posit a special faculty to mediate among the various sensitive powers, Campanella explains, since there is only a single spirit, which runs through the whole sensing body; there is no need for *a* common sense, in other words, for there is but one sense, and it is by nature irreducibly common. As we read in Book Two of the *De sensu rerum et magia*, "the same spirit hears, sees, smells, and tastes, because it flows from one organ to another."[22]

Campanella, however, revises the theory of the senses on more than the question of their count. From his first works to his last, he provides an account of perception that differs fundamentally from the teaching of the tradition. The old doctrine had its basis in the theory of "information" proposed in Aristotle's *De anima*. According to the canonical Scholastic teaching, perception consists in the apprehension of an intelligible form in that which is perceived. The classic analogy was that of the seal, which leaves its immaterial imprint on the wax in which it is impressed: just as the shapeless matter acquires the figure of the seal in form alone, so the perceiving power, for the Scholastics, receives the "species" of the thing perceived, unadulterated by any sensible matter.[23] But such an argument, Campanella affirms, leads to consequences that cannot be maintained. For a sensible form to pass from the perceived to the perceiver, he reasons, the form of the sensed thing would have to be capable of being separated, at least for a moment, from the thing itself, precisely so that it could "inform" the perceiving power. This, however, entails absurdities for the concept of that which perceives, as well as for the notion of that which is perceived. Consider, first, the state of the sensed thing in such a theory. In the moment in which its form passes from it to the sensing power, it would necessarily revert to formlessness and immediately be corrupted. At the same time, the sensing power would inevitably also lose itself: as it received the forms of each of those things it sensed, it would become them, unmade and remade as the wax finds itself reshaped anew with each impression of every different seal.[24]

In the place of the traditional doctrine of sensation by "information," Campanella sets a newer theory, which can be effectively described, by contrast, as a theory of sensation by "mutation."

Developed on the basis of Telesio's natural philosophy, this theory eschews all reference to the apprehension of ideal forms. It defines perception in purely material terms, as the process by which one thing, when placed in proximity to another, acquires something of its physical consistency.[25] "Of many things," Campanella thus writes, with rhetorical insistence, in the *De sensu rerum et magia*, "one alone is well established: there can be no sensation without the sensing being's acquiring a likeness of the sensed" (*non si faccia sensazione, senza che il senziente del sentito similitudine prenda*).[26] What does it mean to feel movement, the philosopher recalls, if not to feel oneself slightly moved, and what does it mean to sense light, if not to sense oneself partly brightened? "Experience," he remarked, "revolts" against the doctrine that "to feel fire, one must acquire the whole form of fire. It suffices to be a little heated."[27]

This fact struck the Italian philosopher as being of capital importance. As Léon Blanchet observed in an important study, for Campanella all perception can be grasped as "the result of a very light modification of the vital spirit, which suffers the external action of things and very faintly reproduces in itself the movements that are proper to them."[28] To feel an external object is to feel, within oneself, the very force of that which one feels outside. It is be touched by it: in this sense, Campanella argued that all perception consists in a tactile act (*tutti li sensi esser tatto*), which transmits to one being the nature of another.[29] The evidence could be extended *ad infinitum*, and the eloquent thinker showed little compunction about curtailing his examples for the purposes of economy. But there is no need to look further, he once commented, than "this pen which writes": "the same object prints itself" (*lo stesso oggetto imprime sè stesso*), leaving the trace of itself in its movements over the blackened sheet.[30]

The trace, for Campanella, is essential. It bears witness to an activity on the part of the sensing being that must not be overlooked if the structure of perception is to be fully grasped. Sensation cannot be reduced to minor mutation alone, for it also implies an active dimension within the mutated being: "the per-

ception of passion" (*perceptio passionis*), in which the slight transformation comes to be registered by the patient, however faintly,
as such. It was a point already repeatedly stressed by Telesio, who
taught that all sensation consisted in "the perception of one's own
passion" (*propriae passionis perceptio*).[31] But Campanella drew
from the principle a novel consequence, which made of the physical alteration that is "mutation" the genesis of a "consciousness,"
albeit one that, in contrast to the Cartesian, cannot be defined by
an act of thought. As perception, all sensation, Campanella reasoned, implies a certain awareness. To sense is to be affected and
"to discern," "to judge," and "to recognize" (*dignotio*), however
dimly, that one has undergone a change.[32]

Such an awareness did not seem to Campanella particularly
human in nature. His most famous proposition was precisely that
there was "a sense of things" (*sensus rerum*), and by all appearances
he meant this claim quite literally. As he clearly stated in the *Compendium physiologiae*, composed toward the end of his life, "We
affirm that the sense [or sensation, *sensus*] with which animals
seem to be equipped and which seems to distinguish them from
inanimate things can be found in every thing."[33] The proof, he
explained, lies "in the reciprocal action" by which all things
"move toward their opposites and flee their opposites."[34] He
developed the thesis in great detail in both his *De sensu rerum et
magia* and in his *Metafisica*, condemning Aristotle and his disciples
for having foolishly restricted the field of perception to the terrain of animal life. Plants, he recalled, react to that which is
around them, growing toward the sun, for example, or away from
it, depending on what they sense themselves to need, and approaching or avoiding those plants toward which they possess a
natural sympathy or antipathy.[35] But the Italian philosopher held
that lesser and greater beings also sense. The movements of
waters show that they, too, perceive the affections they suffer;
magnetism is the proof of perception among stones; the reaction
of air to that which sounds within it tells us much about its powers of sensitivity.... An unbroken chain of perception, for Campanella, stretched from matter, which senses in desiring the forms

171

it lacks, to the sensations of the astral bodies that circulate in the sensing heavens. All the evidence led to a single, startling proposition, which Campanella did not hesitate to formulate repeatedly. "It is necessary to state," the philosopher declared, "that the world is an extremely sensitive animal" (*mundum esse animal maxime sensitivum*).[36] One must simply distinguish in its parts differences of degree, granting that "sensibility is in some things clearer and livelier, in others obscurer and more obtuse."[37]

In the *Metafisica* of his maturity, Campanella drew the single consequence that such a principle implied for the constitution of all things. Sense, he argued in that work, is a principle of existence, without which no thing, earthly or divine, could be. In Book Six of his treatise on first philosophy, he thus explained that the "essence" (*essentia*) of everything that is consists of "sense" (*sensus*), no less than potentiality (*potentia*) and love (*amor*). Without "sense," or, as he also wrote in this work, "sapience" (*sapientia*), and most especially without a sense and sapience of itself, no being could conserve itself and continue to be: no being would be aware of itself, and as a result, no being would know to protect itself as best it could. "Sense," we learn, thus consists in a kind of knowledge. But for Campanella it was not necessarily intellectual in character, nor did it imply the representation of any object. His terminology is in this regard significant: in the *Metafisica*, as elsewhere, consistently employed the Augustinian term *nosse* to describe the awareness that everything possesses of itself, not the *cogitare* that Descartes would soon invoke for the knowledge that the conscious mind possesses in representing its thoughts to itself.

"We see that the existent *is*," Campanella wrote, "because it knows that it is, and there is no existent that does not know itself; for it defends itself against other beings, which are not unknown to it, which are destructive toward it, because sapience is the principle of being and of the conservation of being" (*Ecce videmus quidem ens esse, quia novit esse: et nullum ens reperiri sui inscium; nam pro se pugnat contra non ignota sui destructive, quia essendi et conservandi esse principium sapientia est*).[38] The philosopher found in sensation the ultimate ground of the "self-conservation" (*con-servatio sui*) that Telesio had placed at the foundation of natural philosophy.[39] It amounted to a metaphysical formulation of an old Stoic principle. Tending toward what benefits them and avoiding what harms them, beings preserve themselves, Campanella argued, because they perceive that which affects them and because, there-fore, they simultaneously perceive themselves.

Campanella took pains to distinguish between these two types of perception. They often coincide in fact, but still, he showed, they remain distinct in form. On this point, the Italian philoso-pher departed not only from Aristotle but also from Telesio. It does not suffice, Campanella reasoned, to claim that sensation occurs by means of a "slight mutation," in which the sensing body acquires something of the nature of that which it senses, for in such terms one cannot account for the entire structure of sensa-tion as "the perception of a passion."[40] In any act of sensation, the affection undergone by the sensing power can certainly be under-stood as the result of such a transformation: one being has altered the consistency of another. But the perception in which the sensa-tion comes to be registered as such cannot be explained in terms of "mutation," since it would be contradictory to suppose that one being, while remaining itself, could transfer itself to itself, as heat, for example, passes from the source of warmth to the heated thing. The "perception of a passion" is a perception of another order, for it discloses an essence that is not conveyed from with-out but felt from within: not an "adduced sense" (*sensus additus*), Campanella wrote, but an "innate" or "induced sense" (*sensus inditus*). It reveals the "sense of oneself" (*sensus sui*) shared, dimly or sharply, by everything that exists.[41]

That "adduced sense" and "induced sense" may be simultane-ous in the act of perception is beyond all doubt. The classic exam-ple of feeling heat by feeling oneself heated suffices to illustrate the rule: the external sensation of that which is hot coincides, in this case, with the internal sensation of the alteration in one's own being. But the balance between the two levels of perception is del-icate, and there are times, the philosopher repeatedly suggested, when they may also diverge. It is significant that in discussing the nature of sensation by mutation, Campanella systematically spoke of a "*slight* modification," arguing that, for there to be perception, the perceiving body must be "transmuted in part, and not entirely," by that which it perceives.[42] There were good reasons for the specification. If the transmutation is not partial but complete, the perceiver will become the perceived, and no self will remain to attest to the event of the transformation. An "acquired sense," then, will overcome and efface all "innate sense"; an excessive *sensus additus* will cover over all trace of *sensus inditus*, turning a *sensus sui inditus* into a *sensus sui abditus*. Consider, as an example, the man who is bitten by the rabid dog: overwhelmed by a sensible quality thus transmitted to him, he will subsequently rage like a hound himself, without clearly sensing the transformation he has suffered. At the limit, a perception of excessive strength may even lead to that most extreme alteration in which the "self" itself — at least in one form — vanishes completely: that "mutation in the mode of sensation" (*mutare sentiendi modum*) which Campanella took to define the event of death.[43]

If the modification in perception is not "slight" but too slight, however, induced and adduced perception may also diverge. Take the case of a source of heat so modest as to be barely felt. The being who comes into contact with it will sense it, and so be mutated by it and perceive, in its affected part, the passion of such a mutation, but the perception may still be too minor or too rapid to be registered as such by the sensing spirit. Campanella insisted repeatedly on the point: it is a great error to take that which is too small to be clearly perceived for that which is simply imperceptible. Aristotle held bones, horns, and hairs to be utterly insensitive, but in this he was mistaken: "When they are cut, they feel a certain pain, but on account of their density they do not communicate that passion to the sentient spirit, and the lacerated part does not sufficiently communicate its sense to the other part."[44] It is what happens when fleas bite a man lightly while he sleeps. Such a man "suffers that which he does not perceive" (*pate quel che non sente*), but the bitten part invariably registers the change it has undergone.[45] Everything depends on the degree of "percepti-bility" (*perceptibilitas*) that defines a mutation. Alterations of a certain size will be both undergone and clearly registered by the sensing spirit, but an infinity of more minute transformations will be suffered and perceived too swiftly to be clearly felt as such.

Sensus additus and *sensus inditus*, "acquired sensation" and "innate sensation," passion and its perception may therefore be both joined and disjoined. They may be united in the experience of an alteration sensed as such, but they may also lead apart, as an "adduced sense" overwhelms an "induced sense" or proves too minor a modification for its occurrence to be properly felt. One thing, in any case, is certain: in the "extremely sensitive animal" that is Campanella's world, perceptions are never lacking. Recall-ing and rewriting Kafka's famous apothegm on hope, one might even go so far as to condense the thought of the early modern thinker in the proposition that "there are plenty of sensations — but not for us" (or not, at least, necessarily for us). It is true that they may be ours: there is the case in which the perception of heat coincides with the perception of our own becoming heated. But there is also the case in which wood is heated to the point at which, in combustion, it ceases to be itself, and there are all the minor warmings and coolings that, while felt by the warmed and cool parts of the body, remain too modest to be assigned to any sensing spirit that would take them to be its own. Everywhere, for Campanella, there was mutation, and with it, both "sensation" and "self-sensation," *sensus* and *sensus sui*; but the "selves" did not cease to change.

Campanella was not alone in his age in finding in the world a quantity of perceptions in excess of the conscious minds to which they might be attributed. Francis Bacon, his near contemporary, noted in a work published in 1623 that if one pauses for a mo-ment to examine the many occurrences between bodies, or even within single organisms, one must admit that, as he put it, "per-ceptions" (*perceptiones*) far outnumbered conscious "sensations" (*sensus*). Bacon took the fact be "a matter of great importance," all too hastily overlooked by the classical authorities who had treated the question of sensation. In the conclusion to Book Four of the *De argumentis scientiarum*, he commented on the problem at some length:

> A good explanation of the difference between Perception and Sense should have been prefixed by philosophers to their treatises on Sense and the Sensible, as a matter most fundamental. For we see that all natural bodies have a manifest power of attraction, and also a kind of choice in receiving what is agreeable, and avoiding what is hostile and foreign. Nor am I speaking only of the more subtle perceptions, as when the magnet attracts iron, flame leaps towards naphtha, one bubble coming near another unites with it, rays of light start away from a white object, the body of an animal assimilates things that are useful and excerns things that are not so, part of a sponge attracts water (though held too high to touch it) and expels air, and the like. For what need is there of enumerating such things? Since no body when placed near another either changes it or is changed by it, unless a reciprocal *perception* precede the operation. A body perceives the passages by which it enters; it perceives the force of another body to which it yields; it perceives the removal of another body which held it fast, when it recovers itself; it perceives the disruption of its continuity, which for a time it resists; in short there is Perception everywhere. And air perceives heat and cold so acutely, that its perception is far more subtle than that of the human touch, which yet is reputed the normal measure of heat and cold. It seems then that in regard to this doctrine men have committed two faults; one, that they have for the most part left it untouched and unhandled (though it be a most noble subject); the other, that they who have happened to turn their minds to it have gone too far, and attributed *sense* to all bodies; so that it were a kind of impiety to pluck off the branch of a tree, lest it should groan, like Polydorus. But they should have examined the difference between perception and sense, not only in sensible as compared with insensible bodies (as plants with animals), one body with another; but also in the sensible body itself they should have observed what is the reason why so many actions are performed without any sense at all; why food is digested and

ejected; humours and juices carried up and down; the heart and the pulse beat; the entrails, like so many workshops, perform every one its own work; and yet all these and many other things are done without sense. But men have not seen clearly enough of what nature the action of sense is; and what kind of body, what length of time, or what repetition of impression is required to produce pleasure or pain. In a word, they do not seem at all to understand the difference between simple perception and sense; nor how far perception may take place without sense. Neither is this a dispute about words merely, but about a matter of great importance.[46]

It is tempting to read Bacon's account of those who went "too far, and attributed *sense* to all bodies" as an allusion to the work of the Englishman's Italian counterpart, who had just published that "most celebrated treatise on the doctrine of universally diffused sensation," the *De sensu rerum et magia*.[47] But the differences of doctrine between the two thinkers, however real, should not lead one to overlook the single fact upon which they both insist, and which few before them had chosen to ponder: that "no body when placed near another either changes it or is changed by it, unless a reciprocal *perception* precede the operation," that "in short," as Bacon writes, "there is Perception everywhere" (*ubique denique est Perceptio*), even — or especially — in the absence of any clear awareness and "sense." It is in the midst of perceptions irreducible to consciousness that sentient animals, for Bacon as for Campanella, find themselves: amidst an infinity of perceptions "performed without any sense at all," from those which attest to the relations between sensible and insensible bodies to those carried out within individual bodies, by which "food is digested and ejected; humours and juices carried up and down; the heart and the pulse beat; [and] the entrails, like so many workshops, perform every one its own work."

But it is not enough, Bacon insists, to remark on the ubiquity of perception. That fact raises a philosophical question that "men have not seen clearly enough": the nature of the "action of sense." It is a question the English philosopher was among the first to

pose as such. Since the seventeenth century, it has not been resolved once and for all, but it has provoked more than a single
response, developed over the course of centuries. One among
them found its expression in the project formulated in the same
years by Descartes: to sunder the problem of "perception" utterly
from that of "sense," setting the unconscious actions carried out
in the mechanical world against the conscious acts performed by
the cogitating "I," as extended being may be opposed, in the most
implacable metaphysical terms, to thinking being. Another response found its first formulations in Campanella and Bacon. Its
project was a fundamentally different one: to locate the genesis of
sense in perception itself, by investigating "*how far* perception
may take place without sense," and at what point, consequently,
an unconscious affection may pass into a conscious sensation.
This project, in contrast to the Cartesian, sought to conceive of
"the difference between perception and sense" not as an opposition but as a threshold, not as a fixed barrier but as a porous membrane, which both joined and disjoined the senseless and the
sensate, linking every state of consciousness to the infinity of
unconsciousness from which it arose and to which it could always
return. In time, this project was to lead far, to terms and terrains
neither Campanella nor Bacon could have imagined and, inevitably, to the discovery of more perceptions still, unidentified in
the "extremely sensitive animal" that was the early modern
world.

CHAPTER EIGHTEEN

Of the Merits of Missiles

In which Leibniz differs from Descartes and from Locke, calling
to Mind slow yet forceful Movements most worthy of Attention

Mathematician no less than metaphysician, logician as well as
diplomat, theologian, jurist, and, not least, philologist, excelling
with particular distinction in the study of Chinese, Gottfried Wilhelm Leibniz cultivated many of the branches of learning known
to his age, and there were few to which he can be said to have
failed to add much in one, if not several, of the European languages to which he entrusted his reflections. It is perhaps only
natural that among the multiple subjects on which the seventeenth-century German thinker pronounced himself more than
once was the venerable field to which he no doubt knew he had
contributed in numerous ways: the history of learning. His remarks on this subject could be as penetrating, and as startling, as
on any other. In a characteristically brief and provocative note
that has not always received the attention it deserves, Leibniz
once suggested that the inventions of the philosophers of early
modernity could be best understood in terms traditionally reserved for artifacts of a somewhat narrower nature: weapons
and, in particular, the technologically sophisticated instruments
of modern warfare.[1]

One may distinguish, Leibniz explained, between at least two
types of arms in science. A first set of conceptual inventions in
modern physics and metaphysics can be admired for its speed. A
second set, by contrast, can be praised for its intensity. The members of the first class of philosophical and scientific creations fol-

low the course of the lead ball (*pila plumbeua*) shot by a sling or a firearm. They are very quick; therein lies their strength. They suffer, however, from an unfortunate and ultimately insurmountable limitation: no matter how speedy, they are capable of penetrating only relatively soft objects. The second sort of theoretical creation can be compared to the missile released by the catapult (*catapulta missus*). Such a projectile moves, to be sure, at a speed slower than that of lead balls. Yet despite its lesser velocity, it possesses a virtue denied the pellets shot by the sling and gun: a missile, after all, is nothing if not forceful and, as a consequence, can pierce almost any object. In his short tract, Leibniz did not hesitate to furnish examples for the types of weapons he had identified. Among the makers of lead balls in science, he wrote, one must class Descartes, for his theories of physics, and Hobbes, on account of his moral philosophy. For examples of philosophical missiles catapulted in the early modern age, one may instead turn to Campanella and to Bacon. Their thought, Leibniz remarked, adding a metaphor to his simile, "reaches to the heavens," while that of Descartes and Hobbes barely "creeps along the ground."[2]

These likenesses were, of course, polemical, and they may well have been intended to provoke. But it would be an error to conclude that Leibniz unequivocally distanced himself from that earliest "creeper" of philosophical modernity, Descartes, and from the disciples who came to make of his earthbound theories the principles of a veritable Cartesian school, from Louis de La Forge to Nicolas Malebranche and Antoine Arnauld. There are good reasons why historians of philosophy have traditionally considered Leibniz, like his close contemporary Spinoza, a major figure in the rationalist tradition of modern thought inaugurated by Descartes; between the Leibnizian and the Cartesian philosophies there are unmistakable points of doctrinal proximity, if not identity. These largely concern the nature of that "thinking thing" which the early modern philosophers took the human soul to be and, more precisely, the activity of the elusive being with which they identified it: "the mind" (*mens*), or, as it came to be called in the terminology of the new Cartesian vernacular, "the spirit" (*l'esprit*).

Like Descartes before him, Leibniz understood the mind to be both immaterial and immortal. He also held it to be distinct by nature from the body, moved by principles that owed nothing to the rules of corporeal form. And he did not tire of reaffirming, finally, that in its intellectual power the mind drew on sources of knowledge that could not be reduced to sense perception. To be sure, Leibniz did not doubt that "our external senses" (*nos sens externes*), as he called them, were of importance for the apprehension of "particular objects and their qualities, such as colors, sounds, odors, tastes, and certain qualities of touch that are called hot, cold, and so on."[3] But, he added, "there are other, more intelligible conceptions," which exceed the action of any individual external sense. An example is "the idea of number," which cannot be apprehended by any of the external senses: sight, for example, no less than touch. To explain such perceptions, Leibniz argued, invoking a classic concept, one must turn to a faculty of greater abstraction: "the common and internal sense" (*le sens commun et interne*).[4] And he repeatedly insisted that the intellect of man benefits above all from that "natural light" (*Lumière Naturelle*) that is its "understanding" (*entendement*): the power by which the mind, naturally furnished with innate and intellectual ideas, may come to grasp the necessary truths that found all the demonstrative sciences, from arithmetic to geometry and mechanics.[5]

On the surface, at least, Leibniz also agreed with the Cartesians on a principle that was fundamental to the teachings of their school: the principle, namely, that "the mind always thinks" (*mens semper cogitat*). For the disciples of Descartes, the truth of such a proposition could hardly be doubted. They taught that intellection constituted the primary attribute and essence of the mind. It is because we think, consciously representing ideas to ourselves, they maintained, that our human being must be considered "cogitating being" (*res cogitans*), in opposition to that other order of substance that is "extended being" (*res extensa*). Descartes himself, to be sure, can be understood to have suggested more than a single position on a number of the more delicate aspects of his theory of cogitation, particularly those that involve the problem of representations without determinate objects. Several pages in *The Passions of the Soul*, for example, suggest the existence of cogitations, particularly of the will, that cannot be referred to any movements other than those of the soul itself.[6] But the questions raised by such ambiguities did not touch the fundamental Cartesian thesis on the structure of the conscious power. Without its thoughts, Descartes and his students always taught, the mind would not be one.

This was one principle the thinkers of the seventeenth century did not all grant. In 1690, John Locke, who was but a few years older than Leibniz, questioned it in the most forceful of terms. "Whether this," the English philosopher wrote in Book Two of *An Essay Concerning Human Understanding*, "*that a Soul always thinks*, be a self-evident Proposition, that every Body assents to at first hearing, I appeal to Mankind."[7] Locke did not hesitate to state his own view on the subject: "I confess my self," he wrote with modesty, "to have one of those dull Souls, that doth not perceive it self always to contemplate *Ideas*."[8] Locke was willing to concede "that the Soul in a waking Man is never without thought, because it is the condition of being awake."[9] But unlike the "infinite Author and Preserver of things," human beings, Locke noted, must inevitably "slumber and sleep."[10] Then they may dream and, to a certain extent, thus perceive and retain thoughts of a kind. "But how *extravagant* and incoherent for the most part they are," Locke commented, "how little conformable to the Perfection and Order of a rational Being, those who are acquainted with Dreams, need not be told."[11] In any case, he added, in sleep even those most "frivolous and irrational" of visions may also cease. "Most Men," Locke judged, "pass a great part of their Sleep without dreaming"; at least one gentleman he once knew himself, "that was bred a Scholar," "had never dream'd in his Life, till he had that Fever, he was then newly recovered of, which was about the Five or Six and Twentieth Year of his Age."[12] The conclusion was in Locke's eyes clear. "Though thinking be supposed never so much the proper Action of the Soul; yet it is not necessary," he reasoned, "to suppose, that it should be always thinking, always in Action." For it is no "more necessary," Locke explained, "for the *Soul always to think*, than for the Body always to move; the perception of *Ideas* being (as I conceive) to the Soul, what motion is to the Body, not its Essence, but one of its Operations."[13]

Leibniz knew Locke's *Essay* well. He appears to have taken note of it very soon after its publication in 1690, and once he could acquire Pierre Coste's French translation of the treatise, which appeared in Amsterdam in 1700, he was able to give the greatest of care to the reading of the English "Philosophical Essay, in which it is Shown," as the French subtitle read, "what is the Extent of our certain Knowledges and the Manner by which we Reach them."[14] Leibniz's reflections on the English treatise found their final form in the *New Essays on Human Understanding*, which are thought to have been completed in 1709 or soon thereafter. But the German philosopher appears to have formulated much of the substance of his response to Locke a good decade earlier. A letter he wrote to Thomas Burnett in 1698 already contains a brief reflection on *An Essay Concerning Human Understanding*, which expresses, in condensed form, many of the arguments that would later fill the chapters of the four volumes of the *New Essays*. From his letter to his friend, it appears that Leibniz was especially provoked by the second book of Locke's *Essay* and, in particular, its refutation of the Cartesian thesis that the mind is always thinking.

The argument of the English philosopher had left Leibniz quite unconvinced. "I confess," Leibniz explains to Burnett, "that I share the sentiment of those who believe that the soul always thinks." But Leibniz offers to do more than communicate his views on the subject. He announces in his letter that he can also demonstrate the fact with reference to the very phenomenon invoked by Locke: the dormant state. Leibniz admits the existence of dreamless sleep; he even grants that "there are people who do not know what it is to dream."[15] But from the absence of all known dreams, he continues, one ought not to infer that there has been a cessation of all movement in the soul. He presents the matter first of all as one of principle. Just as in the science of corporeal forms one must accept the existence and perpetual persistence of "small bodies and insensible movements" (*petits corps et les mouvements insensibles*) by virtue of which an absolute absence of movement cannot be conceived, so in the study of the mind one must grant that there are minute perceptions "that are not noticeable enough for one to remember them": the equivalent, in psychology, of particles in physics.[16] With a terminological and conceptual invention that was to have the greatest of philosophical consequences, Leibniz called these minute modifications "small perceptions" (*petites perceptions*).[17] They form a class of psychological affections overlooked by the philosophers of consciousness: perceptions that are by nature "too weak to be noticed, although they are always retained, and this amidst such a heap of infinite other small perceptions that we have continually" (*parmy un tas d'une infinité d'autres petites perceptions que nous avons continuellement*).[18]

Leibniz adduces a host of evidence that, to him, testifies beyond all doubt to the existence of such "small perceptions." Consider those people "who have slept in a cold place": they notice, when they awaken, that they had a "confused and weak sensation" while asleep. The philosopher draws another case from his own experience: "I know a person who wakes up whenever a lamp that he keeps lit in his room at night goes out.... Here, however," Leibniz continues, "is something more precise, which makes it clear that if one did not always have perceptions, one could never be awoken from sleep." Imagine a sleeping man suddenly awoken by the sound of his name being called by many people all at once. "Suppose," moreover, "that the voice of each on its own would not be enough to wake him up, but that the noise of all these voices together wakes him. Now take one among them." May one truly claim that the sleeping man has not heard it, simply because he did not know it? "He must have been touched by this voice in particular," Leibniz reasons, "since the parts are in the whole, and if each one, on its own, is nothing at all, the whole will be nothing too. Nevertheless, the man would not have woken had he heard one voice alone, and this," the philosopher adds, "without ever having remembered that he was called." The one voice must, therefore, have been heard, even if it was not heard as such. Leibniz draws the one conclusion he takes to be admissible: its audition was simply too minute to be clearly represented by the conscious mind.[19]

To the contemporary reader, such "small perceptions" may seem above all to contest the Cartesian theory of the "thinking thing" that is the human soul. And this they certainly did, as Leibniz knew well. But in the works the German philosopher wrote in response to Locke, Leibniz himself turned to the infinitesimal affections he had identified for a different end: to offer an altogether novel defense of the rationalist principle that "the mind always thinks." The pages Leibniz sent to Burnett in 1698 already contained the essence of the argument, which, with an astonishing rhetorical and logical turn, placed the "small perceptions" Descartes and his disciples could never have accepted in the service of an ostensible vindication of the Cartesian principle Locke had challenged. Here Leibniz offers at once a reformulation and a transformation of the Cartesian principle. His insistence on the incessant activity of the mind quickly reveals itself to be, in truth, a vindication of an uninterrupted "thinking" carried out beyond — or, rather, beneath — all the conscious acts of a clearly cogitating mind. "I confess that I share the sentiment of those who believe the soul to think always," Leibniz writes, adding, "although its thoughts are often too confused and too weak for it to remember them distinctly."[20]

In his *Essay*, Locke, in a sense, had already considered the possibility of such "thoughts." It was, in his eyes, beyond all doubt that there are times when thinking beings cease to think, and he was convinced that these times flatly refute the rationalist theory of a perpetually cogitating soul. "Thus," Locke wrote, "methinks, every drowsy Nod shakes their Doctrine, who teach, That the Soul is always thinking."[21] But the English philosopher did not underestimate his opponents; nor did he undervalue their commitment to the official claims of their school. He envisaged an argument with which, if obliged to answer before the reality of the "drowsy Nod," they might seek to dispel the incontrovertible evidence of *"sleep without dreaming."* " 'Twill perhaps be said," he wrote, "That the *Soul thinks,* even *in* the soundest *Sleep, but the Memory retains it not."* This was a hypothesis Locke, for his part, found difficult to entertain. "That the Soul in a sleeping Man should be this moment busy a thinking, and the next moment, in a waking Man, not remember, nor be able to recollect one jot of all those Thoughts, is very hard to conceive."[22] The philosopher also wondered what the purpose of such "thinking" could be, since, as he curtly remarked, "to think often, and never to retain it so much as one moment, is a very useless sort of thinking." If the soul "has no memory of its own Thoughts; if it cannot lay them up for its own use, and be able to recal them upon occasion; if it cannot reflect upon what is past, and make use of its former Experiences, Reasonings, and Contemplations, to what purpose," Locke asked, "does it think?"[23]

But, Locke added, there is still more that can be said against the existence of such immemorial activities in the mind. The author of *An Essay Concerning Human Understanding* raised an objection of principle, which, to him, excluded the very supposition of thoughts of which thinkers might themselves be unaware. For who, quite simply, could ever testify to them? "I would be glad, also to learn from these Men," Locke wrote, "who so confidently pronounce, that the human Soul, or which is all one, that a Man always thinks, how they come to know it; nay, *how they come to know, that they themselves think, when they themselves do not perceive it."*[24] The philosopher, of course, was well aware that there could be but a single answer to that question. The soul would have to think and not to think at once; it would have to discern and, at the same time, not to discern that it did so. But then its self-identity would be compromised beyond repair. "To suppose the Soul to think, and the Man not to perceive it," he explained, "is . . . to make two Persons in one Man."[25] A central presupposition of many of the early modern discussions of the nature of thought, Cartesian and anti-Cartesian alike, now comes clearly to light. It is the principle that thinking and consciousness are strictly correlative: that thought, in other words, cannot occur without the thinker's being simultaneously aware of it.

To Locke, the principle was axiomatic, its negation close to inconceivable. "'Tis altogether as intelligible to say," he wrote, "that a body is extended without parts, as that any thing *thinks without being conscious of it*, or perceiving, that it does so." Were one to entertain such a claim, one would be obliged to admit the possibility of a fact that Locke, for one, could or would not tolerate: that within a single man there was more — or less — than that power which he called "Consciousness," and which he defined, in terms that were to be soon canonical, as "the perception of what passes in a Man's own mind." For if there could be thought without its simultaneous apprehension by the thinking being himself, a thing could well occur to a man without being perceived as such; it could "pass in *a* man's mind," simply put, without that mind's being a "man's *own*," which he must by nature know. A sentient being, in short, "could think, and not be conscious of it," just as he could sense without perceiving that he did so: he could be hungry, Locke noted, without "always" feeling it.[26] Again, the philosopher sought to set the possibility aside in establishing that, by definition, it could not be verified by any experimental method. Divination alone, he argued, could establish such facts. "They must needs have a penetrating sight," Locke wrote, with some acerbity, "who can certainly see, that I think, when I cannot perceive it in my self, and when I declare, that I do not; and yet can see, that Dogs or Elephants do not think, when they give all the demonstration of it imaginable, except only telling us, that they do so."[27]

Leibniz, by all accounts, had just such a "penetrating sight." It distinguished him both from Locke and from the disciples of Descartes, whose theses the English philosopher aimed to refute. It was a fundamental principle of the Cartesian school that the defining characteristic of thought is consciousness: as La Forge once wrote, specifying the nature of mental activity with precision, "cognition is not the production of an idea which represents nor its reception in the interior of the soul, but the *consciousness* or perception that one has of this idea."[28] This was a claim with which Locke concurred; this was why it was for him inconceivable that "any thing" could think *without being conscious of it, or perceiving* that it did so. Leibniz dissented. In the *New Essays on Human Understanding*, as elsewhere, he insisted that there was nothing contradictory in the idea of a mind that acted without consciousness. Just as the mirror may reflect an image, more or less clearly, without possessing any awareness of it, so the mind can perceive without any necessary consciousness that it does so. In the preface to the *New Essays*, Leibniz went so far as to assert that, at every moment, the mind, moreover, did nothing else, and this, *ad infinitum*: "There are hundreds of marks that force us to judge that there is at every moment an infinity of perceptions in us," he wrote, "unaccompanied by awareness and unaccompanied by reflection; that is, modifications in the soul itself of which we are not aware."[29]

The claim implied a fundamental inversion of the terms of the rationalist philosophy of mind, as several scholars have amply shown. For the disciples of Descartes, perception constituted a particular kind of awareness; for them, sensation was no less a conscious act than volition or intellection. Leibniz's response was unabashed: "I do not find," he wrote, "that the Cartesians ever proved — or could ever prove — that every perception is accompanied by consciousness."[30] All the evidence, he repeatedly argued, suggested the contrary: that consciousness, in other words, was but one variety of perception, which persisted for the most part without all awareness.[31] Leibniz believed he could illustrate the point compellingly, disproving Descartes no less than Locke. Many examples could be drawn from the state of sleep, in which much may be felt without any clear awareness: the sense of the cold, of the snuffing of a light, of the sound of the single waking voice, too soft to be heard on its own, though still audible when joined to others of its kind. Leibniz could also invoke sensations that remain unnoticed on account of being too familiar. Habit, he observed, can render the perceptible imperceptible as such: consider the case of those who live near a mill or a waterfall, who are

insensitive to its constant sound, although if it were not customary they would no doubt perceive it.[32] But the great sensations
of conscious life, the German philosopher maintained, also point
to the existence of infinitely smaller ones, which lie "hidden"
(cachées) without them.[33] Take the perception of light and color:
What is the distinct sensation of the color blue, for instance, if
not the apprehension of green and yellow, perceived, albeit indistinctly, both at once?[34] And there is that most famous example of
sensation, to which Leibniz turned more than any other: the
sound of the sea. "One would not hear it," the philosopher
pointed out, "if one did not have a small perception of each of
wave" as it broke on the shore, and one would not hear each wave,
in turn, if one did not hear each drop of water. But it is clear that
no human ear could perceive either a single wave or a drop in the
sea with any awareness of doing so.[35]

It was for Leibniz a matter of necessity, which followed from
two principles that, for him, defined the nature of sensation. On
the one hand, he argued, a conscious perception is a totality and,
like any whole, must be composed of parts: by nature it is complex.[36] Such reasoning sustains the claim that to be woken by
many voices one must have heard each, albeit confusedly, and that
to perceive the roar of the sea as one does, "one must hear the
parts that compose the whole, that is, the noises of each wave,
although each of these little noises makes itself known only in the
confused collection of all of them together, and would not be
noticed if the wave that made it were by itself."[37] On the other
hand, Leibniz maintained, every sensation can be understood as
an effect and, as such, must be reducible to a cause; if the effect is
to be perceptible, after all, then the cause must be so too.[38] Just as
the occurrence of the sounds of the waking call and the breaking
waves may all be led back, by natural necessity, to the discrete
events that occasion them, so their perception must include that
of each of their causes: each individual shouting voice, as it produces its own noise, each drop of water moving within the sea,
as it assembles with the others of its kind. A single consequence
follows from both principles: sensations must be said to arise from

perceptions, partial or causal, too minute to be consciously repre-sented by any limited mind. No matter how distinctly they may appear to the conscious spirit, all sensations remain, as Alison Sim-mons has written, "*constitutively* confused": by definition, they contain an infinity of "small perceptions" that escapes every fac-ulty of representation other than the divine.[39]

Time and time again, from treatise and discourse to epistle, draft, and note, Leibniz insisted on the importance of counting this infinity in the theory of the mind. Like those "small num-bers" involved in the calculus he had invented while still studying in Paris, the "small perceptions" of Leibnizian psychology were bound to transform the world of science.[40] Between the way of constant cogitation and the course of its negation, between the partisans of impassive reason and the defenders of variegated experience, the philosopher of the infinitesimal thus cleared a third path, which led to a region of the mind unimagined by both Descartes and Locke: a region in which consciousness and its absence meet in the terrain of incessant and infinitely minute perceptions. In this, the philosopher of the monad was alone in his age. But he had not found his way to "perceptions that are too small to be noticed" without help. Leibniz had drawn the materi-als of his doctrine from the history of learning, which he knew well, availing himself of instruments unexploited by the rational-ists and empiricists of his time: instruments such as those fur-nished him by Campanella, who had so tirelessly argued for the existence and ubiquity of a sense common to all things, both physical and spiritual, and by Bacon, whose new science had pro-grammatically sought to explore the place of conscious sensations in a world of countless perceptions. Undaunted by the apparent march of science, Leibniz had made a strategic, if anachronistic, choice in turning to these authors. He had set aside the technol-ogy of the lead pellet and replaced it, as he well knew, with that of an older epoch: those cumbersome missiles once catapulted into space. In close pursuit of the heavy projectile's slow but forceful movement, the scientist had resolved to follow it as far as it might lead, and as deeply as it might penetrate into that most resilient

and opaque of philosophical objects, which, in his day, was still
something of a novelty: consciousness.

Chapter Nineteen

Thorns

*Another long Chapter, Treating of Leibniz on
Perception, Apperception, and the Existence of infinitely small
and slightly sharp Sensations*

Leibniz himself understood the doctrine of small perceptions he expounded throughout his works to be of metaphysical as well as psychological import. By its minute sensations, "unaccompanied by awareness and unaccompanied by reflection," each soul, he argued, proves itself to be that simple substance to which he gave the name "monad": "a world in shorthand" (*un monde en raccourci*), "an image of the Universe," or, as he also wrote, in greater detail, "a living mirror representing the universe according to its point of view, and above all with respect to its body."[1] The claim touched on a crucial question in early modern philosophy, to which small perceptions constitute the elements of an original and far-reaching answer: that of the relation between the "thinking thing" that is the mind and the "extended thing" that is the body. Leibniz explained in many works, particularly in discussion with the Cartesians of his time, that he knew of no more than "three systems to explain the commerce between the soul and the body." The first, taught by the disciples of Descartes and in the schools, was that of "the influence of one on the other": the soul, somehow physically connected to the body, would cause it to move. The second system was that of the "occasional causes" proposed by Malebranche: in this theory, a "perpetual surveyor," God, would see to it that everything that happened in one was represented in the other. It would be, Leibniz commented, "more or less as if a man were entrusted with the task of always adjusting two mechanical clocks, which on their own would not be capable of adjusting themselves."[2]

The third system was Leibniz's own: a perfect harmony between body and soul, divinely established such that both substances could not but act concomitantly. There would be no influence in this system, and all surveyors, divine and otherwise, would be quite superfluous. The clocks or automatons would be exact by design, ticking in tandem from creation, without any need for the subsequent intervention of a watchmaker. It would be a divine harmony, independently executed by the body and by the soul. "To employ a likeness," Leibniz explained to Arnauld in April 1687, "I would say that this concomitance that I maintain is much like that between different groups of musicians or choirs, who, separately playing parts while positioned in such a way so as not to see each other or even to hear each other at all, nevertheless succeed in being perfectly in harmony [en s'accordant parfaitement] by simply following their notes, each one his own, so that the one who hears them all finds there to be a marvelous harmony there, much more surprising than if there had been a connection between them."[3]

Such a concomitance of substances constitutes the metaphysical foundation of small perceptions, as the philosopher's "divinely granted" spokesman, Theodorus, methodically explains in the New Essays on Human Understanding. The preface to that work already invokes "the book of the illustrious Monsieur Boyle against absolute rest" as evidence that, on experimental grounds, one must accept that "a substance can never be without action, and there is never a body without movement."[4] In Book Two of the New Essays, Theodorus offers a series of examples of such incessant motions within the human body: "the circulation of the blood," notably, and "all the movements that are internal to the viscera." Given the exact and constant harmony between the body and the soul, such corporeal events must imply corresponding affections of the psyche; anything else would compromise the principle of concomitance. "If there were impressions in the body in sleep or during the waking state by which the soul was not at all affected," Theodorus reasons, "one would have to set limits to the union of the soul and the body, as if corporeal impressions required a certain shape and size for them to be felt by the soul; and this is hardly tenable if the soul is incorporeal, since there is no proportion between an incorporeal substance and this or that modification of matter."[5] Nothing that takes place in the corporeal substance can therefore be too small to be felt, at the same time, by the incorporeal: every movement of the blood, every process of digestion, every nerve that affects the body must by necessity have a correlate within the sensing soul, effective even if it remains imperceptible as such.[6]

The bodies and souls of all beasts, for Leibniz, were in this sense alike — those of the two-legged metaphysician no less than those, for example, of a hound. In his lengthy debate with Pierre Bayle, the philosopher therefore explained the doctrine of small perceptions with reference to an example that his Cartesian contemporaries, on their own, would have been a good deal less likely to invoke: the movements affecting a dog that, while "eating his bread" in a state of some delight, suddenly finds himself, much to his dismay, struck on the head by a man with a stick.[7] One ought not to think, Leibniz teaches, that the blow to the body of the dog in itself exerts any influence on his soul. Nor is there any need to invoke the miraculous intervention of a divine will in the moment he is struck on the head, such that the spirit may feel what the head has sadly undergone. If one grants that the soul of the dog, like all others, is "a living mirror representing the universe according to its point of view and above all with respect to its body," one may propose a far more economical explanation of the course of events.

Here as elsewhere in the preestablished world, the movements of the body play out in perfect harmony with those of the soul. Just as the canine body registers the approach of the man behind him, from the point at which he is too far to be heard and smelled to the point at which he lifts his stick behind him to interrupt his meal, so the canine soul perceives each step of the temporal and spatial series in which it, too, is enveloped. "The causes of the movement of the stick," Leibniz explains, "are also represented in the soul exactly and truly, but weakly and by small and confused perceptions, without awareness, that is, without the dog's remarking upon it, for he is affected only imperceptibly."[8] And just as the body of the dog reflects each movement of the man's body, from the point at which it lies far from him to that at which it causes sizeable injury to his own, so the soul of the dog represents them with continuously increasing clarity: at first obscurely, then with greater definition, and finally in a manner "distinguished and strong," altogether adequate, in its relatively clear awareness, to the "distinguished and strong" blow that causes his pain.[9] A single continuum of perpetual perception ties his many affections; from the "pleasure" (*plaisir*) with which he eats his bread to the "pain" (*douleur*) with which he perceives his head wound, sensation, no less than bodily movement, is incessant.

Leibniz dwelled at length on the uninterruptedly sensing state of all animal life, and he did so more than once. His fullest treatment of the subject can be found in the *New Essays*, where, with his customary rhetorical and logical skill, he turned the very terms invoked by his English model against the arguments to whose service they had once been put. In the twenty-first chapter of Book Two of *An Essay Concerning Human Understanding*, "Of Power," Locke considered the problem of "what determines the Will." "The true proper Answer," he had written, "is, The mind." But this was an abstract answer alone, which bore on the "general power of directing, to this or that particular direction," and Locke had anticipated that it might well "satisfy not." For one could still ask, with greater precision, "What moves the mind, in every particular instance, to determine its general power of directing, to this or that particular Motion or Rest?" To this query Locke gave an original answer, which he emphatically repeated: "The motive, for continuing in the same State or Action, is only the present satisfaction in it; The motive to change, is always some *uneasiness*: nothing setting us upon the change of State, or upon any new Action, but some *uneasiness*."[10] On these grounds, he could dismiss the traditional account of the will, whose cause he consequently took to be "not, as is generally supposed, the greater good in view: But some (and for the most part the most pressing) *uneasiness* a Man is at present under." Locke presented it as a condition common to the body and to the mind, a variety of "pain" that could hardly be told apart from "Desire." "All pain of the body, and disquiet of the mind," he argued, "is *uneasiness*: And with this is always join'd Desire, equal to the pain or *uneasiness* felt; and is scarce distinguishable from it."[11]

In Book Two of Leibniz's *New Essays*, Theodorus, speaking of "the celebrated English Author," declares with some appreciation that "this consideration of *uneasiness* is a capital point, where this Author has particularly well shown his penetrating and profound spirit." Theodorus tells us that he chose, for this reason, to ponder the matter "attentively" himself. At first, he admits, a linguistic difficulty impeded his efforts to understand exactly what the English philosopher meant, since, as he recalls, "I was somewhat at a loss as to the meaning of the English word *uneasiness*."[12] Thankfully, "the French interpreter" had added a note to his edition of the *Essay*, in which he explained that "by this English word, the author meant the State of a man, who is not at his ease, the lack of *ease* and tranquility in the soul," and that, for this reason, the English term "uneasiness" could be rendered, if "only imperfectly," by the French word for "disquiet," *inquiétude*.[13]

Theodorus relates that once he had grasped the sense of Locke's term, however, he was overtaken by a further doubt, which obliged him to question the felicity of the English philosopher's diction. Leibniz's spokesman observes that to the degree to which the English term "uneasiness" designates "a displeasure, a sorrow, an incommodity, and, in short, any felt pain," its usage in such a setting runs the risk of propagating some confusion. Strictly speaking, there is no pain in desire: "I would rather say that in desire there is instead a disposition and a preparation for pain."[14] Alluding to the native tongue of his own author, the literary personage adds that one could designate this determining state of the will with greater accuracy by the German term *Unruhe*, "unrest," a word often used for the "disquiet of the clock's pendulum."[15] That expression, in distinction to the English original, applies quite exactly to the movements of the body; all things considered, so, too, does the Gallic term invoked in the French translation, *in-quiétude*, which lacks the connotations of pain present in the English *uneasiness*. Like the perpetually swinging pendulum, our body finds itself by nature in a state of painless but perpetual "disquiet." "It could never be perfectly at ease," we read, "because if it were, a new impression of objects, a small change in the organs, in the vessels and the viscera would once again change the balance, making them exert some effort to return to the best state it can reach; which produces a perpetual combat that makes, so to speak, the *uneasiness [inquiétude]* of our Clock."[16]

From Locke's "uneasiness" to Leibniz's *Unruhe* and *inquiétude*, the translations, therefore, are simultaneously linguistic and conceptual. They allow the state invoked by Locke to furnish Theodorus with the perfect illustration of Leibniz's own theory of the infinitely minute modifications of the perfectly parallel bodily and psychic orders. If one wishes to know exactly what the author of *An Essay Concerning Human Understanding* wished to express, one must then turn, as Theodorus explains, to the terms of the author of the *New Essays on Human Understanding*. "Once again," the literary personage declares, "it is necessary to apply our doctrine of perceptions that are too small for us to be aware of them."[17] "Disquiet" is the natural state of a substance that represents the created world in its totality, but only indistinctly, from its own point of view and, above all, with respect to its body. It is the state of the soul perpetually affected by the countless "small perceptions," in other words, which crowd in on it from its every side, composing its conscious perceptions and simultaneously exceeding them at every point: the infinity of affections that form the indistinct background of every conscious perception, and of which no mind other than the divine could ever fully be aware.

Here, too, Leibniz draws on the possibilities afforded him by the translation of Locke's essay. Discussing the determination of the will, the English philosopher had asserted, in his own terms, that "the greatest present *uneasiness* is the spur to action, that is constantly felt."[18] The French translation Leibniz read renders this "spur" by *aiguillon*, a word that also designates "goad" and "thorn" ("La plus grande inquiétude actuellement présente," Coste had written, "est ce qui nous pousse à agir, c'est l'aiguillon qu'on sent constamment").[19] In Theodorus's able hands, the "spur" passes from the singular to the plural, becoming, in its indefinite multiplicity, the exemplary figure for those small perceptions unanticipated by Locke, as well as Descartes. Such "goads" then appear, in the discourse of philosopher's representative, as the providential gift of nature: the "thorns of desire," "rudiments or elements of pain or, so to speak, half-pains, or (if I may be permitted to express myself to you more forcefully) little unconscious pains."[20] Painless by nature, such "tiny solicitations" pose no threat to the happy life. Quite the contrary, Theodorus explains: "I find that disquiet is essential to the happiness of creatures, since this cannot ever consist in a perfect possession, because that would render creatures insensible and stupid; it must rather consist in a continual and uninterrupted progress toward greater goods, which cannot fail to be accompanied by desire, or continuous disquiet."[21] Acute but infinitely small, the tiny thorns form the sharp edge of Leibnizian optimism. Without some prodding, the philosopher reasoned, one would get nowhere: needles are by nature necessary. But in the best of all possible worlds, their extremities, while effective, need not be sensible, for the providential creator has ensured that, albeit continually goaded on by them, we shall not be obliged to feel their constant pricking.[22]

Leibniz taught that the phenomenon known to modernity as "consciousness" must be situated within this field of thorns. After Campanella and Bacon, no less than Descartes and Locke, the seventeenth-century philosopher was well aware of the necessity of distinguishing between those affections of which sensing beings are aware and those of which they are not: hence the difference between "small perceptions" and "perceptions," between perceptions in the broad sense, in other words, and "sensations" more strictly understood. But Leibniz did not tire of repeating that between the unconscious and the conscious, between the "small" and the large, there lies a difference of degree. It was a fundamental point, involving a principle he considered himself to have been the first to introduce into the field of science, and which he proudly called "my Law of continuity."[23] He explained the thesis programmatically in the preface to the *New Essays*, likening the method he had implemented in the science of the body to that which he would now adopt in the study the soul. "*Insensible perceptions* are as useful in Pneumatics as insensible corpuscles are in Physics," he wrote,

> and it is equally unreasonable to reject either of them on the grounds that they lie beyond our senses. Nothing happens all at once; and it is one of my great and most demonstrated maxims that *nature makes no leaps*. This is what I called the Law of Continuity when I spoke of it in the first "News of the Republic of Letters," and the use of this Law is very considerable in physics. It stipulates that one always passes from the small to the large and back [by passing] through the intermediary, in degrees as in parts, and that a movement is never immediately born from rest, nor can be reduced to it, unless it is by a lesser movement, just as one has never finished tracing a line until one has finished tracing a shorter one, despite the fact that until now those who have stated the laws of movement have failed to notice this law, believing that, in a single moment, one body can receive a movement that is contrary to its preceding one. And all this leads one to think that even *noticeable perceptions* come in degrees out of those which are too small to be noticed.[24]

Of the body or of the soul, all alteration, Leibniz insists, is therefore of a single kind: continuous. Just as every given physical movement emerges from a lesser one, and every traced line, from one slightly shorter, so every conscious perception arises from more minor ones, too small all to be retained and sensed as such. And just as a discrete change in the corporeal world can always be situated at the point at which a process of uninterrupted alteration reaches a certain limit, so awareness arises when a threshold in sensation has been crossed: the threshold of being "noticed."[25]

Up to this point, souls sense, reflecting, without consciousness, the world of which they are the living mirrors. Beyond it, they do more: noticing their minor sensations, they sense them and therefore sense, at the same time, that they do so.

Coining a term that was to have a long life in philosophical and psychological parlance after him, Leibniz called this perception of perceiving "apperception." For him, this was a French word, and he invoked it without undue comment in the major works he entrusted to the Gallic tongue, such as the *New Essays*, the so-called *Monadology*, and the *Principles of Nature and of Grace Founded in Reason*.[26] But the lexicon of the French language in the seventeenth century did not contain it. Not that its form could be mistaken. "Apperception," it was immediately understood, could only be a substantive drawn from the transitive verb often invoked by the thinkers of the early modern period for the act of noticing and being aware of a certain thing: *appercevoir*. This was the verb employed, for example, in the French version of *An Essay Concerning Human Understanding* for passages that contained "to perceive" in the original (where Locke had stated, "Whatsoever the Mind perceives in it self, or is the immediate object of Perception, Thought, or Understanding, that I call *Idea*," Coste thus wrote, "J'apelle idée tout ce que l'Esprit apperçoit en luy-même, toute perception qui est dans nôtre Esprit lors qu'il pense").[27] It was clear, therefore, that Leibniz's "apperception" signified an awareness and consciousness of a kind. But the French language of the seventeenth century already contained two terms that could have been employed for such ideas: the common word *perception*, to which Coste had turned as the French equivalent of Locke's "Perception," and *conscience*, the cognate of the English word "consciousness," which had been regularly invoked by French philosophers of the mind since Descartes. Naturally Leibniz was well acquainted with these terms. One can only conclude that he found them both inadequate to the idea he wished to express, whose novelty demanded a new expression.

The neologism is all the more significant if one recalls the vigor with which Leibniz himself had warned against the invention of technical terms in science. In his lengthy preface to Mario Nizolio's *De veris principiis et vera ratione philosophandi contra pseudophilosophos*, from 1670, he had gone so far as to make of it a methodological principle of good philosophical style. "Technical terms are to be shunned," he wrote, imperatively, "as worse than a dog or a snake."[28] But with the word "apperception," as with that even stranger expression, "monad," he transgressed the law he had proclaimed, embracing wild beasts and introducing into the *langue particulière* of philosophical discourse expressions for which few, if any, equivalents could be found.

"Apperception" was to prove a decidedly difficult term. Not only was it unattested among the expressions of seventeenth-century philosophical psychology. In time, the word also continued to resist translation from the idiom in which Leibniz himself had invoked it. It was only natural that the eighteenth-century philosophers who erected modern scholastic rationalism on the basis of Leibniz's teachings wished to incorporate "apperception" into the official terminology of their doctrine. When Christian Wolff, aiming to systematize the findings of his protector, composed his compendious *Psychologia empirica* in Latin, he therefore translated the French term into the language of the schools as *apperceptio*, duly recording that this had been the noun "used by Leibniz" (*Aperceptionis nomine utitur Leibnitius*).[29] But the accommodation was deceptive, for the treacherous translator went on effectively to dismiss the singular term and its proper concept, explaining that its meaning "coincides" perfectly with that of the central term of the Cartesian tradition: "consciousness" (*conscientia*).[30]

It was largely in this Cartesian sense that "apperception" acquired an established place in the lexicon of modern philosophy. After Wolff, the literal connotations of "perception" in "apperception" gradually ceded their place to those of "thought," as the Leibnizian expression came to be regularly employed for the definition of the conscious and cogitating activity understood, after Descartes, as constituting the essence of the human ego. In a famous passage in the 1787 edition of the *Critique of Pure Reason*, Kant thus invoked the term to define the structure by which the thinking "I" remains identical to itself in the multiplicity of its representations. By "pure apperception, or *original apperception*," we read in "Deduction of the Pure Concepts of the Understanding," one must understand the original "self-consciousness [*Selbstbewußtsein*] which produces the representation *I think* and which must be able to accompany all others, being in all representations the same, while being itself unaccompanied by any other."[31] After such a definition, which made of the Leibnizian term the name of the unity of consciousness, "apperception" could not but play a central role in philosophical discourse, and, from Fichte and Hegel beyond the aftermath of transcendental Idealism, to the new psychologies of Johann Friedrich Herbart and Wilhelm Wundt, the term, while resolutely technical, remained.[32]

The word apperception, however, never lost its original obscurity. It is significant that even after his first *Critique* Kant invoked the expression equivocally and in Latin: in the *Anthropology from a Pragmatic Point of View*, of 1798, he mentioned it in a note as *aperceptio*, or "the consciousness of one's self" (*der Bewußtsein seiner selbst*).[33] And after it had gradually acquired a secure place in the German philosophical and psychological terminologies of the nineteenth century, "apperception" could still provoke some perplexity. Commenting on the elusive expression in a study published in 1900, Anton Sticker, a historian of the notion, remarked that after almost two centuries it still could not be properly rendered by any Germanic equivalent. Like so many of the conceptual creations of the philosopher of Leipzig, he observed, apperception "grew up on foreign-language soil [*auf fremdsprachlichen Boden*]." Subsequently it refused to be repatriated, since it simply could not be successfully "transferred into the mother tongue."[34]

Leibniz himself placed great importance on the concept of apperception. He invoked it programmatically in the treatise known to the tradition as the *Monadology* and in the *Principles of Nature and of Grace Founded in Reason*, both times insisting on its significance in the doctrine of the soul. "It is good," he thus wrote emphatically in the *Principles*, "to distinguish between *Perception*, which is the inner state of the Monad representing external things, and *Apperception*."[35] "The passing state that envelops and represents a multitude in unity or simple substance," we likewise read in the *Monadology*, "is nothing other than *Perception*, which must be well distinguished from apperception."[36] In both of these works, Leibniz associated the activity he had named with psychological states identified by his predecessors and, in particular, with that state called "consciousness" by Descartes. In the *Monadology*, he thus invoked "apperception, *or* consciousness [*conscience*]," and in the *Principles*, he offered a fuller gloss of the term "*Apperception*" as "*Consciousness* [*conscience*], or the reflexive knowledge of this inner state [of the Monad representing external things], which is not at all in all Souls, or always in the same Soul."[37] But both times Leibniz went on to explain that the "consciousness" designated by "apperception" could not be reduced to that of Descartes and his followers. After distinguishing apperception from perception in the *Monadology*, Leibniz thus wrote: "It is in this that the Cartesians are sorely lacking, having counted as nothing those perceptions of which one is not aware [*ayant compté pour rien les perceptions dont on ne s'apperçoit pas*]."[38] The terms of the *Principles* are almost identical: "It is because they lack this distinction," we read there, as Leibniz explains the difference between perception and apperception, "that the Cartesians are lacking, counting as nothing those perceptions of which one is not aware [*en comptant pour rien les perceptions dont on ne s'apperçoit pas*], as the people counts as nothing insensible bodies."[39]

As Josef Capesius long ago observed, the definitions contained in the *Monadology* and the *Principles of Nature and of Grace Founded in Reason* leave little doubt as to the end for which Leibniz introduced the concept of apperception into the philosophy of mind. It was not to indicate the existence in the spirit of such a thing as "consciousness," "which no one would doubt," and for which the philosopher had no need to coin a new name synonymous with the old.[40] Leibniz identified apperception to clear a region within the mind for that which is not apperception and which, by nature less than it, accompanies it at every point: that state of mere "perception" in which there is no awareness but in which there never cease to be "small perceptions of which one is not aware" (*dont on ne s'apperçoit pas*). Apperception may therefore be understood to be "consciousness," as Leibniz indicates repeatedly, and as his pupils, eager to paraphrase, inevitably add. But it is a "consciousness" the Cartesian philosophers of his day, as after it, could not admit. For to accept the Leibnizian notion of "apperception" is to accept its constitutive relation of difference from, not opposition to, "perception." It is to grant, in other words, that both the absence of awareness and its presence must be situated within a single continuum of degrees, composed of an infinity of perceptions too minute to represented by the finite mind as such. It is to allow, quite simply, that within "apperception" there is "perception": that within that noble thing called "consciousness" there are lesser beings incessantly in movement, and that it is by means of alterations to them alone — by means of "a small addition or augmentation" to their unnoticed and immaterial mass — that living beings come to their senses, and that, once sentient, they come to lose them.[41]

The Leibnizian definition of apperception has more than once been believed to represent a decisive step beyond the concept of consciousness promulgated by the disciples of Descartes. The advance can be variously described. One may assert that phenomena proper to the unconscious may now come to be clearly situated within conscious life, or, with perhaps greater justice, one may maintain that the phenomenon of consciousness comes at last to be considered with respect to the unconscious processes from which it intermittently emerges and to which it always returns. Like any philosophical step worthy of the name, however, the Leibnizian account of apperception receded in the history of thought even as it advanced, posing anew a question thought by many to have been long settled. It was, inevitably, the question of the animal. As long as the perceptual activity of the "thinking thing" was understood to be a mode of cogitation, as the Cartesians taught, it shared nothing with the operations observed in the world of beasts. But once the sensation of the conscious mind came to be grasped as an act of "apperception," its relation to animal perception had to change.

Leibniz had been the first to draw the consequence, in the very passages in which he defined the new concept. After distinguishing mere perception from apperception and observing that the followers of Descartes err greatly in "counting as nothing those perceptions of which one is not aware," Leibniz thus writes in the *Monadology*: "It is this which made them believe that only Minds were Monads, and that there were no Souls of Beasts, nor other Entelechies."[42] The terms of the *Principles of Nature and of Grace Founded in Reason*, once again, are almost identical.[43] If there can be perception without apperception, then there is no reason to deny that all animals perceive, and if perception, like appetition, cannot exist except in animate creatures, one must conclude that the inhuman beasts, no less than the human, possess souls.[44] For this reason, Leibniz showed little sympathy with the Cartesian doctrine that "only man truly has a soul." "It is difficult to see," he commented, "why men find it so repugnant to accord to the bodies of other organic creatures immaterial imperishable substances."[45] If the physicist can grant that the substance of an atom cannot ever be corrupted, Leibniz reasoned, there is no reason why the metaphysician cannot grant that the immaterial substance of the beast, like every other, also lasts forever.

In place of the Cartesian opposition between thinking being and extended being, Leibniz set a threefold hierarchy of substances, which, to the modern eye, seems strikingly reminiscent of the medieval typology of life that had its roots in Aristotle. Long after the Scholastic doctrine of vegetative life, sensitive life, and intellectual life was by all appearances superseded, the seventeenth-century thinker distinguished three varieties of monads. First, there are "bare" or "simple monads," which, reflecting the universe without any awareness, perceive but do not apperceive. Then there are those monads in which "sensation is more distinct, and accompanied by memory," namely, beasts. Finally, there are monads gifted with "knowledge of eternal and necessary truths" and the capacity to reason: they are "minds" or "spirits."[46] These points in the seventeenth-century philosophical system are beyond all doubt. But it is far from clear where one ought to situate the capacity Leibniz calls apperception within such an ascent of substance; on this issue, even the ablest interpreters of the Leibnizian corpus have failed to reach an agreement. Many have argued that, for Leibniz, every substance reflects the universe and to this degree "perceives," while the rational monad alone, among all others, can be said to "apperceive." In a comprehensive review of the literature on the subject, Mark Kulstad has baptized this judgment "the standard view."[47] It has certainly been expressed by a number of Leibnizian authorities. Yvon Belaval, Aron Gurwitsch, Robert McRae, and Émilienne Naert, among others, have all concurred that apperception, in the Liebnizian universe, can be attributed to "spirits" alone.[48]

The Leibnizian texts on the question, however, are far from unequivocal, and several suggest that the early modern philosopher may have gone further in according powers of awareness to animals than his twentieth-century readers would grant.[49] There is, for example, the dog discussed in the debate with Bayle, who is interrupted by a blow to his head just as he is "eating his bread." Analyzing the causal series represented by the dog's body and soul, Leibniz explains to his correspondent that when the human stick reaches the dog's head, affecting it with a causal disposition at once "distinguished and strong," the canine soul acts, as ever, in parallel with the body whose affections it represents: "The dog notices it very distinctly," the philosopher writes, "and this is what makes his pain" (literally, the dog "apperceives it very distinctly" [le chien s'en apperçoit très distinctement, et c'est ce qui fait sa douleur]).[50] The canine soul would seem, therefore, to apperceive, if only when in pain. The preface to Leibniz's New Essays, moreover, suggests that there would be nothing unusual about such an event, for it is only with the moment of death that beasts are "reduced to a state of confusion which suspends apperception yet cannot last forever"; and, as Kulstad has compellingly remarked, "apperception" could hardly "be suspended in animals if animals never apperceived in the first place."[51]

A Leibnizian boar, finally, furnishes more evidence still. Distinctly noticing a "person" screaming before him, he seems to decide the issue quite conclusively. Considering the relations between perception, apperception, and understanding, the philosopher himself calls the actions of this wild beast to mind as indubitable proof that animals, although irremediably irrational, do "have the capacity to be aware" or "to apperceive." The crucial passage is to be found in Book Two of the *New Essays*. "Beasts have no understanding [*entendement*]," the polymath explains there, "although they have the capacity to be aware of more noticeable and distinguished impressions [*quoiqu'elles ayent la faculté de s'appercevoir des impressions plus remarquables et plus distinguées*], just as the boar is aware of a person who screams at him and runs straight at this person, of whom he had up to that point only a mere perception, which was confused like all other objects falling before his eyes with rays striking his lens."[52]

Clearly "apperceiving" that which he has to this point only obscurely "perceived," the boar therefore achieves an awareness of a kind. "He," the mute but lucid beast, "is aware of a person who screams at him" (*s'apperçoit d'une personne qui luy crie*). In distinction to many of his predecessors and successors, Leibniz did not take such an "awareness" to be cognitive in nature. The entire stage of the boar scene is one of sensation. From the "mere perception" of the object that falls before the eyes of animal, "with rays striking his lens," to the conscious "apperception" of the vociferous being before him, of whom he is well aware and toward whom he soon charges, it is all a matter of perception. This much could not be clearer. But one may still wonder whether the boar does not also perceive more — and less — than the philosopher himself explicitly indicates in this passage. Between the small sensations of the boar's soul and the distinct sensation of a screaming person, between the infinite affections of the eternal mirror that is the monad and the noticeable image that, however confused, may form on its surface, there must be middle terms. Nature, after all, "makes no leaps," and, as Leibniz always taught, in physics as in psychology, no transition can be without intermediaries: from the smaller to the greater, one must pass through them, "in degrees as in parts," just as "a movement is never imme-diately born from rest, nor can be reduced to it, unless it is by a lesser movement," and "one has never finished tracing a line until one has finished tracing a shorter one," and one has never finished tracing the shorter until one has finished tracing one slightly shorter still.[53] In the transition from the absence of awareness to its presence, such intermediaries, by definition, would belong neither to the obscurity of "mere perceptions" nor to the clarity of "sensation." They would be reducible neither to the drowsy state nor to the lucidity of the waking mind. No longer "small" but not yet "large," they would be perceptions on the threshold of being noticed: thorns almost felt but not as such, their sharp edges barely beginning now to prick. Did the boar feel them? To take the philosopher at his word, the boar must have, although the unthinking beast could hardly be said, in all rigor, to have known it. For the wild animal had traversed the infinitely divisible pas-sage from perception to consciousness; and he must have sensed each small step of the uneasy voyage out, even if, once on the firm ground of apperception, he soon forgot, like the person scream-ing at him, how he ever got there.

CHAPTER TWENTY

To Myself; or, The Great Dane

In which a fearsome Dog famously leaps upon
Jean-Jacques Rousseau, putting an End to an otherwise solitary Walk

Intermediary states of awareness are of more than a single kind. Some, the eternal accompanists of the fall into drowsiness, lead the mind from waking into sleep. Others, by contrast, compose the passages, slow or sudden, by which sentient beings come to be "in their right mind." Like all steps taken, such intermediaries tend not to be noticed. If they are later recalled, it is natural for them to seem in retrospect minor links in a long chain, stations on a road approaching a point with which, by definition, they cannot coincide. "Coming to" is the exemplary case. If this process ever reaches an end, it is in the moment a self recovers itself: the instant in which I come, after sleep, shock, or stupor, to myself. Then it is difficult, if not impossible, to recall the wide expanses that must already have been traversed: all those regions in which a self comes to without yet coming to anything or anyone, let alone to that intimately felt but eminently forgettable being that is "myself."

It may take an event of some rarity, an accident of sorts, for these regions to be glimpsed with any definition. But among animals unanticipated occurrences are never lacking, and even in the moments of the greatest concentration a thinking thing remains vulnerable to startling solicitations of a sensitive nature. Jean-Jacques Rousseau knew this well. In the second chapter of *The Reveries of the Solitary Walker*, he offered a striking illustration of the ways a train of thought can be interrupted by an unforeseen event. The philosopher recalls how, on the afternoon of Thursday, October 24, 1776, he was returning to his home in Paris after a stroll through the "vineyards and prairies" of Ménilmontant. He had decided to take a walk after lunch, setting aside this time to consider the project of composing a possible sequel to the *Confessions*. The countryside outside the city had offered him the "pleasure and interest" that lovely spots always promised him, and in this case the meditative promenade had led to a number of botanical finds he had hardly anticipated — several varieties of plants not to be found in Paris, and three, in particular, which he took care to recollect by name: "the *Picris hieracioides* of the family of *Compositae*," "the *Bupleurum falcatum* of the family of *Umbelliferae*," and "an even rarer plant, especially in cultivated regions, namely, the *Cerastium aquaticum*."[1]

Wandering through the "verdant and smiling countryside," the learned walker had observed many other varieties of flora and fauna too, "whose aspect and enumeration," as he later recalled, "always gave me pleasure." It was all the perfect setting for "peaceful meditations" — until he found himself startled by an unexpected sight. "Some people walking in front of me," he reports, "suddenly separated." From behind them charged a very large dog: a Great Dane, to be precise, running in front of a carriage with such speed and force that "he could hardly have slowed or altered his course," Rousseau recalled, "once he became aware of me." With a quick calculation, the philosopher immediately understood what must be done: he had to leap high into the air, having in an instant "judged," as he explained, "that the sole means I had to avoid being thrown to ground was to make a great jump, of such proportions as to allow the dog to pass beneath me while I was suspended in the air."[2] One can only wonder how the philosopher would have fared had he had the chance to execute his acrobatic plan. As it happened, the charging hound proved faster even than the movements of the thinker's mind, and before he knew it, the solitary walker no longer knew, or even felt, anything at all. "This idea, which was faster than lightning," Rousseau observed, recalling his projected leap into the air, "was the last I had before my accident. I felt neither the blow, nor the fall, nor anything that happened up to the moment in which I came to myself" (*Je ne sentis ni le coup, ni la chute, ni rien de ce qui s'ensuivit jusqu'au moment où je revins à moi*).[3]

That moment came much later. By then dusk was already falling, and the walker, regaining his senses, found himself "in the arms of three or four young people," peasants, one presumes, who had tended to him after his fall. They furnished the writer with the history of the event he later told. "Unable to restrain his momentum," Rousseau recalls, "the Danish Dog had thrown himself against my two legs and, shocking me by his size and his speed, he had made me fall, head first." But it was Rousseau himself who told the more striking tale in *The Reveries*, having been the only one to live it. It involved the condition in which he found himself, as he wrote, repeating a phrase, "when I came to myself" (*lorsque je revins à moi*).[4] That "state" (*état*) was "too singular" not to be now described:

> It was almost night when I regained my senses. I saw the sky, some stars, and a few leaves. This first sensation was a delightful moment. I was still not yet aware of anything other than it. In this instant I was being born again, and it seemed as if everything I perceived was filled with my light existence. Entirely taken up by the present, I could remember nothing; I had no distinct notion of myself as a person, nor had I the least idea of what had just happened to me. I did not know who I was, nor where I was; I felt neither pain nor fear nor anxiety. I watched my blood flowing as I might have watched a stream, without even thinking that the blood had anything to do with me. I felt throughout my whole being such a wonderful calm, that whenever I recall this feeling I can find nothing to compare with it in all the pleasures that stir our lives.[5]

The incomparable feeling of this "first sensation" merits some attention. A condition of awareness without either a clear object or an identifiable subject, it finds the fallen walker in a state of delight and nothing more, as he barely begins to "come to" himself. Although Rousseau now somehow consciously perceives, he still cannot perceive himself with definition, being, as he explains, without any "distinct notion" of himself "as a person." In the richly equivocal terms of his own description, which hover between the transitive and the intransitive dimensions of the reflexive verb, the experience of his delightful "light existence" (*ma legere existence*) shows itself to be one in which he senses nothing and in which, while still without a "self," he may simultaneously also sense nothing but himself: "*je ne me sentois encor que par là*," "I was still not aware of anything other than it," but also "I still did not sense anything other than it," and, more literally, according to the grammar of the verb, "I still did not sense myself by anything other than it."

However singular it may have seemed to the walker himself, the state evoked in the second *Reverie* was not altogether without precedent in the literary tradition. Giorgio Agamben has drawn attention to its striking similarities to a condition described two centuries earlier by Montaigne in Book Two of his *Essays*. There the writer recounted how he had fallen on account of the sudden movements not of a dog but of a horse; conscious while being barely conscious of anything other than himself, he had been led to an experience whose strangeness in the life of the individual he likened less to birth than to death. But the terms with which he described the event bear more than a superficial resemblance to those later employed by Rousseau. "When I began to see again," the essayist recalled in "Of Exercise,"

> it was with a sight so troubled, so weak and dead, that I discerned nothing but light. . . . As for the functions of the soul, they emerged together with those of the body. I saw myself all bloody. . . . It seemed to me that my life held on to me only just at the edges of my lips; I closed my eyes to help myself, it seemed to me, push it outside, and I took pleasure in relaxing and letting myself go. It was an imagination that was barely swimming at the surface of my soul, as tender and weak as the rest. But the truth is that it was not merely painless; it was

even mixed with the sweetness felt by those who let themselves slide into sleep.[6]

One might also understand the eighteenth-century walker's apprehension of his "light existence" in terms of a perception greatly discussed by many of his contemporaries: the perception, that is, that each thinking thing has of its own being. Such a "perception" had been identified in classic terms by Locke, who defined it in his *Essay* as the most fundamental of all intuitions. "Experience convinces us," the English philosopher wrote in the chapter of his treatise called "Of Our Knowledge of Existence," "that *we have an intuitive Knowledge of our own Existence*, and an internal infallible Perception that we are."[7] On this point, Leibniz emphatically concurred. In the corresponding chapter of the *New Essays*, his representative, Theodorus, went so far as to coin a technical term for this specific "Perception," lest it be mistaken for any other: he dubbed it "the immediate apperception of our existence."[8] The French authors of the eighteenth century devoted considerable attention to it in their wake. Invoked by such diverse figures as Turgot, Condillac, and Hemsterhuis, the "sentiment of existence" was well represented in the *Encyclopédie*, published by Diderot and d'Alembert several decades before *The Reveries*. An anonymous entry in this work followed many of the age in assigning the "Perception that we are" to a power of the soul identified long before: the "inner sense," by which "each of us has an intimate sentiment of his own existence."[9] It was an experience considered with particular force in the same years by the *abbé* Joseph-Adrien Lelarge de Lignac, who took it as proof of the falsity of the Cartesian *cogito*. "Our existence," the *abbé* wrote, "is not demonstrated but sensed, despite whatever Monsieur Descartes says. For I am not certain that I exist by the necessity of the consequence in the argument 'I think, therefore I am.' The certainty of existence is prior to the consequence; it is sealed in the word *I*, which contains the awareness of my existence."[10]

Rousseau himself had famously insisted on the priority of "sentiment" or "feeling" (*sentiment*) with respect to knowledge as a general principle, and in *Émile* he declared: "For us, existing is sensing; our sensibility is incontestably prior to our intelligence, and we had feelings before ideas."[11] By all appearances, Rousseau understood the thesis to apply above all to the experience of that thing which is "our being." Only a few chapters after recalling his unfortunate encounter with the Great Dane in the second *Reverie*, the philosopher offered perhaps the most influential of all evocations of "the feeling of existence."[12] In the fifth *Reverie*, he recounted how, while living on the little island of Saint-Pierre in Switzerland, he would often sit by Lake Biel in the evening, delighting in the sounds of the waves lapping the shores. "As evening approached," the philosopher recalled,

> I would climb down from the top of the island and gladly sit at the edge of the lake, on the shore, in some hidden refuge. There the sound of the waves and the movement of the waters focused my senses, sweeping all worries from my soul, immersed in it a delightful reverie in which I was often startled to discover that it had become night. The ebb and flow of this water, its continuous yet undulating sound, relentlessly reached my ears and my eyes, making up in my internal movements for what the reverie extinguished within me. It allowed me to feel my existence with pleasure, without troubling myself to think.[13]

Later in the same *Reverie*, the philosopher sought to define the state with precision. "What does one enjoy," he asked, reflectively, "in such a situation?" The answer followed immediately: "Nothing exterior to oneself, nothing other than oneself and one's own existence, in which, as long as it lasts, one suffices to oneself, like God."[14] He then concluded: "The feeling of existence stripped of any other affection is in itself a precious sentiment of contentment and peace, which alone would be enough to render this existence dear and sweet to whoever knew how to keep away all the sensuous and earthly impressions that always come to distract us and to trouble our enjoyment."[15]

Such an account may have seemed well suited to the state in

which the philosopher found himself in the happy time he spent on the island of Saint-Pierre. But it is certainly far from adequate to the course of events recalled in the earlier and more dramatic chapter of the work, which furnish the first and perhaps most memorable occasion on which the walking philosopher encounters "the feeling of existence stripped of any other affection." For there the injured thinker came to his feeling of existence not by "keep[ing] away all the sensuous and earthly impressions that always come to distract us and to trouble our enjoyment," but in being overtaken by them: by being suddenly and unwittingly knocked to the ground by a large, running dog. There his experience, for this reason, could hardly be qualified as a sentiment of "nothing exterior to oneself, nothing other than oneself and one's own existence, in which, as long as it lasts, one suffices to oneself, like God." As Rousseau recalls, the singular sensation of "light existence" came upon him, as he lay amid unknown "young people," in a moment of the most uncommon self-forgetfulness: "I could remember nothing; I had no distinct notion of myself as a person, nor had I the least idea of what had just happened to me. I did not know who I was, nor where I was."

It would be an error to take these details in the tale of the charging Great Dane to be trivial, for the truth is that they illustrate a principle. It is no accident that the philosopher comes to himself in being thrown to the ground. This was an event of the destruction and survival of the self: "In this instant," the philosopher wrote, in deliberate terms, "I was being born again." It could not, therefore, be the experience of an individual on his own. The perception it brought upon the startled thinker had to imply something "exterior to oneself," something "other than oneself and one's own existence," a thing with respect to which no one could be said to be "like God." Sensitive creatures, after all, can do much, but they cannot bring themselves into the world, and if, as Rousseau suggests, they have an apprehension of the "delightful moment" of their birth, it cannot be a perception of themselves. As the author of the second *Reverie*, if not the fifth, knew well, the "first sensation" must be a "feeling of existence" too "light" to be

217

identified with any thing, let alone that thing that is oneself; it must be a "feeling of existence stripped of any other affection," including that affection that is the sense of self. For newborn creatures, like all others, come to themselves in time, through intermediaries no less decisive for being soon forgotten, and to come to anything and anyone at all, they must already find themselves in an element with which they do not altogether coincide. It is a matter of psychic topography, which the prose of the philosophical walker was among the first to chart. To be in one's right mind, one must already lie in a field, rightly or wrongly, in which there is room for more and less than it: a region in which the solitary thinker is never by himself, and in which another animal, great or little, may always suddenly come running.

CHAPTER TWENTY-ONE

Of Flying Creatures

Wherein Avicenna, Condillac, and Maine de Biran relate startling
Findings made by Men and Statues suspended in Space

More than once in its history, philosophy has led far from the terrain of experience, to terms, concepts, and regions of observation anything but familiar. There is a good reason for this fact. Committed from its inception to exploring that which is most intimate to life, the classical practice of inquiry and invention has had little choice. It has found itself, time and time again, obliged to remove itself from the domain of the everyday to understand it. With a methodical attachment to the necessity of its own alienation, it has made the greatest of efforts to reach a vantage point of considerable strangeness, precisely so as to bring into focus that which tends to be too near to be seen with any clarity. On this matter, even the most cursory survey leaves little doubt. An activity with a long and distinguished tradition, philosophy has developed multiple means of bringing objects close by distancing them. It could even be asserted that its techniques are as many as its major practitioners. One method, among the first to be recorded, consists in regarding the world as one who knows nothing at all about it: Socrates was its virtuoso. Another consists in a procedure of more obvious artifice. This technique abstracts the object of philosophy from its natural environment: it suspends it, to be precise, in the air. Developed to perfection in metaphysics long before being conceived in physics, this operation can be dated to the late tenth or early eleventh century. It was then, somewhere in the region of central Asia that is today divided between Iran and Uzbekistan, that Avicenna conducted a most unexpected experiment in the doctrine of the soul: he propelled a living man into space.

This scientific undertaking was to have a long posterity in the philosophy of the Muslim, Jewish, and Christian Middle Ages. After Avicenna, such diverse figures as Levi ben Gershom, William of Auvergne, Jean de la Rochelle, and Matthew of Acquasparta could all invoke it with ease simply by alluding to the famous figure who had been its subject: "the flying man," as he was commonly called, or, alternately, "the man in the void."[1] Avicenna introduced the experiment in the opening chapter of the first book of the great treatise on the soul known to the Latin tradition as the *Sextus de naturalibus*. Arguing for the essential independence of the soul from the body, he paused at one point, enjoining his readers to follow him in "imagining" a state of some strangeness. It illustrated a fact they most certainly "knew" and "perceived," although they might well have forgotten it. "Let each one of us," he wrote,

> imagine himself created all at once and fully developed, but veiled from seeing external objects, floating in the air or in the void but doing so without feeling the resistance of the air. One's limbs would be separated from one another so that they would not meet or touch each other. Then one would consider whether one would affirm the existence of one's essence [or "the existence of one's self," *wujūd dhātihi*]. There would be no doubt about the affirmation that one's self exists. But one would not affirm along with that any one of one's limbs or internal organs, or one's heart, or one's brain, or any external thing. Nevertheless one would affirm one's own self, but would not affirm of it length, breadth, or depth. If it were possible to imagine in this state one's hand or some other limb, one would not imagine it as a part of one's essence, or as a condition of one's essence. Now, you know that that which is affirmed is different from that which is not affirmed, and that which is deduced is different from that which is not deduced. Therefore, the essence whose existence has been affirmed possesses a property, insofar as [this man] is in himself other than his body and his limbs, which were not affirmed,

and therefore the one who affirms possesses a means to affirm, by virtue of the existence of the soul [*wujūd al-nafs*], as something other than the body, or, more precisely, [as something] without body. Certainly [this man] knows it and perceives it. And if he has forgotten it, he will need to be reminded. [2]

Avicenna summoned the man in the void twice more in his works: later in the same treatise and again in one of his final works, "Book of Directives and Remarks" (*Kitāb al-ishārāt wa'l-tanbīhāt*).[3] The three experiments showed little variation. Each time, the philosopher could observe the same traits in the man he had propelled into space. The flying figure could see and hear nothing about him; he could feel nothing beneath him. He could not even perceive himself to possess a body: his external limbs and his internal organs remained as insensible as the perfectly "temperate air" all around him. But in this utter ignorance of all things corporeal, there remained something the suspended man could still "affirm" with certainty. It was the one thing about him that was itself no thing at all: his existence (*wujūd*), or, more precisely, as the metaphysician emphatically wrote the second and third times he summoned the flying man, "the existence of his own being" (*wujūd anniyyatihi*).[4]

Long influential in the Arabic and the European Middle Ages, Avicenna's doctrine of being was eventually supplanted by others, and if one regards the course of modern philosophy one must conclude that, in time, allusions to the suspended creature who had once been its classic illustration grew ever scarcer. With the passing of the centuries, the renowned "flying man" became a curiosity, if not a total stranger, in the field of thought. But the practice of speculative experimentation survived, and at times the shadow of the medieval figure in the void could flash by where one might hardly expect it.

In 1754, the *abbé* Étienne Bonnot de Condillac published the first edition of his vastly influential *Treatise on Sensations*, in which he sought to resolve a problem that many consider as fundamental as that raised by the medieval philosopher of the Arabic language:

the problem of the genesis of knowledge from experience. That this was a thorny question was immediately noted by Condillac himself in the preface to the work. "We can hardly remember the ignorance in which we were born," he wrote. "It is a state that leaves no traces behind it." The French thinker took this fact to be a matter of principle, which involved the conditions and limits of that which thinking beings can recall. "We remember what we did not know," Condillac explains, "only when we remember having learned it." And we remember having learned a thing, in turn, only when we clearly noted that we had done so. Hence the delicate problem posed by the very inception of knowledge: how could any being be expected to have remarked the fact of learning something for the first time, if until then, by definition, he truly knew nothing at all? "To note that which we learn," the philosopher observes, "one must already know something; one must have perceived oneself to have ideas that one did not before possess."[5] But this, of course, is precisely what a being without all knowledge must lack.

A first effort to resolve the problem led Condillac to compose his great treatise of 1748: the *Essay on the Origin of Human Knowledge*. Eight years later, the philosopher, however, showed some dissatisfaction with the answers he had offered in that work, and in the introductory outline of the *Treatise on Sensations*, he announced that in the intervening years he had found himself obliged to reject the "prejudices" that defined his own earlier inquiry and to replace them with a new account of the problem he had once posed. Here the philosopher claims to have benefited from the companionship of a good friend, Mademoiselle Ferrand, with whom he was at last able to define the method proper to the scientific study of the genesis of knowledge, as well as the sole point of observation from which the passage from ignorance to knowledge could be contemplated with clarity. It was to be an experimental method, although, it must be immediately added, the subject of the experiment was purely fictional in nature: a being much like ourselves but made of marble, gifted with perceptual and intellectual powers that the scientific examiner could progressively diminish in force and in extent, to the point of their total disappearance. To "fulfill our objective," Condillac explains, "we imagined a statue organized on the inside like ourselves, and animated by a mind deprived of any kind of ideas. We supposed, moreover, that the outside, all of marble, was such as not to allow it to employ any of its senses, and we retained the freedom to open them, at our will, to the different impressions to which they are susceptible."[6]

Maker, mover, and student of his own imagined marble marionette, Condillac controlled his experiment in sensation well. The public was no exception: readers, too, had a precise role to play, and their position was exactly defined before the work itself began. In the "Important Note to the Reader," placed after the frontispiece of the *Treatise on Sensations*, the philosopher explained the matter in terms programmatic and pedagogical. "It is very important," Condillac warned, "to put oneself exactly in the place of the statue that we will observe. One must begin existing with it, with only one sense, when it has only one. One must acquire only the ideas that it acquires and develop only the habits that it develops — in a word, one must be only what it is. It will judge things as we do only when it has all our senses and all our experience, and we will judge as it does only when we imagine ourselves to be deprived of all that which is lacking to it." It was a central point, and the author did not hesitate to claim that the comprehension of the treatise as a whole depended on its being fully respected: "I believe the readers who put themselves exactly in its place will have no trouble understanding this work," he wrote. "The others will raise countless objections against me."[7]

The experiment in philosophy may startle the more modern reader, but in the eighteenth century it was far from original in form. Such diverse thinkers as Diderot, Georges-Louis Leclerc de Buffon, and Charles Bonnet, among others, also wrote of statues brought to life, and a contemporary scholar has gone so far as to assert that "all the theoreticians of the eighteenth century referred" to the same fable, the most famous of all being undoubtedly André-François Boureau-Deslandes, whose *Pygmalion, or,*

The Living Statue was published a good thirteen years before the *Treatise on Sensations*.[8] This fact hardly escaped Condillac's contemporaries. A year after the publication of the *Treatise*, Grimm remarked, with some acerbity, that "the poor abbé of Condillac has drowned Monsieur de Buffon's statue in a ton of water."[9] But the German scholar's *boutade* may have been excessively severe. Condillac's experiment with the statue raised at least one philosophical question that had perhaps never before in modernity been formulated with such clarity: the question of the perception that a living being possesses of its own body, or, in the words that introduce the fifth chapter of Book Two of the *Treatise*, "How a Man, Limited to Touch, Discovers His Body, and Learns that There Is Something Outside Him."[10]

This question could not be fully answered on its own terms. It concealed another, as Condillac knew well. To "discover his body," a man must first have discovered "body" in general: if not that which defines corporeality as such, then at least how to recognize it and how to know when bodies are in motion rather than at rest. To this end, the sensations of the statue merely brought to life do not suffice, since they can give it no more than an intimation of its own organic existence. "If our statue is not struck by any body," the philosopher explains, "and if we place it in a tranquil, temperate air, where it feels its heat neither rising nor falling, the statue will be limited to the fundamental feeling [*le sentiment fondamental*], and it will know its existence only by the confused impressions that result from the movement to which it owes its life." The statue perceives but a "uniform sentiment," which admits of no spatial division: "It is as if it existed in a point alone, and it cannot yet discover that it is extended." How, Condillac asks, could the stony object come to know more? It will do no good to intensify the statue's "uniform sensation" by altering the air around it. Then the animate marble thing will simply perceive more cold or more heat, but it will still not have discovered that there is such a thing as body. "A single sensation," after all, "however lively it may be, cannot give the idea of extension to a being that, not yet knowing that it is extended, has not learned to extend this sensation, referring it to the different parts of its body."[11]

Now the philosopher alters his tactics. He begins striking the sensitive statue, seeking to oblige it to learn that, like all bodies, it is composed of parts, each exterior to the other. But the blows to the marble figure are in vain. "If I successively strike the head and the feet," Condillac notes, "I modify the statue's fundamental feeling in several stages; but these modifications are themselves uniform." It is the same if one intervenes on the body of the thing by touching it in more than a single region. Each time the thinker's hand grazes the surface of the stone figure, the statue senses. But it cannot represent the sensation as a perception relative to a part, since the "fundamental feeling gives no sense of the idea of extension." Aiming at an exhaustive demonstration, the philosopher intervenes again: he shakes the statue's arm. "Will it then acquire an idea of movement? Absolutely not," we read, "since it does not yet know that it has an arm, that it occupies a place, nor that it can alter it." Condillac has modified the parts of the body as best he could, and now he has little choice. The thinker resorts to an ancient but well-established experiment. Without any mention of his illustrious Arabo-Persian predecessor, Condillac propels the fictive figure into space. That operation sufficed to grant the medieval flying man the incontrovertible awareness of his own being. But it now fails before the demands placed on the modern marble object, enjoined to feel not that it exists but that it possesses a body divided into many parts. "It is the same," the philosopher concludes, "if I transport it up into the air. Everything in it can then be reduced to an impression that modifies the entire fundamental feeling, and the statue still cannot learn that it moves."[12]

At last the philosopher reveals the solution to the difficulty he has raised. The marble figure, he makes clear, simply needs a hand. If we "give to the statue the use of all its limbs," it will inevitably reach out to touch, and to touch itself: "It will necessarily come to pass that, repeatedly, it places its hands on itself." Then alone will it discover that it has a body. Condillac insists that on its own, the tactile grasp of objects will not suffice to teach the statue what it must learn. Brought against a thing outside itself, the statue's hand will register "solidity": the resistance by which two bodies exclude each other. From this sensation, the stony artifact will in turn derive its idea of the impenetrability of matter. But to sense that it possesses a body of its own, the statue must do still more. It must touch itself, as when it brings its hand against its chest. "Then," the philosopher observes, "its hand and its chest will be distinguished by the sensation of solidity to which each can be referred, and which puts each [sensation] outside the other." Finally the marble being will find itself: "Distinguishing its chest from its hand, the statue will rediscover its *self* [*son moi*] in each of them, since it feels itself in both." This apprehension will be even clearer if other sensations, such as those of heat and cold, are also involved: then the statue, for example, will feel that while its hand is cool, its chest is warm.[13] Condillac admits that, bringing its hand from one part of itself to another, the statue may be unaware that the regions intervening between them belong to its body and form a single whole. But to learn the full truth the marble thing need only "lead its hand all along its arm," following the long limb where it leads. "Without crossing any borders," the philosopher remarks, "on its chest, on its head, etc., under its hand it will feel, so to speak, a continuity of *self*, and this very hand, which unites the various separated parts in a single continuity, will render extension more sensible."[14]

Faithful to the experimental fiction that animates his work, Condillac presents this discovery as the ineluctable result of the statue's own sensitive explorations. In the *Treatise on Sensations*, therefore, it is not the scientist who notes that the marble thing possesses a single divided body. It is, in all rigor, the animated object itself. Turning its exploring hands upon its body, the marble being suddenly employs a striking capacity nowhere explicitly introduced and explained by the scientist, as it immediately knows to name that which it has found. "As soon as the statue brings its hand on its parts," the philosopher writes, "the same sensing being responds in some way from one part to another: *it is I* [*c'est moi*]." And as it learns the full force of that which it has begun to grasp, the marble being begins to repeat itself, with increasing emphasis: "*It is I! It is I, again!*" ("*C'est moi! C'est moi, encore!*").[15]

One cannot but wonder how the statue, unbeknownst to the observer, has learned to speak, not words but sentences, and to name itself by that simple but decisive term: "I." One may also ask about the identity of the "self" invoked in each of the hand's encounters with the body of which it is but a part. At times, the philosopher speaks of the "same sensing being" (*le même être sentant*); one may infer, in such instances, that "the self" is that of the statue as a whole. But Condillac's terms are at other times less clear. When the statue's hand touches something that is not a region of its body, for instance, the philosopher notes that "if the hand says *I*, it does not receive the same response" (*si la main dit moi, elle ne reçoit pas la même réponse*) from that which it has encountered.[16]

Might the hand, as this statement implies, possess a "self," an "I" all its own? If it did, it would be a self still to be linked to — or, alternatively, distinguished from — that of the other felt regions of the body, from which the mobile part, as the philosopher writes, naturally expects to receive some "response." The consequence of such a distinction of selves would be troubling for the argument of the *Treatise*. If the corporeal regions may possess selves of their own, the body may not yet be one; its unity may still remain to be composed and comprehended by the marble being. By all appearances, Condillac, however, was undaunted by the possibility the speaking hand had raised. In the *Treatise*, the philosopher presents the declarations issued by the marble parts as illustrations of the logically ordered steps by which an animate being progressively uncovers itself. The statue discovers extension in the tactile perception of solid or resistant mass; it discovers its own extension in its tactile perception of its parts; finally, it discovers its body in the contiguity of the parts that compose it. Once it has felt the extended solidity that constitutes it, the marble thing, we learn, can then come to know those bodies that lie outside it. "Just as it

227

has formed its body," the philosopher concludes, "the statue forms all other objects."[17]

Later philosophers were less than certain that a sensitive being discovered its body and those of others in such steps. But many followed Condillac in the practice that, knowingly or not, he had adopted from his forgotten medieval predecessor. Like Avicenna long before them, thinkers after Condillac explored the problem of self-knowledge by considering the living being as it finds itself in a strange state: in utter isolation, its body, felt or unfelt, suspended in an empty space. In his 1798 essay *On the Relations Between the Physical and Moral Aspects of Man*, Pierre-Jean-Georges Cabanis, for one, added merely that one need not invoke a flying statue. It suffices, he remarked, to consider the real fetus in its mother's womb. Since, Cabanis explained, "as Condillac has demonstrated," sensuous impressions may lead to the representation of differing objects only when they can be separated and compared by beings who distinguish themselves from them, and since unborn mammals fail to separate themselves from the maternal body in which they lie, they must clearly be said to be lacking in sensations in the full sense of the term. If, therefore, while moving *in utero*, a fetus happens to "encounter the walls of womb, even to be tightly held within them," still it can hardly be said to sense this fact itself.

A few years later, Antoine Louis Claude Destutt de Tracy went a step further, introducing into the discussion a distinction ignored by both Condillac and his immediate successors.[18] The author of the *Treatise on Sensations* argued that before it lays its hands upon itself the marble statue knows nothing of its own body. Touching the things around it, it may be said to experience a "sensation of solidity or resistance" but no more. Destutt de Tracy indicated that on this point the eighteenth-century thinker had taken as equivalent two impressions that are by nature quite distinct.[19] The impression of solidity is indeed a simple perception, and, as Condillac maintained, it implies no self-perception. But to feel "resistance," Destutt de Tracy added, is to feel more. It is to perceive that the solid object responds to the active force exerted upon it, that it reacts, in other words, to the effort made by the touching body. The sensation of resistance thereby furnishes the tactile being with an element unfelt in the impression of solidity. Resistance offers the sensitive animal a perception of itself, gleaned from its encounter with the foreign body under pressure. A decisive consequence for the theory of perception and self-perception then followed, and it applied with equal force to the sensations of the marble creature and to those of the unborn animal. Destutt de Tracy made clear that, firmly planted on the ground or flying "up in the air," within the womb or well outside it, an animate thing has no need to bring its hands upon itself to feel itself. As long as it touches anything at all, it senses the solidity of the objects it touches as well as their resistance to its touch — and so it senses itself.

When Pierre Maine de Biran composed the *Essay on the Influence of Habit on the Faculty of Thinking* in the first years of the nineteenth century, he drew on both Cabanis and Destutt de Tracy in offering a new answer to the question defined in classic terms by Condillac. Starting with his first major work, Maine de Biran set out to explore the nature of the perceiving body and the conditions in which a sensitive being may perceive itself; following a distinguished tradition, he once again imagined a creature flying alone in an empty space. "Supposing that an individual is suspended in the void," Maine de Biran wrote, "and that he shakes his limbs, or that he moves, he will necessarily feel a particular kind of impression, which is born of the resistance that his muscles oppose to him, and of the *effort* made to put them into play."[20] This claim holds for the moving fetus and the flying statue alike. In its invocation of an impression "born of resistance," the statement rests on Destutt de Tracy's distinction between solidity, as the simple perception of an external object, and the complex perception of resistance, which registers that object in its reaction to the touching body. But Maine de Biran's proposition is of greater import than such a summary would imply. For his statement expressly indicates that even in the absence of any solid objects, an animate thing can and must, in Condillac's terms, discover its body. As long as an "individual" accomplishes any action at all, Maine de Biran explains, "he will necessarily feel a particular kind of impression," born of a perception of the one thing that accompanies, accomplishes, and resists his every voluntary motion: his body. In this respect, it makes little difference whether the subject of the experiment is suspended in the void or situated firmly on the ground. If he exerts himself at all, the imagined being will, by necessity, feel "the resistance that his muscles oppose to him"; perceiving the physical mass that responds and reacts to the movement he aims to make, he will necessarily also perceive himself.

Condillac, to be sure, had imagined a perception of this order: a sensation that subsists in the absence of all sensed objects. In the *Treatise on Sensations*, he called it "the fundamental feeling" (*le sentiment fondamental*). It was what the statue felt when placed by the philosopher "in a tranquil, temperate air, where it feels its heat neither rising nor falling": a "confused" impression of existence, in the eighteenth-century thinker's words, resulting from the undifferentiated activities of the vital processes, the organic movements to which the statue "owes its life."[21] Condillac, however, held that such an impression of existence could not furnish the statue with any perception of its body and its parts. That much required a further step: the statue, Condillac maintained, had to begin actively to explore itself. Maine de Biran could not agree. That a hand could be employed as an instrument of knowledge was a point he would gladly grant. But, he added, such an action in turn implies another perception, which the *Treatise on Sensations*, "not going back far enough," had altogether overlooked. As Maine de Biran argued with great force in 1804 in his *Essay on the Division of Thinking*, Condillac's account of the groping hand is in itself hardly complete. For how, after all, did the statue ever come to move its hand? Maine de Biran held this to be the fundamental problem that a doctrine of sensation must confront. "How can any mobile organ whatsoever be moved without being known?"[22]

There can be but a single answer. If the statue knows to move its hand, it is because its "fundamental feeling" has already furnished it some perception of its body, however "confused" it may have seemed to the eighteenth-century thinker. This was a point Maine de Biran would repeat in several works, arguing with particular insistence against Descartes that "the hypothesis of a being who feels and knows its existence without knowing itself to be a body, or to be in a body, is *inadmissible*."[23] Before perceiving anything with its mobile limbs, the statue, therefore, must already perceive its organic mass. The statue need not see itself, or smell itself, or touch itself to sense that it "is a body, or in a body." A single internal sensation will suffice. Sometimes, citing and revising Condillac's own term, Maine de Biran called this impression the "absolute sensation of existence."[24] Most often, he cast this inner faculty as a tactile power. In the *Essay on the Division of Thinking* as well as *On the Relations Between the Physical and Moral Aspects of Man*, he thus alluded to an "affective touch" (*tact affectif*); in *On Immediate Apperception*, he wrote of an "immediate touch" (*tact immédiat*), which was by nature related by a "secret and natural sympathy" to the various affections of the body, which it could "presage" and "foretell" without the use of the external senses.[25] Maine de Biran was also not averse to calling this power by an ancient name, and in two of his principal works he assigned to it a title that had been current long before. There he called it "the inner touch" (*le tact intérieur*).[26]

The French thinker shows every sign of having been aware that by positing such a power within the sensitive being, he broke with a philosophical tradition well established in modernity. He replaced the absolute certainty of the Cartesian *cogito* with the indubitable evidence of an "I sense," shorthand for "I sense myself in my body's resistance to my effort." In one of his last works, the *New Essays in Anthropology*, Maine de Biran thus explained that "if Descartes believed he had laid the first principle of all science, the first self-evident truth, in saying 'I *think*, therefore I *am* (a thinking thing or substance),' we would say, better, more precisely, and this time with the incontrovertible evidence of the inner sense: 'I act, I will or think action, therefore I feel myself cause, therefore I am or I exist really on account of force or action.'"[27] In Maine de

Biran as in Descartes, therefore, the "first principle" remains subjective existence. But whereas for Descartes it is thought, for
Maine de Biran it is a "force" that implies, by definition, an element in which it realizes itself: a body. Hence Maine de Biran's
self-declared incomprehension before the Cartesian attempt to
doubt the existence of the body. "It is impossible," the nineteenth-
century thinker once commented, "to suppose that I can exist and
say 'I' without having the awareness of a proper body, and [it is
impossible to suppose] that I can have an awareness of effort if this
body does not exist."[28]

After Condillac, Leibniz, and Descartes, Maine de Biran thus
defined a fact of awareness he called "immediate apperception":
the indubitable sensation of existence, consisting of the twin
principles of effort and the body that, by nature, resists it. To
illustrate his new theory, he turned to the old fable, now rewrit-
ten in terms no less unmistakable for lacking any reference to the
medieval philosopher who had first called it to mind. "To understand this 'I'... separated from everything that is not it," Maine
de Biran wrote in *On Immediate Apperception*, "let us imagine all
the voluntary muscles contracted in the immobility of the body,
the eyes open in the darkness, the ears straining (*acuta*) in the
silence of nature, the surrounding air tranquil and the external
temperature balanced with that of the surface of the body, all the
inner impressions reduced to the nature tone of organic life,
insensible in their uniform continuity."[29] A single force, he noted,
can then be observed: "effort remains alone" (*l'effort reste seul*).[30]
"Periodically suspended in sleep," this "fundamental mode of
individual personality is always reborn the same." Its presence in
the life of sensitive beings may be intermittent, but its nature cannot change. It is always "the same immediate apperception, the
same 'I,'" always "the same relation of force to resistance."[31]

Over the course of the years in which he wrote his many and
almost exclusively unfinished works, Maine de Biran became increasingly aware of the degree to which this "relation," although
constant, is complex. It was beyond all doubt that the concept of
"immediate apperception" sought, among other things, to re-

spond compellingly to the question raised by Condillac in his *Treatise on Sensations*: "How a Man . . . Discovers His Body." And in this it succeeded in part. If one grants that there is an "absolute sensation of existence" consisting of the relation of a voluntary effort to a physical resistance, one must conclude that once the imagined statue feels the "temperate air" about it, it also feels the resistance of its marble muscles to its effort and so perceives that it has a body on which it acts. But with such an argument Maine de Biran had still not responded fully to the query raised by Condillac. For the *Treatise on Sensations* sought to explain something more than the discovery of the body: that is, the steps by which the animate thing learns that its body is extended and in "parts." This is a process for which Maine de Biran's early works cannot easily account. They explain how a sensitive creature can feel, from the resistance of its muscles to its will, that it possesses a body. But how can a living being perceive, without the use of any external sense, that its body is extended in space, composed of parts distinct from one another? How can the living statue know without looking that its arm, for example, belongs to a different region of its body from its leg?

As François Azouvi has observed, the elements of an answer to this question find their first formulation in a note added in 1805 to the third edition of the *Essay on the Division of Thinking*.[32] Here Maine de Biran writes that "to the uniformity or continuity with which the body resists effort, there must correspond a feeling of a kind of *interior extension* that is at first vague and unlimited."[33] Expended effort now brings to light not merely a body that resists. Exerted force simultaneously reveals a body "immediately perceived in the sole exercise of the muscular sense," which is "especially suited to the apperception of the inner and unlimited space of the *proper body*."[34] Discussions of such an "inner and unlimited space" can be found in almost all the major works Maine de Biran composed after this point. *On Immediate Apperception*, written in 1807, thus defines "general locomotion, or the simultaneous contraction of all the mobile parts obeying a single will," as the correlate of a "*space* or a kind of vague and unlimited *extension* belonging to one's own body," from which the "I" simultaneously "distinguishes itself, in its immediate apperception, without being able to separate itself" fully.[35] The *Essay on the Fundamentals of Psychology*, begun in 1811 and never finished, says still more. Maine de Biran now explains that the uniformity of resistance felt in the body furnishes "the simple and original type of a kind of extension,... a reality as certain as our existence, from which it is inseparable," an inner counterpart to the "space in which our external locomotion exercises itself."[36] The "Note on the Idea of Existence," most probably Maine de Biran's last work, also invokes this singular space: "a kind of immediate, internal localization of sensations or intuitions," by which we know to refer organic affections to different regions of a single body.[37]

A "kind of interior extension," a "kind of vague and unlimited extension," a "kind of localization": these qualifications point to the startling status of this felt region, which constitutes a space within the sensing self and within it alone. Historians of modern thought have rarely noted the strangeness of this concept. Over half a century ago, Raymond Vancourt, for one, drew attention to it, lauding it as clear proof of "the superiority of [Maine's] doctrine with respect to that of Kant." In the same age in which the philosopher of Königsberg regarded "space as a totality given once and for all," Vancourt argued, Maine de Biran, by contrast, "wanted to explain to us the genesis of this space, and he therefore began by showing it to us in its most rudimentary form, from which space will be developed and complicated."[38] It goes without saying that the "form" that may be in life "most rudimentary" is in philosophy the creation of the greatest advancement. Merleau-Ponty, who lectured on Maine de Biran at the École Normale Supérieure in 1947–1948, maintained that the notion of "a kind of vague and unlimited extension" anticipated the more advanced idea the twentieth-century thinker naturally reserved for phenomenology: "a spatiality of the body prior to objective spatiality, a presence of the outside on the inside of consciousness."[39] One might equally well conclude that with this concept Maine de Biran sought to define a "kind of extension" for which the terms of the tradition are inadequate, and for which even the word "space" may be ultimately inappropriate: a dimension felt within the sensing animal that is extended but not limited, composed not of "parts outside each other" (*partes extra partes*), like all portions of properly extended substance, but of what one might term "parts among each other," whose contours, therefore, by nature cannot be defined.

This inner space constitutes the great discovery of the last philosopher to repeat the experiment in the philosophy of the soul first conducted by Avicenna. Simultaneous with the muscular exertion corresponding to all effort, the "kind of interior extension" remains for Maine de Biran inseparable from the lives of sensing beings. Every animal that discovers itself in immediate apperception, in rest or motion, must find itself in this "kind of vague and unlimited *extension*," which surrounds and separates its divided parts; each, to employ the philosopher's own term, must "appropriate" it to itself.[40] But that is already to say too much. How, after all, can one "find" oneself in a dimension "vague and unlimited" by nature, how can one "appropriate" to oneself a thing that cannot be represented as a single whole? Indefinite by definition, the inner extension imagined by Maine de Biran consists of a terrain from which the self must "distinguish itself" and "distinguish" the extended portions that form its body, but from which no self, and no represented part, could ever fully "separate itself."[41] Perceived as "a kind of vague and obscure feeling, tied to every kind of animal or organic life, which for the human animal does not differ from the feeling of the existence or the presence of the extension of his body," this internal space is "the background to which all impressions are referred" and in which each physical affection, to be sensed, must find its place.[42] Hence its perpetual divergence from every sensing and sensed self, its inevitable excess with respect to the animals who would find themselves within it. Just as the figure cannot be identified with the ground, so no "apperception," however immediate, can coincide with the vague infinitude of a region unbounded by nature.[43] A continuity of resistance surrounding and supporting all forceful

beings, this unlimited expanse is the element of all sensitive existence. It is the invisible air that every animal always breathes, and
on account of which even the most terrestrial of creatures may
always find itself, within itself, much like the medieval man: suddenly suspended in an unknown and impenetrable space.

CHAPTER TWENTY-TWO

Coenaesthesis

On the medical Idea of the common Feeling, the bodily
Sense by which animate Beings dimly perceive that they are alive

Coenesthésie, *mare nostrum*, mère de l'absurde.
— Henri Michaux*

The year 1794 saw the publication of a slim volume bearing the brief and perplexing title *Coenesthesis*. It was a doctoral dissertation by one Christian Friedrich Hübner, defended the same year at the University of Halle and composed, in accordance with the academic conventions of the time, in Latin. Several months later, the book was published again, in a German translation by Johann Friedrich Alexander Merzdorff. Now it was preceded by a work by the Swiss physician Daniel de la Roche, which, for its part, bore a much more comprehensible, if prolix, title: *On the Analysis of the Operations of the Nervous System as an Introduction to a Practical Investigation of Neural Maladies*. Both treatises were introduced by the eminent and influential physician and physiologist Johann Christian Reil, who had acted as the director of Hübner's *dissertatio inauguralis*. Perhaps because of the depth of his involvement with the research he had supervised, Reil limited his enthusiastic prefatory remarks to the treatise by Daniel de la Roche, leaving *Coenesthesis* to stand on its own, an addition to the study of the nervous system that went without commentary. But Hübner's work was in fact better served by this reedition than such a

---

* Michaux, *Oeuvres complètes*, vol. 3, *Face à ce qui se dérobe*, p. 856.

description might suggest, for in its German translation, the strangely titled doctoral dissertation found a second name, which could not but call to mind terms that must have been immediately familiar to eighteenth-century specialists of the body and the soul. In its vernacular version, Hübner's work appeared as a contribution to the scientific study of a most classical subject, which had been defined in canonical terms by the philosophers and physicians of Antiquity and the Middle Ages: the shared faculty of sensation. In translation, *Coenesthesis* emerged as an investigation into an altogether intelligible thing: "the common sense," or, in the terms of the original translation, the *Gemeingefühl*.

Readers undaunted by the obscurity of the Latin title would, in any case, have discovered the exact meaning of *coenaesthesis* in the opening pages of the treatise, in which the author clearly defined the object of his study and situated it among the multiple varieties of perception. It suffices to read the second section of the work, "Feeling, or Sensation" (*Gefühl, Empfindung*), to grasp the nature of the phenomenon in question. "To feel," Hübner establishes, is "to undergo alterations of the soul, which are provoked by alterations of the body." To this degree, all sensations are alike. But the author of *Coenesthesis* immediately adds that "as soon as we investigate our *faculty of feeling* more precisely, we discover that it is very diverse." Three kinds of sensory representations, in particular, may be distinguished; together, they form the elements of a single typology of the forms of perception. First, there are perceptual representations of an "external condition," or "the relation of the whole person to the world." These representations the eighteenth-century thinker classes under the classical rubric of "external sensation": *sensatio externa* or *Empfindung*, in the terms of Merzdorff's translation. Then there are perceptual representations of "the spiritual condition: its powers, actions, representations, and concepts," by which the sensing soul distinguishes itself from its own thoughts, "becoming in this way conscious of them." Hübner's term for the faculty responsible for this type of perception is equally traditional. He calls it the "inner sense" (*innerer Sinn*), adding that it is by this power alone that the rational soul "forms imaginative representations and judgments, represents its ideas and concepts, and becomes conscious of them."[1]

One might well expect the account of the types of perception now to be complete: external sensation and the inner sense, after all, would seem to exhaust the varieties of feeling. But Hübner goes on to invoke a third power of perception: that by which the soul, as he writes, "represents *its own bodily condition*," "by means of the nerves that are spread throughout the body."[2] The author shows some signs of having hesitated in naming this third faculty. In a footnote added at this point in the treatise, he observes that the term "feeling" could be understood in a number of ways. It could indicate not only the registration of a sensation by an animate organism but also mere "irritability," as when a part of the body, extracted from the living whole, continues to respond to external stimuli.[3] In German, as in English, moreover, the term "feeling" also retains a privileged tie to one sense among others: touch. To "feel" a thing is very often to encounter it by the tactile power. The word "feeling" (*Gefühl*) may even mean "the sense of feeling" (*Gefühlsinn*), that is, "touch" (*Getast*). The perception of the bodily condition appears to strike Hübner as related to such a tactile sensation, since he chooses to refer to it as a kind of "feeling" (*Gefühl*). But he leaves little doubt that this third variety of perception is to be understood as a "feeling" neither of an external object nor of the internal faculty that is the mind. He argues that the soul's "representations of its own bodily condition" bear witness to a specific faculty, which perceives the organism in its vital activities, and which "touches," therefore, nothing other than the perpetually touching body itself. Hence the name with which the physician and philosopher finally resolves to baptize the third variety of perception, "the object of the present treatise": "*coenaesthesis*, and in the mother tongue, *common feeling* [*Gemeingefühl*]."[4]

In an important essay on the origins of the modern medical concept of general sensation, Jean Starobinski has remarked that "the word *coenaesthesis* is a learned neologism," unattested in any European language before the end of the eighteenth century, when Reil and Hübner appear to have coined it. In its construction and meaning, however, the term is unmistakable: formed by the combination of two Latinized Greek terms, the prefix *coen-* and the word *aesthesis*, it clearly designates a "shared" or "common perception." Starobinski observed, for this reason, that the medical expression should not be mistaken for "synæsthesia," the modern descendant of the classical *sunaisthēsis*, which was widely employed, starting in the nineteenth century, as a psychological designation of sensory associations, such as the perception of sounds or smells as colored.[5] Starobinski warned even more strenuously against taking the eighteenth-century word as equivalent to the structurally similar technical term of the philosophical tradition. "Above all," he wrote, *coenaesthesis* "should not be confused with the *koinon aisthētērion* whose notion was defined by Aristotle: according to the *De Anima*, it belongs to the *koinon aisthētērion* to receive and conjoin all sensations, such that we may perceive a *single* object where the senses relay qualitatively heterogeneous impressions."[6] To be sure, Starobinski conceded, the two terms for "common sensation," ancient and modern both, are made of precisely the same logical elements. Still, he maintained, they must be strictly separated: "The word *coenaesthesis*," he wrote, "while employing the same roots (*koinos*, *aisthēsis*), in no way aims to designate the same function, and Reil had no need to forge a double of the *koinon aisthētērion* (or of the *sensorium commune*), whose concept remained very much alive in the eighteenth century, even if it was the subject of debates and controversies."[7]

The first point made by Starobinski can hardly be contested. The terms "coenaesthesis" and "synaesthesia" differ both etymologically and semantically, and the sensory power identified by Hübner and Reil has little to do with the psychological and neurological associations between the five senses later studied by nineteenth-and twentieth-century scholars. But the force of Starobinski's second claim is less evident. It is certainly true that "Reil had no need to forge a double of the *koinon aisthētērion*," understood as the power by which we "receive and conjoin all sensations, such that we may perceive a *single* object where the senses relay qualitatively heterogeneous impressions." But the conjunction and disjunction of sensible qualities of different types was but one of the diverse activities performed by the Aristotelian "common faculty." The power known to the ancient and medieval thinkers was also responsible for a further operation, unmentioned by Starobinski, presumably because by the eighteenth century it had ceased to be consistently attributed to the *koinon aisthētērion*. The master perceptual power of the philosophical tradition also perceives the fact of perception, allowing sentient beings to sense when they are sensing and, moreover, when they are not. It is difficult not to hear an echo of this sensation in the feeling defined by Hübner and Reil, which registers the bare fact of sensitive existence. Once disjoined from the modern concept of the *sensorium commune* and effaced as such, the central activity of the classical common sense seems to return, in a new guise that is, in truth, the ghostly repetition of its old. The *koinē aisthēsis* of the ancient philosophers thus appears as the coenaesthesis of the modern physicians; the "common sensation" emerges as a "common feeling"; and the "inner touch, by which we perceive ourselves," finds itself redefined as a faculty of "touch" (*Getast*) that apprehends the vital force of the sensing body.

The "feeling" defined by the modern medical treatise calls to mind a number of sentiments discussed by the philosophers of the second half of the eighteenth century. One thinks first of all of the "sense of the co-existence of the body" described in exemplary terms by the *abbé* Lelarge de Lignac in his *Elements of Metaphysics Drawn from Experience* of 1753 and *Testimony of the Inner Sense and of Experience* of 1760, both of which were to exert a profound influence on Maine de Biran.[8] More than a trace of this sensory power can be found in Turgot's entry on existence in the 1756 edition of the *Encyclopédie*. Considering the origins of the consciousness of being, Turgot invoked Descartes, Locke, and Condillac, dwelling, like many others in the eighteenth century, on the important place of perception in the genesis of knowledge. He naturally discussed the senses by which we perceive that which lies beyond us. But he soon set them aside to reflect on other, "so to speak more penetrating senses, which can be referred to the inside of our body." "Of these sensations," he wrote,

> I would make a special class, under the name of *inner touch*, or the sixth sense, and I would class under it the aches that we sometimes feel under our skin, in the powers of our intestines, even in our bones; nausea, the upset that precedes fainting, hunger, thirst, the emotion that accompanies all passion; shudders, either of pain or of desire; finally, the whole multitude of confused sensations that never leave us; the sensations that, so to speak, circumscribe our body, rendering it always present — the sense that metaphysicians, for this reason, have at times called the *sense of the co-existence of our body*.[9]

Four years later, we find a discussion of a similar perceptual power in d'Alembert's *Essay on the Elements of Philosophy.* "Beyond the five senses," the philosopher explains in the seventh *Éclaircissement* of this work, "there is one that may be called *internal*, which is, as it were, intimately spread throughout our substance, and whose seat can be situated at once in all the external and internal parts of our body."[10]

The terms of Hübner's treatise recall such reflections on the "inner touch," but they also move beyond them. The late eighteenth-century German physician rigorously distinguishes the "general feeling" from both the forms of external perception and the "inner sense" of the tradition: in the terms of the medical treatise, coenaesthesis is no more a perception of consciousness than it is a perception of objects distinct from the body. By definition, the "common feeling" is a perception of the living being as such: a sensation of the sensing organism itself. Hübner and Reil's early readers were well aware of this point. The first among them in France may have been Maine de Biran, who composed a set of copious notes on Reil's *Functiones organo animæ peculiares* in the final years of his life. Twenty-one years before the term *cénesthésie* officially entered the lexicon of the French language through an entry in the *Complément du Dictionnaire de l'Académie française* of 1842, Maine de Biran made what appears to be the first mention of the term in the Gallic tongue. "Reil," he commented in 1821, "gives the name 'coenaesthesis' [*coenesthèse*]" to the sensation of "pleasure or pain, which is inseparable from everything that lives," the "general feeling, the composed modality of all the vital impressions inherent in every part" of the living organism.[11] When Sir William Hamilton introduced the learned Latinate word into the English language in the second volume of his *Lectures on Metaphysics and Logic* of 1858, he also defined the term in this technical acceptation, remarking that "the vital sense," as he then called it, had received "from the various authors various synonyms, as *coenaesthesis*, common feeling, vital feeling, etc."[12]

The idea defined by Hübner and Reil was to have a long and distinguished reception. Less than a quarter of a century after the publication of *Coenesthesis* in Latin and in German, its influence can already be detected in a book that ranks among the great works of nineteenth-century science: Jean-Baptiste de Lamarck's *Analytic System of the Positive Knowledges of Man*. Published in Paris in 1820, this text makes no mention of the lesser doctor of Halle, but its account of the types of sensations suggests that its author possessed more than a passing familiarity with Reil's theories of perception. Lamarck gives the name "sensation" to "those phenomena that belong to feeling, and whose *affecting cause* acts solely on the extremities of the nerves it affects," thereby provoking an "agitation" throughout the nerves of the body and transmitting an impression from the extremity of the affected nerve "to the common nucleus of the system of which the nerves are a part." He proceeds to distinguish, in classic fashion, the varieties of sensation. The first among them are "particular sensations." They are defined by the shared trait of "being executed in certain determinate parts of the body and nowhere else," and, if one believes Lamarck, they are no more than four: taste, smell, sight, and hearing.[13]

One cannot but observe that that count includes no reference to the sense of touch. It would be a serious oversight, however, to conclude that the tactile power remains absent from the *Analytic System*. After treating the particular sensations and their proper qualities, the scientist passes to a consideration of the "feeling sense" in terms no less unmistakable for lacking any explicit reference to the power traditionally called touch. The scientist now argues that there is a variety of perception that is fundamentally distinct from "particular sensations," which remains effective in not one but all the multiple parts of the living body, be they internal or external. Its name in the French treatise constitutes an equivalent to the Germanic "common feeling" (*Gemeingefühl*): "general sensation" (*sensation générale*). This is a perception that, in opposition to the enumerated four forms of particular sensation, "can be executed everywhere, on the outside as well as on the inside of the individual." By nature it is indifferent to location: "All the points of the body are almost equally susceptible to it," Lamarck writes, "except the parts of the individual's skeleton, if he possesses one."[14]

Lamarck explains that such a general sensation can be of two sorts. On the one hand, there are forms of common perception that are essentially circumstantial (*sensations circonstancielles*). They can be felt "in degrees, from the weakest, whose impression is the least perceptible, to the most acute pain." Certain affections of this kind, he writes, "are pleasing to us, even pleasurable, and temporarily excite some of our organic functions, on condition of remaining within the limits beyond which they would begin to do us harm; others affect us in an opposite manner; and, finally, others cause us physical pain, suffering of every degree."[15] On the other hand, there is a variety of general perception that by nature cannot cease: "permanent sensation" (*sensation permanente*). "I give this name," the scientist explains,

> to that sensation which is executed in all the sensible parts of the body, in general and without discontinuity, during the entire course of the individual's life. It results from the vital movements, the displacements of fluids, and the frictions brought about by these displacements, frictions which are the result of contacts and the result, therefore, of affecting causes, and which may even produce a special noise that we distinguish very well in our heads, especially when we

are ill. Although extremely weak, these affecting causes are infinitely many and, at the extremities of the nerves leading to all the sensible points of the body, they produce a light agitation in the subtle fluid that they contain, which flows from all the parts to the part housing the central nucleus, thus occasioning a kind of uninterrupted shivering. It is probably to this physical cause that we owe the intimate sentiment of existence which we feel, however obscure it may be.[16]

The permanence of general sensation results, therefore, from that of smaller sensations still: "infinitely many" and "extremely weak" minor vital affections, which bear more than a passing resemblance to the "little perceptions" conceived by the author of the *Monadology*. Together, they form a sensory phenomenon irreducible to the particular regions of the body and the distinct varieties of its impressions; they compose the countless elements of a single sensation, which persists uninterrupted "during the entire course of the individual's life." Imperceptible for the most part, this affection imposes itself on the sensing being exclusively in times of unrest, when it seems, in the terms of the *Analytic System*, to acquire a strangely auditory consistency: to be felt as "a special noise," the sound, as it were, of purely organic subsistence.

Lamarck's definition of permanent sensation is memorable for its elegance and its force, but it can hardly be said to be alone in its age in setting the "common feeling" at the center of the animal's perceptual powers. Nineteenth-century physiologists and psychologists immediately recognized the importance of the investigations into general sensation undertaken by Reil and his students. At times, to be sure, their terms for the phenomenon could vary, as Starobinski has shown.[17] Franz von Paula Gruithuisen, for example, rendered "coenaesthesis" in German by "common sense" (*Gemeinsinn*), rather than by "common feeling" (*Gemeingefühl*), in his *Anthropology* of 1810.[18] Míhaly Ignácz Lenhossék, by contrast, invoked a "corporeal sense" (*sensus corporeus*) in his *Physiology*, published from 1816 to 1818.[19] Karl Friedrich Burdach took "the common feeling" (*Gemeingefühl*) to be the most rudimentary manifestation of "self-feeling" (*Selbstgefühl*), explaining in 1828 that, together with instinct, it constitutes the "seed" of all the "powers of the soul" (*Seelenkräften*).[20] Before long, the perceptual phenomenon identified by the physicians of Halle could no longer be ignored. At most, the doctors of the age could detach it from its pretended inventor, as when Karl Asmund Rudolphi polemically argued in 1830 that "fundamentally, the word 'common feeling' [*Gemeingefühl*] alone belongs to Riel, since the matter was just as well described by Leidenfrost under the name 'life feeling' [*Lebensgefühl*]."[21] The sensation, in any case, remained. Jacob Henle's *Pathological Investigations* of 1840 and *Anatomy* of 1841 both gave a prominent place to coenaesthesis, casting it as the perception of "the tonality of the sensitive nerves" in general, "the sum, the undifferentiated chaos" of all felt sensations.[22] And in his influential treatise of 1850, *The Sense of Touch and the Common Feeling*, Ernst Heinrich Weber naturally dwelled at some length on the concept, which he employed to name "the consciousness of our sensory condition" (*das Bewußtsein unseres Empfindungszustande*).[23]

The importance of the concept of coenaesthesis in the medical disciplines of the second half of the nineteenth century can be measured by the lengthy article devoted to *cenestesi* by Maurizio (Moritz) Schiff in the 1871 Italian *Dictionary of Medical Sciences*. By this point, "common feeling" was a well-known notion, and the lexicographer needed not to introduce it but to limit and define its meanings with precision. In his article, Schiff recalls that the medical term may be employed in at least three distinct senses. The first, as Starobinski has observed, can be traced to Reil: "Coenaesthesis includes all sensations which do not result from the influence of an external agent, and which make us aware of the state and existence of the different parts of our body." The second definition casts the common feeling as consisting of that which cannot be reduced to one of the proper senses: the remainder of sensation, so to speak, left over after all perceptions have been attributed to the particular forms of sensation. Coenaesthesis, in this meaning, can be characterized as "including all the sensations that are due to the nerves responsible for what is called *general* sensibility [*sensibilità generale*], and which are not the effects of the excitation of a *special* organ of sense." Both such definitions identify the common feeling in exclusively negative terms; they make of the shared sense that which cannot be reduced to other feelings, be they those of external objects or those of the particular senses. For this reason, Schiff finds them equally unsatisfactory, and he therefore proposes a third sense. Coenaesthesis may also be understood, he writes, as "the *complex* of all sensations, which, in any given moment, are more or less distinctly transmitted to our consciousness, and which constitute the content of our momentary consciousness."[24] Although Schiff's terminology remains resolutely modern, such a "common feeling" could be aptly named by a term employed over two millennia earlier by Aristotle in his brief treatise *De sensu et sensibilibus*. A "total sense" (*aisthētikon pantōn*), such a "faculty" is receptive to everything the body perceives, by all means, at each moment.[25]

The history of coenesthesis in modern medicine extends well beyond Schiff, and the decades that followed the publication of his article witnessed the emergence of a large literature on the common feeling by physicians, physiologists, psychologists, and neurologists of various methodological and scientific orientations.[26] Of particular importance were the contributions of Théodule Ribot, professor of the Collège de France, founder of the *Revue de philosophie* in France, and the author of numerous influential books on the nature of the mind. Ribot knew the work of his German colleagues well, and his *Contemporary German Psychology*, published in French in 1879, played an important role in disseminating their findings in France.[27] In 1883, he published *Personality Illnesses*, a work that was to go through no fewer than fifteen editions between then and 1914. Chapter One of this work dealt with the problem of "organic maladies": that is, disturbances of the mind involving those structures that Ribot took to constitute "the organic conditions of personality." The first among them was the faculty identified over a century before by Hübner and Reil: in the French psychologist's own terms, "general sensibility, or 'coenesthesis.'"[28]

Ribot dwelled at length on the common feeling, citing the description of it that had been given half a century earlier by Louis Peisse, the first "philosophical physician" in France to demonstrate "that our knowledge of the body is above all subjective."[29] In his edition of Cabanis's *Relations Between the Physical and Moral in Man*, Peisse had argued strenuously for the existence of a "consciousness of the exercise of organic functions." Familiar with the important work of his predecessors, he had turned for assistance to Condillac, theorist of the "fundamental feeling," and to Maine de Biran, philosopher of the "feeling of sensitive existence."[30] The two thinkers furnished Peisse with the elements for a doctrine of the psychological perception of the physiological machine. "It is by it," Peisse had written in 1844, "that the body incessantly seems to the self to be *its own*, and that the spiritual subject feels and perceives itself [*se sent et s'aperçoit*] to exist somehow locally and in the limited extension of the organism. A perpetual and infallible monitor, it renders the state of the soul constantly present to consciousness and thus manifests, in the most intimate manner, the indissoluble tie between psychic life and physiological life."[31]

Physician no less than thinker, Ribot illustrated this doctrine with a host of examples, all of which pointed, in his eyes, to the existence of a purely "organic awareness" (*conscience organique*). Consider those sensations "tied to breathing, the feeling of well-being produced by clean air, and of suffocation in the absence of air." Or observe those impressions linked to "the state of nutrition," such as hunger and thirst, which, "despite appearances, have no precise localization, but rather result from an unease of the entire organism," being in truth "a cry made by the blood that has grown poor." Or take, finally, "the organic sensations that arise from the state of the muscles," such as the feelings of exhaustion and excitement, to say nothing, the psychologist delicately added, of the "organic sensations of the genital apparatus."[32] Such examples were by Ribot's time classic, and they represented but a selection of a well-established and much larger set of common feelings thought to bear witness to the perception of the living body. Other nineteenth-century psychologists, among whom Oswald Külpe, added to their number "complexes of cutaneous sensations," such as tickling, itching, prickling, tingling, and shivering, which could be explained only as "compound mental states, which are the result of the combination of various sensory excitations from the periphery of the body."[33] Others still, more interested in the movements and coordination of the limbs, wrote of a "muscular sense" (*Muskelsinn*), which registered the body in movement and at rest: "kinaesthesis," as H. Charlton Bastian defined it, or "proprioception," as Sir Charles Scott Sherrington would later call it, "our secret sense, our sixth sense."[34]

If Ribot's analysis in *Personality Illnesses* can lay claim to exemplarity, this is above all by virtue of its definition of coenaesthesis as a single sensory phenomenon, a definition that draws on two eminent and influential authorities in nineteenth-century psychology. The first was Henle, who had identified the common feeling in his *Anatomy* as "the sum, the undifferentiated chaos of sensations that are incessantly transmitted from all the points of the body to the *sensorium*."[35] The second was Weber, the great experimental psychologist. Ribot did not provide any precise textual source for Weber's definition, but he made a point of adding that it represented a decisive advance over Henle's conception of coenaesthesis. "With greater precision," we read, "E.-H. Weber meant by the word *coenaesthesis* an internal sensibility, an inner touch which furnishes the *sensorium* with information about the mechanical and chemico-organic state of the skin, the mucous and serous membranes, the viscera, the muscles, and the joints."[36]

Although Ribot himself did not dwell on it, the contrast between the two definitions is striking. It cannot but raise the question of the nature of the common feeling as a single physiological and psychological phenomenon. Henle's definition, after all, presents "coenesthesis" as a name for all sensation, without distinction: "the sum, the undifferentiated chaos of sensations that are incessantly transmitted from all the points of the body to the *sensorium*." Weber, by contrast, casts the shared sense as one among significant: coenaesthesis, he affirms, can be most exactly defined as "*an* internal sensibility, *an* inner touch which furnishes the *sensorium* with information about the mechanical and chemico-organic state of the skin, the mucous and serous membranes, the viscera, the muscles, and the joints."

All of perception and but one of its elements, the fundamental organ of sensation yet still a sensory power of its own: the paradoxical status of the nineteenth-century common feeling once more recalls the ancient common sense, which consistently resisted being represented either as the entire aesthetic power or as one of its many parts. In later modernity, however, the classic problem of the single central sense acquired a new urgency. Reinterpreted as "an inner touch" that furnished the *sensorium* with a perception of "the vital movements, the displacements of fluids, and the frictions brought about by these displacements, frictions which are the result of contacts and the result, therefore, of affecting causes, and which may even produce a special noise that we distinguish very well in our heads, especially when we are ill," the common sense now opened onto a thing the classical and medieval philosophers had never known as such: the living organism, defined as the object of a single sensation. But what kind of object of sensation could the animate body be? This was a question Aristotle and his many pupils had never raised. It belonged to the scientists of the nervous system after Reil, and it was they who were forced, time and time again, to confront it.

From Hübner to Ribot, from the German neurology of the eighteenth century to the French psychiatry of the nineteenth, "coenesthesis" remained the name of both the solution and the difficulty: the cipher of that sense by which animate beings dimly feel they are alive. This was a perplexing perception from the start, and with time its obscurity could never entirely be dispelled. Clearly the shared feeling could not be referred to any single part of the body, since it was "common" by definition. But it also could not be defined with any precision as the perception of a totality. The sense of the skin, for some, of the intestines, for others, of the viscera, the muscles, the blood, for others still, coenaesthesis, "permanent sensation," could certainly be a feeling of diverse things; for many, it was a feeling of all things together, sensed in a single moment. But it could never clearly be defined as the perception of the body as a whole. The medical terminology was to this degree exact: the common feeling was, above all, a "general perception." The attribute in that phrase merits some attention. Above all, it cannot be taken as equivalent to another: a total perception or, even worse, "a feeling of totality" (*Totalitäts-gefühl*), as some physicians hastily concluded.[37] That there is a perception that may be called "general" means, in truth, no more than this: there is a perception that cannot be referred to any single object; there is a sensation that, while felt, cannot be defined as the representation of one part or one set of parts and that cannot, perhaps, be defined as the representation of "one" living being at all. This, to be sure, was a startling conclusion, most of all for those who aimed to refer all physical sensations to the multiple regions of the single sensing organism. In time, however, coenesthesis would reveal itself to be a stranger sentiment than those who first identified it may have thought. As the modern disciplines of the body and the mind sped toward ever more startling discoveries in the final years of the nineteenth century, the sciences of sensing life soon found themselves confronted with a thing for which terms and notions, medical and philosophical, could not easily be found: a thinking thing that generally sensed its living body to be much more and less than, by all scientific accounts, it could ever be.

CHAPTER TWENTY-THREE

Phantoms

In which Bodies feel Parts they do not possess, and alternately
fail to feel those Parts that are truly theirs

The July 1866 issue of *The Atlantic Monthly* contained an article of singular literary and scientific interest. It was unsigned, but its opening sentence clearly suggested that its author could be identified with the figure named by its lapidary title: "The Case of George Dedlow."[1] The beginning of the work explained why the "case" now appeared in a periodical destined for a wide and general readership. "The following notes of my case," the article began, "have been declined on various pretexts by every medical journal to which I have offered them." The author conceded that he could well understand why this could have been so. "There was, perhaps, some reason in this," he immediately added, "because many of the medical facts which they record are not altogether new, and because the psychical deductions to which they have led me are not in themselves of medical interest."[2] The truth was that the "notes" George Dedlow had assembled contained findings that far exceeded the terrain of the modern science of the living body. They revealed nothing less than "metaphysical discoveries," as the author himself called them, which he was determined to "set forth" for the education and edification of the interested public.

The "case" consisted largely of a grim tale, which was more than a little violent. The son of an Indiana physician, George Dedlow studied medicine in his father's office, obtaining formal training at Jefferson Medical College, in Philadelphia, in 1859 and

1860. In normal circumstances, he would have completed his medical education at that same institution, but with the "outbreak of the Rebellion," his father's means were drastically reduced, leaving him little choice but to interrupt his studies. Since "the demand for army surgeons at this time became very great," however, the young Dedlow, while still not a graduate, succeeded in finding a position as assistant surgeon to the Tenth Indiana Volunteers. Soon, having "contracted a strong taste for army life, and, disliking cavalry service," he sought and obtained the position of first lieutenant in the Seventy-ninth Indiana Volunteers.

This decision was to lead to a most unfortunate end. Attacked by Confederate fighters while alone near the Cumberland River below Nashville, the young lieutenant was shot in both arms. Within an hour, he recalls, he felt a terrible sensation in one of his wounded limbs. His right hand and forearm seemed "perfectly insensible," except for a single fact: the "dead right hand" continued to produce in him a "strange burning." Eventually he was brought to "one of the Rebel hospitals near Atlanta," where he was treated "throughout with great kindness." But six weeks later, when the condition of his right arm had not changed, the physician treating him resolved that the limb must be removed.

There followed "weary months of monotonous prison life in the South." Then, in August 1863, Dedlow was exchanged and, "after the usual thirty days' furlough," returned to his regiment. He was now promoted to captain, but his luck did not change. One month later, he was wounded at the Battle of Chickamauga Creek, south of Chattanooga, Tennessee, in which, as he recalls, "my regiment took a conspicuous part."[3] Shot again, he lost consciousness and awoke, lying in a hospital tent, to a gruesome surprise:

> I got hold of my own identity in a moment or two, and was suddenly aware of a sharp cramp in my left leg. I tried to get at to rub it with my single arm, but, finding myself too weak, hailed an attendant. "Just rub my left calf," said I, "if you please."
>
> "Calf?" said he, "you ain't none, pardner. It's took off."
>
> "I know better," said I. "I have pain in both legs."

"Wall, I never!" said he. "You ain't got nary leg."

As I did not believe him, he threw off the covers, and, to my horror, showed me that I had suffered amputation of both thighs, very high up.

"That will do," said I, faintly.[4]

A month later, the patient was transferred from his small hospital in Chattanooga to Nashville, where he "filled," in his words, "one of the ten thousand beds of that vast metropolis of hospitals." There he suffered "the final misfortune." In the third week of his stay in the "metropolis," an epidemic of gangrene broke out in his ward. Before long, his one wounded arm was infected, entailing an inevitable consequence: "At last, as a final resort, the remaining arm was amputated at the shoulder joint." Dedlow recalls that "against all chances," he once again survived the operation, only to regain consciousness in a frightening new form. "I recovered," he reports, "to find myself a useless torso, more like some strange larval creature than anything of human shape."[5]

At this point, George Dedlow's bodily losses were complete. But the literary and medical "case" was still far from its conclusion, and the author had yet to unveil the most startling of the "discoveries" he made. Benefiting from the benevolent intervention of a friend of his father's, "the late Governor Anderson," the "useless torso" found himself transferred in January 1864 to Philadelphia, where he entered that medical institution on South Street generally known by the "not very pleasing title of Stump Hospital." Renewing his old interest in the science of the body, Dedlow now sought to glean knowledge about the physical and psychological state he shared with so many others who had survived the war. "I amused myself, at this time," he writes, "by noting in my mind all that I could learn from other limbless folk, and from myself, as to the peculiar feelings which were noticed in regard to lost members." It is at this point that the veteran made a startling discovery, which he explains to the untrained readers of *The Atlantic Monthly* at some length:

I found that the great mass of men who had undergone amputations for many months felt the usual consciousness that they still had the lost limb. It itched or pained, or was cramped, but never felt cold or hot. If they had painful sensations referred to it, the conviction of its existence continued unaltered for long periods; but where no pain was felt in it, then, by degrees, the sense of having that limb faded away entirely. I think we may to some extent explain this. The knowledge we possess of any part is made up of the numberless impressions from without which affect its sensitive surfaces, and which are transmitted through its nerves to the spinal nerve-cells, and through them, again, to the brain. We are thus kept endlessly informed as to the existence of parts, because the impressions which reach the brain are, by a law of our being, referred by us to the part from which they came. Now, when the part is cut off, the nerve-trunks which led to it and from it, remaining capable of being impressed by irritations, are made to convey to the brain from the stump impressions which are as usual referred by the brain to the lost parts, to which these nerve-threads belonged. In other words, the nerve is like a bell-wire. You may pull it at any part of its course, and thus ring the bell as well as if you pulled at the end of the wire; but, in any case, the intelligent servant will refer the pull to the front door, and obey it accordingly. The impressions made on the cut ends of the nerve, or on its sides, are due often to the changes in the stump during healing, and consequently cease as it heals, so that finally, in a very healthy stump, no such impressions arise; the brain ceases to correspond with the lost leg, and, as *les absents ont toujours tort*, it is no longer remembered or recognized. But in some cases, such as mine provided at last to my sorrow, the ends of the nerves undergo a curious alteration, and get to be enlarged and altered. This change, as I have seen in my practice of medicine, passes up the nerves towards the centres, and occasions a more or less constant irritation of the nerve-fibres, producing neuralgia, which is usually referred to that part of the lost limb to which the affected nerve belongs. This pain keeps the brain ever mindful of the missing part, and, imperfectly at least, preserves to the man a consciousness of possessing that which he has not.[6]

The "limbless folk" of Stump Hospital furnished Dedlow with the incontrovertible empirical evidence of the experience he himself knew well: that of the persistence after amputation of sensation in the "lost limb." The erstwhile physician presents it as the result of an interruption in the "correspondence" that defines the perceptual apparatus, a breakdown in the ordered "conversation" that ties the healthy body to its brain. After the removal of the sensitive surfaces of the injured parts, the larger "nerve-trunk" to which the extreme parts were once connected still remains; in the absence of its earlier edges, it continues to transmit confused impressions to the brain. This is so, Dedlow explains, most of all in those cases in which the surviving nerve-ends are "enlarged and altered." Then the neural extremities, active in irritation, render the "brain ever mindful of the missing part." Hence, the reader infers, the feeling of burning in the "dead hand" Dedlow himself experienced, as well as the "sharp cramp" he felt in his lost leg, which can now be identified as instances of neuralgia in "missing parts." Hence, too, one presumes, the impressions the "larval creature" continued to retain long after losing both arms and legs, which preserve to him "a consciousness of possessing that which he has not."

The stay in Stump Hospital proves, therefore, an instructive period in Dedlow's unhappy life. But it brings him more than the discovery of sensation in the truncated part; now, at last, he begins to recover after the multiple amputations he has suffered. Through the regular administration of morphine to the sensitive portions of his skin, the pain he once felt in his right arm decreases, and, he recounts, in time "the sense of the existence of that limb gradually disappeared, as did that of my legs also."[7] Now he begins to experience "still more remarkable" feelings, psychological affections that follow on the heels of his newly regained physical health, such as it is:

> I found to my horror that at times I was less conscious of myself, of my own existence, than used to be the case. This sensation was so novel, that at first it quite bewildered me. I felt like asking some one

257

constantly if I really were George Dedlow or not; but, well aware how absurd I should seem after such a question, I refrained from speaking of my case, and strove more keenly to analyze my feelings. It was, as well as I can describe it, a deficiency in the egoistic sentiment of individuality.

Dedlow himself seems to have believed such psychological affections of absence to be the counterparts of the physical losses he had suffered, which were severe. In total, he surmises, "about one half of the sensitive surface of my skin was gone, and thus much of relation to the outer world destroyed"; many parts of his brain, moreover, which are normally concerned with locomotion and the movements of the limbs, "must be out of employ and, like other idle things, degenerating rapidly." The healthy patient concludes that, quite simply, his vital "economy" has been damaged beyond repair. Having lost part of his body, he imagines he will be forever sentenced to a sentiment of a corresponding loss in his "own existence." "Haunted and perplexed" by "the strange want," he finds himself increasingly "moody and wretched."[8]

It is in this state that George Dedlow encounters a man who promises him relief of a higher nature. While still a patient in Stump Hospital, Dedlow meets "a tall, loosely made person, with a pale face, light eyes of a washed-out blue tint, and very sparse whiskers," of whom he adds, moving on to the man's head, "I should have said, as a phrenologist, Will feeble, — emotional, but not passionate, — likely to be enthusiast, or weakly bigot." This man has suffered no amputation, although he does carry "one arm in a sling." As a result of a gunshot wound to his shoulder, he suffers from "what the doctors call paralysis of the median," as he explains to Dedlow. But that ailment seems to trouble him little, and he declares that as soon as his "time's out," he will "go back to Kearsage and try on the school-teaching again." The "loosely made person" tells Dedlow of the solace he has taken in an institution he calls the "New Church." "It's a great comfort for a plain man like me," he explains, "when he's weary and sick, to be able to turn away from earthly things, and hold converse daily with the great and good who have left the world."[9] Dedlow agrees that such communication would be consoling, "if only one could believe it"; provoked by the erstwhile physician's doubt, the ardent believer immediately promises Dedlow the proof he requires, if only he will come to a meeting of the new ecclesiastical institution.

Lent an ambulance by a well-meaning surgeon, Dedlow finds himself shortly thereafter, with his "new comrade," "in a house in Coates Street, where a 'circle' was in the daily habit of forming." There is a medium, around whom sit a small group of initiates: "a flabby man, with ill-marked baggy features, and injected eyes"; "a female, — authoress, I think, of two somewhat feeble novels"; "a pallid, care-worn girl"; and several others Dedlow does not deign to describe in detail. One after another, the members of the congregation ask the medium to summon a spirit, concentrating on the memory of a departed one, while uttering no names. Soon it is Dedlow's turn. Asked to "think of a spirit," "a wild idea," he tells us, "came into my head. I answered, 'I am thinking as you directed me to do.'" It is not long before the summoned spirit manifests itself. But it is, strangely, double, and its name, when spelled by the raps on the table, reveals itself to be numerical in nature: "4, 3, 6, 8; then a pause, and 3, 4, 8, 7."[10]

Questions put to the spirit disclose letters before the numbers, which, when transcribed by the "authoress," reveal the hidden identities of the dear departed: "UNITED STATES ARMY MEDICAL MUSEUM, NOS. 4368, 3487." As the medium looks up "with a puzzled expression," Dedlow names the two spirits he has summoned back to life:

> "Good gracious!" said I, "they are *my legs! My legs!*"
>
> What followed, I ask no one to believe, except those who, like myself, have communed with the beings of another sphere. Suddenly I felt a strange return of my self-consciousness. I was re-individualized, so to speak. A strange wonder filled me, and, to the amazement of every one, I arose, and, staggering a little, walked across the room on limbs invisible to them or me. It was no wonder I staggered, for, as I briefly reflected, my legs had been nine months in the strongest

alcohol. At this instant all my new friends crowded around me in astonishment. Presently, however, I felt myself sinking slowly. My legs were going, and in a moment I was resting on my two stumps upon the floor. It was too much. All that was left of me fainted and rolled over senseless.

The "Case" ends shortly thereafter, but not before Dedlow has assured his readers that the apparition of the absent limbs was both transitory and unrepeated. "I am now at home in the West," he comments, "surrounded by every form of kindness and every possible comfort; but alas! I have so little surety of being myself, that I doubt my own honesty in drawing my pension." One hope alone seems to sustain him as he takes leave of his reader. "It is needless to add," he concludes, "that I am not a happy fraction of a man; and that I am eager for the day when I shall rejoin the lost members of my corporeal family in another and happier world."[11]

"The Case of George Dedlow" met with astonishing success among the public of *The Atlantic Monthly*. Workers in the office of the surgeon general looked for the name of the pathetic "larval creature" among their records; many raised money to help support him; a subscription was taken out under his name; sympathetic readers sought to visit the "useless torso" in person at the mythic Stump Hospital of Philadelphia. But it was not to be, for a simple reason: there was no George Dedlow. Although he did not disclose the truth for many years after the publication of the "Case," the author of the work was in fact Silas Weir Mitchell, the great nineteenth-century scientist unanimously elected in 1874 to the position of the first president of the American Neurological Association.[12] Like Dedlow, Weir Mitchell was the son of a physician and had been a young man at the start of the Civil War. By 1861, however, he had finished his medical training, and when he did reach the Stump Hospital, it was as a surgeon, not a patient. He was not seriously wounded in the war, and, in contrast to the sad soldier of his "Case," he suffered no amputations. He studied "the limbless folk," however, with unprecedented attention, and in the works of his maturity he dedicated to them extended studies, which would earn him international acclaim. "The Case of George Dedlow" was the first of these. A literary fantasy of missing parts, it announced contributions in neurology that would forever transform the study of the living organism.

To be sure, many of the physiological and psychological phenomena described in chilling terms in Weir Mitchell's "Case" were not unknown at the time of its publication, at least to those trained in the medical sciences. Accounts of the loss of limbs, the persistence of sensations after the removal of bodily parts, and the wondrous restitution of severed members can all already be found in the literature and hagiography of the Middle Ages, the most well-known and often-cited examples being Peter of Grenoble's leg, John of Damascus's hand, and Gundrada's famous nose and lip, lost and miraculously recovered by divine favor.[13] The sixteenth-century French army surgeon Ambroise Paré was the first of the modern physicians to discuss the phenomenon when, in a chapter of his *Ten Books of Surgery*, he called attention to a "thing worthy of admiration, which is almost unbelievable to those who have not had experience of it" (*chose digne d'admiration, et quasi incredible à gens qui de ce n'ont expérience*): the fact, namely, that "long after an amputation is conducted, patients say they still feel pain in the dead and amputated parts."[14]

After Paré, references in philosophical and medical literature to the pain felt in absent limbs were far from uncommon. Discussing the essential uncertainty of sensory experience in the *First Meditation*, Descartes famously remarked that he had "learned from some persons whose arms and legs have been cut off, that they sometimes seemed to feel pain in the part which had been amputated."[15] In 1798, the German physician Aaron Lemos devoted an entire treatise to the explanation of what he called "the continuing pain of an amputated limb" (*Dolorem membri amputati remanentem explicat*).[16] And historians of science have recorded numerous references to the same phenomenon in the medical literature of the nineteenth century, the most far-reaching of whom was perhaps Charles Bell, who argued in the 1820s and 1830s that the perception of a missing limb was to be explained with reference to a sensory faculty beyond the classic five forms of perception: a sense of muscular effort and general exertion, by which "we know the relative position of an object to ourselves."[17]

It is nonetheless Weir Mitchell who has traditionally been credited with having offered the first great analysis of the sensory delusions provoked by the amputation of limbs in the terms of modern neurology. It was certainly he who named the phenomenon for posterity. His first scholarly contribution to the subject was an essay of 1871, published in *Lippincott's Magazine*, which bore the title "Phantom Limbs." Five years after "The Case of George Dedlow," this essay returned to the memorable setting of the gruesome tale. "Towards the end of the great rebellion," Weir Mitchell writes at the opening of this essay, "there existed in South street, Philadelphia, a hospital of several hundred beds, which was devoted altogether to the lodging and care of men in need of artificial limbs. It was known as the 'Stump Hospital,' and was certainly full of the strangest interest for even the least thoughtful observer." The neurologist notes that "the feelings and delusions entertained by men who have lost members have often been the subjects of casual notice in surgical treatises, from Ambroise Paré's time to our own." But he argues that "even in the best books there is as yet no clear and detailed statement as to this subject, which for interest alike popular and scientific is hardly to be surpassed, even in this time of scientific sensationalism."[18] It is this statement that Weir Mitchell seeks now to give.

"Phantom Limbs" begins by recalling a work of fiction: "an article," as Weir Mitchell calls it, "published in *The Atlantic Monthly* which purported to be the autobiography of an officer who had survived the loss of all his limbs.... This sketch," the physician comments, offered an "account of the sensations of men who have lost a limb or limbs." To this degree, it constituted a pertinent point of reference now. But the physician immediately adds that the author of the 1866 article, whom he does not name, "certainly could never have conceived it possible that his humorous sketch, with its absurd conclusion, would for a moment mislead any one"; as a neurologist, Weir Mitchell now takes it upon himself to "correct such erroneous beliefs as were caused by this *jeu d'esprit*." He observes that, from the physician's point of view, "the chief interest of the matter arises out of the fact that the 'stump,' as we call it — for, curiously enough, we have in medical language no Latin synonym for this term — is liable to the most horrible neuralgias, and to certain curious spasmodic maladies." It also tends, as "has long been known to surgeons," to continue to provoke in the sufferer a sensation of the missing limb. "Only about five per cent of the men who have suffered amputation never have any feeling of the part as being still present." All others continue, in one way or another, to sense it, some forgetting it in time, but most retaining "a sense of its existence so vivid as to be more definite and intrusive than is that of its truly living fellow-member."[19]

One year later, in 1872, Weir Mitchell published his last and perhaps greatest contribution to the scientific field he did so much to define: *Injuries of Nerves and Their Consequences*. The final chapter of this book, "Neural Maladies of Stumps," contains an extended treatment of sensory hallucinations, those "sensorial delusions to which persons are subject in connection with their lost limbs."[20] Here his terms are close, at times even identical, to those of "Phantom Limbs." As he did in that essay, the scientist dwells at length on the spectral quality of the absent limb. "Nearly every man who loses a limb," he explains in the 1872 book, "carries about with him a constant or inconstant phantom of the missing member, a sensory ghost of that much of himself, and sometimes a most inconvenient presence, faintly to be felt at times, but ready to be called up to his perception by a blow, a touch, or a change of wind."[21] "There is something almost tragical, something ghastly," he wrote in 1871, "in the notion of these thousands of spirit limbs haunting as many good soldiers, and every now and then tormenting them with the disappointments which arise when, the memory being off guard for a moment, the keen sense of the limb's presence betrays the man into some effort, the failure of which of a sudden reminds him of the loss."[22] Like a specter, the phantom limb can fade away, only to return unexpectedly years after its disappearance, and to vanish again, but even when felt as present, the neurologist explains, the absent member cannot clearly be situated with respect to the seen body, being "rarely felt as a whole."[23] With the sensed body, without being one with it, the "ghostly members" introduce into the field of perception a startling sensation that seems hardly one all.

Since Weir Mitchell's time, great scientific attention has been devoted to the analysis of phantom limbs. Today, readers interested in the startling medical phenomenon may consult a vast and varied literature on its various dimensions: neurological, psychological, psychoanalytic, and philosophical. They may also learn from several valuable studies about the history of investigations into the persistent pain of the amputated part.[24] It has perhaps never been noted, however, that in the same years in which the American neurologist published his famous accounts of sensory hallucinations of missing limbs, a French psychiatrist offered the first descriptions of a class of "sensorial delusions" that were at least as curious. Like the illusions identified by Weir Mitchell, these perceptions troubled the understanding of living beings' physiological and psychological senses of their own bodies.

When the eleventh volume of the *Archives de neurologie* appeared in 1882, it contained an extended medical study by a student of Paul Broca and Jean-Martin Charcot whose name remains to this day little known outside France.[25] He was Jules Cotard, and he began his essay with a tribute to Charles Lasègue, a physician who had published "an important report" in 1856 on melancholic ailments, paying particular attention to persecution delirium. Cotard recalled that the 1860s and 1870s had witnessed significant progress in research into the diverse symptoms and structures of melancholia. As evidence, he cited the works of Bénédict Auguste Morel, Achille Foville, Henri Legrand du Saulle, and especially Jules Falret, who had recently presented a summary of the successive phases and evolution of mental and nervous illnesses before the Société Médico-psychologique.[26] But the author immediately added that much more was still to be learned in the study of melancholia, which was by 1882 well advanced.

Scholars "have offered careful descriptions of simple melancholia, melancholia with stupor, and anxious melancholia; they have established that these forms are often intermittent, that sometimes they become continuous and chronic." Nonetheless, Cotard wrote, "the characteristics and the successive phases of the delirium that end in this chronic state have not, to my knowledge, been the object of any study equivalent to the study offered for persecution delirium."[27]

Cotard declared that he would now "exhibit a particular development of delirium," to which, in accordance with scientific custom, he proceeded to assign a technical name: "negation delirium." He quickly explained the designation. "If one asks them what their name is," Cotard wrote, introducing the ailing patients he would now discuss, "they do not have one." If one asks them their age, "they do not have an age." "Where were they born? They were not born. Who were their father and mother? They have no father, mother, and no children." But these negating melancholics presented the physician with a further characteristic, which was even stranger, for it touched on the physiological object of medicine itself: the body. When asked if they suffered from headaches, stomachaches, "pains in any part of the body whatsoever," the delirious patients answered in terms no less astonishing for their simplicity. "They have no head. They have no stomach. Some," Cotard wrote, "have no body."[28]

A few pages later, the psychiatrist offered a summary typology of the ailments he believed he had identified. Before introducing a host of clinical evidence, he explained that he would adopt a threefold system of classification, distinguishing among several categories of a single malady: "cases in which negation delirium presents itself in its simplicity"; those in which negation delirium is, by contrast, "symptomatic of general paralysis"; and those in which negation delirium is associated with persecution delirium, constituting "forms of complex alienation," such as "ideas of ruin, guilt, distrust, and persecution" which "almost all other authors" had failed to tell apart from straightforward melancholic delirium. As an illustration, Cotard offered a selection of clinical cases drawn from the notes he has taken as a practicing physician at the psychiatric center of Vanves in the 1860s, 1870s, and 1880s:

> Madame E., fifty-four years of age, married, mother, is put in the Vanves medical center June 15, 1863, after having made various suicide attempts. Madame E. is in a state of anxious agitation.... She imagines that she has a shrunken throat and a displaced heart. In paroxysms of agitation, she cries out and complains aloud, always repeating the same sentences. All her organs have been displaced; she cannot do anything about it....
>
> 1864. — Same delirium, same anxious paroxysms, with the continual repetition of the same formulaic phrases. Madame E.... is lost; she no longer has a head; she no longer has a body....
> The negation delirium becomes ever more forceful. Madame E.... has neither arms nor legs. All the parts of her body have been transformed....[29]
>
> Madame C., forty-three years of age, married, mother, entered the Vanves health center in November, 1880.... Madame C. believes she no longer has a stomach; she believes that her organs have been destroyed and attributes this destruction to an emetic that was in fact administered to her.... Madame C. claims that her throat has been removed, that she no longer has a stomach, that she no longer has any blood.[30]
>
> Monsieur A., forty-eight years of age, put in the Vanves health center in March, 1879, following a suicide attempt, is in a state of intense anxious agitation.... His brain has turned soft; his head is like a hollow nutshell. He has no penis; he has no testicles; he no longer has anything at all.[31]
>
> Monsieur C., forty-five years of age, of a sturdy constitution, married, father.... Sometime near March, 1880, he began to express negative and completely absurd ideas.... Brought to Vanves in April, 1880.... Monsieur C. insists that he is not married, that he does not have children, that he has neither a father nor a mother, that he has no name.... Monsieur C. resists all care taken as to his body; he

refuses to don clothing because his whole body is nothing other than a large nut. He refuses to eat, for he has no mouth; he refuses to walk, for he has no legs.[32]

Cotard published reports of a total of eleven such cases, to which he added a series of bibliographic indications for further study, as well as a synoptic table in which he presented the similarities between the negation delirium he had observed and the persecution delirium considered by others before him.[33] By the conclusion of the second portion of his study, which bore the programmatic title "Du délire des négations" (On Negation Delirium), the defining traits of the new ailment were beyond all doubt. The various melancholic patients the French psychiatrist had observed all suffered, in different ways, from a single sensory delusion: with great insistence, they felt the lack of bodily parts that they nevertheless did, by all objective accounts, possess.

Cotard's two-part paper of 1882 was followed by three further clinical and theoretical contributions to the study of forms of melancholic delirium: "Loss of Mental Vision in Anxious Melancholia," published in 1884; "On the Psychosensorial or Psychomotor Origin of Delirium," from 1887; and "Enormity Delirium," which appeared in 1888.[34] That year, the psychiatrist's contributions abruptly ended: the French physician had been assiduously treating his own daughter at Vanves when he acquired and succumbed to a case of diphtheria. Three years later, in 1892, his colleagues dedicated the third annual conference of their association for the study of mental illness to his memory.[35] The report on the "conference of Blois," as it is called, contains mention of contributions by such figures as Falret, Garnier, Charpentier, and Jules Séglas, who had himself published a response to Cotard's "Negation Delirium," titled "Anxious Melancholia with Negation Delirium," as early as 1887.[36] It is at this point that the psychological phenomenon identified by Cotard can be said to enter the clinical vocabulary of nineteenth-century French psychiatry as a whole, above all through its definition as a "psychic state proper to the chronically anxious" and, therefore, less as a "delirium" in its own right than as a "syndrome": "Cotard syndrome," as Emmanuel Régis baptized it at the 1892 conference, and as it would subsequently be known.[37]

Discussing the curious syndrome in a lecture called "Negation Delirium in Anxious Melancholia" given and published in 1894, Séglas argued that the ailment identified by Cotard could, in fact, manifest itself in several distinct forms, which ought to be clearly separated by the clinician and the theorist.[38] Each form of the malady could be defined, he argued, by the type of object it involved. An anxious melancholic may deny aspects of his or her "moral or intellectual personality": "He then declares, for example, that 'he no longer has a heart, no longer has feelings, no longer has a mind, and no longer thinks.'" He may also negate objects in the external world. "One shows him a flower," for instance, "and he denies that it is a flower; there is nothing around him, neither things nor people; he is in a void." And, finally, he may deny his "physical personality." "This," Séglas wrote, "is the hypochondriac of negation," the figure so vividly evoked in Cotard's first essay. "The patient says: 'I no longer have blood; I no longer have veins; I no longer have a brain; I no longer have genital organs. I am as empty as a cupboard.'"[39]

On the surface, to be sure, such symptoms of unease may appear remarkable and even quite unique. They seem a far cry, it could be said, from those described by Weir Mitchell in the aftermath of the American Civil War. And some differences between the sensory delusions identified in the United States and those described in France are certainly beyond all doubt. The first of the two ailments is neurological in nature and can be explained with reference to the functions and dysfunctions of the sensory apparatus in its physiological structure. The second malady, which is, rather, psychiatric and psychological, points to an anxious melancholia. But the sensation of the phantom limb and the perception of the negated part also bear resemblances that can hardly be denied. To be more precise, one seems to be the mirror image of the other. A moment's reflection suffices to grasp the point. Those who suffer from "neural maladies of stumps" feel limbs they do not possess as if they did; those who suffer from the "delirium of negation" sense the limbs they do possess as if they did not. One might easily multiply such formulations. The patients described by Weir Mitchell sense in their bodies a presence none but they can see; those identified by Cotard, instead, sense in their bodies absences that none but they will grant. The first of the two sets feel themselves to possess that which, by all accounts, they lack; the second feel themselves to lack that which, by all appearances, they do possess.

In all these variously deluded sensations, the reality of one fact cannot be denied. The nineteenth-century perceptions of parts, present and absent alike, remit those who feel them to a being, affirmed or negated, that is neither a thinking thing within them nor an extended thing beyond them, neither their own consciousness and mind nor any worldly object clearly external to themselves. In feeling themselves to be more and less than they seem beyond all doubt to be, the veteran and the melancholic patient bear witness to a common difficulty of representing the nature and parts of their own organic mass. They can all be said to suffer from disturbances of the shared feeling that was coenesthesis; they all fall prey to disorders of the single "vital sense" thought to inform the mind of the parts and portions of the body that is its own. To this degree, the nineteenth-century medical figures also cast a new light upon it. Feeling the presence of limbs where they are absent, sensing the absence of parts where they are present, the patients described by Weir Mitchell and by Cotard reveal the "general perception" to be a thing the physicians before them could hardly have anticipated. For that perception, the ailing figures all suggest, is the perception of a phantom: a being that, whether felt in presence or in absence, is, by scientific standards, none.

"Delusion" is one name for such a feeling, which cannot be referred to any object seen or named by the specialists in the study of the body and the soul. And the neurological and psychiatric figures described by Weir Mitchell and by Cotard seem without a doubt to have been in part deceived about the internal and external extensions of the bodies they called their own. But the truth of the matter is more complex than such a summary judgment would suggest. For however deranged they seemed and still seem today, the nineteenth-century sensations contained at least one veritable "metaphysical discovery," which concerned the nature of the general perception of organic existence as such. All the men and women who felt themselves to be where they were not, and all those who failed to feel themselves to be where they nevertheless did seem to be, perceived one fundamental fact that few scientists and scholars in their age and after it have registered with equal force: the ultimate delusion may be to believe that sentient beings, in sickness or in health, could perceive their bodies to be wholes composed of anything but ghostly parts.

CHAPTER TWENTY-FOUR

The Anaesthetic Animal

Of modern Psychiatry and its Discovery of People who sense,
with much Conviction, that they do not exist

There can be little doubt that in ethics, as in other domains, the classical philosophers differed among themselves. But from a modern standpoint, there seems at least one point on which they can be said largely to have concurred. The ancient thinkers all assumed that an ethical being is by nature a sensitive being, consigned from birth to a life in which perceptions, misleading or propitious, cannot be avoided. This may well be why, in their books on the good and happy life, the classical philosophers sought precisely to define the nature of sensitive impressions and the forms by which they are best mastered. Like all affections of the body and the soul, sensations were to be correctly understood and ordered, since, in any case, they could never altogether be set aside. To be sure, the medical authorities of Antiquity were familiar with states in which perceptual activities could cease. These were pathologies of insensibility, for which the classical physicians employed several technical terms: *mōrōsis, agrupnos kōma, lethargus,* and *anaesthesia,* all names for conditions close to the general numbness that defines the modern psychiatric and neurological category of "stupor."[1] But the philosophers, for their part, seem to have considered such cases barely worthy of mention, and their works contain few serious discussions of the possibility that human beings might find themselves, for one reason or another, lacking in sensations.

271

A brief passage of the *Nicomachean Ethics* is exemplary in this regard. It can be found in the third book of the treatise, where Aristotle offers an extended account of virtue, vice, and the sensations of pleasure and pain. Excessive feelings of enjoyment and hurt, Aristotle affirms, lead naturally to profligacy (*akolasia*). This vice can be opposed to two virtues: temperance (*sōphrosunē*), the proper enjoyment of pleasure in moderation, and courage (*andreia*), the endurance of a pain that cannot be avoided.[2] At this point, the Philosopher pauses to add a note on method. He concisely recalls that abuses of sensation are vices of excess, not debility, for he judges it unlikely, if not impossible, that people would feel less, rather than more, than they ought. "Men erring on the side of deficiency as regards pleasures, and taking less than a proper amount of enjoyment in them," he writes, "are scarcely to be found." In his eyes, it is, quite simply, a matter of nature: "Such insensibility," he explains, "is not human" (*ou gar anthrōpikē estin hē toiautē anaisthēsia*). But there is more: it is not even animal. "Even the lower beasts," the philosopher continues, "discriminate in food, and like some kinds and not others; and if there be a creature that finds nothing pleasant, and sees no difference between one thing and another, it must be very far removed from humanity." Hence the absence of any term for such hypothetical beings: "As people of this type hardly ever occur," Aristotle curtly concludes, "we have no special name for them."[3]

By the first half of the nineteenth century, "people of this type" began to be found, and it was not long before they were also named. They were discovered with some astonishment and excitement by psychiatrists, whose observations and analyses gradually led to the identification of forms of insensibility that Aristotle, for one, most likely never imagined. Étienne Esquirol has traditionally been considered the first to have described the new medical phenomenon. In his *Mental Illnesses Considered from Medical, Hygienic, and Medico-Legal Perspectives* of 1838 the French physician reported that he had treated "many patients" who all reported, in similar terms, that they had lost the various forms of sensation that had once been theirs. "I hear, I see, I touch," they would explain to him, "but I am not as before; things do not come to me; they cannot be identified with my being; a thick veil, a cloud has changed the color and aspect of things."[4]

> The functions and acts of ordinary life are still left to me, but in every one of them there is something lacking — that is, the sensation which is proper to them.... Each of my senses, each part of my proper self is as if it were separated from myself and can no longer afford me any sensation. This impossibility seems to depend upon a void which I feel in the front of my head and to be due to a diminished sensibility over my whole body, for it seems to me that I never actually reach the objects that I touch. I no longer experience the internal feeling of the air when I breathe.... My eyes see and my spirit perceives, but the sensation of what I see is completely absent.[5]

Also in 1838, A. Zeller recorded strikingly similar findings. He had treated five patients, all of whom "complained in almost the same terms of a lack of sensations." "To them," he wrote, "it was a total lack of feelings, as if they were dead."[6] By 1845, Griesinger could write of the same symptoms as the signs of a new malady: in his words, "a very different kind of anaesthesia" from the one known to the medical tradition. Citing the patient seen by Esquirol, Griesinger commented that "we sometimes hear the insane, especially melancholics, complain of a very different kind of anaesthesia.... 'I see, I hear, I fear,' they say, 'but the object does not reach me; I cannot receive the sensation; it seems to me that there is a wall between me and the external world.'"[7]

The medical literature on the subject was greatly enriched in 1873. This was the year that the Hungarian psychiatrist Maurice Krishaber published a monograph on a physiopsychological malady that deeply troubled the faculties of sensation as a whole. "I have gathered together a great number of observations," Krishaber wrote at the opening of the work, "on a nervous illness which has not been described, and which affects an invariable type. I designate it by the name of cerebro-cardiac neuropathy."[8] The patients described by the Hungarian physician suffered from various symptoms, several of which had been recorded by Esquirol. The subject of the second "observation" recorded in the book, once a colonel in the English army, explained to Krishaber that he could no longer perceive the world about him as he had always done. He was now sentenced, as he declared, to a "sense of *profound isolation*": "I felt as if I was almost entirely separated from the world," he explained, "and as if there was some barrier between me and it."[9]

The subject of Krishaber's thirty-eighth and final "observation" found himself in an even more drastic state. He reported that, while awake and "drinking only the purest water," he could not escape "sensations of dreaming, emptiness, drunkenness." As he fell ill, his senses seemed to grow progressively weaker and more deranged. "I could feel," he recalled to Krishaber, "that my senses were perverted and giving me a false idea of what lay around me." He could no longer distinguish by sight between "apparitions" and "the real world," and his "troubles of hearing" were "even more pronounced." "I could not recognize the place of origin of sounds," he declared, "and not only the voice of my interlocutors, but even my own voice seemed to be coming from far away; all my impressions were so strange that I was as if constantly *stunned*. Very often it seemed to me that my head was no longer attached to my body, and it was the same with my legs, which seemed to move without the intervention of my will."[10]

Krishaber's book, titled *On Cerebro-Cardiac Neuropathy*, was clearly a medical study, but it touched on questions that interested thinkers no less than physicians. It quickly found a public well beyond the psychiatric profession, the most famous and influential of its readers being Hippolyte Taine. Taine's interest in the monograph was such that he wrote to the physician to ask him for access to the medical records of his published "observations." Krishaber obliged, and news of the medical monograph, as a result, found its way into a lengthy appendix of Taine's widely read treatise *On Intelligence*.[11] Here Taine announced in an extended note, "On the Elements and the Formation of the Idea of the Self," that "under the name of cerebro-cardiac neuropathy,

Dr. Krishaber describes an illness in which one can see very well how the idea of the self is made and unmade."[12]

Taine began by recalling that, as Krishaber presents it, "the visible symptom" of the malady is above all one of perception: "a perversion of sensations," to be precise, no more and no less. "This perversion," Taine explained, "does not touch judgment, reason, memory, and the other activities that surpass raw sensation. All those functions remain intact."[13] Strictly speaking, therefore, the patient cannot be said to be mad. He has merely lost his senses. "But," Taine continued,

> since the illness almost always arrives all at once, the effect is immense. One cannot do better than to compare the state of the patient to that of a caterpillar that, keeping all its ideas and all its memories of being a caterpillar, all of a sudden became a butterfly, with the senses and sensations of a butterfly. Between the old state and the new, between the first self, which belongs to the caterpillar, and the second, which belongs to the butterfly, there is a profound scission, a complete rupture. The new sensations cannot be integrated into any earlier series; the patient can no longer interpret them or make use of them; he no longer recognizes them and they are unknown to him. Two strange conclusions then follow. The first consists in saying: *I am not.* The second, which follows a little later, consists in saying: *I am another.*[14]

A "perversion of sensation" thus leads ineluctably to the demise and doubling of the self: once new perceptions can no longer be inscribed in the "series" of the old, the patient, while still a cogent and cogitating being, no longer feels that he is himself.[15] To Taine, the medical finding was in this sense of great philosophical import, and he did not hesitate to assert that "this little tale [*ce petit récit*]," as he termed Krishaber's thirty-eighth observation, "is more instructive than a metaphysical work on the substance of the self." "Thus," he concluded, "the *I*, the moral person, is a product of which sensations are the primary factors.... When these sensations suddenly become other, the self

275

becomes other and appears as *another*; they must then become the same again for the self to become the same and once again appear as the same."[16] That thesis, to be sure, was speculative in character. But, Taine commented, "here experience confirms theory; and, in effect, according to Dr. Krishaber, 'the particular perturbation by virtue of which the patient to a certain point loses the feeling of his own person does not cease until the sensorial troubles to which it is linked also cease.'"[17]

Krishaber was hardly the last nineteenth-century psychiatrist to report cases of speaking beings asserting, with much conviction, that they had ceased to sense and to sense themselves. Without mentioning the inventor of "cerebro-cardiac neuropathy," Schäfer, for example, reported in a psychiatric paper published in 1880 that he had treated patients who "complained of suffering" but refused to refer their pain to any portion of a felt body: "They relate it explicitly to an emptiness, hollowness in their head, or in the pit of their stomach."[18] Schäfer believed such subjects to suffer from a variety of melancholy to which he gave a new name: *melancholia anaesthetica*.[19] And in 1896, Ribot described a similar set of symptoms, which he treated as examples of "doubt delirium" (*le délire du doute*): an "absolute skepticism, which," he argued, "bears not only on ideas, abstract concepts, memories, thoughts, but even on perceptions."[20] "I exist," one of the French professor's patients had exemplarily declared, "but outside real life and despite myself.... Something which seems to be my body at times incites me to act as before; but I cannot truly believe that my actions are real.... My individuality has completely disappeared. The way in which I see things makes me incapable of recognizing them, of feeling that they exist. Even while touching and seeing, the world seems to me to be a huge hallucination.... I am perfectly conscious of the absurdity of these judgments, but I cannot surmount them."[21]

It was Ludovic Dugas who coined the most famous term for the cluster of symptoms of insensibility famously described and commented on by Esquirol, Krishaber, Taine, and Ribot. In an article published in the *Revue philosophique de Paris et l'étranger* in

1898, Dugas announced that he would discuss a type of illness "which we have often had the occasion to observe, to which attention has often been brought," and which, he commented, "may even be said to be classic." He nevertheless argued that the medical phenomenon still remained to be correctly understood and named, both by patients and by their physicians. As an example, Dugas recalled Ribot's patient, who had claimed that the world seemed to him "a huge hallucination." "The subject believes that he is explaining his case in saying he dreams," Dugas commented, "and, on our side, we believe that we understand what he is saying by that." But the truth is the patient and the physician now fall prey to the same delusion. To dream is to take a hallucination to be real. The victim of "doubt delirium" suffers, in truth, from an inverse illusion: the subject of "a *reverse dream*," he takes reality to be a hallucination.[22] Unlike the dreamer, the anaesthetic subject therefore affirms nothing. At best, he "doubts," as Ribot had claimed.

Dugas, however, went further. "Is the word 'doubt,'" he asked, "exact?" Such a usage would imply that the patient is uncertain about the existence of things. But "in reality the subject does not doubt things; he is simply a stranger to them, or, if one prefers, things seem strange to him." On this matter, Dugas cited Taine approvingly. The patient in question is not mad, and he can discuss his delusions with considerable cogency. But still Dugas would not grant Taine's claim that the ailment constituted a "perversion of sensations," for the subject's sensations, he argued, never ceased. They simply seemed fundamentally "strange," beginning with those involving the patient's own mind and body. The subject's voice "sounds *strange* to his ears"; it seems to "come from afar." And so it is, Dugas wrote, with each of his acts: "When he speaks, when he acts and when he senses, the subject cannot believe that it is he who speaks, who acts and who senses. He is, as it were, detached from what he experiences, and he is stunned to experience it." Hence the designation Dugas adopted for this curious condition, which involves neither dreaming nor doubt: "To this state in which the self feels its own acts escaping it and

277

becoming strange," Dugas asserted, "I will give the name *alienation of personality* or *depersonalization*."[23]

"Depersonalization" was soon to become a central term in psychiatric discourse. Dugas himself played an important role in arguing for the neologism as the proper designation of the "classic" illness of the age. After devoting several papers in the 1890s to "cases of depersonalization," in 1911 he published a book on the subject with F. Moutier that bore the simple title *Dépersonnalisation*.[24] But although Dugas was certainly responsible for the medical usage, he was not the first to employ the curious expression in print. He had drawn the term, as he later made clear, from a work that was not medical but literary and philosophical in nature: Henri-Frédéric Amiel's *Fragments of an Intimate Journal*. In an entry from July 8, 1880, a year before his death, the Swiss writer had written in his diary, "At present I can contemplate existence more or less beyond the grave, from the beyond; everything is strange to me; I can be outside my body and my self; I am *depersonalized*, detached, away" (*à présent je puis considérer l'existence à peu près comme d'outre-tombe, comme d'au-delà; tout m'est étrange; je puis être en dehors de mon corps et de mon individu, je suis* dépersonnalisé, *détaché, envolé*). Such words were strong and striking, as Amiel, placing the term "depersonalized" in italics, was well aware. The literary author had clearly anticipated that they might be read as a confession of delusion. "Is this madness?" the writer therefore asked after recording his "depersonalized" state. The answer was unambiguous. "No," he wrote. "Madness is the impossibility of returning to one's equilibrium after erring in foreign forms, after dangerous visits to invisible worlds. Madness is not being able to judge oneself and to stop oneself. But it seems to me that my mental transformations are nothing other than philosophical experiments."[25]

Dugas seems to have taken these "philosophical experiments" as the record of psychological states in need of psychiatric elucidation, for by all appearances he understood the 1880 journal entry to be "a literal description of Amiel's mental experience," as Mauricio Sierra and German E. Berrios have observed.[26] But the force of Amiel's own note of explanation can hardly be denied. The idea of an "alienation of personality," a state of being "detached, away" from one's own self, acquires its full meaning when considered as a hypothesis concerning the nature and limits of eminently philosophical notions: the self, the person, and that elusive being known since the seventeenth century by the name of "consciousness." No less than Krishaber's "little tale," Amiel's remarks bore on the metaphysical question of what Taine had called "the substance of the self." Like Krishaber's "cerebro-cardiac" observations, moreover, they suggested that the problem had been fundamentally misunderstood on at least one point: its "substance." If the self could be "detached, away," then it could by no means be presupposed as permanently present; if the "person," in the terms of nineteenth-century psychiatry, could be "alienated" within a speaking subject, then it could not be said to be strictly necessary to conscious life. In the science of the mind, the discovery of "cases of depersonalization" implied nothing less. Human beings, it now seemed, could live well after the demise of their "selves," and they could reason, with the lucidity of the sane, in the absence of their own "persons."

This conclusion followed from the clinical accounts published by Esquirol, Krishaber, and Ribot, but it also resonated with more general principles in the psychiatric science of the age. It was, in a certain sense, anticipated by the most philosophical of the modern French psychiatrists, Pierre Janet, who had formulated a new program for psychology in his major work of 1889, *Psychological Automatism*. This book sought to bring the methods and findings of experimental science to bear on phenomena that had rarely been examined with precision: "the inferior forms of human activity." Trained as a philosopher, Janet knew well that the very idea of "inferior forms of human activity" was hardly admissible in the terms of at least one major current of modern thought, namely, Cartesianism. In the first chapter of his book, therefore, he made his own position perfectly clear. "Some philosophers," he wrote, "following the Cartesians, have represented consciousness as something invariable and immutable, without nuances and without degrees. For Descartes, thought existed complete, with doubt, reflection, reasoning and language; otherwise it did not exist at all and found itself replaced by mechanism pure and simple, by extension and movement." But another philosopher of the modern age, he continued, had disagreed, opposing the Cartesian doctrine of the mind in implacable terms. "Leibniz, on the contrary," Janet recalled, "in this profound philosophy, to which all the physical and moral sciences seem to return us, had a completely different conception of consciousness. He admitted an infinite number of degrees, and some of these forms seemed to him so inferior to normal thought that 'human minds are like little gods compared to them.'"[27]

For Janet, as for Leibniz, to posit such "an infinite number of degrees" in the mind was not to contest the reality of thought. It was, instead, to situate the cogitative activity within a continuum of mental states that stretches from reasoned reflection to unconscious forms no less important for their relative "inferiority." "Let us take human consciousness in its regular and realized form," Janet urged, "and successively remove all the perfections it has acquired, but which are not essential to it."[28] Much will be left below reason, which stands at the "most elevated level" of mental activity. Immediately beneath it, one will encounter perception, intact and complete in the absence of all cognition. Consider, as an illustration, what happens when one opens one's eyes and, on the basis of a number of diverse sensations, perceives that one is standing before a tree. This is certainly "a psychological phenomenon of some complexity," which involves the correlation of numerous distinct sensations of form, size, color, and position; still, it is not a reasoned thought. And beneath such perception one reaches a more minor form of human activity still: sensation. Janet observed that this act has at times been described as "the simple phenomenon that occurs in *me* when *I* see, when I hear, etc." But such a definition of sensation, he wrote, "contains one term too many: it is the word *me*, the word *I*." The truth is that if one considers sensations from "an exclusively psychological perspective, if one considers the *self* not as a being or a cause, one will be obliged to think that there are sensations without a self, that there can be phenomena of vision despite the fact that no one says: 'I see.'" The idea of the self, Janet noted, is "an extremely complicated psychological phenomenon," which implies a host of factors: memories of our past experience, our abilities, our body, our powers, "even our name." "If one considers a simple sensation, it contains nothing at all of that and it is not sufficient on its own to form such a complex idea."[29]

"This truth," Janet observed, had been expressed by "a great number of philosophers." He recalled that Cudworth, Bonnet, and Buffon were all willing to grant animals "feeling without thought" (*le sentiment sans la pensée*), a thing inconceivable were sensation not in itself independent of reasoned reflection. Above all, he invoked Maine de Biran, that "precursor of scientific and experimental psychology," who in his late *Anthropology* defined "affection" as "that which remains of a complete sensation after one has separated from it all individual personality."[30] But by Janet's time, psychiatric science had confirmed the fact: blackouts, nervous crises, hypnotic sleep, and fainting fits all furnished the philosopher with examples of states in which the mind persists beyond any consciousness of a self. Here Janet could cite an illustrious contemporary: "During a fainting spell," Alexandre Herzen had explained in his study of the brain and cerebral activity of 1887, "it is psychic nothingness, the total absence of consciousness; then one begins to have a vague, unlimited, infinite feeling, a feeling of existence in general, without any delimitation of one's own individuality, without the slightest trace of any distinction between the *I* and the non-*I*."[31]

It can hardly be considered surprising that Janet showed the greatest of interest in the phenomenon designated by Dugas as "depersonalization." This condition could be understood to provide a perfect illustration of one of the fundamental principles of *Psychological Automatism*: that mental activity can persist in the diminution and even absence of any *I*. And, when Janet published *Obsessions and Psychasthenia*, in 1903, he devoted considerable attention to the "alienation of the person" as an exemplary variety of mental infirmity. In a major portion of the book devoted to "feelings of incompletion" (*sentiments d'incomplétude*), he turned at several points to the famous cases described by Esquirol, Krishaber, Dugas, and Ribot, citing his predecessors and the phenomena they had exhaustively reported. First he dealt with the alienated subjects in a section called "Feelings of Incompletion in Intellectual Operations," as he focused on "feelings of incomplete perception"; then he invoked them in a section titled "Feelings of Incompletion in Emotion," concentrating on "feelings of indifference"; finally, he considered them in a section called "Feelings of Incompletion in Personal Perception," where he also cited Jules Séglas's work on obsession. In a concluding treatment of "feelings of complete depersonalization," Janet wrote that "what characterizes the feeling of depersonalization ... is that the subject feels his person to be incomplete, unrealized. 'I cannot reach the idea of my person,'" he cited one of his patients as explaining, "'I cannot reach myself.'"[32]

Janet put great emphasis on the importance of understanding such claims properly. It would be an error, he maintained, to take the ailing patients simply at their word. For they did not truly mean it, as they themselves were, in the final analysis, aware. "In the end," Janet wrote of the depersonalized subjects, with some severity, "they all know well that they are not really doubled, and they know that they are not dead; despite their often exaggerated expressions, they do not have a positive feeling of multiplicity and death." Such a feeling, the philosopher-psychiatrist wrote, would be "contradictory and unachievable." The "completely depersonalized" subjects feel, in truth, a sentiment that Janet presented as decidedly more coherent but that, to the untrained reader, may seem no less strange. If one believes the physician, the alienated subjects perceive, with painful clarity, that they are not more but less than one. "What they really have," Janet thus explained, "is a negative feeling of not being unitary enough, of not being alive enough, of not being real enough. This is what they ought to say, and indeed one can get them to say it easily enough if one insists a bit: 'I do not feel the reality of my person enough.'"[33]

Janet turned to the same alienated subjects again in one of his final and most important works, *From Anguish to Ecstasy: Studies on Beliefs and Feelings*, published in two volumes in 1926 and 1928. Now he considered them all subjects of a single experience: "a negative feeling, such as a feeling of absence, and the disappearance of normal feelings," which, for the purposes of economy, Janet designated by the single name of "feelings of emptiness" (*sentiments du vide*).[34] These are feelings of weakened and deranged powers of perception, which involve both things sensed and the sensing thing that is the body and its mind. One patient complains, for instance, that "objects have become all flat"; in a "neighboring form" of the ailment, Janet wrote, "things grow small and draw away to infinity," as when another subject tells him "the Eiffel Tower has grown so small that one would think oneself in Lilliput."[35] Other patients describe a troubled sense of corporeal space, with clear symptoms of "Cotard syndrome": "a patient . . . complains of not being able to feel certain parts of his body and not being able to recognize the position of his limbs."[36] And in the most radical cases, patients declare that they no longer feel themselves at all. "I have lost myself," Anna, "a girl of twenty-four years of age," tells Janet. "It is funny to have the same face and the same name, and not to be the same person." In a similar predicament, Laetitia assures the physician that he has never truly seen "the real Laetitia." "If I knew where she was, I'd show her to you," she assures the doctor, "but I can't find her." "Zd.," once a captain and the father of a family, "is always moaning 'because he no longer finds himself in his old skin, which he preferred to this one.'" "I can't find myself," he explains to his physician. "It is not I who am sick; it is not I who am sad; it is not I who am old; it is not I who am a child; I am not I at all. What is lacking is myself. It is terrible to elude oneself, to live and not to be oneself" (*Je ne retrouve moi-même. Je ne suis pas Moi malade, je ne suis pas Moi triste, je ne suis pas Moi vieilli, je ne suis pas Moi enfant, je ne suis pas Moi du tout. Ce qui me manque, c'est moi-même, c'est terrible de s'échapper à soi-même, de vivre et de n'être pas soi-même*).[37]

In *From Anguish to Ecstasy*, Janet offered a new interpretation of the nature of such sentiments of absence. It followed from a principle he had held for many years: the "essential point," in his words, "that a scientific psychology must consider psychological facts as actions and express them in terms of action."[38] From such a perspective, he could regard feelings of emptiness as symptoms of a "disorder" (*trouble*) in the functions that define the activity of the mind. These, he maintained, are of two levels. First, there are "primary actions": the immediate results of "stimulation from the external world," be it the jerk of a knee or the memory provoked by the sight of a familiar object.[39] Then there are "secondary actions." These may formally resemble primary actions, but the stimulus that provokes them is not external but internal. "If, when asked a question, I answer absent-mindedly with a silly remark," Janet explains, "that remark constitutes a primary action"; if, "immediately afterward, I murmur 'Idiot!' to myself," that act, by contrast, may be termed secondary.[40] Secondary actions, the psychiatrist explains, thus tie primary actions to one another. Constantly responding to primary responses, secondary actions form "a host of echoes and harmonics," "thousands of resonances," in which each of the primary actions "brutally determined by the external world" can be integrated into a single "impression of life, spontaneity, and even certainty." When secondary action fails, therefore, the effect is immediate. "Primary action, however correct, feels strange in isolation." Abstracted from the flow of secondary actions that is their element, perceptions, memories, acts, and impressions no longer seem to exist "in the real world." This was a fact that Captain Zd. had already noted "with various metaphors." He complained of the "discomfort he felt on account of 'the suppression of that continual murmuring, that bright swarming that used to fill his mind and that was now replaced by the back of his brain.'"[41]

Those terms are striking, not least for the echo they contain of a scientific concept with which Janet, if not Captain Zd. himself, was no doubt quite familiar: "permanent sensation," that activity of the living organism which Lamarck believed to be "executed in all the sensible parts of the body, in general and without discontinuity, during the entire course of the individual's life," which "results from the vital movements, the displacements of fluids, and the frictions brought about by these displacements ... and which may even produce a special noise that we distinguish very well in our heads."[42] Bereft of the "secondary action" of the mind, the depersonalized patient would seem to be shorn, by that same token, of this permanent sensation: devoid of the common faculty defined by the modern medical and psychological tradition and reduced, therefore, to exclusively particular perceptions. And, to be sure, many of the nineteenth- and twentieth-century psychiatrists viewed "feelings of emptiness" as precisely that: symptoms of a malady of coenesthesis, a "coenesthopathy," to employ the term coined by Ernest Dupré and Paul Camus in 1907 as a name for "alterations of common or internal sensibility, that is, disorders involving those sensations that incessantly reach the brain from all the parts of the body."[43]

Janet himself would not grant that the "feelings of emptiness" to which he had devoted such care were indeed instances of "perturbations" of the common feeling. This was an interpretation of the phenomenon that antedated his work on the subject and which could be found in many of the first theorists of the condition, who had treated symptoms of insensibility as signs of an ailment of the perceptual power as a whole. But the understanding of "depersonalization" as a disorder of the common feeling also outlasted Janet; it continued to furnish psychiatrists with elements of an analysis of the symptoms of what had once been dubbed "anaesthetic melancholia" well into the second half of the twentieth century. Paul Schilder and Henri Baruk, for example, drew on the idea of "coenesthopathy" to define a host of symptoms intimately related to those described by the nineteenth-century physicians: symptoms such as "impressions of emptiness," "sensations of lack, deficit in existence," "feelings of death," and delusional perceptions of the disappearance of the "feeling of life and the existence of bodily or spiritual personality, either entirely or partially."[44]

In time, the idea of a disorder of the common feeling naturally gave way to others as explanations of the "alienation of the person." From the 1950s to our time, new accounts of the nature and causes of "depersonalization phenomena" have proliferated, not least because the symptoms they seek to define have continued to grow increasingly widespread.[45] But the hypothesis of "coenesthopathy" merits consideration nonetheless. The truth is that it is more than one medical theory among others advanced in the course of the development of modern psychiatry. If one understands the "common feeling" of the modern physicians as a last figure of the common sense defined and discussed in classic terms by Aristotle and his pupils, its "pathologies" in the nineteenth and twentieth centuries appear in a new light. "Coenesthopathy" emerges as nothing less than the illness of the master sense of the tradition. The grave and perhaps terminal ailment of the primary power of the sensible soul, this disorder of the "common feeling" threatens the thinking animal with the specter of a life from which the sense of sensing has all but disappeared: a life of conscious cogitation in the absence of any perception of being alive. Hence the clarity of this ailing state, which leaves the subject a power of thinking all the more distressing for its irrefutable lucidity. As Baruk wrote in an important paper of 1951, stressing the irreducibility of such a state to madness, in "true coenaesthopathies," "the patient knows perfectly that his body lives and functions, but he no longer has any feeling of it."[46]

That state breaks fundamentally with the account of animal life defined and elaborated to this point. The condition of the alienated patient may admit perceptions, but those of the proper senses alone: individual feelings can remain, but the common feeling and its once incessant "special noise" must now cease. This state could be variously described, in each of the idioms of the theory of the sensing soul. To cite and rewrite the classic example of Antiquity, one might say that in such a condition, in contrast to the one described in the *De anima*, "we see and we hear, but we do not sense that we are seeing and we do not sense that we are hearing." Or, to venture forward in history with one's terms: there may be perceptions, both unconscious and conscious, but no apperception of the act of perceiving itself, at least insofar as such an "apperception" may be distinguished from the strictly intellectual activity of cogitation. Consciousness, resolutely cognitive, now remains alone. Hence the sound mind of the subject, which persists in knowledge beyond the absence of any sense of sensing: he "knows perfectly that his body lives and functions, but he no longer has any feeling of it."

This may seem a strange state, and, in the course of the millennial reflection on the nature of the speaking living being in the West, there is no doubt that it is novel. But it can also be said to have been in part anticipated by the tradition. One metaphysical determination of human nature now reaches its fulfillment. The animal vanishes from man: in a speaking being, thought and existence remain, at last absolved of the animal power that was the sense of life. Such an "absolution," to be sure, can seem a parody of fulfillment, but that makes it no less fulfillment of a sort. Augustine's vision now comes to pass in terms more radical than any he himself might have imagined. Some fourteen hundred years after the bishop composed his many works, the faculty he took to be the hallmark of the dominating and dominated being triumphs over all: "knowledge of life" (*scientia vitae*) persists in the total absence of the animal awareness that was the "sensation of life" (*sensus vitae*), as the "inner sense" of brutes gives way to a reason altogether unadulterated by perception. Cartesian consciousness, too, now appears in a new form, at once verified and carried to an extreme. With the discovery of those "doubting" people who do not feel that they feel and do not feel that they even are, one may at last point to subjects who reason, in purity, without sensing that they do so; one may indicate the incontrovertible evidence of cogitating beings who think that they exist, even — or especially — when they cannot be said, with any rigor, to sense it. At the limit, one reaches the absolute certainty of an intellectual power divested of everything at all that can be perceived — not least existence. "Laetitia," the young woman who taught Janet what he knew of feelings of emptiness, attained this point: "Undoubtedly, I think," she once explained to her physician, recalling and rewriting Descartes's *dictum*, "but I do not exist" (*sans doute je pense, mais je n'existe pas*).[47]

The final irony, however, is that the new state of mind described by the modern physicians can at times bear more than a striking resemblance to the very condition whose definitive absence it seems to mark: the condition, namely, of the sensing being. All the authors who discuss the cessation of perception first identified by Esquirol suggest, at least at points, that its symptoms are themselves signs of a perceptual activity. It is the cerebro-cardiac patient who recalls, for example, how he felt "almost entirely separated from the world," and it is the depersonalized subjects who sense, with clarity, that they no longer sense and no longer sense themselves. Janet's own term had said it all. If one takes the expression "feelings of emptiness" literally, one must admit that they are still "feelings" of a kind: liminal feelings, to be sure, that touch upon the edge of the tactile world, but sensible impressions nonetheless.

One might compare such perceptions without object to the activity of the soul identified long before: the sense of not sensing illustrated by the eyes of the *De anima* in the dark, the *sunaisthēsis* described by Themistius and Priscian, the "sensation of no trace at all" that spurs on the Chrysippean hound in pursuit of his prey. But one should make no mistake. Those classic perceptions were the acts of animal souls in good health, which, to appropriate their natures to themselves, sensed when they failed to employ their senses no less than when they succeeded. The modern subjects who perceive that they no longer perceive, by contrast, are the patients of a medical science that takes as its object the debilitating illnesses of the body and the mind. They are the "alienated" of modernity, but their illnesses are no aberration. For their many maladies shelter a truth about a faculty lacking to the healthy in modernity. In their ailments, the variegated class of insensitively sensing subjects bears witness to the final form in which the "common sense" of the tradition survives in our age. Their pathologies are the last remnants of "permanent perception": glimmers of a general sensation felt, however dimly, by the aesthetic animal under anaesthesia.

It would not be difficult to find others of their kind well after them, from the later decades of the twentieth century to this day. One may think, first of all, of the many psychological cases that have not ceased to grow in our time: from the "absence of grief" and "as if" syndromes described by Helene Deutsch, for instance, to the multiple "dissociation disorders" of contemporary psychiatry.[48] But one may go much further. Are the great affects of the twentieth century, the sensible impressions discovered then and not before, not all feelings of the progressive retreat and vanishing of all feeling? The "poverty of experience" (*Erfahrungsarmut*) identified by Benjamin, the state of "being left empty" (*Leergelassenheit*) said by Heidegger to define the "deep boredom" we all know, the overwhelming insomniac impression of the bare fact that "there is" (*il y a*), described by Lévinas as an absolute "experience of depersonalization": these basic impressions are the fundamental feelings of a culture that has bid farewell to the primary perceptual power of the tradition.[49] They are the affects that belong to animals who strive to think and to think about themselves with increasing might but who no longer sense that they sense, if not in perceiving, at the limit, that their ailing perceptions are, in truth, of nothing and of no one.

Without any inner touch save that by which we perceive that we do not perceive ourselves, we come later and with duller senses still. Our world is by now the inverted image of the ancient: people erring on the side of excess of sensation are "scarcely to be found," and those individuals who feel "less than a proper amount" of enjoyment and pain in life grow more numerous with each day. Hence the new names and figures of being without affect in our works of literature and in the catalogues and handbooks of our medical and psychiatric sciences; hence the unfeeling faces and bodies that fill our screens, our books, and our newspapers with ever greater force. A common insensibility, however "inhuman" it may have seemed to Aristotle, has become the rule: we are all, to rewrite Musil's famous phrase, "men without perceptual qualities." Some may wish to deny the fact; others may lament it as an evil of the present; still others may celebrate it as the triumph of a resilience of the mind and body unseen until now. But the truth is that a transformation in the speaking living being poses a challenge to thought that can hardly be avoided. Just as the ethics of Antiquity naturally departed from the forms of human sensibility it took to be self-evident, so ours today must begin with an investigation into the absence among thinking beings of any "general perception": how it came about and where its vanishing may still lead. Any ethics worthy of the name must confront the promise and the threat contained in the sensation that today we may no longer, or may not yet, sense anything at all.

CHAPTER TWENTY-FIVE

Untouchable

An End to the Work, containing what the Reader may,
perhaps, expect to find in it

Avicenna's *Book of Definitions* (*Kitāb al-ḥudūd*) contains an account of the various qualities that distinguish the surfaces of solids. A concise but thorough treatment, it consists of a discussion of five terms. First, the philosopher specifies the nature of the rough (*al-khašin*). "This is a solid [*jirm*]," he writes, "whose surface is divided into parts whose positions are diverse." Next, he defines the smooth (*al-'amlas*): "This is a solid whose surface," by contrast, "is divided into parts whose positions are equal." Third in the series is the hard (*al-ṣulb*), a thing whose outer layer can be defined by a new trait: that of "letting its surface be pushed toward the inside with difficulty." As such, the hard may be opposed first of all to the soft (*al-layyin*), "a solid which receives this push with ease." But the hard as well as the unqualifiedly soft may be distinguished from the last type of surface to be considered among the class, the tender (*al-rakhw*). "This is a soft solid," the philosopher explains, "which is ready to come apart."[1]

Aristotle held our flesh to be a thing of this last nature. It suffices to consider the varieties of animal skin, he once affirmed, to conclude that the human's is the most tender of them all. "Human flesh," we read in a laconic but unequivocal formulation in Book Beta of the *De partibus animalium* (On the Parts of Animals), is simply "the softest [*malakōtatē*] kind of flesh there is."[2] Hence the fragility and vulnerability of the speaking living being's body. Devoid of all natural armor and the formidable weaponry of the other beasts, the upright walker on two feet enters the world exposed to its harsh elements by virtue of his unprotected and largely uncovered skin, which consists of the subtlest of membranes. But in the natural order no debility is entirely in vain, and the truth is that the extreme tenderness of human flesh serves a final cause. Its delicacy allows for the excellence of at least one of the rational animal's five senses: touch. Stressing the unsurpassed softness of human flesh in the *De partibus animalium*, Aristotle thus immediately adds that "this is because man's sense of touch is much more delicate [*aisthētikōtaton*] than that of any other creature." He recalls this fact at several points. In Book Alpha of the *Historia animalium*, he writes, "The most acute [*akribestatēn*] of all man's senses is the sense of touch, and the second is taste; in other senses many animals surpass him."[3] And in the fourth chapter of the *De sensu et sensibilibus*, he affirms, in the briefest of terms, that "our sense of touch is more acute [*akribestatēn*] than that of any other living being."[4] Alexander of Aphrodisias knew it well, and explained the fact by reference to the exceptional "good temperament" of the human body. "In his touch," the great commentator of Antiquity writes in his own *De anima*, "man is extraordinarily sensitive [*akribestatēn aisthēsin ekhomen*], since he possesses a body that is particularly well tempered [*eukraton malista einai to sōma autōi*] . . . , on account of which he has the most subtle touch [*tēn haphēn akribestatēn*], which is extended, one may say, throughout the entire body which possesses that felicitous temperament [*eukrasian*], so much so that among human beings an innate subtlety of touch seems to be the sign of a good nature [*euaisthēsia*]."[5]

Aristotle's treatise on the soul suggests that the delicacy of human flesh may be responsible for a further distinction still, which surpasses even the level of general sensation. Considering the nature of the olfactory faculty in Chapter Nine of Book Beta of the *De anima*, the Philosopher notes that it is by nature difficult to offer a full treatment of the subject, since "this sense with us is not highly discriminating, far less so indeed than with many animals."[6] Taste is a different matter, and for a simple reason. "Taste is itself a form of touch," Aristotle writes, recalling the terms of his other works, and "man possesses touch as the most acute of the senses [*tautēn d'ekhein tēn aisthēsin ton anthrōpon akribestatēn*]; whereas in other senses man lags behind many other animals, in touch he distinguishes himself from the others."[7] Now the Philosopher advances a striking claim: "This is why he is the most intelligent of living beings [*dio kai phronimōtaton esti tōn zōiōn*]. The sign of this is to be found in the fact that within the human species, individuals are well endowed and poorly endowed with this sensory power, but not with any other. Those who possess hard skin are poorly endowed with thought [*aphueis tēn dianoian*]; and those who possess soft skin, by contrast, are well endowed [*euphueis*] with it."[8] This passage may well startle the contemporary reader. At least one eminent twentieth-century scholar, an editor of the *De anima*, no less, has commented that "the remark at 421a 22 ff. on the connection between touch and intelligence seems of very dubious validity."[9] Among the ancient commentators, however, the unlikely "remark" formed the kernel of a well-accepted doctrine. Discussing the "particularly good temperament" of the human body in his own treatise on the soul, Alexander, for example, does not hesitate to attribute to the subtlety of man's touch the distinction of his entire soul. It is because of his "extraordinarily sensitive touch," Alexander writes, that "man's entelechy and his perfection, which is the soul, is better and more perfect than that of other animals."[10] Themistius draws the connection to the faculty of thought in explicit terms. "In acuity of touch, we surpass each and every animal," he asserts. "That is also why a human being is the most intelligent of animals, and his temperament [*krasis*] is better suited to judgment."[11] Philoponus concurs, adding that common usage supports the link between the tenderness of the flesh and the power of the intellect. Commenting on the passage in the *De anima*, he notes that we naturally refer to fools as "'hard-fleshed ones' or pachyderms [*pakhudermoi*]."[12]

One might still wonder why it is the acuity of touch, among all the senses, that testifies to the unique strength of the human mind. Is it not the lofty faculty of sight, as we are always told, that distinguishes man from the other beasts, which makes of him the

293

seer, the gazer, the contemplator par excellence? The query would seem well founded: Aristotle himself, after all, suggests in both the *Nicomachean Ethics* and the *Metaphysics* that vision may be a nobler sense than touch.[13] But in the ancient doctrine the power to think finds its roots in the tactile faculty and nowhere else. Thomas Aquinas explains the point in detail in his commentary on the classic treatise, where he too affirms that the "pre-eminence of touch in man is the reason why man is the wisest of animals"; "moreover, among men it is in virtue of fineness of touch, and not of any other sense, that we discriminate the mentally gifted from the rest."[14]

The thirteenth-century doctor does not doubt that if one compares touch and sight, one must conclude that "sight is the more spiritual sense, and reveals better the differences between things."[15] Nevertheless, he holds that there are two grounds for the privilege of touch in matters intellectual. He draws one reason from the tradition of Alexander, although he does not refer to him by name. "A fine touch," Thomas writes, "is an effect of a good bodily constitution or temperament... Now," he reasons, "nobility of soul follows from a well-balanced physical constitution, because forms are proportionate to their matter; it follows that those whose touch is delicate are so much the nobler in nature and the more intelligent."[16] Another reason Thomas draws directly from the teachings of his master. "Touch," Thomas writes, recalling the classic Aristotelian doctrine, "is the basis of sensitivity as a whole; for obviously the organ of touch pervades the whole body, so that the organ of each of the other senses is also an organ of touch, and the sense of touch by itself constitutes a being as sensitive." This fact alone, he observes, suffices to distinguish the primary power from all others. If one grants the fundamental position of the tactile faculty in the order of the animal soul, one must conclude that "the finer one's sense of touch, the better, strictly speaking, is one's sensitive nature as a whole, and consequently the higher one's intellectual capacity. For a fine sensitivity is a disposition to a fine intelligence." This much cannot be said of any other sense: "exceptionally good hearing or sight," for instance, "does not imply that the sensitivity as a whole is finer, but only that it is so in one respect."[17]

The *Metaphysics* goes still further in the association of thought and touch. When Aristotle in this work defines the most fully realized of all intellectual acts, the activity proper to a god, he invokes no power other than that of the tactile being. The greatest of all intelligences, we read in a decisive passage of Book Lambda, "becomes the intelligible by touching and by thinking, in such a way that intelligence and intelligible become the same" (*noētos gar gigneti thinganōn kai noōn, hōste tauton nous kai noēton*).[18]

What would it mean for touch to be the root of thinking and for thinking, in turn, to be in its most elevated form a kind of touch? Elements of an answer could certainly be sought in the doctrine of the tactile faculty developed by Aristotle and his successors. Like touch, one might conclude, thought has no proper object, no clear organ of operation, and no medium to call its own, if not one that vanishes from perception in the act of thinking. Other responses to the question, however, are equally admissible. One might turn to later terms proposed to define the nature of touch, such as those invoked in a fragmentary note, from May 1960, appended to Merleau-Ponty's unfinished and posthumously published final work, *The Visible and the Invisible*:

To touch and to touch oneself (to touch oneself = touching-touched [*touchant-touché*]). They do not coincide in the body: the touching is never exactly the touched. This does not mean that they coincide "in the mind" or at the level of "consciousness." There must be something other than the body for the junction to be made. It is made in the *untouchable*. That which belongs to the Other which I will never touch. But that which I will never touch, he too does not touch; no privilege of the self over the other here. It is therefore not *consciousness* that is untouchable — "consciousness" would be something positive, and then there would be another beginning, there is another beginning, of the duality of the reflecting and the reflected, like that of the touching and the touched. The untouchable is not a touchable that happens to be inaccessible; the unconscious is not a representation that happens to be inaccessible. The negative here is not a *positive that is elsewhere* (something transcendent). It is a true negative.[19]

This note can be read as a compressed effort to explain a single fact: that however intimately they may be joined in a tactile act committed by one body on itself, the touching and the touched "do not coincide." Even when I lay one hand upon the other, the touching member, in other words, "is never exactly the touched." A medium, no matter how subtle it may seem, must separate the two tactile terms, even as it grants them the element in which they may meet.

Merleau-Ponty names this medium "the untouchable." Irreducible both to the felt body and to the mind, conscious or unconscious, it constitutes the indistinct terrain in which the "junction" between the touching and the touched comes to pass. As Merleau-Ponty defines it in his note, such an "untouchable" is, quite clearly, withdrawn from tactility not accidentally but essentially. "It is not a touchable that happens to be inaccessible," the philosopher therefore specifies with pedagogical precision. It is "not a positive that is elsewhere (something transcendent)" but "a true negative." There can be no doubt: the untouchable, for this reason, retreats from the field of touch in allowing it. But such a summary nevertheless runs the risk of philosophical inadequacy, for the nature of the untouchable medium of touch is in fact still more complex. The truth of the matter is that every touching and touched term solicits and encounters this element, precisely as that "in which" all contact comes to pass; every grasp, be it forceful or gentle, exerts itself upon it and within it. Despite its structural inaccessibility, the medium of touch is therefore not impassive; in Merleau-Ponty's words, it is not "something transcendent." One might even maintain that, since no contact is immediate and "the touching is never exactly the touched," one never truly encounters anything but it. The ultimate element of all touch, it remains no less untouchable for being incessantly, always, and already touched.

Aristotle, for his part, gives no name to the element of touch.

Nor does he specify the nature of the dimension common to the tactile power of the animal and the contact proper to the intellectual act. But there is at least one passage in his works in which he identifies a thing apprehended by perception and by thought, which neither faculty, sensitive or intellectual, could ever fully grasp. It is the fact of the living being's own existence — or, more simply put, its life. Like Murr long after him, Aristotle holds it to be a source of joy. "Life," the Philosopher maintains, "is a thing good and pleasant in itself" (*to de zēn tōn kath'auto agathōn kai hēdeōn*).[20] That, he explains, is why to feel affection for the intimate "other self" (*heteros autos*) that is the friend is above all to feel affection for the good and pleasant thing that is his life: to sense an existence jointly and in common. "If life itself is good and pleasant [*agathon kai hēdu*]," the Philosopher reasons in Book Theta of the *Nicomachean Ethics*,

> as it appears to be, because all men desire it, and virtuous and supremely happy men most of all, since their way of life is the most desirable and their existence the most blissful; and if one who sees senses [*aisthanetai*] that he is seeing, one who hears [senses] that he is hearing, one who walks [senses] that he is walking, and similarly for all the other cases there is something that perceives that we are in activity [*esti ti to aisthanomenon hoti energoumen*], so that whenever we sense, we sense that we are sensing, and whenever we think, we [sense] that we are thinking, and to sense that we are sensing or thinking is to sense that we exist [*hoti esmen*] (for existence, as we saw, is sensation or thinking [*to gar einai ēn aisthanesthai ē noein*]); and if to sense that one is alive [*hoti zēi*] is a pleasant thing in itself (for life is a thing essentially good, and to sense that one possesses a good thing is pleasant); and if life is desirable, and especially so for good men, because existence [*to einai*] is good for them, and so pleasant (because they are pleased by the sensation of what is intrinsically good); and if the virtuous man feels toward his friend in the same way as he feels toward himself (for his friend is an other self [*heteros gar autos*]) — then, just as a man's own existence [*to auton einai*] is desirable for him, so, or nearly so, is his friend's existence

also desirable. But, as we saw, it is the sensation of oneself as good that makes existence desirable, and such sensation is pleasant in itself. Therefore a man ought also jointly to sense his friend's existence [*sunaisthanesthai ara dei kai tou philou hoti estin*], and this is attained by their living together and conversing and communicating their thoughts to each other. [21]

Although it cannot be said to have been altogether ignored by modern scholars, this capital passage in the Aristotelian treatise on friendship has yet to receive the attention it deserves.[22] As Giorgio Agamben has shown, it presents the principles that constitute "the ontological basis" for the theory of friendship as a whole: that there is, namely, a sensation of existence (an *aisthēsis* of "the fact of that we exist" and "the fact that one is alive"); that this sensation, moreover, is a source of joy ("good and pleasant in itself," "pleasant" and "desirable"); and that, finally, this sensation is shared, as an irreducibly "joint perception" (literally, a *sunais-thēsis*) between those two selves who "live together and converse and communicate their thoughts to each other."[23]

The passage in the *Ethics*, however, contains still more. It also presents a searing sketch of the primary power repeatedly invoked in Aristotle's many treatises on the soul: that central capacity in the sensing thinking being thanks to which "one who sees senses that he is seeing, one who hears [senses] that he is hearing, [and] one who walks [senses] that he is walking," "so that," in the philosopher's own words, "whenever we sense, we sense that we are sensing, and whenever we think, we [sense or think] that we are thinking." But now one question concerning the master sense cannot be avoided. By what power of perception can we be said to sense not only "that we are sensing" but also, as the *Ethics* has it, "that we are thinking"? The formulation has no equivalent in Aristotle's works on the nature of the soul, and it raises a problem that can hardly be avoided. One could suppose, to be sure, that a second activity is implied in the sentence: there could be, in other words, an unstated verb that corresponds to thought as sensing corresponds to sensation. Thomas, glossing the passage in his commentary on the *Ethics*, opts for such an interpretation: "We sense that we are sensing," he writes, explaining the words of the Philosopher, "and we think that we are thinking" (*sentimus nos sentire et intelligimus nos intelligere*).[24] But such a reading ultimately changes little. In this passage, the difference between sensation and thought, so stressed by Aristotle elsewhere, seems to fade away: the repeated invocation of "sensation *or* thought" (*aisthanesthai ē noein*) suggests the two activities are in this setting interchangeable. The "faculty" that grasps them both is resolutely singular; according to the letter of the treatise, there is but one power, both in sensation and in thought, that "senses that we are in activity." In his paraphrase, it should be added, Thomas himself lends little weight to the distinction he draws. Although he differentiates the sense of sensing from the thought of thinking, he still believes them to open onto a single terrain: our life. "When we sense that we are sensing and when we think that we are thinking," the angelic doctor concludes, "we sense and we think that we are" (*sentimus et intelligimus nos esse*).[25]

Our being is the common element to which both perception and intellection ultimately lead. Element, but not object: for neither the faculty of sensation nor that of thought could grasp the fact "that we are" (*nos esse*) as one thing among others. That fact is untouchable, although, "not something transcendent," it continues to be grazed by those who touch within the terrain of "sensation or thought" that it enables. Imperceptible as such, our life remains, for this reason, like the "matter" and the "place" (*khōra*) of Plato's *Timaeus*, "perceptible with an absence of perception" (*met'anaisthēsias hapton*), "touchable," in the terms of Calcidius's classic translation of the dialogue into Latin, "without the sense of touch" (*sine tangentis sensu tangi*).[26] This may be the reason why it is approachable only in the redoubled form repeated by Aristotle and Thomas. That which cannot be represented as any single thing reveals itself, at the limit, in the barest of perceptions without object: in the mere sense "that we are sensing" and in the simple thought "that we are thinking." This, too, may be the reason why the fact of our existence seems to Aristotle, as to the writing cat, a thing "sweet" and "pleasant in itself." Only the untouchable can be touched with pleasure. That is one joy reserved to beings of tender flesh, whose feeling surface is always "ready to come apart." They are never so hardened as to be untouched by the untouchable in which they move, nor so thoughtless as to be indifferent to the sweetness they may fail to sense.

Notes

NOTE ON TRANSLATIONS

Wherever possible, I have indicated English translations of works cited in the notes and used them in quotations. On occasion, I have silently modified published versions in accordance with the originals.

Unless otherwise noted, all translations are my own.

An earlier version of "Murriana" was published in *Grey Room* 24 (Fall, 2006), pp. 8–15. "Company" appeared in a slightly different form in *October* 117 (2006), pp. 35–43.

CHAPTER ONE: MURRIANA

    1. Hoffmann, *Lebensansichten des Katers Murr*, p. 15.

    2. Hoffmann, *Lebensansichten des Katers Murr*, p. 16.

    3. Hoffmann, *Lebensansichten des Katers Murr*, p. 16.

    4. Kafka, "Ein Bericht für eine Akademie," *Gesammelte Werke*, vol. 1, p. 244.

    5. Hegel, *Jenaer Realphilosophie*, pp. 181–82.

    6. Hegel, *Werke*, vol. 1, pp. 24–25.

    7. Hoffmann, *Lebensansichten des Katers Murr*, pp. 32–33.

    8. Hoffmann, *Lebensansichten des Katers Murr*, p. 33.

    9. Hoffmann, *Lebensansichten des Katers Murr*, p. 35.

    10. Hoffmann, *Lebensansichten des Katers Murr*, p. 42.

    11. Robert Schumann to Simonin de Sire, March 15, 1839, *Kreisleriana*, p. iii.

12. Hoffmann, *Lebensansichten des Katers Murr*, p. 10.

13. Hoffmann, *Lebensansichten des Katers Murr*, pp. 51 and 56.

CHAPTER TWO: THE AESTHETIC ANIMAL

1. On *suneidēsis* and the Greek vocabulary of conscience, see Cancrini, *Syneidesis*. See also, among others, Seel, "Zur Vorgeschichte des Gewissens-Begriffes"; Snell, review of *Syneidesis-Conscientia*; Dupont, "Syneidesis"; and Mondolfo, *La comprensione del soggetto umano*, pp. 514–24. On the philosophical terminology for the phenomenon, see also Siebeck, "Der Begriff des Bewusstseins"; Jung, "Syneidesis, conscientia, Bewusstsein"; and Lloyd, "Nosce Teipsum and Conscientia."

2. See the classic article by Schwyzer, "'Bewusst' und 'Unbewusst' bei Plotin." See also Smith, "Unconsciousness and Quasiconsciousness in Plotinus."

3. In Christian Wolff's 1720 essay *Vernünfftige Gedanken von Gott, der Welt und der Seele des Menschen*, one finds four graphically distinct renditions of the term: *Bewußt sein*, *Bewußsein*, *Bewußt-sein*, and *bewußt Sein*. See "Bewußtsein" in Ritter, Gründer, Gabriel, and Eisler (eds.), *Historisches Wörterbuch der Philosophie*, vol. 1, p. 888.

4. See, among many others, Hamlyn, "Aristotle's Account of Aisthesis," pp. 6–7, and Solmsen, "αἴσθησις in Aristotelian and Epicurean Thought."

5. See Kahn, "Sensation and Consciousness in Aristotle's Psychology," p. 23 n.62.

6. Hippocrates, *On the Sacred Disease*, chs. 10–20, *Hippocrates*, vol. 2, cited in Kahn, "Sensation and Consciousness in Aristotle's Psychology," p. 23 n.62.

7. Kahn, "Sensation and Consciousness in Aristotle's Psychology," p. 23 n.62; see also Solmsen, "αἴσθησις in Aristotelian and Epicurean Thought," pp. 616–18.

8. Plato, *Theaetetus* 184–86. On this passage, see, among others, Cooper, "Plato on Sense-Perception and Knowledge"; Burnyeat, "Plato on the Grammar of Perceiving"; Frede, "Observations on Perception in Plato's Later Dialogues."

9. Plato, *Theaetetus* 156.

10. Plato, *Timaeus* 64a2.

11. Frede, "Observations on Perception in Plato's Later Dialogues," p. 4.

12. Plato, *Apology* 50c.

13. Solmsen, "αἴσθησις in Aristotelian and Epicurean Thought," p. 616.

14. Aristotle, *De anima* 2.4, 3.9–11, 3.4–8.

15. Cf. Aristotle, *De insomniis* 2.459a15–17, which, with an apparent reference

to *De anima* 3.1, goes so far as to identify imagination and *aisthēsis* in one sense: "while imagination is the same as perception, the being of each differs" (*esti men to auto tōi aisthētikōi to phantastikon, to d' einai phantastikōi kai aisthētikōi heteron*).

16. Kahn, "Sensation and Consciousness in Aristotle's Psychology," pp. 5–6. As Kahn indicates, this summary of *De anima* excludes 3.3, on the imagination, and 3.12–13, which considers the relation of the faculties among themselves.

17. Aristotle, *De anima* 434a27.

18. *Ibid.*, 413b1.

19. *Ibid.*, 413b1–2: *to men oun zēn dia tēn arkhēn tautēn [trophēn] huparkhei tois zōsi, to de zōion dia tēn aisthēsin prōtōs.*

20. *Ibid.*, 416b33. Here Aristotle indicates that he has already said as much (*kathaper eirētai*), but it is not entirely clear which passage he has in mind. Marchl (*Des Aristoteles Lehre von der Tierseele*, [Metten: 1897], p. 17 n.3) suggested it is *Physics* 7.2; Essen (*Das zweite Buch der aristotelischen Schrift*, p. 36 n.1) and, after him, Rodier (*Aristote*, p. 248), as well as Hamlyn (Aristotle, *De Anima Books II and III*, p. 99) believe it is instead *De anima* 2.4.415b.24. Cf., later, 424a: *to gar aisthanesthai paskhein ti estin.*

21. On Aristotle's terminology, see Kosman, "Perceiving that We Perceive," p. 595; cf. Hamlyn, "Aristotle's Account of Aisthesis in the *De Anima*," pp. 7–8, and Aristotle, *De Anima Books II and III*, pp. xvii–xviii.

22. See Aristotle, *De anima* 2.7, esp. 418a–418b13. On the development of the doctrine of the transparent in Antiquity and the Middle Ages, see Vasiliu, *Du Diaphane*.

23. Aristotle, *De anima* 424a2.

24. This is the basis of the so-called "*logos* doctrine" of *De anima* 2, by which Aristotle has been said to elaborate on theories of several of his predecessors. See Modrak, *Aristotle*, pp. 56–62.

25. Rodier (*Aristote*, pp. 338–39) notes that for reasons of method, touch, as the most elementary of the senses, might be most logically treated first, although in the order of Aristotle's analysis it comes last.

26. Aristotle, *De anima* 2.2.413b4–5.

27. *Ibid.*, 3.13.435b4–5.

28. If one believes such readers of Aristotle as Thomas Aquinas and Albertus Magnus, the power of touch founds not only the existence but also the operation of the remaining four senses. See Thomas Aquinas, *In Aristotelis librum De anima commentarium* 2.19.484–85, and Albertus Magnus, *Opera Omnia*, vol. 7, pt.

1, p. 135. Cf. the discussion of the subject in Movia, "Tatto e pensiero in un passo del 'De Anima,'" *Due studi sul De Anima di Aristotele*, p. 68.

29. Aristotle, *De anima* 2.11.423a25–27.

30. *Ibid.*, 2.11.423b7.

31. *Ibid.*, 2.11.423b7 and 8.

32. *Ibid.*, 2.11.423b20–22, 2.7.419a13–14, 2.7.419a18–20.

33. *Ibid.*, 2.11.423b14–15.

34. *Ibid.*, 2.11.423b22–24.

35. On Aristotle's definition of senses by their objects, see Sorabji, "Aristotle on Demarcating the Five Senses."

36. Aristotle, *De anima* 422b23–27.

37. Aristotle, *De generatione et corruptione* 2.329b18. On the possible reductions of this list, see Sorabji, "Aristotle on Demarcating the Five Senses," p. 85 n.34.

38. Aristotle, *De generatione et corruptione* 422b32–34.

39. Aristotle, *De anima* 2.10.422b17.

40. *Ibid.*, 3.13.435a18.

41. Aristotle, *De generatione et corruptione* 2.2.329b6–7.

42. Aristotle, *De anima* 2.11.423b26–27.

CHAPTER THREE: THE PRIMARY POWER

1. See Rodier, *Aristote*, p. 341, and Aristotle, *De anima*, Hicks edition, p. 422; *Über die Seele*, p. 130; *De anima*, Ross edition, p. 268.

2. On the reception of the *De anima* in the Arab world, see Gätje, *Studien zur Überlieferung der aristotelischen Psychologie im Islam*; cf. also Peters, *Aristoteles Arabus*, pp. 40–45. A classical Arabic translation of the treatise has been published by 'Abdarrahmān Badawī: see Aristotle, *Aristūtālīs Fī'l-nafs*; in this form, however, the segmentation of the Aristotelian text has been made to conform to that of its standard modern editions. As Hicks indicates (Aristotle, *De anima*, p. 422), Zabarella also began Book Gamma with what is now *De anima* 3.4.

3. Aristotle, *De anima* 2.6.418a17–18; cf. 3.1.425a16.

4. On "accidental" or "incidental" sensation, see *ibid*, 2.6.418a21–25 and 3.1.425a24–30.

5. *Ibid.*, 2.6.418a8–19.

6. *Ibid.*, 3.1.425a16–17.

7. *Ibid.*, 3.2.426b10–11.

8. *Ibid.*, 3.2.426b12–14.

9. On the sense of the "discernment" invoked by Aristotle for the senses, see Ebert, "Aristotle on What Is Done in Perceiving," which argues, on compelling philological and philosophical grounds, against the traditional and still widespread rendering of *krinein* as "judgment."

10. Aristotle, *De anima* 3.2.426b10ff.

11. *Ibid.*, 3.2.425b12–15.

12. *Ibid.*, 3.2.425b15.

13. *Ibid.*, 3.2.427a27.

14. Aristotle, *De sensu et sensibilibus* 7.448b5–8.

15. *Ibid.*, 7.449a8–20.

16. Aristotle, *De somno et vigilia* 2.455a12–21.

17. *Ibid.*, 2.455a22–23.

18. See Aristotle, *Parva naturalia*, Ross edition; Nuyens, *L'évolution de la psychologie d'Aristote*; and Block, "Order of Aristotle's Psychological Writings" and "Three German Commentators on the Individual Senses."

19. Aristotle, *De anima* 3.2.427a27, *De memoria et reminiscentia* 450a10, and *De partibus animalium* 686a27. Some have found the phrase, in addition, in *De anima* 3.2.431b5, but this can be done only if one refers the term *aisthēsis* to a *koinē* whose occurrence in the text at this point has been questioned — most notably by Hamlyn, who has gone so far as to affirm that "there is every reason why the word should be deleted from the text" ("Koine Aisthesis," p. 195). On the Arabic and Hebrew terminology for the sense, see Wolfson, "Internal Senses in Latin, Arabic and Hebrew Philosophic Texts"; on the Hebrew terminology, cf. Moses of Salerno, *Un glossario filosofico ebraico-italiano del XIII secolo*, p. 130 (where it is said that Moses of Salerno has *sensus communis* correspond not to *ḥush meshutaf* but to *da'ath meshutaf*).

20. Michael of Ephesus, *In Parva naturalia commentaria*, p. 48. On this interpretation, see the remarks in Wiesner, "Unity of the Treatise *De Somno*," esp. pp. 244–47. Chrétien has deemed this interpretation "certainly questionable from the point of view of philological exactitude" (*L'appel et la réponse*, p. 129). But the eleventh-century Byzantine commentator is quite exact: he has merely paraphrased the Aristotelian dictum (*De somno* 455a20–21) according to which the *kurion aisthētērion hama tōi haptikōi malista huparkhei*.

21. Kahn, "Sensation and Consciousness in Aristotle's Psychology," p. 22; Sorabji, "Body and Soul in Aristotle," p. 68; Modrak, "Aristotelian Theory of Consciousness?" p. 160.

22. Blumenthal, *Aristotle and Neoplatonism in Late Antiquity*, p. 137.

23. Hamlyn, "Koine Aisthesis," pp. 207–208.

24. Aristotle, *De Anima Books II and III*, p. xiii. On this and related matters, see Hardie, "Concepts of Consciousness in Aristotle."

25. Kahn, "Sensation and Consciousness in Aristotle's Psychology," p. 21.

26. Kosman, "Perceiving that We Perceive," p. 499. Cf. Schiller, "Aristotle and the Concept of Awareness in Sense Perception," and, *contra* Kosman, Catherine Osborne, "Aristotle, *De Anima* 3.2."

27. Modrak, "Aristotelian Theory of Consciousness?" pp. 161, 168, 160.

28. Aëtius, *Placita* 4.8.7, *Stoicorum veterum fragmenta*, frag. 2.852: *Hoi Stōikoi tēnde tēn koinēn aisthēsin entos haphēn prosagoreuousi, kath' hēn kai hēmōn autōn antilambanometha.*

CHAPTER FOUR: THE CIRCLE AND THE POINT

1. Aristotle, *De anima* 3.1.424b22–23.

2. Aristotle, *De somno et vigilia* 2.455a12–21.

3. Aristotle, *De anima* 3.2.425b12–17: *hōst' epi tēs prōtēs touto poiēteon.*

4. *Ibid.*, 3.2.426b17–19.

5. Aristotle, *De sensu et sensibilibus* 7.448b8–9: *anangkē ara hen ti einai tēs psukhēs, hōi hapanta aisthanetai.*

6. Aristotle, *De anima* 3.2.426b29–426a2.

7. *Ibid.*, 3.2.427a5a–b.

8. *Ibid.*, 3.2.427a9–14. The presence of *kekhōrismena* at 427a14 is contestable; see the *apparatus criticus* in the Ross edition.

9. See Simplicius, *On Aristotle's Physics* 707.33, and John Philoponus, *On Aristotle's Prior Analytics* 136.20. On Alexander, see Sharples, "Alexander of Aphrodisias."

10. For the Greek text, see Alexander of Aphrodisias, *Alexandri Aphrodisiensis*, pp. 94.10–98.15; English in *Quaestiones*, pp. 57–63.

11. Original in Alexander of Aphrodisias, *Alexandri Aphrodisiensis*, vol. 2, pt. 2, p. 96, l. 11; English in *Quaestiones*, p. 60.

12. Original in Alexander of Aphrodisias, *Alexandri Aphrodisiensis*, vol. 2, pt. 2, p. 96, ll. 1–28; English in *Quaestiones*, p. 60.

13. Original in Alexander of Aphrodisias, *Alexandri Aphrodisiensis*, vol. 2, pt. 1, p. 63, ll. 6–12; English in *De Anima of Alexander of Aphrodisias*, p. 76.

14. Themistius, *Themistii in libros Aristotelis De Anima paraphrasis*, p. 86, l.

18; English in *On Aristotle On the Soul*, p. 109. For the Arabic translation of Themistius's *Paraphrase*, see Lyons (ed.), *Arabic Translation of Themistius' Commentary*; 1973); cf. also Browne, "Ad Themistium Arabum." For the Latin translation by William of Moerbeke, see Themistius, *Commentarie sur le traité De l'âme*.

15. For the Arabic Avicenna, see Avicenna, *Psychologie d'Ibn Sīnā*, vol. 1, p. 159 (B153r); the Latin text can be found in *Avicenna latinus*, vol. 1, p. 87, l. 20. For Averroës, see Averroës, *Averrois Cordubensis*, sec. 149.16, p. 356, *Middle Commentary on Aristotle's De anima*, sec. 260, pp. 100–102, and p. 196 n.290, and *Talkhīs kitāb al-nafs*, p. 55, l. 16.

16. Plotinus, *Ennéades*, vol. 4, pt. 6, p. 196: *dei toinun touto hōsper kentron einai, grammas de sumballousas ek periphereias kuklou tas pantakhothen aisthēseis pros touto perainein, kai toiouton to antilambanomenon einai, hen on ontōs*. On Plotinus and the Aristotelian figure, see Bréhier's notes to the passage in *ibid.*, pp. 195 and 196; cf. Paul Henry, "Une comparaison"; and see Moraux, review of Donini, *Tre studi sull'aristotelismo*, n.1.

17. Original in Alexander of Aphrodisias, *Alexandri Aphrodisiensis*, vol. 2, pt. 1, p. 63, ll. 12–25; English in *De Anima of Alexander of Aphrodisias*, p. 76.

18. Aristotle, *De Anima Books II and III*, p. 128.

19. Rodolfo Mondolfo, "L'unité du sujet dans la gnoséologie d'Aristote," p. 323.

20. Aristotle, *De anima* 3.2.426b22.

21. *Ibid.*, 3.2.427a15–16.

22. *Ibid.*, 3.2.426b24–29.

23. Bywater, "Aristotelia III," esp. pp. 55–56, where the sentence in question is characterized as a "parenthetical note merely thrown in to prevent a misconception."

24. On the point and the instant in Aristotle's *Physics*, see, 4.10.218a19; 4.11.220a4; 4.13; 6.1.231b6 and 233b35–234a24. Brentano long ago called attention to the proximity between the *De anima*'s simile and that of the *Physics*: see *Die Psychologie des Aristoteles*, pp. 91–92. In this he was challenged by Neuhaeuser (*Aristoteles' Lehre von dem sinnlichen Erkenntnisvermögen*, pp. 45–46), as well as by Rodier after him (*Aristote*, pp. 394–95). On the historical importance of Aristotle's determination of the essence of time, see, most famously, the concentrated footnote to the penultimate paragraph of the last chapter of *Being and Time*: Heidegger, *Sein und Zeit*, pp. 405–406. Cf. Jacques Derrida, "Ousia et grammè: Note sur une note de *Sein und Zeit*," pp. 31–78.

25. See Aristotle, *De memoria et reminiscentia* 451a14–17.

26. Aristotle, *De anima* 3.2.426b25–28.

27. On time and "untime," see Hamacher, "Des contrées des temps."

CHAPTER FIVE: *SENTIO ERGO SUM*

1. The passage fills Aristotle, *De sensu et sensibilibus* 7.448a–19–448b17.

2. *Ibid.*, 7.447b22–24.

3. In Porphyry, *On Ptolemy's Harmonics* 3, l. Düring edition, p. 63, l. 19; now in Theophrastus, *Theophrastus of Eresus*, vol. 2, text 716, pp. 562–73, pp. 565–66.

4. Aristotle, *De sensu et sensibilibus* 7.448a26–28.

5. *Ibid.*, 7.448a30–448b2.

6. *Ibid.*, 7.448a16–17.

7. Bréhier, "Une forme archaïque du 'Cogito ergo sum.'"

8. Mondolfo, "L'unité du sujet dans la gnoséologie d'Aristote," pp. 361–62.

9. Greek in Alexander of Aphrodisias, *Commentaria in Aristotelem Graeca*, vol. 3, pt. 1, p. 148, ll. 9–10; English in *On Aristotle on Sense Perception*, p. 134.

CHAPTER SIX: SLEEP

1. Aristotle, *De somno et vigilia* 1.454a21–22.

2. *Ibid.*, 1.454a24–26.

3. *Ibid.*, 1.454a26–29.

4. Aristotle, *De anima* 3.4.430a5–6: *tou de mē aei noein to aition episkepteon.*

5. Aristotle, *De somno et vigilia* 1.454a9–10.

6. *Ibid.*, 1.454a4–11.

7. See *ibid.*, 2.455b35–456a4.

8. On the debates of the commentators on the subject, see Wiesner, "Unity of the Treatise *De Somno*," esp. pp. 254–63.

9. Gershom ben Solomon, *The Gate of Heaven* (שער השמים) 9.66b, cited by Blumberg in the notes to his translation of Averroës, *Epitome of Parva naturalia*, p. 97. On the explanation and its apparent novelty, see the remarks in Robinson, "Gershom ben Solomon of Arles' *Sha'ar ha-Shamayim*," esp. pp. 265–67.

10. Michael of Ephesus, *In Parva naturalia commentaria* 48.9–10.

11. Aristotle, *De somno et vigilia* 2.455a11–12.

12. See *ibid.*, 2.455a15–23.

13. *Ibid.*, 2.455b8–13.

14. *Ibid.*, 2.455a32–455b2.

15. *Ibid.*, 2.455b2–7.

16. Aristotle, *De insomniis* 2.460b28–461a4 and 460b5–11.

17. *Ibid.*, 2.459a24–28.

18. *Ibid.*, 2.459b5–7: *dio to pathos estin ou monon en aisthanomenois tois aisthētēriois, alla kai en pepaumenois, kai en bathei kai epipolēs.*

19. *Ibid.*, 2.459b3–5.

20. *Ibid.*, 2.459b13–18.

21. *Ibid.*, 1.459a8–10.

22. Aristotle, *De somno et vigilia* 2.456a26.

23. Aristotle, *De insomniis* 3.462a6-7.

CHAPTER SEVEN: AWAKENING

1. Proust, *À la recherche du temps perdu*, pp. 14–15; English in *Swann's Way*, pp. 5–6.

2. Proust, *À la recherche du temps perdu*, p. 15; *Swann's Way*, p. 5. Cf. the appearance of the dreaming and dreamt animal in the second half of *À l'ombre des jeunes filles en fleurs*: "On dit que nous voyons souvent des animaux en rêve, mais on oublie que presque toujours nous y sommes nous-mêmes un animal privé de cette raison qui projette sur les choses une clarté de certitude" (*À la recherche du temps perdu*, p. 645).

3. Valéry, *Cahiers*, vol. 28, p. 625: "Il n'est pas de phénomène plus excitant pour moi que le réveil. Rien ne *tend* à donner une idée plus extraordinaire de . . . *tout*, que cette autogenèse — Ce commencement de ce qui fut — qui a, lui aussi, son commencement = *Ce qui est*, — et ceci n'est que choc, stupeur, contraste." The passage can also be found in the two-volume Robinson edition of the *Cahiers*, vol. 2, p. 198. On Valéry and waking, see Valerio Magrelli, *Vedersi vedersi*, esp. pp. 160–70.

4. Valéry, *Cahiers*, vol. 21, p. 669; Robinson edition, vol. 2, p. 181: "Qu'est ce que la veille? C'est de *re-trouver*. Ce RE notation essentielle."

5. Valéry, *Cahiers*, vol. 8, p. 843; Robinson edition, vol. 2, p. 181: "S'*éveiller* c'est — se re-*trouver*"; vol. 7, p. 794; Robinson edition, vol. 1, p. 1243: "Le fait capital de mémoire est de se retrouver au réveil, de retrouver son corps et soi"; vol. 11, p. 413; Robinson edition, vol. 2, p. 124.

6. *Ibid.*, vol. 11, p. 119; Robinson edition, vol. 1, p. 1239.

7. *Ibid.*, vol. 22, p. 405; Robinson edition, vol. 1, p. 1074: "*La grande affaire*

de la function ψ est de re-*connaître*, re-*constituer* — re — *trouver, dont la capitale est*
SE REconnaître, SE REssaisir, — etc. à partir de toute situation initiale ou événe-
ment — premier — par nature."

8. *Ibid.*, vol. 16, p. 249; Robinson edition, vol. 1, p. 1250.

9. *Ibid.*, vol. 14, p. 600; Robinson edition, vol. 1, p. 121: "Je me réveille le toujours surpris."

10. *Ibid.*, vol. 11, p. 517; Robinson edition, vol. 2, p. 127.

11. Benjamin, *Gesammelte Schriften*, vol. 5, p. 492: "Es ist eine der still-
schweigende Voraussetzungen der Psychoanalyse, daß der konträrer Gegensatz
von Schlaf und Wachen für die empirische Bewußtseinsform des Menschen
keine Geltung hat, vielmehr einer unendlichen Varietät konkreter Bewußtseinszustände weicht, die durch alle denkbaren Gradstufen des Erwachtseins aller
möglichen Zentren bedingt sind."

12. *Ibid.*, p. 495: "Das kommende Erwachen steht wie das Holzpferd der
Griechen im Troja des Traumes."

CHAPTER EIGHT: COMPANY

1. Aristotle, *Eudemian Ethics* H.12.1254b24, and *Nicomachean Ethics*
9.9.1170b4. On the sense of *sunaisthanesthai* in these passages, see Cancrini,
Syneidesis, pp. 18–19; Schwyzer, "'Bewusst' und 'Unbewusst' bei Plotin," pp.
355–66; Pierre Rodrigo, "Synaisthanesthai," pp. 35–51; and Fraisse, *Philia*, esp.
pp. 238–45. On the term *sunaisthēsis*, see also Badalamenti, "Ierocle stoico," esp.
pp. 85–92; cf. Sorabji, *Philosophy of the Commentators*, pp. 159–60, which alludes
to Aristotle's mention of *sunaisthēsis* with reference to insects in *Historia animalium* 534b18. On Aristotle's *Nicomachean Ethics* 9.9, see Chapter Twenty-five,
"Untouchable."

2. Galen, *On the Therapeutic Method* 8.1 (10.875.14 Kühn).

3. Aretaeus, *Aretaeus* 2.9.2 (Hude edition, p. 30, l. 25); 4.2.4 (Hude edition,
p. 66, l. 10).

4. Polybius 5.72.5; Philo Judaeus, *De virtutibus* 76; Sextus Empiricus, *Adversus mathematicos* 9.68. For these and other references, see Schwyzer, "'Bewusst'
und 'Unbewusst' bei Plotin," pp. 356–57. Cf. Jung, "Syneidesis, conscientia,
Bewusstsein," pp. 537–39.

5. Aristotle, *De anima* 3.2.425b11–12.

6. Original in Alexander of Aphrodisias, *Alexandri Aphrodisiensis*, vol. 2, pt.
2, p. 91, ll. 28–29; English in *Quaestiones*, p. 54.

7. Alexander of Aphrodisias, *Alexandri Aphrodisiensis*, p. 91, ll. 29–31; *Quaestiones*, p. 54.

8. Alexander of Aphrodisias, *Commentaria in Aristotelem Graeca*, vol. 3, pt. 1, p. 148, ll. 9–10; English in *On Aristotle on Sense Perception*, p. 134.

9. *hē men dē sunaisthēsis tou aisthanesthai ginomenē en tōi tēn aisthēsin hama te [tēi] tou aisthētou kai tēs idias peri to aisthēton energeias aisthanesthai. dio ex anagkēs hepetai panti tōi aisthanomenōi sunaisthanesthai kai heautou aisthanomenou tōi hepesthai tēi aisthēsei aisthanomenēi tinos tōn aisthētōn exō ontos to hama kai heautēs aisthanesthai.* Original in Alexander of Aphrodisias, *Alexandri Aphrodisiensis*, p. 93, ll. 18–22; English in *Quaestiones*, p. 56.

10. See, among many others: Hadot, "La théorie de la perception," esp. pp. 63–71, where *sunaisthēsis* appears at some times as "conscience," at others as "conscience de soi"; Philoponus, *On Aristotle On the Soul*; Huby renders the term as "consciousness" in her translation of Priscian, *On Theophrastus on Sense-Perception.* Elsewhere, Huby adopts "self-awareness" as a translation of the term: see Theophrastus, *Theophrastus of Eresus*, vol. 4, pp. 81–82.

11. Alexander of Aphrodisias, *On Aristotle on Sense Perception*, pp. 36 and 163.

12. English translation in Alexander of Aphrodisias, *Quaestiones*, p. 54.

13. On *sunaisthēsis* in Plotinus's *Enneads* (4.4; 5.1; 5.3; 5.4; 5.6), see Schwyzer, "'Bewusst' und 'Unbewusst' bei Plotin"; Schroeder, "Synousia, Synaisthesis and Synesis" and "Conversion of Consciousness"; Becker, *Plotin und das Problem der geistigen Aneignung*, esp. pp. 21–40; Lautner, "Rival Theories of Self-Awareness in Late Neoplatonism"; and Smith, "Unconsciousness and Quasi-consciousness in Plotinus."

14. Aristotle, *De anima* 3.2.425b21–22. It is perhaps in relation to this passage that one must understand Aristotle's statement that the sense of sight, like every other, has two objects: "the visible and the invisible" (*ibid.*, 2.11.424a10–12: *eti d'hōsper horatou kai aoratou ēn pōs hē opsis, homoiōs de kai hai loipai tōn antikeimenōn, houto hē haphē tou haptou kai anaptou.*)

15. The full passage reads as follows: *phaneron toinun hoti oukh haplōs legetai to aisthanesthai. kai gar hotan mē horōmen, tēi opsei krinomen kai ou monon phōtos alla kai skotous sunaisthanometha, all' oukh hōsautōs. hēi toinun aisthēsei aisthanometha hoti oukh horōmen, tēi autēi tautēi aisthēsei aisthanometha kai hoti horōmen, hautē de estai hē opsis.* Original in Themistius, *Themistii in libros Aristotelis De Anima paraphrasis*, p. 83, ll. 22–26; English in *On Aristotle On the Soul*, p. 105.

16. *hēi toinun aisthēsei aisthanometha hoti oukh horōmen, tēi autēi tautēi aisthēsei aisthanometha.* Themistius, *Themistii in libros Aristotelis De Anima paraphrasis,* p. 83, ll. 24–25; *On Aristotle On the Soul,* p. 105.

17. Original in Priscian, *Metaphrasis in Theophrastum,* p. 21, ll. 32–33; English in *On Theophrastus on Sense-Perception,* p. 31.

18. Priscian, *Metaphrasis in Theophrastum,* p. 22, l. 1; *On Theophrastus on Sense-Perception,* p. 31.

19. Priscian, *Metaphrasis in Theophrastum,* pp. 21, l. 32–22, l. 16; *On Theophrastus on Sense-Perception,* p. 31.

CHAPTER NINE: *HISTORIA ANIMALIUM*

1. See Aristotle, *Metaphysics* 4.5.1009b21–31, and *De anima* 1.2.404b1–6 and 405a8–16, and 3.427a19–29. Cf. Theophrastus, *On Sense-Perception,* p. 23.

2. Aristotle, *De anima* 1.2.404b1–5.

3. Cf. Agamben's analysis of the "anthropological machine" in *L'aperto.*

4. Aëtius 4.5.12 (*Dox. Gr.* 392.4–7).

5. Diogenes of Apollonia frag. 4, in Diels-Kranz.

6. Plato, *Laws* 961d.

7. Plato, *Timaeus* 42d–b and 91d–c, *Republic* 376b, and *Statesman* 263d. On Plato and animals, see the classic work by Dierauer, *Tier und Mensch in der Antike,* pp. 66–99. See also Sorabji's helpful summary in *Animal Minds and Human Morals,* pp. 9–12.

8. Plato, *Theaetetus* 186b–c.

9. See, among others, Sorabji, *Animal Minds and Human Morals,* pp. 11–12. For Aristotle's claims that animals lack *logos,* see *De anima* 3.3.428a24, *Eudemian Ethics* 2.8.1224a27, *Politics* 7.13.1332b5, *Nicomachean Ethics* 1.7.1098a3–4; on *logismos,* see *De anima* 3.10.433a12; on *dianoia,* see *De partibus animalium* 1.1.641b7; on *nous,* see *De anima* 1.2.404b4–6; on *doxa,* see *De anima* 3.3.428a19 –24 and *De memoria et reminiscentia* 450a16. On Aristotle and animals, see, among many others, Dierauer, *Tier und Mensch in der Antike,* pp. 100–61; Fortenbaugh, "Aristotle"; and, most recently, Labarrière, *Langage, vie politique et movement des animaux.*

10. See Fortenbaugh, who believes such cases to "exhibit a Platonic influence," in "Aristotle."

11. Aristotle, *Historia animalium* 6078a13–16.

12. *Ibid.,* 612b21–27, 614b18–20, 618z25–28.

13. Sorabji, *Animal Minds and Human Morals*, p. 13. The reference is to Aristotle, *Historia animalium* 9.631a27. Plutarch's Autobulus will dwell at some length on this "as if" (*hōsanei*): "As for those who foolishly affirm that animals do not feel pleasure or anger or fear or make preparations or remember, but that the bee 'as it were' remembers [*hōsanei mnēmoneuein*] and the swallow 'as it were' prepares her nest and the lion 'as it were' grows angry and the deer 'as it were' is frightened — I do not know what they will do about those who say that beasts do not see or hear, but 'as it were' hear and see; that they have no cry but 'as it were'; nor do they live at all but 'as it were.' For these last statements (or so I believe) are no more contrary to plain evidence than those that they have made." *De sollertia animalium* 961E–F, in Plutarch, *Moralia*, vol. 12, pp. 332–35. The objection appears again in Porphyry, *De abstinentia* 3.22.5 (see *De l'abstinence*, pp. 180–81).

14. Aristotle, *De anima* 2.2.413b24–27.

15. *Ibid.*, 2.2.413b21–24.

16. *Ibid.*, 3.7.431a10–12.

17. *Ibid.*, 2.2.413b3–4.

18. Plotinus, *Ennead* 4.3[28].24.21–13; cf. 5.8[31].11.13: *ta de hēmōn kai hēmeis anaisthētoi*, "that which is ours and we ourselves are not objects of sensation." On these passages, see Schroeder, "Synousia, Synaisthaesis and Synesis," esp. pp. 682–83.

19. Original in John Philiponus, *Ioannis Philoponi*, p. 464, ll. 20–26; English in *On Aristotle on the Soul*, p. 40.

20. On Plutarch of Athens's psychology, see Blumenthal, "Plutarch's Exposition of the *De Anima*," and Lautner, "Rival Theories of Self-Awareness in Late Neoplatonism" and "Plutarch of Athens on *koinē aisthēsis* and Phantasia."

21. On this text, see Bernard, "Philoponus on Self-Awareness."

22. Simplicius, *Simplicii in libros Aristotelis De anima commentaria* pp. 187, ll. 27–28: *to de aisthanesthai hoti aisthanometha anthrōpou moi monon idion einai dokei.*

23. Hadot, "Aspects de la théorie de la perception chez les Néoplatoniciens," p. 68.

24. Original in Alexander of Aphrodisias, *Alexandri Aphrodisiensis*, p. 93, ll. 18–22; English in *Quaestiones*, p. 56.

CHAPTER TEN: APPROPRIATION

1. Diogenes Laertius, *Lives* 7.183, vol. 2, pp. 292–93: *ei mē gar ēn Khrusippos, ouk an ēn stoa.*

2. *Ibid.*, 7.180, pp. 288–89: *houtō d'epidoxos en tois dialektikois egeneto, hōste dokein tous pleious hoti ei para theois ēn [hē] dialektikē, ouk an allē ēn hē Khrusippeios.*

3. *Ibid.*, The life is contained in 7.179.1–185.11.

4. Plutarch, *De sollertia animalium* 980a-b, *Moralia*, pp. 444–45.

5. Aristotle, *Historia animalium* 5.547b14–17, pp. 150–51: *hai de pinnai orthai phuontai ek tou bussou en tois ammōdesi kai borborōdesin, ekhousi d' en hautais pinnophulaka, hai men karidion, hai de karkinion. hou steriskomenai diaphtheirontai thatton;* "Pinnae grow erect out of their *byssus* in sandy and muddy places. They have inside them a 'pinna-guard'; some of them have a small card, some a small crab; and if they are deprived of it they quickly perish."

6. See Chrysippus, *Oeuvre philosophique*, vol. 2, frags. 727–31 (=*SVF* 2.729a, 729b, 729, 730).

7. Thompson, *Glossary of Greek Fishes*, pp. 200–202.

8. Athenaeus, *Deipnosophistai* 3.38.6–15, in Chrysippus, *Oeuvre philosophique*, frag. 728 (=*SVF* 2.729a).

9. Cicero, *De natura deorum* 2.123–24, in Chrysippus, *Oeuvre philosophique*, frag. 730 (=*SVF* 2.729); Plutarch, *De sollertia animalium* 980a8-b8, in Chrysippus, *Oeuvre philosophique*, frag. 729 (=*SVF* 2.729b).

10. Cicero, *De natura deorum* 2.123–24, in Chrysippus, *Oeuvre philosophique*, frag. 730 (=*SVF* 2.729); Plutarch, *De sollertia animalium* 980a8–b8, in Chrysippus, *Oeuvre philosophique*, frag. 729 (=*SVF* 2.729b).

11. Plutarch, *De sollertia animalium* 980b, *Moralia*, pp. 444–45.

12. Cicero, *De natura deorum* 2.123–24: "In quo admirandum est congressune aliquo inter se an iam inde ab ortu natura ipsa congregatae sint?"

13. Long, "Soul and Body in Stoicism," p. 49.

14. Seneca, Epistle 124.21: "Nullo modo prodesse possum magis quam si tibi bonum tuum ostendo, si te a mutis animalibus separo, si cum deo pono"; *Lettere a Lucilio*, vol. 2, p. 976.

15. Cicero, *De officiis* 1.105.

16. This was the basis of the orthodox Stoic proposition that the ancient vegetarians, such as Porphyry, could not accept: that, as Chrysippus is said to have written in the first book of his treatise on justice, "there can be no justice

toward the other animals, for the differences between them are too great." Diogenes Laertius, *Lives* 7.129 (= *SVF* 3.367).

17. The *hormē* and *aisthēsis* of Stoic animals have often been thought to represent a reworking of the *orektikon* and *aisthēsis* of their Aristotelian homologues (see Aristotle, *De anima* 3.10.433a9, 433a20, 433a27, 433b39, and *Nicomachean Ethics* 7.8.1150b28). See Long, "Soul and Body," p. 46 (who alludes to the division between the *kinētikon* and *aisthēsis*), and "Representation and the Self in Stoicism," pp. 105–106. On the two animal faculties among the Stoics, see, for example, Origen, *De principiis* 3.12–3, in Chrysippus, *Oeuvre philosophique*, frag. 996 (=*SVF* 2.988 and 990). On the difference between *aisthēsis* and *phantasia* in Stoicism (the one implying "assent," *sunkatathesis* or *adsensio*, the other not), see Long, "Representation and the Self in Stoicism," esp. pp. 104–11; on contemporary debates over Stoic animals and their capacity or incapacity to assent, see the summary in Sorabji, *Animal Minds and Human Morals*, pp. 40–44.

18. Pohlenz, "Die Oikeiosis," *Grundfragen der stoischen Philosophie* p. 11; Pembroke, "Oikeiōsis," pp. 114–15.

19. Striker, "The Role of *Oikeiosis* in Stoic Ethics," p. 145.

20. See Sorabji, *Animal Minds and Human Morals*, p. 122.

21. Kerferd, "Search for Personal Identity," p. 180.

22. Pembroke, "Oikeiōsis," p. 115.

23. Kerferd, "Search for Personal Identity," pp. 181–82.

24. Herodotus 6.54 and Thucydides 3.86; on these passages, see Kerferd, "Search for Personal Identity," p. 181.

25. See Pembroke, "Oikeiōsis," p. 115 n.1, which refers to Herodotus 4.148.1, Thucydides 1.36.1 and 2.65.3, Aeneas Tactitus 24.5, and Plato, *Laws* 843e1 and *Sophist* 223b1. Cf. Görgemanns's remarks in "*Oikeiōsis* in Arius Didymus," p. 184.

26. Pembroke, "Oikeiōsis," p. 116. Pembroke believes *oikeousthai* to be a "middle" (*ibid.*, p. 115). Görgemanns, by contrast, treats it as a "passive," citing as clear evidence the aorist: *oikeiōthēn* ("*Oikeiōsis* in Arius Didymus," p. 184).

27. Görgemanns, "*Oikeiōsis* in Arius Didymus," p. 184.

28. See Pembroke's remarks on the subject, "Oikeiōsis," p. 116.

29. On the theory of *philautia* and the setting in which Aristotle developed his concept, see Gantar, "Amicus sibi I" and "Amicus sibi II." On the Delphic imperative, see Courcelle, *Connais-toi toi-même.*

30. Here I follow those scholars who prefer *sunaisthēsis* to *suneidēsis* as a *lec-*

tio: Pohlenz, "Die Oikeiosis," p. 7, esp. n.1; Schwyzer, "'Bewusst' und 'Unbe-wusst' bei Plotin," pp. 354–55; Pembroke, "Oikeiōsis," pp. 119 and 142 n.25; Inwood, "Hierocles," p. 169 n.19. Other have retained *suneidēsis*: see, for example, the edition edited by Arnim: *SVF* 3.178.

31. Diogenes Laertius, *Lives* 7.85 (=*SVF* 3.178).

32. Cicero, *De finibus bonorum et malorum* 3.5.16 (=*SVF* 3.182), Rackham edition, pp. 232–34.

33. Kerferd, "Search for Personal Identity," p. 185.

34. On "that which is first by nature," see the classic study by Philippson, "Das 'Erste Naturgemäße." On the structure of arguments from the moment of birth in Greek thought, see Jacques Brunschwig, "Cradle Argument," pp. 113–44 and, on the Stoics in particular, pp. 128–44.

35. Striker, "Role of *Oikeiōsis* in Stoic Ethics," p. 153.

36. Even such an authoritative commentator as Kerferd can describe the living being "appropriated to itself" as "an animal, which, through its consciousness of itself, is itself" ("Search for Personal Identity," p. 185). Cf. Long's comments on the subject in "Representation and the Self in Stoicism," esp. pp. 117–20.

37. Cicero, *De finibus bonorum et malorum*, p. 233.

38. See *ibid.*, 3.5.16 (=*SVF* 3.182); more generally, it remains of help to consult von Arnim's *Ethica IV, De appetitu et selectione*, sec. 2, "De primo appetitu et prima conciliatione," *SVF* 3.178–89.

39. Stobaeus 2.88.18 (=*SVF* 3.173); Diogenes, *Lives* 7.113; 129 (=*SVF* 3.396; 716). See Pembroke, "Oikeiōsis," p. 130 and, for further references, p. 146 n.78.

40. Plutarch, *De stoicorum repugnantiis* 12, p. 1038 (=*SVF* 3.724 and 1.197 [2]).

41. Porphyry, *De abstinentia* 3.19.2, p. 174 (=*SVF* 1.197 [1]).

42. Seneca, Epistle 121.5, *Lettere a Lucilio*, vol. 2, p. 942.

43. *Ibid.*, Epistle 121.6, p. 944.

44. *Ibid.*, Epistle 121.7, p. 944.

45. *Ibid.*, Epistle 121.8, p. 944.

46. *Ibid.*

47. As Brunschwig has observed ("Cradle Argument," p. 136 n.43), the definition represents a "cumulative summary of the four Stoic 'categories' (*hupo-keimenon poion pros ti pōs ekhon*)." Cicero also employs for *sustasis* the Latin term *status*.

48. Seneca, Epistle 121.10, p. 944.

49. *Ibid.*, Epistle 121.11, p. 944.

50. *Ibid.*, Epistle 121.17, p. 948.

51. On the care of the self, see the classic study by Foucault, *Le souci de soi*, esp. pp. 53–94. It is of consequence for Foucault's analysis that he left unexamined the question of animal nature, to the point of maintaining, with reference to Epictetus (1.16.1–3), that the care of the self could be effectively defined as "the proper of man" (*Le souci de soi*, p. 65).

52. Seneca, Epistle 121.18, p. 948.

53. In Alexander of Aphrodisias, *Alexandri Aphrodisiensis*, p. 150.25 (=*SVF* 3.183).

54. Philippson ("Das 'Erste Naturgemäße,'" pp. 455–56) and Pohlenz ("Die Oikeiosis," p. 9) understand the passage to allude to a difference of doctrine between Zeno and Chrysippus, but one may also take both statements as the expressions of a single view, most "precisely and elegantly" stated, as Alexander suggests, in the second form. Cf. the remarks in Pembroke, "Oikeiōsis," pp. 145–46 n.77.

CHAPTER ELEVEN: ELEMENTS OF ETHICS

1. See Diels and Schubart, *Didymos*, p. ix.

2. On the acquisition of the papyrus, see ibid. Cf. the paleographical account in the introduction to A. A. Long and Guido Bastianini's edition of Hierocles, "Ethica Moralia," in Adorno (ed.), *Corpus dei papiri filosofici*, pp. 270–81.

3. See Diels and Schubart, *Didymos*.

4. Arnim, *Stoicorum veterum fragmenta*, to which one may add the fourth volume, *Indices*, published by Adler in 1924.

5. Hierocles, *Hierokles Ethische Elementarlehre*.

6. Aulus Gellius, *Noctes Atticae* 9.5.8.

7. See Praechter, *Hierokles der Stoiker*, which established that Hierocles the Stoic, the source of the fragments in Stobaeus, was to be distinguished from Hierocles of Alexandria, the Neoplatonist of the fifth century. See the summaries of the debates on the subject in Badalamenti, "Ierocle stoico," pp. 53–57, and, more recently and exhaustively, Adorno (ed.), *Corpus dei papiri filosofici*, pp. 282–83. For Arnim's position, see Hierocles, *Hierokles Ethische Elementarlehre*, pp. xiv–xv.

8. On the title to the work, see the summary of scholarship on the subject in Adorno (ed.), *Corpus dei papiri filosofici*, pp. 373–74.

9. *Ibid.*, 1.1–2, p. 296.

10. *Ibid.*, 1.32–36, p. 300.

11. On Hierocles's terminology of perception, see Badalamenti, "Ierocle stoico," and see the note to the modern translation in Hierocles, "Ethica Moralia," in Adorno (ed.), *Corpus dei papiri filosofici*, p. 295, which explains that the three Greek terms in the work (*aisthēsis*, *sunaisthēsis*, and *antilēpsis*) will be rendered by the single modern expression "perception," on the grounds that Hierocles himself clearly uses such diverse forms "interchangeably, as if they were synonyms," and any attempt to distinguish them in the Italian translation runs the risk of distorting the original meaning. Cf. also Long, "Hierocles on Self-Perception." On the importance given by Hierocles to self-perception, see Inwood, "Hierocles."

12. Inwood, "Hierocles," esp. p. 154; cf. Long, "Hierocles on Self-Perception."

13. Cf. Sextus Empiricus, *Adversus mathematicus* 7.162 (=*SVF* 2.63).

14. Adorno (ed.), *Corpus dei papiri filosofici*, 6.1–3, p. 334.

15. *Ibid.*, 6.2–6, p. 334.

16. Pembroke, "Oikeiōsis," p. 118.

17. See Sextus Empiricus, *Adversus mathematicus* 7.191 and 6.3. On Hierocles and the Skeptic argument, see Brunschwig, "Cradle Argument," p. 142 n.52, and Badalamenti, "Ierocle stoico," pp. 68–70.

18. Montaigne, "Apologie de Raimond Sebond," *Oeuvres complètes*, p. 571: "Les Cyrenayens tenoyent que rien n'estoit perceptible par le dehors, et que cela estoit seulement perceptible qui nous touchoit par l'interne attouchement."

19. Adorno (ed.), *Corpus dei papiri filosofici*, 5.61, p. 332, and 6.6–10, p. 334. On the logical structure of this reasoning, see Brunschwig, "Cradle Argument," pp. 142–43.

20. Adorno (ed.), *Corpus dei papiri filosofici*, 4.54–58, p. 324.

21. For what follows, see *ibid.*, 4.60–5.19, pp. 326–28.

22. Kannicht and Snell (eds.), *Fragmenta adespota*, 416, 2.

23. Adorno (ed.), *Corpus dei papiri filosofici*, 5.24–25, p. 328.

24. *Ibid.*, 5.23–24, p. 328.

25. Brunschwig ("Cradle Argument," p. 141 n.51) has called attention to the form of this proof, which can be formalized as follows: "if S_1 is that S that has most chance of being P, and if S_1 is not P, then no S is P." As Brunschwig notes, the strategy is mentioned in Aristotle's *Topics* (3.119b31–34) and employed once by Sextus Empiricus, *Adversus mathematicus* 7.411.

26. Adorno (ed.), *Corpus dei papiri filosofici*, 1.37–40, p. 300. The identity of Hierocles's antagonists has been a subject of some dispute: see Inwood, "Hierocles," pp. 167–83, and Long and Bastianini's notes in Adorno (ed.), *Corpus dei papiri filosofici*, pp. 390–96.

27. Adorno (ed.), *Corpus dei papiri filosofici*, 1.50–51, p. 302.

28. Seneca, Epistle 121.12, *Lettere a Lucilio*, vol. 2, p. 946.

29. Adorno (ed.), *Corpus dei papiri filosofici*, 1.52–2.1, pp. 302–304.

30. Hierocles, *Hierokles Ethische Elementarlehre*, pp. xx–xxi.

31. Inwood, "Hierocles," p. 159.

32. Adorno (ed.), *Corpus dei papiri filosofici*, 2.5–18, p. 304–306.

33. *Ibid.*, 2.20–31, and 2.34–46, pp. 306–308.

34. *Ibid.*, 2.47–48, p. 308.

35. *Ibid.*, 2.58–3.2, p. 310. On Hierocles and his deer, see the remarks in *ibid.*, p. 406, which refer the reader to the corresponding treatment of the animal's antlers in Aristotle, *Historia animalium* 9.5, Pliny, *Historia naturalis* 8.117, Phaedrus 1.12, and Babrius 43.12–15.

36. See Adorno (ed.), *Corpus dei papiri filosofici*, 2.58–3.2, pp. 405–406; on Hierocles's *argumentum ex mirabilibus*, cf. also Inwood, "Hierocles," pp. 164–67.

37. Adorno (ed.), *Corpus dei papiri filosofici*, 2.58–3.2, p. 405.

Chapter Twelve: The Hound and the Hare

1. Sextus Empiricus, *Outlines of Pyrrhonism* 1.69, pp. 40–41.

2. *Ibid.*

3. See *ibid.* It is presumably "fifth" in that its terms are five: "Either A, or B, or C; if not A, or B, then necessarily C." Plutarch calls it not "disjunctive" (*diezeugmenon*) but "indemonstrable" (*anapodeiktos*) in *De sollertia animalium* 969b, *Moralia*, pp. 376–77. For its form, see Diogenes, *Lives* 7.81. Cf. the corresponding passage in Philo Judaeus, *De animalibus* 45; *Alexander*, pp. 138–39.

4. Sextus Empiricus, *Outlines of Pyrrhonism* 1.69, pp. 40–41.

5. Porphyry, *De abstinentia* 3.6.3–4; *De l'abstinence*, p. 159; Philo, *De animalibus* 45 and 84; Aelian, *De natura animalium* 6.59.

6. Philo, *De animalibus* 45, Alexander; pp. 138–39.

7. Pohlenz, *Die Stoa*, vol. 2, p. 49; Dierauer agrees (*Tier und Mensch*, p. 222).

8. Montaigne, "Apologie de Raimond Sebond," *Oeuvres complètes*, pp. 440–41.

9. Samuel Clarke, "The Lives of Thirty Two English Divines," *A General*

Martyrologie, 3rd ed. (London: Printed for William Birch, 1677), pp. 80–81, cited in Costello, *Scholastic Curriculum*, p. 25.

10. Plutarch, *De sollertia animalium* 969b, *Moralia*, pp. 378–79.

11. Philo, *De animalibus* 83; Alexander, pp. 184–85.

12. Montaigne, *Oeuvres complètes*, p. 441.

13. Cited in Costello, *Scholastic Curriculum*, p. 26.

CHAPTER THIRTEEN: LIFE SCIENCE

1. Ovid, *Tristia* 1.3.12.

2. Augustine's *De libero arbitrio* appears to have been written over the course of several years: the first book is thought to have been completed in 388, the third and final volume in 395.

3. Augustine, *De libero arbitrio* 2.3.7.20, *La felicità; La libertà*, p. 168. All subsequent references to the *De libero arbitrio* are to this edition.

4. *Ibid.*

5. See, among others, Matthews, "Si fallor, sum."

6. Augustine, *De libero arbitrio* 2.3.7.21, p. 168.

7. *Ibid.*, 7.22, p. 168.

8. *Ibid.*, 7.24, p. 170.

9. *Ibid.*, 8.25, p. 170.

10. *Ibid.*, pp. 170–72.

11. *Ibid.*

12. *Ibid.*, 8.16, p. 172.

13. *Ibid.*, 2.4.10.38, p. 178.

14. *Ibid.*, 2.3.9.33, pp. 174–76.

15. *Ibid.*, 2.4.10.38, p. 178.

16. *Ibid.*, 2.4.10.39, p. 178.

17. *Ibid.*, 2.3.9.29, p. 172. Augustine's *Confessions* contain references to a faculty of similar names: in Book One Augustine writes of an *interior sensus* "that preserves the fullness of the five senses [*custodiebam interiore sensu integritatem sensuum meorum*]" (1.20), and in Book Seven he alludes to an *interior vis* that reproduces external objects within the soul (*interior vis, cui sensus coporis exteriora nuntiaret*) (7.17).

18. For an overview of Augustine's possible precedents, see O'Daly, *Augustine's Philosophy of Mind*, pp. 102–105, and Augustine, *De magistro; De libero arbitrio*, pp. 566–67.

19. Wolfson, "Internal Senses," p. 252.

20. Aristotle, *De somno et vigilia* 2.455a22–23, and *De anima* 2.11.423 b22–24.

21. See, for instance, Adorno (ed.), *Corpus dei papiri filosofici*, 6.1–3, p. 334.

22. Aëtius, *Placita* 4.8.7 (=*SVF* 2.852). The suggestion may have been first made by Fazlur Rahman, who also cites Alexander's invocation of "inner sensible qualities" in his *De anima* (see Alexander of Aphrodisias, *Alexandri Aphrodisiensis*, p. 68.31–69): Avicenna, *Psychology*, pp. 77–78.

23. Augustine, *De trinitate* 9.6.9.954, *La trinité*, p. 48, and *De libero arbitrio* 2.4.10.40, p. 178.

24. *Ibid.*, 1.7.16.52, p. 118.

25. *Ibid.*,1.7.16.53–56, p. 118.

26. *Ibid.*, 1.7.16.57, p. 120.

27. *Ibid.*, 1.7.17.59, p. 120.

28. See Bermon, *Le cogito*, p. 60.

CHAPTER FOURTEEN: THE UNNAMED KING

1. See Gutas, *Greek Thought, Arabic Culture*, p. 1.

2. On the sociopolitical conditions of the translation movement, see *ibid.*

3. Gutas dates the inception of Greco-Arabic studies to the formal proposal for research made by the Royal Society of Sciences and Humanities in Göttingen in 1830 ("ut collingantur notitiae de versionibus auctorum Graecorum Syriacis, Arabicis, Armeniacis, Persicis, quarum versionum historiâ accuratâ adhuc caremus") (*ibid.*, p. xiii).

4. *Ibid.*, p. 2.

5. On the "afterlife" of Antiquity in Islam, see the classic anthology by Rosenthal, *Das Fortleben der Antike im Islam*.

6. On philosophy as the "science of sciences," see the classic statement by Averroës (Ibn Rušd): *Book of the Decisive Treatise.* Cf. Heller-Roazen, "Philosophy before the Law."

7. On the transmission of the Aristotelian psychological works to the Arab world, see Aristotle, *Fī 'l-nafs*; Peters, *Aristoteles Arabus*, pp. 40–45; Gätje, *Studien zur Überlieferung der aristotelischen Psychologie*; Guerrero, *La recepción árabe del "De Anima"*; and Aristotle, *Aristoteles' De anima.*

8. Wolfson, "Internal Senses," p. 252.

9. *Ibid.*, pp. 254–55.

10. Wolfson believed the classifications of the Arabic and Hebrew thinkers

to be traceable to a Galenic source, and he adduced considerable terminological evidence for his hypothesis, but this remained a hypothesis, no more. See *ibid.*

11. English in Altmann and Stern, *Isaac Israeli*, pp. 135–36. For the Hebrew text, see Fried, *Sefer ha-yesodot*, p. 53. The Latin text can be found, in part, in Fried's notes: the passage cited is from *Sefer*, p. 53 n.3c: "um sit medius inter sensum visibilem scilicet corporeum et informatum qui est in anteriori parte cerebri nominatuum phantasia."

12. *Ibid.*

13. See Wolfson, "Internal Senses," pp. 274–75.

14. Al-Fārābī, *Kitāb ārā' ahl al-madīna al-fāḍila*, pp. 88–89.

Chapter Fifteen: Psychology of the 449th Night

1. Richard F. Burton, *The Book of the Thousand Nights and a Night*, vol. 5, p. 219. On the use of medical knowledge in this tale, see Strohmaier, "Avicennas Lehre von den 'inneren Sinnen,'" and Brandenburg, *Die Ärzte des Propheten*, pp. 183–87.

2. On Fārābī's classifications and the origin of the *virtus aestimativa*, see Wolfson, "Inner Senses," pp. 267–76.

3. Thomas Aquinas, *Summa theologiae* 1.Q78.A4, sec. 6.

4. See Wolfson, "Inner Senses," pp. 271–81.

5. For the Arabic text, see Avicenna, *Psychologie d'Ibn Sīnā*, vol. 1, p. 44. The Latin text can be found in *Avicenna latinus*, vol. 1, p. 87.20.

6. Avicenna, *Kitāb al-Najāt* 4.1, Arabic in *Psychologie d'Ibn Sīnā*, vol. 1, p. 157 (P182r).

7. See Pines, "La conception de la conscience de soi," esp. pp. 35–56.

8. Avicenna, *De anima* 3.8, cited in Gérard Verbeke's introduction to *Avicenna latinus*, p. 50*.

9. For the Arabic, see Avicenna, *Psychologie d'Ibn Sīnā*, vol. 1, p. 159 (B153r); Latin in *Avicenna latinus*, vol. 2, p. 5.57–59.

Chapter Sixteen: The Fountain and the Source

1. See, in particular, Jean de la Rochelle, *Tractatus de divisione multiplici potentiarum animae*; Alexander of Hales, *Expositio super tres libros Aristotelis De anima*; and Kilwardby, *On Time and Imagination*.

2. On Averroës and the inner senses, see Gätje, "Die 'inneren Sinne' bei Averroes."

3. Albertus Magnus, *Opera omnia*, vol. 7, pt. 1, *De anima*, lib. 2, tract. 4, ch.

6, p. 155; ch. 8, pp. 158–59; and ch. 10, "De Probatione sensus communis per hoc quod componit et dividit inter sensato diversorum sensuum," pp. 161–63.

4. *Ibid.*, ch. 11, p. 164.

5. *Ibid.*, ch. 12: *Et est digressio declarans, qualiter sensus communis est medietas omnium sensibilium*, pp. 164–65.

6. *Ibid.*

7. Pseudo-Dionysius the Areopagite, *De divinis nominibus* 13.n.2, and *Patrologia Graeca* 3.977d; Simon, p. 432.70–73: "sicut omnia in seipso prae-habens et supermanens secundum unam impausabilem et eandem et superple-nam et imminorabilem largitionem"; see Eustathius of Nicaea, *In Primum Aristotelis Moralium ad Nicomachum* 1096a10–14; Mercken, p. 68.69–71, cited in de Libera, "Le sens commun," p. 495.

8. Albertus Magnus, *Opera omnia*, vol. 7, pt. 1, p. 165.

9. See the title of *ibid.*, ch. 12.

10. Eckhart, *Werke*, vol. 2, p. 328. Cf. also *L'oeuvre latine de Maître Eckhart*, p. 487.

11. D'Arckel, *Li ars d'amour*, vol. 1, pt. 2, ch. 7 of sec. 1, "Cis capitles deter-mine du sens commun," pp. 198–99: "Li communs sens si est une puissance ki comprent toutes les propres choses, ki les sens particulars muevent. Et cil sens particuliers u singulars de dehors, si descendent dou commun sens ki est par en dedens; ensi con diverses lignes issent d'un cercle de c'un moïelon d'un cercle, issent à toutes parties de ce ciercle. Et ensi les sanlances des choses par les sin-gulars sens senties, sunt au sens commun raportées; par lesqueles moïennes il juge des propriétés des singulars sens, et dessoivre et destinte entre les diverses choses diversement par les sens senties, si comme nos, entre blanc et douc, dis-ons on lait. Dont disons-nous ke li sens communs est li fontaine et li sourgons de tous les sens singulars, ouquel tot li movement sensible sunt rapporté, si comme en fin derraine. Ceste possance a aucune chose en tant k'ele est sens, et aucune en tant k'ele est communs. En tant ke sens est, il rechoit des choses la sanlance sans matère et toutes voies de matère présente. En tant que communs est, il a deux choses: l'une si est li jugements de la chose sentie, par lequele nous connis-sons ke nous sommes sentant: ensi que quant nous nous jugoon véans et oïans a l'uevre d'aucun autre sens faisant; la seconde si est comparer les diverses choses senties ensanle, et deviser; ensi que dire: checi est douc et che plus douc. Ci lais est blans et si est dous. Et iche a-il pour ce k'a lui sunt raportées toutes les nuances des choses senties par cascun sens singular. Est cest virtue metent aucun

en la derantraine partie de la cervel, là li nerf sentant de cink sens singulars s'asanlent. Li autre le metent ou cuer, pour çou k'il est fontaine et racine de vie."

12. Thomas Aquinas, *Commentaria in Aristotelem*, p. 349.

CHAPTER SEVENTEEN: PERCEPTION EVERYWHERE

1. Aristotle, *De anima* 3.1.424b23: *hoti d' ouk estin aisthēsis hetera para tas pente (legō de tautas opsin, akoēn, osphrēsin, geusin, haphēn)*, "sensum autem nullum alium esse praeter hos quinque visum, inquam, auditum, odoratum, gustum et tactum."

2. For a helpful overview, see Armogathe, "Les sens," esp. pp. 175–76.

3. Thomas Aquinas, *Opusc.* 43.4, and *Summa theologiae* 1a.Q78.A4. See Armogathe, "Les sens," p. 181.

4. Shakespeare, sonnet 141, v. 9.

5. Burton, "Of the Sensible Soul," *Anatomy of Melancholy*, pt. 1, sec. 1, mem. 2, sub. 6, p. 157.

6. See the second *regula*: "Circa illa tantum objecta oportet versari, ad quorum certam et indubitatam cognitionem nostra ingenia videntur sufficere," in Descartes, *Oeuvres*, vol. 10, pp. 359–62.

7. Descartes, *Principles of Philosophy* 1.9.

8. Descartes, *Oeuvres*, vol. 7, p. 160, ll. 7–10. On this passage, and the status of *cogitatio* in Descartes more generally, see Marion, "La pensée rêve-t-elle? Les trois songes ou l'éveil du philosophe," *Questions cartésiennes*, vol. 1, pp. 7–36.

9. For a succinct account of Descartes's notion of machine-animals, see Guéroult, "Animaux-machines et cybernétique," pp. 33–40; on the debates provoked by the thesis of "animal machinery," see Baertschi, *Les rapports de l'âme et du corps*, pp. 292–311, and Dagognet, *L'animal selon Condillac*.

10. Burton, *Anatomy of Melancholy*, pt. 1, sec. 1, mem. 2, sub. 7, p. 159.

11. A number of Cartesian texts could be read as transpositions to the level of cogitation of problems once posed in terms of sensation: the *Second Meditation* is perhaps the most obvious case. For suggestive remarks on the sensitive dimensions of the Cartesian *cogitatio*, see Marion, "Le cogito s'affecte-t-il? La générosité et le dernier *cogito* suivant l'interprétation de Michel Henry," *Questions cartésiennes,* vol. 1, pp. 153–87, esp. pp. 164–72.

12. Descartes, *Oeuvres* vol. 8, p. 356, ll. 23–26. For an overview of the appearances of the term in the Cartesian corpus, see Gilson, *Index scolastico-cartésien*, pp. 263–69.

13. Armogathe, "Les sens," p. 182.

14. Descartes, *Regula XII*, *Oeuvres*, vol. 10, p. 414, ll. 1–3; *Dioptrics*, *Oeuvres*, vol. 6, p. 109, l. 14; cf. p. 129, l. 22, and p. 141, l. 17. On the invocation of the common sense in the *Regulae*, see Marion, "La déconstruction de l'eidos et la construction de l'objet (sec. 18–24)," *Sur l'ontologie grise de Descartes*, pp. 113–47, esp. pp. 122–26, and Beyssade, "Le sens commun."

15. Descartes, *Le monde*, *Oeuvres*, vol. 11, p. 176–77; *La Description du corpus humain*, *Oeuvres*, vol. 11, p. 227; Descartes to Mersenne, Dec. 24, 1640?, *Oeuvres*, vol. 3, p. 263.

16. Descartes, *Oeuvres*, vol. 7, p. 32, ll. 17–19.

17. Descartes, *Les passions de l'âme*, 1.32. See Beyssade, "Le sens commun," p. 70. The term does appear in this work (*Oeuvres*, vol. 11, pp. 385–86), as Armogathe notes ("Les sens," p. 183), but its use in this passage seems not to be technical.

18. The most famous of such cases can be found in Descartes, *Discours de la méthode*: see *Oeuvres*, vol. 6, p. 77, ll. 3–9.

19. On the history of the term "common sense," see the article in Ritter, Gründer, Gabriel, and Eisler (eds.), "Sensus Communis," *Historisches Wörterbuch*, vol. 9, pp. 622–75, esp. pp. 639–62, for the modern period. The use of the expression for "sound judgment" is already attested to for the Roman period: it has been noted that Cicero, for instance, writes of the necessity of a common sense (*principio necesse erat sensu exsistere unum communemque omnium*) (Cicero, *Timaeus* 12.44), that in *De rerum natura* Lucretius founds certain truths on the self-evidence of the *communis sensus* (Lucretius, *De rerum natura*, 1.422–25), and that Quintilian and Seneca both invoke a *sensus communis hominum* (Quintilian, *Institutio oratoria* 1.2.29; Seneca, Epistle 1.5.4); see "Sensus Communis," pp. 629–34. On the rhetorical ideal of common sense in the modern period, see also Gadamer, *Truth and Method*, pp. 19–29.

20. Campanella, *De sensu rerum et magia*, bk. 2, ch. 17, pp. 90–93.

21. Telesio, *De rerum natura*, bk. 1, ch. 6, vol. 1, p. 68.

22. Campanella, *De sensu rerum et magia*, p. 91.

23. See Aristotle, *De anima* 2.12.424a17–24.

24. See the argument in the *Realis philosophia epilogistica* (Frankfurt: [n.p.], 1623), 1.42. Cf. the acute remarks in Gilson, "Notes sur Campanella."

25. See, for example, Campanella, *De sensu rerum et magia*, bk. 2, ch. 15, pp. 79–86.

26. *Ibid.*, p. 79.

27. *Ibid.*, p. 80.

28. Blanchet, *Campanella*, p. 270.

29. Campanella, *De sensu rerum et magia*, bk. 2, ch. 12, pp. 68–74. On this point he differs from Telesio, who had maintained that hearing, in contrast to the other senses, could not be reduced to touch: see *De rerum natura* 7.8, vol. 3, p. 282. Cf. Luigi de Franco, *Introduzione a Bernardino Telesio*, p. 295.

30. Campanella, *De sensu rerum et magia*, bk. 2, ch. 15, p. 81.

31. Telesio, *De rerum natura* 1.34, p. 50; cf. 7.2, p. 276 and 5.7.

32. See Campanella, *De sensu rerum et magia*, 2.15 and 1.4; cf. *Compendium physiologiae*, 27.2, p. 106: "Est enim est sensibilis obietcti dignogtio ex percepta passione ab ea; cf. the formulation in Epilogo magno," p. 367.

33. Campanella, *Compendium physiologiae* 27.1, published as *Compendio di filosofia della natura*, p. 106: "Sensum, quo videntur cuncta animalia praedita esse, distinguique ab inanimatis, in omni re dicimus reperiri."

34. Campanella, *Compendium physiologiae*, 27.4, p. 108.

35. Campanella, *De sensu rerum et magia*, 3.14, pp. 213–19.

36. Campanella, *Metafisica*, bk. 6, ch. 7, art. 1, vol. 2, p. 100; cf. *De sensu rerum et magia*, bk. 1, ch. 9, p. 26.

37. Campanella, *Compendium physiologiae* 27.11, p. 108: "Sensus in aliis rebus est clarior et vivacior, in aliis obscurior et obtusior."

38. Campanella, *Metafisica*, bk. 6, ch. 7, art. 1, vol. 2, p. 88.

39. On Telesio and self-conservation, see Mulsow, *Frühneuzeitliche Selbsterhaltung*.

40. Campanella, see *Metafisica*, bk. 6, ch. 8, art. 3.

41. See *ibid.*, art. 4, vol. 2, pp. 130–36. Campanella's terms vary, but the distinction of perceptions remains constant: *innatus* and *inditus* are repeatedly opposed to *acquisitus*, *illatus*, *superadditus*, and *additus*. Before Campanella, Agostino Donio had already written in like terms of a *sensus abditus*: see Fiorentino, *Bernardino Telesio*, vol. 1, pp. 321–41, esp. p. 329. On the relations between *sensus additus* and *sensus abditus* in Campanella, see also Isoldi Jacobelli, *Tommaso Campanella*, esp. pp. 65–84.

42. Campanella, *Epilogo magno*, p. 367. Campanella's formulations are consistent: cf. *De sensu rerum et magia* 2.15, p. 79: "Non potersi far senso per informazion perfettiva solo, come Aristotile disse, nè ci esser senso agente, nè il senso pura potenza incorporea, ma ente passibile, e sentire per mutazione poca e per argomento."

43. Campanella, *Metafisica*, bk. 6, ch. 7, art. 1, vol. 2, p. 98.

44. *Ibid*., art. 3, vol. 2, pp. 112–14.

45. Campanella, *De sensu rerum et magia*, bk. 1, ch. 4, p. 12.

46. Bacon, *De argumentis scientiarum*, bk. 4, ch. 3, *Works*, vol. 1, pp 353–55: "Atque differentiam inter Perceptionem et Sensum bene enucleatam debuerant philosophi tractatibus suis de Sensu et Sensibili praemittere, ut rem maxime fundamentalem. Videmus enim quasi omnibus corporibus naturalibus inesse vim manifestam *percepiendi*; etiam electionem quandam amica amplectendi, inimica et aliena fugiendi. Neque nos de subtilioribus perceptionibus tantum loquimur; veluti cum magnes ferrum allicit; flamma ad naphtham assilit; bulla bullae approximate coït; radiatio ab objecto albo dissilit; corpus animalis utilia assimilat, inutilia excernit; spongiae pars (etiam super aquam elevate) aquam attrahit, aërem expellit; et hujusmodi. Etenim quid attinet talia enumerare? Nullum siquidem corpus ad aliud admotum illud immutat au ab illo immutatur, nisi operationem praecedat Perceptio reciproca. *Percipit* corpus meatus quibus se insinuat; *percipit* impetum alterius corporis cui cedit; *percipit* amotionem alterius corporis a quo detinebatur, cum se recipit; *percipit* divulsionem sui continui, cui ad tempus resistit; ubique denique est Perceptio. Aër ver Calidum et Frigidum tam acute *percipit*, ut ejus Perceptio sit longe subtilior quam tactus humani; qui tamen pro calidi et frigidi norma habetur. Duplex igitur deprehenditur circa hanc doctrinam hominum culpa; alia, quod eam intactam et intractatam (cum tamen sit res nobilissima) plerumque reliquerunt; alia, quod qui huic contemplationi forte animum adjecerunt longius quam par est provecti sunt, et *Sensum* corporibus omnibus tribuerunt; ut piaculum fere sit ramum arboris avellere, ne forte instar Polydori ingemiscat. At debuerant illi Differentiam Perceptionis et Sensus, non tantum in comparatione sensibilium ad insensibilia, secundum corpus integrum, explorare, (veluti plantarum et animalium); verum etiam in corpore ipso sensibili animadvertere, quid in causa sit cur tot actiones expediantur absque omni tamen Sensu; cur alimenta digerantur, egerantur; humores et succi sursum deorsum ferantur; cor et pulsus vibrent; viscera sua quaeque opificia, sicut officinae, producant; et tamen haec omnia, et complura alia, absque Sensu fiant? Verum homines non satis acute, qualis sit actio Sensus, viderunt; atque quod genus corporis, quae mora, quae conduplicatio impressionis ad hoc requirantur, ut dolor vel voluptas sequatur? Denique differentiam inter Perceptionem simplicem et Sensum nullum modo nosse videntur; nec quatenus fieri possit Perceptio absque Sensu. Neque enim haec verborum tantum controversia

est, sed de re magni prorsus momenti." English in Bacon, *Philosophical Works*, pp. 496–97.

47. John Robertson, for his part, judges such a possibility "unlikely" (*ibid.*, p. 497n), given the proximity in the dates of the publication of Campanella's work and Bacon's.

CHAPTER EIGHTEEN: OF THE MERITS OF MISSILES

1. See Leibniz, *Opera omnia*, vol. 6, p. 303.

2. "Quid *Cartesio* in physicis, *Hobbio* in moralibus acutius? At si ille Bacono, hic *Campanellae* comparetur, apparet illos humi repete; hos magnitudine cogitationum, consiliorum, imò destinationum assurgere in nubes, ac pene humanae potentiae imparia moliri" (*ibid*). Leibniz alludes at several points to Campanella: see "Theodicy," *Die philosophischen Schriften*, vol. 6.1, sec. 150, p. 199; "Guilielmi Pacidii plus ultra," *Die philosophischen Schriften*, vol. 7, p. 52; "Antibarbarus Physicus pro philosophia reali contra renovationes qualitatum scholasticarum et intelligentiarum chimaericarum," *Die philosophischen Schriften*, vol. 7, p. 339; *Opera omnia*, vol. 5, pp. 260 and 421, vol. 1, pp. 71 and 240. On Leibniz and Campanella, see Blanchet, *Campanella*, pp. 549–54.

3. Leibniz, "Sur ce qui passe les sens et la matière," *Die philosophischen Schriften*, vol. 6, p. 488.

4. See *ibid.*, p. 493; "Lettre sur ce qui passe les sens et la matière," *Die philosophischen Schriften*, vol. 6, p. 493; Leibniz to Queen Sophie Charlotte of Prussia, "Lettre touchant ce qui est independant des Sens et de la Matière," *Die philosophischen Schriften*, vol. 6, pp. 499–508.

5. See Leibniz, "Sur ce qui passe les sens et la matiere," *Die philosophischen Schriften*, vol. 6, esp. p. 490, as well as the letters to Queen Sophie Charlotte of Prussia that follow it (*Die philosophischen Schriften*, pp. 491–538).

6. For an argument for the limits of intentional experience in Descartes, see Marion, "Le Cogito s'affecte-t-il? La générosité et le dernier cogito suivant l'interprétation de Michel Henry," *Questions cartésiennes*, vol. 1, esp. pp. 164–78.

7. Locke, *Essay Concerning Human Understanding*, bk. 2, ch. 1, sec. 10, p. 109.

8. *Ibid.*, p. 108.

9. *Ibid.*, sec. 11, p. 109.

10. *Ibid.*, sec. 9, p. 108.

11. *Ibid.*, sec. 16, p. 113.

12. *Ibid.*, sec. 15, p. 112.

13. *Ibid.*, sec. 9, p. 108.

14. Locke, *Essai philosophique concernant l'entendement humain.*

15. Leibniz, "Echantillon de Reflexions sur le II. Livre de l'Essay de l'Entendement de l'homme," *Die philosophischen Schriften*, vol. 5, p. 23.

16. *Ibid.*, pp. 23–24.

17. On Leibniz's theory of small perceptions, see, among others, Herbertz, *Die Lehre vom Unbewussten*, esp. pp. 29–68; Jalabert, "La psychologie de Leibniz"; and Kulstad, "Two Arguments on *Petites Perceptions*," and "Some Diffficulties in Leibniz's Definition of Perception."

18. Leibniz, "Echantillon de Reflexions sur le II. Livre," p. 23.

19. *Ibid.*

20. *Ibid.*

21. Locke, *Essay Concerning Human Understanding*, bk. 2, ch. 1, sec. 13, p. 111.

22. *Ibid.*, sec. 14, p. 111.

23. *Ibid.*, sec. 15, p. 112.

24. *Ibid.*, sec. 18, p. 114.

25. *Ibid.*, sec. 19, p. 115.

26. *Ibid.*

27. *Ibid.*, pp. 115–16.

28. La Forge, *Traitté de l'esprit de l'homme*, p. 97.

29. Leibniz, preface to *Nouveaux essais sur l'entendement*, *Die philosophischen Schriften*, vol. 5, p. 46: "Il y a mille marques qui font juger qu'il y a une infinité de *perceptions* en nous, mais sans apperception et sans reflexion, c'est à dire des changements dans l'ame même dont nous ne nous appercevons pas."

30. Leibniz, "Considérations sur les Principes de Vie, et sur les Natures Plastiques," *Die philosophischen Schriften*, vol. 6, p. 543.

31. See the illuminating essay by Simmons, "Changing the Cartesian Mind," esp. pp. 40–47.

32. Leibniz, preface to *Nouveaux essais sur l'entendement*, *Die philosophischen Schriften*, vol. 5, p. 47.

33. Leibniz, *Nouveaux essais sur l'entendement*, bk. 4, ch. 17, sec. 13, *Die philosophischen Schriften*, vol. 5, p. 470.

34. See *ibid.*, bk. 2, ch. 9, sec. 4, p. 121.

35. Leibniz to Queen Sophie Charlotte, *Die philosophischen Schriften*, vol. 6, p. 515. Cf. also "Sur l'Essay de l'entendement humain de Monsieur Lock," *Die*

philosophischen Schriften, vol. 5, p. 16; preface to *Nouveaux essais sur l'entende-ment*, *Die philosophischen Schriften*, vol. 5, p. 47; "Discours sur la métaphysique," sec. 33, *Die philosophischen Schriften*, vol. 4, p. 459.

36. For a classic statement, see Leibniz's letter to Masson, *Die philosophis-chen Schriften*, vol. 6, p. 628.

37. Leibniz, preface to *Nouveaux essais sur l'entendement*, *Die philosophischen Schriften*, vol. 5, p. 47: "Pour entendre ce bruit comme l'on fait, il faut bien qu'on entende les parties qui composent ce tout, c'est à dire les bruits de chaque vague, quoyque chacun de ces petits bruits ne se fasse connoistre que dans l'assemblage confus de tous les autres ensemble, c'est à dire dans ce mugisse-ment même, et ne se remarqueroit pas si cette vague qui le fait, estoit seule."

38. See, for example, Leibniz, "Monadologie," sec. 23, *Die philosophischen Schriften*, vol. 6, p. 610.

39. Simmons, "Changing the Cartesian Mind," p. 63.

40. On Leibniz, the infinitesimal method and its history, see Cohen's classic 1883 study, "Das Princip der Infinitesimal-Methode und seine Geschichte"; cf. the critical reviews and remarks by Frege, *Kleine Schriften*, pp. 99–102, and Rus-sell, *Principles of Mathematics*, secs. 315–24, pp. 338–45.

CHAPTER NINETEEN: THORNS

1. See Leibniz, "Eclaircissement des difficultés que M. Bayle a trouvées dans le systeme nouveau de l'union de l'ame et du corps," *Die philosophischen Schriften*, vol. 4, p. 562. See, among many other passages, *ibid.*, p. 532. Numerous other texts could be equally cited: see, among others, Leibniz to Arnauld, Nov. 28/Dec. 8, 1686, and April 1687; "Monadologie," sec. 62, *Die philosophischen Schriften*, vol. 6, pp. 607–23; "Discours sur la métaphysique," sec. 33, *Die philosophischen Schriften*, vol. 4, p. 459.

2. See Leibniz, *Die philosophischen Schriften*, vol. 4, p. 520; cf. the letter to Lady Masham in *ibid.*, vol. 2, p. 355.

3. Leibniz to Arnauld, April 30, 1678, in *ibid.*, vol. 2, p. 95.

4. Leibniz, preface to *Nouveaux essais sur l'entendement*, *Die philosophischen Schriften*, vol. 5, p. 46.

5. Leibniz, *Nouveaux essais sur l'entendement*, bk. 2, ch. 1, sec. 15, *Die philosophischen Schriften*, vol. 5, p. 106.

6. Cf. Leibniz's remarks on the subject in his letters to Arnauld: *Die philosophischen Schriften*, vol. 2, pp. 90 and 340–41.

7. Leibniz, "Eclaircissement des difficultés," esp. pp. 531–32.

8. *Ibid.*, p. 532.

9. See *ibid.*; cf. the similar passage, this time without the dog, in *ibid.*, pp. 546–47.

10. Locke, *Essay Concerning Human Understanding*, bk. 2, ch. 21, sec. 29, p. 249.

11. *Ibid.*, sec. 31, pp. 250–51.

12. Leibniz, *Nouveaux essais sur l'entendement*, bk. 2, ch. 20, sec. 6, *Die philosophischen Schriften*, vol. 4, pp. 150–51.

13. *Ibid.*; see Locke, *Essai philosophique*, pp. 193 and 177.

14. Leibniz, *Nouveaux essais sur l'entendement*, bk. 2, ch. 20, sec. 6, *Die philosophischen Schriften*, vol. 4, p. 151.

15. *Ibid.*, p. 153.

16. *Ibid.*

17. *Ibid.*, p. 151.

18. Locke, *Essay Concerning Human Understanding*, bk. 2, ch. 21, sec. 40, p. 258.

19. Locke, *Essai philosophique*, p. 200.

20. Leibniz, *Nouveaux essais sur l'entendement*, bk. 2, ch. 20, sec. 5, *Die philosophischen Schriften*, vol. 4, pp. 151–52.

21. *Ibid.*, ch. 21, sec. 36, p. 175.

22 *Ibid.*, bk. 2, ch. 20, sec. 5, p. 151.

23. See Leibniz's letter to Varignon, Feb. 2, 1702, Leibniz, *Die mathematischen Schriften*, vol. 4, p. 93. On Leibniz and the law of continuity, see Philonenko, "La loi de continuité." pp. 261–86.

24. Leibniz, preface to *Nouveaux essais sur l'entendement*, *Die philosophischen Schriften*, vol. 5, p. 49.

25. See the analysis of pleasure and pain in Leibniz, *Nouveaux essais sur l'entendement*, bk. 2, ch. 21.

26. On the formation of the term "apperception," see Capesius, *Der Apperceptionsbegriff bei Leibniz*; Sticker, *Die Leibnizischen Begriffen*; and Kulstad, *Leibniz on Apperception, Consciousness, and Reflection*.

27. Locke, *Essay Concerning Human Understanding*, bk. 2, ch. 8, sec. 8, p. 134. Cf. *ibid.*, bk. 2, ch. 9, sec. 1, p. 143: "For in bare naked *Perception*, the Mind is for the most part, only passive, and what it perceives, it cannot help perceiving," which Coste translated as follows: "Car dans ce qu'on nomme simplement

Perception l'Esprit est, pour l'ordinaire, purement passif, ne pouvant éviter d'appercevoir ce qu'il apperçoit actuellement" (Locke, *Essai philosophique*). See Capesius, *Der Apperceptionsbegriff*, p. 9 n.1.

28. Leibniz, *Sämtliche Schriften und Briefen*, ser. 6, vol. 2, p. 420. On Leibniz and Nizolio, see Fenves, "Of Philosophical Style," esp. pp. 71–76.

29. Wolff, *Psychologia empirica*, sec. 25. See Capesius, *Der Apperceptionsbegriff*, p. 20. As Capesius notes (p. 16), the term had already been translated into Latin as *aperceptio* in the posthumous edition of *Monadology* published by the Leipziger Acta Eruditorum of 1721.

30. Wolff, *Psychologia empirica*, sec. 25.

31. Kant, *Kritik der reinen Vernunft* (Critique of Pure Reason), Analytic of Concepts, sec. 16, B132.

32. See the brief summary in Capesius, *Der Apperceptionsbegriff*, pp. 20–25.

33. Kant, *Anthropology*, sec. 4, *Werke*, vol. 12, *Schriften zur Anthropologie, Geschichtsphilosophie, Politik und Pädagogik*, pt. 2, pp. 416–17n.

34. Sticker, *Die Leibnizischen Begriffen*, p. 4.

35. Leibniz, *Principes de la nature et de la grace fondés en raison*, sec. 12, *Die philosophischen Schriften*, vol. 6, p. 600.

36. Leibniz, *Monadology*, sec. 14, *Die philosophischen Schriften*, vol. 6, p. 608.

37. Leibniz, *Principes de la nature et de la grace fondés en raison*, sec. 12, p. 600.

38. Leibniz, *Monadology*, sec. 14, p. 608.

39. Leibniz, *Principes de la nature et de la grace fondés en raison*, sec. 12, p. 600.

40. Capesius, *Der Apperceptionsbegriff*, p. 16.

41. On small additions, see Leibniz, *Nouveaux essais sur l'entendement*, bk. 2, ch. 9, sec. 4, *Die philosophischen Schriften*, vol. 5, p. 121; cf. the famous letter to Queen Sophie Charlotte of Prussia, in which the thought of the "Self" (*Moy*) is said to "add something to the objects of the senses" (*Die philosophischen Schriften*, vol. 6, pp. 483, 493, 502).

42. Leibniz, *Monadology*, sec. 14, *Die philosophischen Schriften*, vol. 6, pp. 608–609.

43. Leibniz, *Principes de la nature et de la grace fondés en raison*, sec. 12, p. 600.

44. On perception and appetition as the hallmarks of the soul, see, among other passages, Leibniz, *Monadology*, sec. 19, p. 610.

45. Leibniz, "Considerations sur les Principes de Vie, et sur les Natures Plastiques" *Die philosophischen Schriften*, vol. 6, p. 542.

46. See Leibniz, *Monadology*, sec. 14–30, pp. 608–12. See the helpful summary in Gennaro, "Leibniz on Consciousness and Self-Consciousness," pp. 361–64.

47. Kulstad, "Leibniz, Animals, and Apperception," later incorporated into the same author's *Leibniz on Apperception, Consciousness, and Reflection*, pp. 16–52.

48. See Belaval, *Études leibniziennes*, p. 143; Gurwitsch, *Leibniz*, p. 123; McRae, *Leibniz*, esp. ch. 3; Naert, *Mémoire et conscience chez Leibniz*, p. 37.

49. In addition to Kulstad, *Leibniz on Apperception, Consciousness, and Reflection*, see Gennaro, "Leibniz on Consciousness and Self-Consciousness," esp. pp. 361–64; Simmons, "Changing the Cartesian Mind," esp. p. 54n.; Jalabert, "La psychologie de Leibniz," p. 472.

50. Leibniz, "Eclaircissement des difficultés," *Die philosophischen Schriften*, vol. 4, p. 532.

51. Leibniz, preface to *Nouveaux essais sur l'entendement*, *Die philosophischen Schriften*, vol. 5, p. 48; Kulstad, "Leibniz, Animals, and Apperception," p. 29.

52. Leibniz, *Nouveaux essais sur l'entendement*, bk. 2, ch. 21, sec. 5, *Die philosophischen Schriften*, vol. 5, p. 159: "C'est pourquoy les bestes n'ont point d'entendement, au moins dans ce sens, quoyqu'elles ayent la faculté de s'appercevoir des impressions plus remarquables et plus distingués, comme le sanglier s'apperçoit d'une personne qui luy crie et va adroit à cette personne, dont il n'avoit eu déja auparavant qu'une perception nue, mais confuse comme de tous les autres objets, qui tomboient sous ses yeux, et dont les rayons frappoient son cristallin." It is Kulstad's merit to have called attention to this example (see "Leibniz, Animals, and Apperception," p. 28).

53. On "degrees in all things," see Leibniz, "Considerations sur la doctrine d'un Esprit Universel Unique," p. 537. On degrees of perception, see Brandom, "Leibniz and Degrees of Perception."

Chapter Twenty: To Myself; or, The Great Dane

1. Rousseau, *Oeuvres complètes*, vol. 1, p. 1003.

2. *Ibid.*, pp. 1003–1005.

3. *Ibid.*: "Cette idée plus prompte que l'éclair et que je n'eus le temps ni de raisonner ni d'executer fut la dernière avant mon accident. Je ne sentis ni le coup, ni la chute, ni rien de ce qui s'ensuivit jusqu'au moment où je revins à moi."

4. *Ibid.*

5. *Ibid*: "La nuit s'avançoit. J'apperçis le ciel, quelques étoiles, et un peu de verdure. Cette prémiére sensation fut un moment délicieux. Je me ne sentois encor que par là. Je naissois dans cet instant à la vie, et il me sembloit que je remplissois de ma legere existence tous les objets que j'appercevois. Tout entier au moment present je ne me souvenois de rien; je n'avois nulle notion distincte de mon individu, pas la moindre idée de ce qui venoit de m'arriver; je ne savois ni qui j'étois ni où j'étois; je ne sentois ni mal, ni crainte, ni inquietude. Je voyais couler mon sang comme j'aurois vu couler un ruisseau, sans songer seulement que ce sang m'appartins en aucune sorte. Je sentois dans tout mon être un calme ravissant auquel chaque fois que je me rappelle je ne trouve rien de comparable dans toute l'activité des plaisirs connus."

6. Montaigne, "De l'exercitation," bk. 2, ch. 6: *Essais*, "Quand je commençai à y voir, ce fut d'une vue si trouble, si faible et si morte, que je ne discernais encore rien que la lumière.... Quant aux fonctions de l'âme, elles naissaient avec le même progrès que celles du corps. Je me vis tout sanglant.... Il me semblait que ma vie ne me tenait plus qu'au bout des lèvres; je fermais les yeux pour aider, ce me semblait, à la pousser hors, et prenais plaisir à m'alanguir et à me laisser aller. C'était une imagination qui ne faisait que nager superficiellement en mon âme, aussi tendre et aussi faible que tout le reste, mais à la vérité non seulement exempte de déplaisir, ains mêlée à cette douceur que sentient ceux qui se laissent glisser au sommeil." Cf. Agamben, *Infanzia e storia*, pp. 34–37.

7. Locke, *Essay Concerning Human Understanding*, bk. 4, ch. 9, sec. 1, pp. 618–19.

8. Leibniz, *Nouveaux essais sur l'entendement*, bk. 4, ch. 9, sec. 2, *Die philosophischen Schriften*, vol. 5, p. 415.

9. See Denis Diderot and Jean Le Rond d'Alembert (eds.), *Encyclopédie, ou, Dictionnaire raisonné des sciences, des arts et des métiers* (Paris: Briasson, 1751–1765), s.v. "Sens intime." D'Alembert defined it in his *Elements of Philosophy* of 1759 as a faculty lying "beyond the five senses, which can be called internal, which is, so to speak, intimately diffused in our substance, and whose seat is at once in all the external and the internal parts of our body" (See d'Alembert, *Essai sur les éléments de la philosophie* (1759), *Oeuvres philosophiques*, p. 259. On the theory of the inner sense in the eighteenth century, see Gusdorf, "L'inversion des priorités: Le sens intime," *Naissance de la conscience romantique*, pp. 285–316; on d'Alembert and the *Encylopedia*, see pp. 301–303.

10. Lelarge de Lignac, *Éléments de métaphyisique*, p. 39: "Notre propre exis-

tence n'est pas démontrée, elle est sentie, quoi qu'en dise M. Descartes; car je ne suis pas certain que j'existe par la nécessité de la conséquence de cet argument: Je pense, donc j'existe. La certitude de l'existence est antérieure à la conséquence; elle est renfermée dans ce mot *je*, lequel comprend la conscience de mon existence." On Lelarge de Lignac's doctrine of the inner sense, see Gusdorf, *Naissance de la conscience romantique*, pp. 302–307.

11. See, for example, Rousseau, *Émile*, bk. 4, *Oeuvres complètes*, vol. 4, p. 600: "Exister, pour nous, c'est sentir; notre sensibilité est incontestablement antérieure à notre intelligence, et nous avons eu des sentiments avant des idées."

12. On the "sentiment of existence" and the Fifth Reverie, see Starobinski, *Jean-Jacques Rousseau*, pp. 306–308; Mortier, "À propos du sentiment de l'existence"; and Poulet, "Le sentiment de l'existence et le repos."

13. Rousseau, *Oeuvres complètes*, vol. 1, p. 1045: "Quand le soir approchait je descandais des cimes de l'Ile et j'allois volontiers m'asseoir au bord du lac, sur la gréve, dans quelque azyle caché; là le bruit des vagues et l'agitation de l'eau fixant mes sens et chassant de mon ame toute autre agitation la plongeoient dans une réverie delicieuse où la me surprenoit souvent sans que je m'en fusse apercu. Le flux et reflux de cette eau, son bruit continu mais renflé par intervalles frappoint sans relâche mon oreille et mes yeux, suppleaient aux mouvements internes que la rêverie éteignoit en moi et suffisaient pour me faire sentir avec plaisir mon existence, sans prendre la peine de penser."

14. *Ibid.*, p. 1047.

15. *Ibid*: "De quoi jouit-on dans une pareille situation? De rien d'extérieur à soi, de rien sinon de soi-même et de sa propre existence, tant que cet état dure on se suffit a soi-même comme Dieu. Le sentiment de l'existence depouillé de toute autre affection est par lui-même un sentiment précieux de contentement et de paix qui suffiroit seul pour rendre cette existence chére et douce à qui sauroit écarter de soi toutes les impressions sensuelles et terrestres qui viennent sans cesse nous en distraire et en troubler ici bas la douceur."

CHAPTER TWENTY-ONE: OF FLYING CREATURES

1. On the posterity of the experiment in the Latin West, see the remarks in Gilson's classic essay, "Les sources gréco-arabes de l'augustinisme avicennisant," esp. pp. 38–42.

2. Avicenna, *Sextus de naturalibus* 1.1; the Arabic text can be found in Avicenna, *Psychology*, p. 16. In my rendition of the passage, I have benefited from

the versions offered by Druart in "The Soul and Body Problem: Avicenna and Descartes," *Arabic Philosophy and the West*, p. 32, as well as by Bakoš in Avicenna, *Psychologie*, vol. 2, pp. 12–13.

3. The second appearance of the flying man is in the *Psychology* of the *Shifā'* 5.7: see Avicenna, *al-Nafs*, p. 225, ll. 2–6. The third appearance is in *Kitāb al-ishārāt wa'l-tanbīhāt*, Forget edition, p. 119. On the man in the void more generally, see Marmura, "Avicenna's Flying Man"; Arnaldez, "Un précédent avicennien du 'cogito' cartésien?"; Druart, "Soul and Body Problem"; Pines, "La conception de la conscience de soi"; Furlani, "Avicenna e il 'Cogito, ergo sum' di Cartesio"; and Galindo-Aguilar, "'L'homme volant' d'Avicenne," pp. 279–95.

4. In Avicenna's *Psychology* of *al-Shifā'* 5.7, we thus read: "If a human being were to be created at all once, with his limbs separated such that he did not see them, and if it so happened that he did not touch them and that they did not touch each other, and if he heard no sound, he would be ignorant of the existence of the whole of his organs, but he would know the existence of his own being as one thing [*wujūd anniyyatihi shay'an*], while being ignorant of the former things." In the *Ishārāt*, we find a slightly different use of the same term: "If you imagine your essence [or "yourself," *dhātika*] created in its first creation, mature and whole in mind and body, and if it is supposed to be in such a position and physical circumstance as not to perceive its parts, with its limbs not touching each other but being rather spread apart, [and if it is supposed that it is momentarily that this self is] momentarily suspended in temperate air, you will find that it will be unaware of everything except the consistency of its own being [*thubūt anniyyathihā*]." The formation, use, and value of the technical term *anniyya* have been the subject of much discussion among historians of Arabic philosophy: see Frank, "Origin of the Arabic Philosophical Term 'Anniyat'"; Alonso Alonso, "La 'al-anniyya' de Avicena" and "La 'al-anniyya' y el 'al-wujûd' de Avicena"; d'Alverny, "Anniyya-anitas"; Simon van den Bergh, "Anniyya," in Gibb (ed.), *Encylopaedia of Islam*; and Goichon's translation of Avicenna's *Kitāb al-ishārāt wa'l-tanbīhāt*, commentary in bk. 10, ch. 3, n.3, and pp. 303–307.

5. Condillac, *Traité des sensations*, p. 10.

6. *Ibid.*, p. 11.

7. *Ibid.*, p. 9.

8. Dagognet, *L'animal selon Condillac*, p. 7.

9. Nov. 1, 1755, *Correspondance littéraire, philosophique et critique* (Paris: Garnier, 1877), vol. 3, p. 111, cited in *ibid.*, p. 8n.

10. Condillac, *Traité des Sensations*, bk. 2, ch. 5, p. 101.

11. *Ibid.*, ch. 2, pp. 91–92.

12. *Ibid.*, pp. 92–93.

13. *Ibid.*, pp. 102–104.

14. *Ibid.*, p. 104: "Mais s'il lui arrive de conduire sa main le long de son bras, et sans rien franchir, sur sa poitrine, sur sa tête, etc., elle sentira, pour ainsi dire, sous sa main, une continuité de *moi*; et cette même main, qui réunira, dans un seul continu, les parties auparavant séparées, en rendra l'étendu plus sensible."

15. *Ibid.*, p. 105.

16. *Ibid.*

17. *Ibid.* Cf. Condillac's modifications in the 1798 edition of the *Treatise*: Condillac, *Oeuvres philosophiques*, vol. 1, pp. 255–56; see Le Roy, *La psychologie de Condillac*, pp. 142ff.

18. See Azouvi, *Maine de Biran*, pp. 49–50.

19. See Destutt de Tracy, "Mémoire sur la faculté de penser" (1798) and "Dissertation sur quelques question d'idéologie" (1798), rpt. in Destutt de Tracy, *Mémoire sur la faculté de penser*, esp. pt. 1 of "Mémoire," "De la manière dont nous acquérons la connaissance des corps extérieurs et du nôtre" (pp. 37–64).

20. Maine de Biran, *Oeuvres*, vol. 2, *Mémoires sur l'influence de l'habitude*, p. 40: "L'individu qui agite ses membres, ou se meut, le supposât-on suspendu dans le vide, éprouvera nécessairement une espèce particulière d'impression, qui naît de la résistance opposée par ses muscles, et de l'*effort* fait pour les mettre en jeu."

21. Condillac, *Traité des sensations*, bk. 2, ch. 2, p. 91.

22. Maine de Biran, *Oeuvres*, vol. 3, *Mémoire sur la decomposition de la pensée*, p. 137. See the penetrating analysis in Henry, *Philosophie et phénoménologie du corps*, pp. 81–105.

23. Maine de Biran, "Notes sur l'*idéologie* de M. de Tracy," *Oeuvres*, vol. 11, pt. 3, *Commentaires et marginalia, dix-neuvième siècle*, p. 2: "L'hypothèse d'un être qui sentirait et connaîtrait son existence sans se sentir un corps ou dans un corps, est *inadmissible*; c'est l'hypothèse de Descartes renouvelée par Condillac et Tracy."

24. *Ibid.*, vol. 3, p. 134.

25. *Ibid.*, vol. 6, *Rapports du physique et du moral de l'homme*, p. 110. See Azouvi's commentary, p. 97.

26. See *ibid.*, vol. 3, p. 294, and vol. 6, p. 110.

27. *Ibid.*, vol. 10, pt. 2, *Dernière philosophie: Existence et anthropologie*, p. 77:

"Si Descartes crut poser le premier principe de toute science, la première verité évidente par elle-même, en disant: je *pense*, donc je *suis* (chose ou substance pensante), nous dirons mieux, [d'une manière] plus determine, et cette fois avec l'évidence irrécusable du sens intime: j'agis, je veux ou je pense l'action, donc je me sens *cause*, donc je suis ou j'existe réellement à titre de cause ou de force." On this "primitive fact," see Baertschi, *Les rapports de l'âme et du corps*, pp. 134–39; cf. also Tilliette, "Nouvelles réflexions sur le cogito biranien."

28. Maine de Biran, *Oeuvres*, vol. 11, pt. 1: *Commentaires et marginalia: Dix-septième siècle*, p. 36: "Supposition impossible qu'ainsi je puisse exister et dire *moi*, sans avoir la conscience du corps propre, et que je puisse avoir cette conscience de l'effort si le corps n'existe pas. Je peux bien rêver que je marche pendant que je suis dans le repos du sommeil, mais non pas que j'ai un corps sur lequel ma volonté agit, pendant que ce corps n'existe pas."

29. *Ibid.*, vol. 4, *De l'aperception immédiate: Mémoire de Berlin 1807*, p. 137: "Pour concevoir ce *moi* phenomenal dans le sens unique et individuel de son aperception immédiate, séparée de tout ce qui n'est pas elle, supposons tous les muscles volontaires contractés dans l'immobilité du corps, les yeux ouverts dans les ténèbres, l'ouïe tendue (*acuta*) dans le silence de la nature, l'air ambient en repos et la temperature extérieure en équilibre avec celle de la surface du corps, toutes les impressions internes réduites au ton naturel de la vie organique, insensibles dans leur continue uniformité."

30. *Ibid.*, pp. 137–38: "L'effort reste seul, et avec lui, le moi phenomenal pur ou réduit à son aperception immédiate interne."

31. *Ibid.*, p. 137.

32. See Azouvi's enlightening commentary: *Maine de Biran*, p. 227.

33. Maine de Biran, *Oeuvres*, vol. 3, p. 432: "Au déploiement unique de cet effort commun, à l'uniformité ou à la continuité de résistance organique, doit correspondre le sentiment d'une sorte d'*étendue intérieure* d'abord vague et illimité."

34. *Ibid.*, vol. 11, pt. 1, p. 73: "Quoique la connaissance précise de la situation des parties du corps les unes par rapport aux autres, telle que nous l'avons par le sens de la vue et du toucher, ne soit pas comprise immédiatement dans le simple exercice musculaire, on ne peut douter néanmoins que ce dernier sens ne soit spécialement approprié à l'aperception de l'espace intérieure et illimité du *corps propre*."

35. *Ibid.*, vol. 4, pp. 124–25. Cf. *ibid.*, vol. 7, pt. 1, p. 142.

36. *Ibid.*, vol. 7, *Essai sur les fondements de la psychologie*, pt. 1, p. 142.

37. *Ibid.*, vol. 10, pt. 2, *Dernière philosophie, existence et anthropologie*, p. 260: "Il faut bien remarquer ici toute la différence qui existe entre cette espèce de localisation immédiate, intérieure, des sensations ou des intuitions que nous prétendons rattacher uniquement au sens de l'effort, comme l'expérience ci-dessus semble propre à le démontrer, et cette autre localisation externe et média-te, par laquelle nous rapportons les différentes impressions du dehors aux parties de notre corps connues extérieurement par la vue comme peuvent l'être les objets ou corps étrangers."

38. Vancourt, *La théorie de la connaissance*, p. 39.

39. Merleau-Ponty, *L'union de l'âme et du corps*, pp. 67–68.

40. On Maine's invocations of "appropriation," see Azouvi, *Maine de Biran*, p. 239.

41. Maine de Biran, *Oeuvres*, vol. 4, p. 125: "Cet espace *intérieur* du corps propre — dont le *moi* phénoménal se distingue, dans son aperception immédiate, sans pouvoir s'en séparer par l'intuition externe — sera le lieu des modifications simplement affectives — qui ne peuvent être senties ou perçues sous une autre *forme* ou sans que l'être individual les rapports hors de lui à quelque partie de son organisation."

42. *Ibid.*, vol. 10, pt. 2, p. 256: "Cette espèce de sentiment vague et obscure, lié à tout mode de vie animale ou organique, ne diffère point pour l'homme ani-mal de celui de l'existence ou de la presence de l'étendu de son corps; c'est le fond auquel toutes les impressions senties se rattachent, et elles ne sont vérita-blement senties dans le tout de l'animal qu'en tant qu'elles affectent une partie de l'étendue organique du corps vivant et modifient ou changent son étant, c'est-à-dire le ton actuel de sa vie ou de sa sensibilité propre."

43. On the irreducibility of apperception to affection and Maine's theory of differing orders of immediacy, see Azouvi, "L'affection et l'intuition." Not to have registered the noncoincidence of the "I" to its experienced body remains the great limitation of Henry's study of Maine de Biran, as several scholars have indicated: see Montebello, *La décomposition de la pensée*, pp. 126–31; Baertschi, *L'ontologie de Maine de Biran*, pp. 80–88; and Azouvi, *Maine de Biran*, pp. 234–40.

CHAPTER TWENTY-TWO: COENAESTHESIS

1. Hübner, *Coenesthesis*, sec. 2; German in Roche, *Zergliederung der Verrich-*

tungen des Nervensystems, vol. 2, pp. 228–29. On the *dissertatio* of 1794, see Schiller, "Coenesthesis." Schiller has argued that the true author of the opusculum was in fact Reil (see pp. 511–12).

2. Hübner, *Caenesthesis*, sec. 2; Roche, *Zergliederung der Verrichtungen des Nervensystems*, pp. 228–29.

3. The distinction between irritability and sensibility can be traced to Haller: see his *Dissertation sur les parties irritables et sensibles des animaux*. On Haller's concept of irritability and its reception, see Baertschi, *Les rapports de l'âme et du corps*; cf. Canguilhem's remarks in "La physiologie animale," esp. pp. 608–609.

4. Hübner in de la Roche, *Zergliederung der Verrichtungen des Nervensystems*, vol. 2, pp. 228–29.

5. Starobinski, "Le concept de cénesthésie," pp. 3–4. Cf. Starobinski's related essay, "Brève histoire de la conscience du corps."

6. Starobinski, "Le concept de cénesthésie," p. 3.

7. *Ibid.*, pp. 3–4.

8. See Lelarge de Lignac, *Éléments de métaphysique* and *Le témoignage du sens intime*; for Maine de Biran's notes on Lelarge de Lignac, see Maine de Biran, *Oeuvres*, vol. 11, pt. 2, *Commentaires et marginalia: Dix-huitième siècle*, pp. 59–94. Cf. Azouvi, "Genèse du corps propre," and Baertschi, *Les rapports de l'âme et du corps*.

9. Turgot, "Existence," p. 261: "Il ne faut pas omettre un autre ordre de sensations plus pénétrantes, pour ainsi dire, qui rapportées à l'intérieur de notre corps, en occupant même quelquefois toute l'habitude, semblent remplir les trois dimensions de l'espace, & porter immédiatement avec elle l'idée de l'étendue solide. Je ferai de ces sensations une classe particulière, sous le nom de *tact intérieur* ou *sixième sens*, & j'y rangerai les douleurs qu'on ressent quelquefois dans l'intérieur des chairs, dans la capacité des intestins, & dans les os mêmes; les nausées, le malaise qui précède l'évanoüissement, la faim, la soif, l'émotion qui accompagne toutes les passions; les frissonnements, soit de douleur, soit de volupté; enfin cette multitude de sensations confuses qui ne nous abandonnent jamais, qui nous circonscrivent en quelque sorte notre corps, qui nous le rendent toûjours présent, & que par cette raison, quelques metaphysiciens ont appellées *sens de la coexistence de notre corps*." On Turgot's article and his doctrine of "penetrating sensations," see Grimsley, "Turgot's Article 'Existence,'" esp. pp. 130–31.

10. d'Alembert, "Essai sur les éléments de philosophie," *Oeuvres philosophiques, historiques et littéraires*, vol. 2, "Éclaircissement VII," pp. 154–64, esp.
pp. 159–60: "Mais outre les cinq sens, il est un qu'on peut appeler *interne*, qui est
comme intimement répandu dans notre substance, et dont le siège se trouve à-
la-fois dans toutes les parties externes et internes de notre corps" (p. 159).

11. Maine de Biran, "Écrits sur la physiologie," *Oeuvres*, vol. 9, *Nouvelles considérations sur les rapports du physique et du moral de l'homme*, p. 125: "Je citerai,
comme exemple le mieux approprié à mon but actuel, le passage où le célèbre
physiologiste allemande Reil, caractérise de la manière la plus remarquable les
modes vraiment simples de ce sens immédiate qui est aussi, selon lui, le fait propre du plaisir ou de la douleur, inséparable de tout ce qui vit. Reil donne à ce
sens le nom expressif de *coenesthèse*, ce qui veut dire sentiment d'ensemble,
mode composé de toutes les impressions vitales inhérentes à chaque partie de
l'organisation." In his introduction to this volume, Baertschi comments that, to
his knowledge, "Biran is the first author in France to use these works by Reil"
(*ibid.*, p. xix).

12. See "Coenaesthesis," in Murray (ed.), *Compact Edition of the Oxford English Dictionary*, vol. 1, p. 457. For Hamilton's works, see Hamilton, *Works of
Thomas Reid, D.D.* Cf. the citation from Sully's *Illusions*, first published in 1881:
"That mass of organic feelings which constitutes what is known as *coenasthesis*,
undefined consciousness, the product of the vital sense" (p. 197).

13. Lamarck, *Système analytique*, pp. 177 and 180–83.

14. *Ibid.*, pp. 184–90.

15. *Ibid.*, pp. 188–89.

16. *Ibid.*, p. 187: "*Sensation permanente*: je nomme ainsi celle qui s'exécute
dans tous les points sensibles du corps, et en général sans discontinuité, pendant
le cours entier de la vie de l'individu. Elle résulte des mouvements vitaux, des
déplacements des fluides, des frottements qu'ils exécutent dans ces déplacements qui sont les suites de contacts et par conséquent de causes affectantes, et
qui même produisent un bruit particulier que nous distingons fort bien dans la
tête, surtout lorsque nous sommes malades. Ces causes affectantes, quoique
extrêmement faibles, étant infiniment multipliées, produisent à l'extrémité des
nerfs qui se rendent à tous les points sensibles du corps, une légère agitation
dans le fluide sensible qu'ils contiennent, laquelle vient aboutir de toutes parts à
celui qui renferme le foyer commun, et y occasionne une sorte de frémissement
sans interruption. C'est probablement à cette cause physique qu'est dû le senti-

ment intime d'existence que nous éprouvons, quelque obscure qu'il soit."

17. See Starobinski, "Le concept de cénesthésie," pp. 4–5.

18. Gruithuisen, *Anthropologie*, secs. 475–85.

19. Lenhossék, *Physiologia medicinalis*, vol. 4, bk. 2, ch. 4, sec. 1, "De sensu corporeo," secs. 470–84.

20. Burdach, *Die Physiologie als Erfahrungswissenschaft*, vol. 2, sec. 472, p. 784; *Der Mensch*, sec. 232.

21. Rudolphi, *Grundriß der Physiologie*, vol. 2, pt. 1, sec. 269, pp. 48–49: "Im Grunde gehöhrt aber Reil blos das Wort Gemeingefühl, denn die Sache ist von Leidenfrost under der Benennung *Lebensgefühl* ebenso dargestellt."

22. See the citations in Ribot, *Les maladies de la personnalité*, p. 22.

23. Weber, *Tastsinn und Gemeingefühl*, pp. 119–28; an English translation can be found in Weber, *E.H. Weber on the Tactile Senses*, pp. 213–18.

24. Schiff, "Cenestesi," pp. 626–27.

25. See Aristotle, *De sensu et sensibili* 7.449a8–20.

26. See, among others, O. Funke and E. Hering, "Tatsinn und Gemeinge-fühl," in Hermann, *Handbuch der Physiologie*, vol. 3, pt. 2, esp. pp. 289–315; Kröner, *Das körperliche Gefühl*, esp. ch. 2, "Das Gemeingefühl"; Morselli, *Manuale di semejotica*, vol. 1, esp. pp. 542–47 ("Cenestesi"); Bertrand, *L'aperception du corps humain*; Beaunis, *Les sensations internes*, esp. pp. 152–56.

27. Ribot, *La psychologie allemande contemporaine*.

28. Ribot, *Les maladies de la personnalité*, pp. 20 and 22.

29. *Ibid.* See Cabanis, *Rapports du physique*, pp. 108–10.

30. Cabanis, *Rapports du physique*, p. tk.

31. *Ibid.*, p. 23.

32. Ribot, *Les maladies de la personnalité*, pp. 25–26.

33. Külpe, *Outlines of Psychology*, which appeared in German in 1883 and was translated into English by Edward Bradford Titchener: see esp. sec. 23, "Analysis of the Common Sensations: The 'Static Sense,'" pp. 146–52.

34. On the muscular sense, see Jones, "Development of the 'Muscular Sense' Concept." For Sherrington's notion of proprioception, see Sherrington, *Integrative Action*, pp. 335–43, and *Man on His Nature*, pp. 323–58.

35. Henle, *Allgemeine Anatomie*, p. 728. In Ribot's own translation: "C'est la somme, le chaos non débrouillé des sensations qui de tous les points du corps sont sans cesse transmises au sensorium" (*Les maladies de la personnalité*, p. 22). That citation seems traceable to Weber's *Tastsinn und Gemeingefühl*: see Schiller,

"Coenesthesis," pp. 503–504.

36. Ribot, *Les maladies de la personnalité*, p. 22: "Plus précis, E.–H. Weber entendait par ce mot: une sensibilité interne, un toucher intérieur qui fournit au sensorium des renseignements sur l'état mécanique et chimico-organique de la peau, des muqueuses, des viscères, des muscles, des articulations."

37. The expression is Philip Franz von Walther's: see Schiller, "Coenesthesis," p. 509.

CHAPTER TWENTY-THREE: PHANTOMS

1. Weir Mitchell, "Case of George Dedlow." Cf. Canale, "Civil War Medicine."

2. Weir Mitchell, "Case of George Dedlow," p. 1.

3. *Ibid.*, p. 4.

4. *Ibid.*, p. 5.

5. *Ibid.*

6. *Ibid.*, p. 6.

7. *Ibid.*, p. 7.

8. *Ibid.*, p. 8.

9. *Ibid.*, p. 9.

10. *Ibid.*, pp. 9–11.

11. *Ibid.*, p. 11.

12. On the history of the text and the revelation of its author, see Lovering, *S. Weir Mitchell*, and Rein, *S. Weir Mitchell as a Psychiatric Novelist*.

13. See the valuable sourcebook edited by Price and Twombly, *Phantom Limb Phenomenon*.

14. Paré, *Oeuvres complètes*, vol. 2, bk. 10, ch. 19, "Des signes des mortifications parfaits," p. 221. On Paré, see Keil, "Sogennante Erstbeschreibung."

15. See Finger and Hustwit, "Five Early Accounts," p. 678.

16. See the reprint and translation of Lemos's *dissertatio inauguralis medica*: Price and Twombly (eds.), "Phantom Limb." Cf. Finger and Hustwit, "Five Early Accounts," pp. 678–79.

17. Bell, "On the Motions of the Eye," p. 178. Cf. the commentary in Finger and Hustwit, "Five Early Accounts," p. 681.

18. Weir Mitchell, "Phantom Limbs," pp. 563–64.

19. *Ibid.*, pp. 564–65.

20. Weir Mitchell, *Injuries of Nerves*, p. 348.

21. *Ibid.* Cf. the similarly worded passage in Weir Mitchell, "Phantom Limbs," p. 565.

22. Weir Mitchell, "Phantom Limbs," pp. 565–66.

23. Weir Mitchell, *Injuries of Nerves*, p. 350.

24. See, among a great number of others, Ramachandran and Blakeslee, *Phantoms in the Brain*; Schilder, *Image and Appearance of the Human Body*; and Merleau-Ponty, *Phénoménologie de la perception*.

25. Cotard, "Du délire des négations." On Cotard and his "syndrome," see, among others, Cacho, *Le délire des négations*; Czermak, *Passions de l'objet*, ch. 11 "Signification psychanalytique du syndrome de Cotard," pp. 205–36. Cf. the remarks in Lacan, *Le moi dans la théorie de Freud*, pp. 275–81.

26. See especially Falret, "Du délire de persécution," "Des aliénés persécutés raisonnants et persécuteurs," and *Études cliniques*.

27. Cotard, "Du délire des négations," p. 25.

28. *Ibid.*, p. 26.

29. *Ibid.*, pp. 39–40.

30. *Ibid.*, pp. 43–44.

31. *Ibid.*, p. 45.

32. *Ibid.*, p. 47.

33. See *ibid.*, pp. 50–53.

34. Cotard, "Perte de la vision mentale," "De l'origine psycho-sensorielle ou psychomotrice du délire," and "Du délire d'énormité."

35. See Cotard, Camuset, and Séglas, *Du délire des négations aux idées d'énormité*, pp. 77–166; cf. Cacho, *Le délire des négations*, pp. 135–97.

36. Jules Séglas, "Mélancolie anxieuse avec délire des négations," *Le progrés médical* (1887), pp. 417–19.

37. On the identification of the "syndrome," see Cacho, *Le délire des négations*, pp. 164–69, and, on the distinction between the delirium and the syndrome, p. 169.

38. Jules Séglas, "Le délire des négations dans la mélancolie," lecture given Feb. 25, 1894, summarized by H. Meige in *Journal des connaissances médicales* 30, 31, and 32 (1894), now in Cotard, Camuset, and Séglas, *Du délire des négations aux idées d'énormité*, pp. 179–207.

39. *Ibid.*, p. 185.

CHAPTER TWENTY-FOUR: THE ANAESTHETIC ANIMAL

1. See Berrios, "Stupor," esp. p. 679.

2. Aristotle, *Nicomachean Ethics* 3.10–11.1117b23–1118b35.

3. *Ibid.*, 3.11.1119a6–13.

4. Esquirol, *Des maladies mentales*, vol. 1, p. 414. Esquirol described the patient as suffering from "lypomania," a malady often seen as a precursor to depression.

5. Esquirol's patient as quoted by Griesinger, *Die Pathologie und Therapie*, p. 157.

6. Zeller, "Über einige Hauptpunkte," pp. 524–25.

7. Griesinger, *Die Pathologie und Therapie*, p. 67.

8. Krishaber, *De la névropathie cérébro-cardiaque*, p. 1.

9. *Ibid.*, "Observation 2," p. 14.

10. *Ibid.*, "Observation 38," pp. 151–52.

11. Taine, *De l'intelligence*, vol. 2, pp. 465–74.

12. *Ibid.*, p. 465.

13. *Ibid.*

14. *Ibid.*, p. 466.

15. On the closely related problem of multiple personality, see Hacking, *Rewriting the Soul*.

16. Taine, *De l'intelligence*, p. 474.

17. *Ibid.* The citation represents a slightly modified form of a sentence in Krishaber, *De la névropathie cérébro-cardiaque*, p. 181.

18. Schäfer, "Bemerkungen zur psychiatrischen Formenlehre," p. 242.

19. *Ibid.* Cf. the remarks in Sierra and Berrios, "Depersonalization," pp. 219–20.

20. Ribot, *La psychologie des sentiments*, pp. 366–67. On "doubt delirium," see also Ball, "De la folie du doute," *Leçons sur les maladies mentales*, lecture 31, pp. 605–21.

21. Ribot, *La psychologie des sentiments*, p. 367.

22. Dugas, "Un cas de dépersonnalisation," p. 500.

23. *Ibid.*, pp. 501–502.

24. In addition to "Un cas de dépersonnalisation," see Dugas, "Dépersonnalisation et fausse mémoire," and Dugas and Moutier, *La dépersonnalisation*.

25. Amiel, *Fragments d'un journal intime*, vol. 1, pp. 292–93.

26. Sierra and Berrios, "Depersonalization," p. 216.

27. Janet, *L'automatisme psychologique*, pp. 36–37.

28. *Ibid.*, p. 37.

29. *Ibid.*, p. 39.

30. *Ibid.*, pp. 41–42.

31. *Ibid.*, p. 43.

32. Janet, *Les obsessions et la psychasthénie*, pp. 281–87, 298–301, 305–11 (for the introduction to this section), 318. Cf. also Janet, "Perte du sentiment de la personnalité," "Dépersonnalisation et possession chez un psychasthénique," and "Le sentiment de la dépersonnalisation."

33. *Ibid.*, p. 318.

34. Janet, *De l'angoisse à l'Extase*, vol. 2, pt. 1, ch. 2, pp. 44–126.

35. *Ibid.*, p. 62.

36. *Ibid.*, p. 99. Here Janet relies on Foerster's account of "somatopsychosis": see Foerster, "Ein Fall von elemantarer allgemeiner Somatopsychose."

37. Janet, *De l'angoisse à l'extase*, vol. 2, p. 56.

38. *Ibid.*, p. 101.

39. See, in particular, *ibid.*, pp. 106–107.

40. *Ibid.*, p. 122.

41. *Ibid.*, p. 126.

42. Lamarck, *Système analytique*, p. 187.

43. Dupré and Camus, "Les cénesthopathies," p. 616.

44. See Baruk, "Le sentiment de la personnalité." For Schilder's treatments of depersonalization, see *Selbstbewusstsein und Persönlichkeitsbewusstsein*, esp. chs. 1 and 2, pp. 23–186; cf. Schilder, *Image and Appearance of the Human Body* and *Psychoanalysis, Man, and Society*. For a later treatment of Cotard syndrome together with depersonalization, see Resnik, "Syndrome de Cotard."

45. On the history of the syndrome, see, above all, Sierra and Berrios, "Depersonalization." For important and informative contributions to the analysis of the phenomenon, see, among others, Pick, "Zur Pathologie des Ich-Bewusstsein"; Mayer-Gross, "On Depersonalization"; Dide, "Dépersonnalisation, déréalisation, aproprioceptivité"; Krapf, "Sur la dépersonnalisation"; Cattell, "Depersonalization Phenomena"; Cattell and Cattell, "Depersonalization"; Weckowicz, "Depersonalization"; Ackner, "Depersonalization"; Sierra and Berrios, "Phenomenological Stability of Depersonalization"; and, finally, the entry on depersonalization in American Psychiatric Association, *Diagnostic and Statistical Manual of Mental Disorders*, 4th ed.

46. Baruk, "Le sentiment de la personnalité," p. 403.

47. Janet, *De l'angoisse à l'extase*, p. 6.

48. For Deutsch's classic studies, see "Absence of Grief," "On a Type of Pseudo-Affectivity (the 'As If' Type)," and "Clinical and Theoretical Aspects of 'As If' Characters," *Therapeutic Process*, pp. 193–207 and 215–20. On Deutsch's "as if," see the remarks in Lacan, *Les psychoses*, p. 218.

49. For Benjamin: see his famous 1933 essay, "Erfahrung und Armut," *Gesammelte Schriften*, vol. 2, pt. 1, pp. 213–19; for Heidegger, see *Die Grundbegriffe der Metaphysik*, esp. pp. 199–238; for Lévinas, see, among many other texts, *De l'existence à l'existant*, p. 112.

CHAPTER TWENTY-FIVE: UNTOUCHABLE

1. See Avicenna, *Livre des définitions*, entries 52, 53, 54, 55, pp. 35–36 (Arabic) and 51–52 (French).

2. Aristotle, *De partibus animalium* 6.660a11–14: *malakōtatē d'hē sarx hē tōn anthrōpōn hupērkhen. touto de dia to asithētikōtaton eina tōn zōiōn tēn dia tēs haphēs aisthēsin.*

3. Aristotle, *Historia animalium* 1.15.494b16: *ekhei de akribestatēn anthrōpos tōn aisthēseōn tēn haphēn, deuteran de tēn geusin. en de tais allais leipetai pollōn.*

4. Aristotle, *De sensu et sensibili*, 4.441a2–3. The entire passage (440b32–441a4) reads as follows: *toutou d' aition hoti kheiristēn ekhomen tōn allōn zōiōn tēn osphrēsin kai tōn en hēmin autois aisthēseōn, tēn d' haphēn akribestatēn tōn allōn zōiōn. hē de geusis haphē tis estin.*

5. Original in Alexander of Aphrodisias, *Alexandri Aphrodisiensis*, vol. 2, pt. 1, pp. 51.25–52.7.

6. Aristotle, *De anima* 2.9.421a7–12.

7. *Ibid.*, 421a19–20.

8. *Ibid.*, 421a21–27. On the passage, see the enlightening essay by Movia, "Tatto e pensiero in un passo del 'De Anima,'" *Due studi sul De Anima*, pp. 61–84.

9. Aristotle, *De anima*, Hamlyn edition, p. 110.

10. Alexander of Aphrodisias, *Alexandri Aphrodisiensis*, vol. 2, pt. 1, p. 52.2–4.

11. Original in Themistius, *Themistii in libros Aristotelis De Anima paraphrasis*, p. 68.4; English in *On Aristotle On the Souls*, p. 88.

12. Greek in Philoponus, *Ioannis Philoponi: in Aristotelis De anima libros commentaria*, p. 388.33–34, cited in Movia, "Tatto e pensiero," p. 66.

13. See Aristotle, *Nicomachean Ethics* 10.5.1175b36–1176a1 and *Metaphysics* 2.1.980a27.

14. Thomas Aquinas, *In Aristotelis librum De anima commentarium*, sec. 483; English in *Commentary on Aristotle's De Anima*, sec. 483.

15. *Ibid.*, sec. 484.

16. *Ibid.*, sec. 485.

17. *Ibid.*, sec. 484.

18. Aristotle, *Metaphysics* 12.7.1072b20–25; cf. *Metaphysics* 10.1051b24.

19. Merleau-Ponty, *Le visible et l'invisible*, pp. 307–308: "Toucher et se toucher (se toucher = touchant-touché). Ils ne coïncident pas dans le corps: le touchant n'est jamais exactement le touché. Cela ne veut pas dire qu'ils coïncident 'dans l'esprit' ou au niveau de la 'conscience.' Il faut quelque chose d'autre que le corps pour que la jonction se fasse: elle se fait dans *l'intouchable*. Cela d'autrui que je ne toucherai jamais. Mais ce que je ne toucherai jamais, il ne le touche pas non plus, pas de privilège du soi sur l'autre ici, ce n'est donc pas la *conscience* qui est l'intouchable — 'La conscience,' ce serait du positif, et à propos d'elle recommencerait, recommence, la dualité du réfléchissant et du réfléchi, comme celle du touchant et du touché. L'intouchable, ce n'est pas un touchable en fait inaccessible, — l'inconscient, ce n'est pas une representation en fait inaccessible. Le négatif n'est pas un *positif qui est ailleurs* (un transcendant) — C'est un vrai négatif."

20. Aristotle, *Nicomachean Ethics* 9.9.1170a20–21.

21. *Ibid.*, 1170a20–1170b13. Cf. the closely related passage in Aristotle, *Eudemian Ethics* 7.12.1244b24–1245a27.

22. Authors who have discussed the metaphysical dimensions of the discussion include Fraisse, *Philia,* pp. 238–45, and Rodrigo, "Synaisthanesthai," who provides a summary account of the literature on the subject.

23. See Agamben, "L'amicizia," pp. 9–15.

24. Thomas Aquinas, *Opera Omnia*, vol. 48, p. 540.

25. *Ibid.*

26. Plato, *Timaeus* 52b2; for Calcidius's translation, see Calcidius, *Timaeus* CCCXLV.

Bibliography

Ackner, Brian, "Depersonalization: I, Aetiology and Phenomenology," *Journal of Mental Science* 100 (1954), pp. 838–53.

Adorno, Francesco (ed.), *Corpus dei papiri filosofici greci e latini (CPF): Testi e lessico nei papiri di cultura greca e latina*, pt. 1, *Autori noti*, v. 1 (Florence: Olschki, 1992).

Alder, Maximilianus, *Stoicorum veterum fragmenta: Vol. 1V, Quo indices continentur. . .* (Stuttgart: Teubner, 1924).

Agamben, Giorgio, *Infanzia e storia: Distruzione dell'esperienza e origine della storia* (Turin: Einaudi, 1978).

————, "L'amicizia," in *I filosofi e l'amore*, ed. Fausto Pellecchia (Cassino: Edizioni dell'università degli studi di Cassino, 2003), pp. 9–15.

————, *L'aperto: L'uomo e l'animale* (Turin: Bollati Boringhieri, 2002).

Alexander of Aphrodisias, *Alexandri Aphrodisiensis praeter commentaria scripta minora*, vol. 2, pt. 1, *De Anima liber cum mantissa*, ed. Ivo Bruns (Berlin: Reimer, 1887).

————, *Alexandri Aphrodisiensis praeter commentaria scripta minora*, ed. Ivo Bruns, vol. 2, pt. 2, *Quaestiones, De fato, De mixtione* (Berlin: Reimer, 1892).

————, *Commentaria in Aristotelem Graeca*, vol. 3, pt. 1, *Alexandri in librum De Sensu commentarium*, ed. Paul Wendland (Berlin: Reimer, 1901).

————, *The De Anima of Alexander of Aphrodisias: A Translation and Commentary*, ed. and trans. Athanasios P. Fotinis (Washington, DC: University Press of America, 1979).

————, *On Aristotle on Sense Perception*, trans. Alan Towey (London: Duckworth, 2000).

————, *Quaestiones*, 2 vols., trans. Robert W. Sharples (Ithaca, NY: Cornell University Press, 1992–94).

Albertus Magnus, *Opera omnia*, 37 vols., ed. Bernhard Geyer (Monasterii Westfalorum: Aschendorff, 1951–).

Alembert, Jean Le Rond d', *Oeuvres philosophiques, historiques et littéraires*, 18 vols. (Paris: Bastien, 1805).

Alexander of Hales, *Expositio super tres libros Aristotelis De anima* (Oxford: Theodoricus Rood, 1481).

Altmann, A., and S.M. Stern, *Isaac Israeli: A Neoplatonic Philosopher of the Early Tenth Century* (Oxford: Oxford University Press, 1958).

Alverny, Marie-Thérèse d', "Anniyya-Anitas," in *Mélanges offerts à Etienne Gilson* (Toronto: Pontifical Institute of Mediaeval Studies, 1959), pp. 59–91, rpt. in *Avicenne en Occident* (Paris: Vrin, 1993), pp. 43–91.

Alonso Alonso, Manuel, "La 'al-anniyya' de Avicena y el problema de la esencia y existencia," *Pensamiento* 14 (1958), pp. 311–45.

————, "La 'al-anniyya' y el 'al-wujûd' de Avicena y el problema de esencia y existencia (fuentes literarias)," *Pensamiento* 14 (1958), pp. 311–46.

American Psychiatric Association, *Diagnostic and Statistical Manual of Mental Disorders*, 4th ed. (Washington, DC: American Psychiatric Association, 1994).

Amiel, Henri-Frédéric, *Fragments d'un journal intime*, vol. 1, 7th ed. (Geneva: Georg, 1897).

Arckel, Jean d', *Li ars d'amour, de vertu et de boneurté, par Jehan le Bel*, ed. Jules Petit, 2 vols (Brussels: Devaux, 1867–69).

Aretaeus of Cappadocia, *Aretaeus*, ed. Karl Hude (Leipzig: Teubner, 1923).

Aristotle, *Aristūtālīs Fī' l-nafs*, ed. 'Abdarrahmān Badawī, 2nd ed. (Beirut: Dār al-qalam, 1980).

————, *De anima*, ed. and trans. R.D. Hicks (Cambridge: Cambridge University Press, 1907).

————, *De anima*, ed. David Ross (Oxford: Clarendon, 1961).

————, *Parva naturalia*, ed. W.D. Ross (Oxford: Clarendon, 1955).

————, *De anima Books II and III*, trans. D.W. Hamlyn (Oxford: Clarendon, 1968).

————, *De l'âme*, ed. Antonio Jannone, trans. and notes by Edmond Barbotin (Paris: Belles Lettres, 2002).

————, *Historia animalium*, 3 vols., trans. A.L. Peck (Cambridge, MA: Harvard University Press, 1965–).

————, *On the Soul*; *Parva naturalia*; *On Breath*, trans. W.S. Hett (Cambridge, MA: Harvard University Press, 1957).

————, *Petits traités d'histoire naturelle*, ed. and trans. René Mugnier (Paris: Belles Lettres, 2002).

————, *Über die Seele*, ed. and trans. Willy Theiler, 2nd ed. (Berlin: Akademie-Verlag, 1966).

Armogathe, Jean-Robert, "Les sens: Inventaires médiévaux et théorie carté-sienne," in Joël Biard and Roshdi Rashed (eds.), *Descartes et le Moyen Âge* (Paris: Vrin, 1997), pp. 175–84.

Arnaldez, Roger, "Un précédent avicennien du 'cogito' cartésien?" *Annales islamologiques* 11 (1972), pp. 341–49.

Arnim, Hans von, *Stoicorum veterum fragmenta* (Leipzig: Teubner, 1903).

Arnzen, Rüdiger, ed., *Aristoteles, De anima: Eine verlorene spätantike Para-phrase in arabischer und persischer Überlieferung; Arabischer Text nebst Kommentar, quellengeschichtlichen Studien und Glossaren* (Leiden: Brill, 1998).

Augustine of Hippo, *De magistro*; *De libero arbitrio*, ed. and trans. Goulven Madec, 3rd ed. (Paris: Desclée de Brouwer, 1976). *La felicità; La libertà*, trans. Riccardo Fedriga and Sara Puggioni (Milan: Rizzoli, 1995).

————, *La trinité, Livres VIII–XV*, trans. Paul Agaësse (Paris: Institut d'études augustiniennes, 1991).

Averroës (Ibn Rušd), *Averrois Cordubensis: Commentarium magnum in Aristotelis De anima libros*, ed. F. Stuart Crawford (Cambridge, MA: Mediaeval Academy of America, 1953).

————, *The Book of the Decisive Treatise Determining the Connection Between the Law and Wisdom; and, Epistle Dedicatory*, trans. and ed. Charles E. Butter-woth (Provo, UT: Brigham Young University Press, 2001).

————, *Epitome of Parva naturalia*, trans. Harry Blumberg (Cambridge, MA: The Mediaeval Academy of America, 1961).

————, *Middle Commentary on Aristotle's De anima*, ed. Alfred L. Ivry (Provo, UT: Brigham Young University Press, 2002).

————, *Talkhīs kitāb al-nafs*, ed. Aḥmad al-Ahwānī (Cairo: Maktaba al-nahḍa al-miṣrīya, 1950).

Avicenna (Ibn Sīnā), *Avicenna latinus: Liber de anima, seu Sextus de naturalibus*, 2 vols., ed. Simon van Riet (Louvain: Peeters, 1968–).

————, *Kitāb al-ishārāt wa'l-tanbīhāt*, ed. Jacques Forget (Leiden: Brill, 1892).

————, *Livre des Directives et Remarques (Kitāb al-ishārāt wa'l-tanbīhāt)*, ed. and trans. A.M. Goichon (Beirut/Paris: Vrin, 1951).

————, *Livre des définitions*, ed. and trans. A.M. Goichon (Cairo: Publications de l'Institut français d'archéologie orientale du Caire, 1963).

————, *al-Nafs*, ed. George C. Anawati and Sa'īd Zayid (Cairo: Organisation générale des imprimeries gouvermentales, 1975).

————, *Psychologie d'Ibn Sīnā (Avicenne) d'après son oeuvre aš-Šifā'*, 2 vols., ed. and trans. Ján Bakoš (Prague: Éditions de l'Académie tchécoslovaque des sciences, 1956).

————, *Psychology: An English Translation of Kitāb an-Najāt, Book 2, Chapter 6, with Historico-Philosophical Notes and Textual Improvements on the Cairo Edition*, ed. Fazlur Rahman (Oxford: Oxford University Press, 1952).

Azouvi, François, "L'affection et l'intuition chez Maine de Biran," *Études philosophiques* 1 (1982), pp. 79–90.

————, *Maine de Biran: La science de l'homme* (Paris: Vrin, 1995).

————, "Genèse du corps propre chez Malebranche, Condillac, Lelarge de Lignac et Maine de Biran," *Archives de philosophie* 45, no. 1 (1982), pp. 85–107.

Bacon, Francis, *The Philosophical Works of Francis Bacon*, ed. John M. Robertson (London: Routledge, 1905).

————, *The Works of Francis Bacon*, ed. Robert Leslie Ellis, Douglas Denon Heath, and James Spedding, 15 vols. (New York: Hurd and Houghton, 1862–79).

Badalamenti, Guido, "Ierocle stoico e il concetto di ΣΥΝΑΙΣΘΗΣΙΣ," *Annali del Dipartimento di filosofia* 3 (1987), pp. 53–97.

Baertschi, Bernard, *L'ontologie de Maine de Biran* (Fribourg: Éditions universitaires, 1982).

————, *Les rapports de l'âme et du corps: Descartes, Diderot et Maine de Biran* (Paris: Vrin, 1992).

Ball, Benjamin, *Leçons sur les maladies mentales*, 2nd ed. (Paris: Asselin & Houzeay, 1890).

Baruk, Henri, "Le sentiment de la personnalité: La dépersonnalisation et la cénesthésie; Nouvelles données psycho-physiologiques," *Annales médico-psychologiques* 109 (1951), pp. 393–407.

Beaunis, Henri Étienne, *Les sensations internes* (Paris: Alcan, 1889).

Becker, Otfrid, *Plotin und das Problem der geistigen Aneignung* (Berlin: de Gruyter, 1940).

Belaval, Yvon, *Études leibniziennes: De Leibniz à Hegel* (Paris: Gallimard, 1976).

Bell, Charles, "On the Motions of the Eye, in Illustration of the Uses of the Muscles and Nerves of the Orbit," *Philosophical Transactions of the Royal Society of London* 113 (1823), pp. 166–87.

Benjamin, Walter, *Gesammelte Schriften*, 7 vols., ed. Hermann Schweppenhäuser and Rolf Tiedemann (Frankfurt: Suhrkamp, 1972–89).

Bermon, Emmanuel, *Le cogito dans la pensée de Saint Augustin* (Paris: Vrin, 2001).

Bernard, Wolfgang, "Philoponus on Self-Awareness," in Richard Sorabji (ed.), *Philoponus and the Rejection of Aristototelian Science* (London: Duckworth, 1987), pp. 154–63.

Berrios, German E., "Stupor: A Conceptual History," *Psychological Medicine* 11 (1981), pp. 677–88.

Bertrand, Alexis, *L'aperception du corps humain par la conscience* (Paris: Baillière, 1880).

Beyssade, Jean-Marie, "Le sens commun dans la *Règle XII*: Le corporel et l'incorporel," *Descartes au fil de l'ordre* (Paris: Presses Universitaires de France, 2001), pp. 69–88.

Blanchet, Léon, *Campanella* (Paris: Alcan, 1920).

Block, Irving, "The Order of Aristotle's Psychological Writings," *American Journal of Philology* 82, no. 1 (1961), pp. 50–77.

———, "Three German Commentators on the Individual Senses and the Common Sense in Aristotle's Psychology," *Phronesis* 9, no. 1 (1964), pp. 58–63.

Blumenthal, Henry J., *Aristotle and Neoplatonism in Late Antiquity: Interpretations of the "De Anima"* (London: Duckworth, 1996).

———, "Plutarch's Exposition of the *De Anima* and the Psychology of Proclus," in *De Jamblique à Proclus: Neuf exposés suivis de discussions* (Geneva: Hardt, 1975), pp. 12–147.

Brandenburg, Dietrich, *Die Ärzte des Propheten: Islam und Medizin* (Berlin: Edition Q, 1992).

Brandom, Robert B., "Leibniz and Degrees of Perception," *Journal of the History of Philosophy* 19, no. 4 (1981), pp. 447–79.

Bréhier, Émile, "Une forme archaïque du 'Cogito ergo sum,'" *Revue philosophique* 10 (1942), pp. 143–44.

Brentano, Franz, *Die Psychologie des Aristoteles insbesondere seine lehre vom ΝΟΥΣ ΠΟΙΗΤΙΚΟΣ* (1867; Darmstadt: Wissenschaftliche Buchgesellschaft, 1967).

Browne, G.M. "Ad Themistium Arabum," *Illinois Classical Studies* 11 (1986), pp. 223–45.

Brunschwig, Jacques, "The Cradle Argument in Epicureanism and Stoicism," in Malcolm Schofield and Gisela Striker (eds.), *The Norms of Nature: Studies in Hellenistic Ethics* (Cambridge: Cambridge University Press, 1986), pp. 113–44.

Burdach, Karl Friedrich, *Die Physiologie als Erfahrungswissenschaft*, 2 vols. (Leipzig: Voss, 1835–38).

—————, *Der Mensch nach den verschiedenen Seiten seiner Natur: Eine Anthropologie für das gebildete Publicum* (Stuttgart: Balz, 1837).

Burnyeat, Myles, "Plato on the Grammar of Perceiving," *Classical Quarterly* 26 (1976), pp. 29–51.

Burton, Richard F., *A Plain and Literal Translation of the Arabian Nights' Entertainments, Now Entitled The Book of the Thousand Nights and a Night*, 9 vols. (Tehran: Burton Club, 1885).

—————, *The Anatomy of Melancholy*, ed. Holbrook Jackson (New York: New York Review of Books, 2001).

Bywater, Ingram, "Aristotelia III," *Journal of Philology* 17 (1888), pp. 53–79.

Cabanis, P.J.G., *Rapports du physique et du moral de l'homme* (Paris: Baillière, 1844).

Cacho, Jorge, *Le délire des négations: Psychopathologie du syndrome de Cotard, de la mélancolie anxieuse à la folie systématisée* (Paris: Association freudienne internationale, 1993).

Calcidius, *Timaeus*, ed. J.H. Waszink (London: Warburg Institute, 1975).

Campanella, Tommaso, *Compendio di filosofia della natura [Compendium physiologiae]*, ed. Germana Ernst, trans. Paolo Ponzio (Rimini: Rusconi, 1999).

—————, *De sensu rerum et magia*, ed. Antonio Bruers (Bari: Laterza, 1925).

—————, *Epilogo magno (Fisiologia italiana)*, ed. Carmelo Ottaviano (Rome: Reale accademia d'Italia, 1939).

—————, *Metafisica*, ed. Giovanni Di Napoli, 3 vols. (Bologna: Zanichelli, 1967).

Canale, D.J., "Civil War Medicine From the Perspective of S. Weir Mitchell's 'The Case of George Dedlow,'" *Journal of the History of the Neurosciences* 11, no. 1 (2002), pp. 11–18.

Cancrini, Antonia, *Syneidesis: Il tema semantico della con-scientia nella Grecia antica* (Rome: Ateneo, 1970).

Canguilhem, Georges, "La physiologie animale," in René Taton (ed.), *Histoire générale des sciences*, vol. 2, *La science moderne (de 1450 à 1800)*, ed. Georges Allard (Paris: Presses Universitaires de France, 1958), pp. 594–619.

Capesius, Josef, *Der Apperceptionsbegriff bei Leibniz und dessen Nachfolgern: Eine terminologische Untersuchung* (Hermannstadt: Drotleff, 1894).

Cattell, James P., "Depersonalization Phenomena," in Silvano Arieti (ed.), *American Handbook of Psychiatry*, vol. 3 (New York: Basic Books, 1966), pp. 88–102.

———, and J.S. Cattell, "Depersonalization: Psychological and Social Perspectives," in Silvano Arieti and Eugene B. Brody (eds.), *American Handbook of Psychiatry*, 2nd ed., vol. 3, *Adult Clinical Psychiatry* (New York: Basic Books, 1974), pp. 766–99.

Chrétien, Jean-Louis, *L'appel et la réponse* (Paris: Minuit, 1992).

Chrysippus, *Oeuvre philosophique*, 2 vols., ed. and trans. Richard Dufour (Paris: Belles Lettres, 2004).

Cicero, Marcus Tullius, *De finibus bonorum et malorum*, trans. H. Rackham (Cambridge, MA: Harvard University Press, 1931).

Cohen, Hermann, *Das Princip der Infinitesimal-Methode und seine Geschichte: Ein Kapitel zur Grundlegung der Erkenntniskritik, Werke*, ed. Helmut Holzhey, vol. 5 (Hildesheim: Olms, 1978).

Condillac, Étienne Bonnot de, *Oeuvres philosophiques*, 3 vols., ed. Georges Le Roy (Paris: Presses Universitaires de France, 1947).

———, *Traité des sensations; Traité des animaux* (Paris: Fayard, 1984).

Cooper, John M., "Plato on Sense-Perception and Knowledge (*Theaetetus* 184–186)," *Phronesis* 15 (1970), pp. 123–46.

Costello, William T., *The Scholastic Curriculum at Early Seventeenth-Century Cambridge* (Cambridge, MA: Harvard University Press, 1958).

Cotard, Jules, "De l'origine psycho-sensorielle ou psychomotrice du délire," *Annales médico-psychologiques* (1887), pp. 351–57.

———, "Du délire d'énormité," *Annales médico-psychologiques* (1888), pp. 465–69.

———, "Du délire des négations," *Archives de neurologie* 4, no. 11 (1882), pp. 314–44; rpt. in J. Cotard, M. Camuset, and J. Séglas, *Du délire des négations aux idées d'énormité* (Paris: Harmattan, 1997).

———, "Perte de la vision mentale dans la mélancolie anxieuse," *Archives de neurologie* 7, no. 21 (1884), pp. 345–350.

———, M. Camuset, and J. Séglas, *Du délire des négations aux idées d'énormité* (Paris: Harmattan, 1997).

Courcelle, Pierre, *Connais-toi toi-même: De Socrate à Saint Bernard*, 3 vols. (Paris: Études augustiniennes, 1975).

Czermak, Marcel, *Passions de l'objet: Études psychanalytiques des psychoses* (Paris: Clims, 1986).

Dagognet, François, *L'animal selon Condillac: Une introduction au "Traité des animaux" de Condillac* (Paris: Vrin, 2004).

Derrida, Jacques, "Ousia et grammé: Note sur une note de *Sein und Zeit*," *Marges de la philosophie* (Paris: Minuit, 1972), pp. 31–78.

Descartes, René, *Oeuvres de Descartes*, 11 vols., ed. Charles Adam and Paul Tannery (Paris: Vrin, 1996).

Destutt de Tracy, Antoine Louis Claude, *Mémoire sur la faculté de penser: De la Métaphysique de Kant* (Paris: Fayard, 1992).

Deutsch, Helene, "Absence of Grief," *Psychoanalytic Quarterly* 6 (1937), pp. 12–22.

———, *The Therapeutic Process, the Self, and Female Psychology*, ed. Paul Roazen (New Brunswick, NJ: Transaction, 1992).

Dide, M., "Dépersonnalisation, déréalisation, aproprioceptivité: Esquisse anatomo-clinique," *Annales médico-psychologiques* 96 (1938), pp. 95–103.

Diels, Hermann, and Walther Kranz (ed.), *Die Fragmente der Vorsokratiker, griechisch und deutsch*, 8th ed. (Berlin: Weidmann, 1956).

Diels, H., and W. Schubart (eds.), *Didymos, Kommentar zu Demosthenes (Papyrus 9780), nebst Wörterbuch zu Demosthenes' Aristocratea (Papyrus 5008)* (Berlin: Weidmann, 1904).

Dierauer, Urs, *Tier und Mensch in der Antike: Studien zur Tierpsychologie, Anthropologie und Ethik* (Amsterdam: Grüner, 1977).

Diogenes Laertius, *Lives of Eminent Philosophers*, 2 vols., trans. R.D. Hicks (Cambridge, MA: Harvard University Press, 1950).

Druart, Thérèse-Anne (ed.), *Arabic Philosophy and the West: Continuity and Interaction* (Washington, DC: Center for Contemporary Arab Studies, Georgetown University, 1988).

Dugas, Ludovic, "Un cas de dépersonnalisation," *Revue philosophique de Paris et l'étranger* 45 (1898), pp. 500–507.

———, "Dépersonnalisation et fausse mémoire," *Revue philosophique de Paris et l'étranger* 46 (1898), pp. 423–25.

———, and F. Moutier, *La dépersonnalisation* (Paris: Alcan, 1911).

Dupont, J., "Syneidesis: Aux origines de la notion chrétienne de conscience morale," *Studia hellenistica* 5 (1948), pp. 130–32.

Dupré, Ernest, and Paul Camus, "Les cénesthopathies," *L'encéphale* 12 (1907), pp. 616–31.

Ebert, Theodor, "Aristotle on What Is Done in Perceiving," *Zeitschrift für philosophische Forschung* 37, no. 2 (1983), pp. 181–98.

Eckhart, Meister, *L'Oeuvre latine de Maître Eckhart*, vol. 1: *Commentaire de la Genèse, précédé des Prologues*, ed. Alain de Libera, Edouard Wéber, and Emilie Zum Brunn (Paris: Cerf, 1984).

———, *Werke*, 2 vols., ed. Niklaus Largier (Frankfurt: Deutscher Klassiker, 1993).

Esquirol, Étienne, *Des maladies mentales considérées sous les rapports medical, hygiénique et medico-légal*, 2 vols. (Paris: Baillière, 1838).

Essen, Ernst, *Das zweite Buch der aristotelischen Schrift über die Seele* (Jena: Neuenhahn, 1894).

Everson, Stephen (ed.), *Psychology* (Cambridge: Cambridge University Press, 1991).

Falret, Jules, "Des aliénés persecutés raisonnants et persécuteurs," *Annales médico-psychologiques* 19 (1878), pp. 414–15.

———, "Du délire de persécution chez les aliénés raisonnants," *Annales médico-psychologiques* 20 (1878), pp. 396–400.

———, *Études cliniques sur les maladies mentales et nerveuses* (Paris: Baillière et fils, 1890).

Fārābī, Abū Naṣr al-, *Kitāb ārā' ahl al-madīna al-fāḍila*, ed. Albert Naṣrī Nādir, 7th ed. (Beirut: Dār al-Mashriq, 1987).

Fenves, Peter, "Of Philosophical Style," *Boundary 2* 30, no. 1 (2003), pp. 67–87.

Finger, Stanley, and Meredith Hustwit, "Five Early Accounts of Phantom Limb in Context: Paré, Descartes, Lemos, Bell, and Mitchell," *Neurosurgery* 52, no. 3 (2003), pp. 675–86.

Fiorentino, Francesco, *Bernardino Telesio; ossia, Studi storici su l'idea della natura nel risorgimento italiano*, 2 vols. (Florence: Monnier, 1872–74).

Foerster, Otfreid, "Ein Fall von elemantarer allgemeiner Somatopsychose (Afunktion der Somatopsyche): Ein Beitrag zur Frage der Bedeutung der Somatopsyche für das Wahrnehmungsvermögen," *Monatsschrift für Psychiatrie und Neurologie* 14 (1903), pp. 189–205.

Fortenbaugh, William W., "Aristotle: Animals, Emotion, and Moral Virtue," *Arethusa* 4 (1971), pp. 137–65.

357

Foucault, Michel, *Histoire de la sexualité*, vol. 3, *Le souci de soi* (Paris: Gallimard, 1984).

Fraisse, Jean-Claude, *Philia: La notion d'amitié dans la philosophie antique; Essai sur un problème perdu et retrouvé* (Paris: Vrin, 1974).

Franco, Luigi de, *Introduzione a Bernardino Telesio* (Catanzaro: Rubbettino, 1995).

Frank, Richard M., "The Origin of the Arabic Philosophical Term 'Anniya,'" *Cahiers de Byrsa* 6 (1956), pp. 181–201.

Frede, Michael, "Observations on Perception in Plato's Later Dialogues," *Essays in Ancient Philosophy* (Minneapolis: University of Minnesota Press, 1987), pp. 3–8.

Frege, Gottlob, review of *Das Princip der Infinitesimal-Methode und seine Geschichte: Ein Kapitel zur Grundlegung der Erkenntnisskritik* by Hermann Cohen, *Zeitschrift für Philosophie und philosophische Kritik* 87 (1885), rpt. in *Kleine Schriften* (Hildesheim: Olms, 1990), pp. 99–102.

Furlani, G., "Avicenna e il 'Cogito, ergo sum' di Cartesio," *Islamica* 3 (1927), pp. 53–72.

Gadamer, Hans-Georg, *Truth and Method*, trans. rev. by Joel Weinsheimer and Donald G. Marshall, 2nd rev. ed. (New York: Continuum, 2004).

Galindo-Aguilar, E., "'L'homme volant' d'Avicenne et le 'Cogito' de Descartes, *Institut des Belles Lettres Arabes* 21 (1958), pp. 279–95.

Gantar, Kajetan, "Amicus sibi I: Zur Entstehungsgeschichte eines ethischen Begriffs in der antiken Literatur," *Živa antika* 16 (1966), pp. 135–74.

———, "Amicus sibi II," *Živa antika* 17 (1967), pp. 49–80.

Gätje, Helmut, "Die 'inneren Sinne' bei Averroes," *Zeitschrift der Deutschen Morgenländischen Gesellschaft* 115, no. 2 (1965), pp. 255–93.

———, *Studien zur Überlieferung der aristotelischen Psychologie im Islam* (Heidelberg: Winter, 1971).

Gennaro, Rocco J., "Leibniz on Consciousness and Self-Consciousness," in Rocco J. Gennaro and Charles Huenemann (eds.), *New Essays on the Rationalists* (New York: Oxford University Press, 1999), pp. 353–71.

Gibb, H.A.R. (ed.), *Encylopaedia of Islam*, 12 vols. (Leiden: Brill, 1986).

Gilson, Étienne, *Index scolastico-cartésien*, 2nd rev. ed. (Paris: Vrin, 1979).

———, "Les sources gréco-arabes de l'augustinisme avicennisant," *Archives d'histoire doctrinale et littéraire du Moyen Âge* 4 (1929), pp. 5–107.

———, "Notes sur Campanella," *Annales de philosophie chrétienne* 165 (1913), pp. 491–513.

Görgemanns, Herwig, "*Oikeiōsis* in Arius Didymus," in William W. Fortenbaugh (ed.), *On Stoic and Peripatetic Ethics: The Work of Arius Didymus* (New Brunswick, NJ: Transaction, 1983), pp. 165–89.

Griesinger, Wilhelm, *Die Pathologie und Therapie der psychischen Krankheiten* (Stuttgart: Krabbe, 1845).

Grimsley, Ronald, "Turgot's Article 'Existence' in the *Encyclopédie*," in Will Moore, Rhoda Sutherland, and Enid Starkie (eds.), *The French Mind: Studies in Honour of Gustave Rudler* (Oxford: Clarendon, 1952), pp. 126–51.

Gruithuisen, Franz von Paula, *Anthropologie; oder, Von der Natur des menschlichen Lebens und Denkens für angehende Philosophen und Aerzte* (Munich: Lentner, 1810).

Guéroult, Martial, "Animaux-machines et cybernétique," *Études sur Descartes, Spinoza, Malebranche et Leibniz*, 2nd ed. (Hildesheim: Olms, 1997), pp. 33–40.

Guerrero, Rafael Ramón, *La recepción árabe del "De Anima" de Aristoteles: al-Kindi y al-Farabi* (Madrid: Consejo superior de investigaciones científicas, 1992).

Gurwitsch, Aron, *Leibniz, Philosophie des Panlogismus* (Berlin: de Gruyter, 1974).

Gusdorf, Georges, *Naissance de la conscience romantique au siècle des Lumières* (Paris: Payot, 1976).

Gutas, Dimitri, *Greek Thought, Arabic Culture: The Graeco-Arabic Translation Movement in Baghdad and Early 'Abbāsid Society (2nd–4th/ 8th–10th centuries)* (London: Routledge, 1998).

Hacking, Ian, *Rewriting the Soul: Multiple Personality and the Sciences of Memory* (Princeton, NJ: Princeton University Press, 1995).

Hadot, Ilsetraut, "Aspects de la théorie de la perception chez les Néoplatoniciens: Sensation (aisthesis), sensation commune (koinè aisthesis), sensibles communs (koiná aistheta) et conscience de soi (synaisthesis)," *Documenti e studi sulla tradizione filosofica medievale* 8 (1997), pp. 33–85.

Haller, Albrecht von, *Dissertation sur les parties irritables et sensibles des animaux*, trans. S.A.D. Tissot (Lausanne: Bosquet, 1755).

Hamacher, Werner, "Des contrées des temps," in Georg Christoph Tholen and Michael O. Scholl (eds.), *Zeit-Zeichen*: *Aufschübe und Interferenzen Zwischen Endzeit und Echtzeit* (Weinheim, Germany: VCH, Acta Humaniora, 1990), pp. 29–36.

Hamilton, William, *The Works of Thomas Reid, D.D., now fully collected, with selections from his unpublished letters*, 2 vols. (Edinburgh: Maclachlan and Stewart, 1846).

Hamlyn, D.W., "Aristotle's Account of Aisthesis in the *De Anima*," *Classical Quarterly* 9, no. 1 (1959), pp. 6–16.

———, "Koine Aisthesis," *Monist* 52, no. 2 (1968), pp. 195–209.

Hardie, W.F.R., "Concepts of Consciousness in Aristotle," *Mind* n.s. 85 (1976), pp. 388–411.

Hegel, G.W.F., *Jenaer Realphilosophie: Vorlesungsmanuskripte zur Philosophie der Natur und des Geistes von 1805–1806*, ed. Johannes Hoffmeister (Hamburg: Meiner, 1967).

———, *Werke*, 21 vols., ed. Eva Moldenhauer and Karl Markus Michel (Frankfurt: Suhrkamp, 1986).

Heidegger, Martin, *Die Grundbegriffe der Metaphysik: Welt, Endlichkeit, Einsamkeit* (Frankfurt: Klostermann, 1983).

———, *Sein und Zeit* (Halle: Niemeyer, 1929).

Heller-Roazen, Daniel, "Philosophy before the Law: Averroës's *Decisive Treatise*," *Critical Inquiry* 32, no. 3 (2006), pp. 412–42.

Henle, Jacob, *Allgemeine Anatomie: Lehre von den Mischungs- und Formbestandtheilen des menschlichen Körpers* (Leipzig: Voss, 1841).

Henry, Michel, *Philosophie et phénoménologie du corps*, 4th ed. (1965; Paris: Presses Universitaires de France, 2001).

Henry, Paul, "Une comparaison chez Aristote, Alexandre et Plotin," in E.R. Dodds (eds.), *Les sources de Plotin* (Geneva: Fondation Hardt, 1960), pp. 429–49.

Herbertz, Richard, *Die Lehre vom Unbewussten im System des Leibniz* (Halle: Niemeyer, 1905).

Hermann, Ludimar, *Handbuch der Physiologie*, 6 vols. (Leipzig: Vogel, 1879–83).

Hierocles, "Ethica Moralia," *Hierokles Ethische Elementarlehre (Papyrus 9780): Nebst den bei Stobäus erhaltenen Ethischen Exzerpten aus Hierokles*, ed. Hans von Arnim (Berlin: Weidmann, 1906).

———, "Ethica Moralia," in Francesco Adorno (ed.), *Corpus dei papiri filosofici greci e latini (CPF): Testi e lessico nei papiri di cultura greca e latina*, pt. 1, *Autori noti*, vol. 2 (Florence: Olschki, 1992).

Hippocrates, *Hippocrates*, vol. 2, *Prognostic, Regimen in Acute Diseases, The Sacred Disease, The Art, Breaths, Law, Decorum, Physician, Dentition, Postscript*, trans. W.H.S. Jones (Cambridge, MA: Harvard University Press, 1923).

Hoffmann, E.T.A., *Lebensansichten des Katers Murr: Nebst fragmentarischer Biographie des Kapellmeisters Johannes Kreisler in zufälligen Makulaturblättern* (Frankfurt: Insel, 1976).

Hübner, Christian Friedrich, *Coenesthesis: Dissertatio inauguralis medica...*, (Halle: Typis Bathianis, 1794).

Inwood, Brad, "Hierocles: Theory and Argument in the Second Century AD," *Oxford Studies in Ancient Philosophy* 2 (1984), pp. 151–84.

Isoldi Jacobelli, Angelamaria, *Tommaso Campanella: "Il diverso filosofar mio"* (Rome: Laterza, 1995).

Israeli, Isaac "Book of Elements," in Salomon Fried, *Sefer ha-yesodot: Das Buch über der Elemente; Ein Beitrag zur jüdischen Religionsphilosophie des Mittelalters...* (Frankfurt: Kaufmann, 1900).

Jalabert, Jacques, "La psychologie de Leibniz: Ses caractères principaux," *Revue philosophique de la France et de l'étranger* 136 (1946), pp. 453–72.

Janet, Pierre, *L'automatisme psychologique: Essai de psychologie expérimentale sur les formes inférieures de l'activité humaine*, 10th ed. (Paris: Alcan, 1930).

———, *De l'angoisse à l'extase: Etudes sur les croyances et les sentiments*, 2 vols. (Paris: Alcan, 1926–28).

———, "Dépersonnalisation et possession chez un psychasthénique" (with F. Raymond), *Journal de psychologie* 1 (1904), pp. 28–37.

———, *Les obsessions et la psychasthénie*, vol. 1. (Paris: Alcan, 1903).

———, "Perte du sentiment de la personnalité" (with F. Raymond), *Journal des practiciens* 12 (1898), pp. 625–30.

———, "Le sentiment de la dépersonnalisation," *Journal de psychologie* 5 (1908), pp. 514–16.

———, and Fulgence Raymond, *Les obsessions et la psychasthénie*, vol. 2 (Paris: Alcan, 1903).

Jean de la Rochelle, *Tractatus de divisione multiplici potentiarum animae*, ed. Pierre Michaud-Quentin (Paris: Vrin, 1964).

Jones, E.G., "The Development of the 'Muscular Sense' Concept during the Nineteenth Century and the Work of H. Charlton Bastian," *Journal of the History of Medicine and Allied Sciences* 27, no. 3 (1972), pp. 298–311.

Jung, Gertrud, "Syneidesis, conscientia, Bewusstsein," *Archiv für die gesamte Psychologie* 89 (1933), pp. 525–40.

Kafka, Franz, *Gesammelte Werke*, 12 vols., ed. Hans-Gerd Koch (Frankfurt: Fischer Taschenbuch, 1994).

Kahn, Charles H., "Sensation and Consciousness in Aristotle's Psychology," in Jonathan Barnes, Malcolm Schofield, and Richard Sorabji (eds.), *Articles on Aristotle*, vol. 4, *Psychology and Aesthetics*, pp. 1–31.

Kannicht, Richard and Bruno Snell (eds.), *Fragmenta adespota: Testimonia volumini 1 addenda, indices ad volumina 1 et 2* (Göttingen: Vandenhoeck & Ruprecht, 1981).

Kant, Immanuel, *Werke*, 12 vols., ed. Wilhelm Weischedel (Frankfurt: Suhrkamp, 1960).

Keil, G., "Sogennante Erstbeschreibung des Phantomschmerzes von Ambroise Paré," *Fortschritte der Medizin* 108 (1990), pp. 62–66.

Kerferd, G.B. "The Search for Personal Identity in Stoic Thought," *Bulletin of the John Rylands University Library of Manchester* 55 (1972), pp. 177–97.

Kilwardby, Roger, *On Time and Imagination: De tempore; De spiritu phantastico*, 2 vols., ed. P. Osmund Lewry (Oxford: Oxford University Press, 1987–93).

Kosman, L.A., "Perceiving that We Perceive: On the Soul III, 2," *Philosophical Review* 84, no. 4 (1975), pp. 499–519.

Krapf, Ernesto, "Sur la dépersonnalisation," *L'encéphale* 40, no. 3 (1951), pp. 217–27.

Krishaber, M., *De la névropathie cérébro-cardiaque* (1873; Nendeln: Kraus Reprint, 1978).

Kröner, Eugen, *Das körperliche Gefühl: Ein Beitrag zur Entwicklungsgeschichte des Geistes* (Breslau: Trewendt, 1887).

Külpe, Oswald, *Outlines of Psychology: Based upon the Results of Experimental Investigation*, trans. Edward Bradford Titchener (London: Sonnenschein, 1895).

Kulstad, Mark, "Leibniz, Animals, and Apperception," *Studia Leibnitiana* 13, no. 1 (1981), pp. 25–60.

———, *Leibniz on Apperception, Consciousness, and Reflection* (Munich: Philosophia, 1991.)

———, "Some Diffficulties in Leibniz's Definition of Perception," in Michael Hooker (ed.), *Leibniz: Critical and Interpretative Essays* (Minneapolis: University of Minnesota Press, 1982), pp. 65–78.

———, "Two Arguments on *Petites Perceptions*," *Rice University Studies* 63, no. 4 (1977), pp. 57–68.

Labarrière, Jean-Louis, *Langage, vie politique et movement des animaux: Études aristotéliciennes* (Paris: Vrin, 2004).

Lacan, Jacques, *Le moi dans la théorie de Freud et dans la technique de la psychanalyse*, 1954–1955, ed. Jacques-Alain Miller (Paris: Seuil, 1978).

———, *Les psychoses*, 1955–1956, ed. Jacques-Alain Miller (Paris: Seuil, 1981).

La Forge, Louis de, *Traitté de l'esprit de l'homme, de ses facultez et fonctions, et de son union avec le corps* (1666; facsimile rpr., Hildesheim: Olms, 1984).

Lamarck, Jean-Baptiste de, *Système analytique des connaissances positives de l'homme* (Paris: Presses Universitaires de France, 1988).

Lautner, Peter, "Plutarch of Athens on *koinē aisthēsis* and Phantasia," *Ancient Philosophy* 20, no. 2 (2000), pp. 425–46.

———, "Rival Theories of Self-Awareness in Late Neoplatonism," *Bulletin of the Institute of Classical Studies* 39 (1994), pp. 107–16.

Leibniz, Gottfried Wilhelm, *Opera Omnia*, 6 vols., ed. Louis Dutens (1768; Hildesheim: Olms, 1989).

———, *Die mathematischen Schriften*, 7 vols., ed. C.J. Gerhardt (1849–63; Hildesheim: Olms, 1962).

———, *Die philosophischen Schriften*, 7 vols., ed. C.J. Gerhardt (1875–90; Hildesheim: Olms, 1978).

———, *Sämtliche Schriften und Briefe* (Berlin: Akademie, 1923).

Lelarge de Lignac, Joseph-Adrien, *Éléments de métaphysique tirés de l'expérience; ou, Lettres à un matérialiste sur la nature de l'âme* (Paris: Desaint & Saillant, 1753).

———, *Le témoignage du sens intime et de l'expérience opposé à la foi profane et ridicule des fatalistes modernes*, 3 vols. (Auxerre: Fournier, 1760).

Lenhossék, Míhaly Ignácz, *Physiologia medicinalis*, 5 vols. (Pest: Trattner, 1816–18).

Le Roy, Georges, *La psychologie de Condillac* (Paris: Boivin, 1937).

Lévinas, Emmanuel, *De l'existence à l'existant*, 2nd ed. (Paris: Vrin, 1998).

Libera, Alain de, "Le sens commun au XIIIe siècle: De Jean de la Rochelle à Albert le Grand," *Revue de Métaphysique et de Morale* 4 (1991), pp. 475–96.

Lloyd, A.C., "Nosce Teipsum and Conscientia," *Archiv für Geschichte der Philosophie* 45, no. 2 (1964), pp. 188–200.

Locke, John, *Essai philosophique concernant l'entendement humain*, ed. Émilienne Naert, trans. Pierre Coste (1700; Paris: Vrin, 1998).

———, *An Essay Concerning Human Understanding*, ed. Peter H. Nidditch (Oxford: Oxford University Press, 1975).

Long, A.A., "Representation and the Self in Stoicism," in Stephen Everson (ed.), *Psychology* (Cambridge: Cambridge University Press, 1991), pp. 102–20.

———, "Hierocles on Self-Perception," *Stoic Studies* (Cambridge: Cambridge University Press, 1996), pp. 250–63.

————, "Soul and Body in Stoicism," *Phronesis* 27, no. 1 (1982), pp. 34–57.

Lovering, Joseph P., S. *Weir Mitchell* (New York: Twayne, 1971).

Lyons, M.C. (ed.), *An Arabic Translation of Themistius' Commentary on Aristotle's De Anima* (Oxford: Cassirer, 1973).

Magrelli, Valerio, *Vedersi vedersi: Modelli e circuiti visivi nell'opera di Paul Valéry* (Turin: Einaudi, 2002).

Maine de Biran, Pierre, *Oeuvres*, 13 vols., ed. François Azouvi (Paris: Vrin, 1984).

Marchl, Paul, *Des Aristoteles Lehre von der Tierseele* (Metten: n.p., 1897)

Marion, Jean-Luc, *Questions cartésiennes*, 2 vols. (Paris: Presses Universitaires de France, 1991–96).

————, *Sur l'ontologie grise de Descartes: Science cartésienne et savoir aristotélicien dans les Regulae*, 2nd rev. ed. (Paris: Vrin, 1981).

Marmura, Michael, "Avicenna's Flying Man in Context," *Monist* 69, no. 3 (1986), pp. 383–95.

Matthews, G.B., "Si fallor, sum," in R.A. Markus (ed.), *Augustine: A Collection of Critical Essays* (Garden City, NY: Anchor, 1972), pp. 151–67.

Mayer-Gross, W., "On Depersonalization," *British Journal of Medical Psychology* 15 (1935), pp. 103–22.

McRae, Robert, *Leibniz: Perception, Apperception, and Thought* (Toronto: University of Toronto Press, 1976).

Merleau-Ponty, Maurice, *Phénoménologie de la perception* (Paris: Gallimard, 1945).

————, *L'union de l'âme et du corps chez Malebranche, Biran et Bergson*, 2nd rev. ed. (Paris: Vrin, 2002).

————, *Le visible et l'invisible, suivi de notes de travail*, ed. Claude Lefort (Paris: Gallimard, 1964).

Michael of Ephesus, *In Parva naturalia commentaria*, ed. Paul Wendland (Berlin: Reimer, 1903).

Michaux, Henri, *Oeuvres complètes*, 3 vols., ed. Raymond Bellour with Ysé Tran (Paris: Gallimard, 1998–2004).

Modrak, Deborah K.W., "An Aristotelian Theory of Consciousness?" *Ancient Philosophy* 1, no. 2 (1986), pp. 160–69.

————, *Aristotle: The Power of Perception* (Chicago: University of Chicago Press, 1987).

Mondolfo, Rodolfo, *La comprensione del soggetto umano nell'antichità classica*, trans. Lavinia Bassi (Florence: Nuova Italia, 1958).

————, "L'unité du sujet dans la gnoséologie d'Aristote," *Revue philosophique de la France et de l'étranger* 143 (1953), pp. 359–78.

Montaigne, Michel de, *Oeuvres complètes*, ed. Albert Thibaudet and Maurice Rat (Paris: Gallimard, 1962).

Montebello, Pierre, *La décomposition de la pensée: Dualité et empirisme chez Maine de Biran* (Grenoble: Millon, 1994).

Moraux, Paul, review of *Tre studi sull'aristotelismo nel secolo II d. C.* by Pierluigi Donini, *Gnomon* 50, no. 6 (1978), pp. 532–36.

Morselli, Enrico, *Manuale di semejotica delle malattie mentali: Guida alla diagnosi della pazzia per i medici, i medici-legisti e gli studenti*, vol. 1, *Generalità: Esame anamnestico, somatico e fisiopatologico degli alienati*, 2nd ed. (Milan: Vallardi, 1898).

Mortier, Roland, "À propos du sentiment de l'existence chez Diderot et Rousseau: Notes sur un article de l'*Encyclopédie*," *Diderot Studies* 6 (1964), pp. 183–95.

Moses ben Solomon of Salerno, *Un glossario filosofico ebraico-italiano del XIII secolo*, ed. Giuseppe Sermoneta (Rome: Ateneo, 1969).

Movia, Giancarlo, *Due studi sul De Anima di Aristotele* (Padua: Antenore, 1974).

Mulsow, Martin, *Frühneuzeitliche Selbsterhaltung: Telesio und die Naturphilosophie der Renaissance* (Tübingen: Nimeyer, 1998).

Murray, James Augustus Henry, *The Compact Edition of the Oxford English Dictionary* (Oxford: Oxford University Press, 1971).

Naert, Émilienne, *Mémoire et conscience chez Leibniz* (Paris: Vrin, 1961).

Neuhaeuser, Joseph, *Aristoteles' Lehre von dem sinnlichen Erkenntnisvermögen und seinen Organen* (Leipzig: Koschny [Heimanns], 1878).

Nuyens, François, *L'evolution de la psychologie d'Aristote* (Louvain: Institut supérieur de philosophie, 1948).

O'Daly, Gerard, *Augustine's Philosophy of Mind* (London: Duckworth, 1987).

Osborne, Catherine, "Aristotle, *De Anima* 3.2: How Do We Perceive That We See and Hear?" *Classical Quarterly* n.s. 33, no. 2 (1983), pp. 401–11.

Paré, Ambroise, *Oeuvres complètes*, 3 vols., ed. Joseph François Malgaigne (Paris: Baillière, 1840).

Pembroke, S.G., "Oikeiōsis," in A.A. Long (ed.), *Problems in Stoicism* (London: Athlone, 1974), pp. 114–49.

Peters, F.E., *Aristoteles Arabus: The Oriental Translations and Commentaries on the Aristotelian Corpus* (Leiden: Brill, 1968).

Philippson, Robert, "Das 'Erste Naturgemäße,'" *Philologus* 87 (1932), pp. 445–66.

Philo Judaeus (Philo of Alexandria), *Alexander: vel De ratione quam habere etiam bruta animalibus (De animalibus) e versione armeniaca*, ed. and trans. Abraham Terian (Paris: Cerf, 1988).

Philonenko, Alexis, "La loi de continuité et le principe des indiscernables: Étude leibnizienne," *Revue de métaphysique et de morale* 72, no. 3 (1967), pp. 261–86.

Philoponus, John, *Ioannis Philoponi in Aristotelis De anima libros commentaria*, ed. Michael Hayduck (Berlin: Reimer, 1897).

———, *On Aristotle On the Soul* 3.1–8, trans. William Charlton (London: Duckworth, 2000).

Pick, Arnold, "Zur Pathologie des Ich-Bewusstsein: Studie aus der allgemeinen Psychopathologie," *Archiv für psychiatrie und nervenkrankheiten* 38 (1909), pp. 22–33.

Pines, Shlomo, "La conception de la conscience de soi chez Avicenne et chez Abu'l-Barakat al-Baghdadi," *Archives d'histoire doctrinale et littéraire du Moyen Âge* 29 (1954), pp. 21–98.

Plotinus, *Ennéades*, 7 vols., ed. Émile Bréhier (Paris: Belles Lettres, 1924–38).

Plutarch, *Moralia*, trans. Harold Cherniss and William C. Helmbold, vol. 12 (Cambridge: Harvard University Press, 1957).

Pohlenz, Max, *Grundfragen der stoischen Philosophie* (Göttingen: Vandenhoeck & Ruprecht, 1940).

———, *Die Stoa: Geschichte einer geistigen Bewegung*, 2 vols., 2nd ed. (Göttingen: Vandehoeck & Ruprecht, 1955–59).

Porphyry, *De l'abstinence*, vol. 2, *Livres II et III*, ed. and trans. Jean Bouffartigue and Michel Patillon (Paris: Belles Lettres, 2003).

———, *Porphyrios kommentar zur Harmonielehre des Ptolemaios*, ed. Ingemar Düring (Göteborg, Elanders, 1932).

Poulet, Georges, "Le sentiment de l'existence et le repos," in Simon Harvey (ed.), *Reappraisals of Rousseau: Studies in Honor of R.A. Leigh* (Manchester: Manchester University Press, 1980), pp. 37–45.

Praechter, Karl, *Hierokles der Stoiker* (Leipzig: Dietrich, 1901).

Price, Douglas B., and Neil J. Twombly, *The Phantom Limb Phenomenon: A Medical, Folkloric, and Historical Study; Texts and Translations of 10th to 20th Century Accounts of the Miraculous Restoration of Lost Body Parts*, trans. Mary

Chamberlain Osborne (Washington, DC: Georgetown University Press, 1976).

———— (eds.), *The Phantom Limb: An 18th Century Latin Dissertation* (Washington, DC: Georgetown University Press, 1972).

Priscian, *Metaphrasis in Theophrastum*, ed. Ingram Bywater (Berlin: Reimer, 1886).

————, *On Theophrastus on Sense-Perception*, trans. Pamela Huby (London: Duckworth, 1997).

Proust, Marcel, *À la recherche du temps perdu*, ed. Jean-Yves Tadié (Paris: Gallimard, 1999).

————, *Swann's Way*, trans. Lydia Davis (New York: Penguin, 2004).

Ramachandran, V.S., and Sandra Blakeslee, *Phantoms in the Brain: Probing the Mysteries of the Human Mind* (New York: William Morrow, 1998).

Rein, David, *S. Weir Mitchell as a Psychiatric Novelist* (New York: International University Press, 1952).

Resnik, S., "Syndrome de Cotard et dépersonnalisation," *L'information psychiatrique* 46, no. 5 (1970), pp. 461–74.

Ribot, Théodule, *Les maladies de la personnalité*; (Paris: Alcan, 1885).

————, *La psychologie allemande contemporaine*; *École expérimentale* (Paris: Baillière, 1879).

————, *La psychologie des sentiments* (Paris: Alcan, 1896).

Ritter, Joachim, Karlfried Gründer, Gottfried Gabriel, and Rudolf Eisler (eds.), *Historisches Wörterbuch der Philosophie*, 12 vols. (Basel: Schwabe, 1971–).

Robinson, James T., "Gershom ben Solomon of Arles' *Sha'ar ha-Shamayim*: Its Sources and Use of Sources," in Steven Harvey (ed.), *The Medieval Hebrew Encyclopedias of Science and Philosophy: Proceedings of the Bar-Ilan University Conference* (Dordrecht: Kluwer, 2000), pp. 248–74.

Roche, Daniel de la, *Zergliederung der Verrichtungen des Nervensystems als Einleitung zu einer praktischen Untersuchung der Nervenkrankheiten*, trans. Johann Friedrich Alexander Merzdorff (Halle: Curtschen Buchhandlung, 1794–95).

Rodier, Georges, *Aristote, "Traité de l'âme": Commentaire* (1900; Paris: Vrin, 1985).

Rodrigo, Pierre, "Synaisthanesthai: Le point sensible de l'amitié parfaite chez Aristote," *Philosophie* 12 (1986), pp. 35–51.

Rosenthal, Franz, *Das Fortleben der Antike im Islam* (Zurich: Artemis, 1965).

Translated by Emile and Jenny Marmorstein as *The Classical Heritage in Islam* (Berkeley: University of California Press, 1975).

Rousseau, Jean-Jacques, *Oeuvres complètes*, 5 vols., ed. Bernard Gagnebin and Marcel Raymond (Paris: Gallimard, 1959–69).

Rudolphi, Karl Asmund, *Grundriß der Physiologie* (Reutlingen: Mäckenschen, 1830).

Russell, Bertrand, *The Principles of Mathematics* (Cambridge: Cambridge University Press, 1903).

Schäfer, "Bemerkungen zur psychiatrischen Formenlehre," *Allgemeine Zeitschrift für Psychiatrie* 36 (1880), pp. 214–78.

Schiff, Maurizio (Moritz), "Cenestesi," in Paolo Mantegazza (eds.), *Dizionario delle scienze mediche* (Milan: Brigola, 1871–), vol. 1, pt. 2, pp. 626–32.

Schilder, Paul, *The Image and Appearance of the Human Body: Studies in the Constructive Energies of the Psyche* (New York: International University Press, 1950).

———, *Psychoanalysis, Man, and Society*, ed. Lauretta Bender (New York: Norton, 1951).

———, *Selbstbewusstsein und Persönlichkeitsbewusstsein: Eine psychopathologische Studie* (Berlin: Springer, 1914).

Schiller, Francis, "Coenesthesis," *Bulletin of the History of Medicine* 58, no. 4 (1984), pp. 496–515.

Schiller, Jerome, "Aristotle and the Concept of Awareness in Sense Perception," *Journal of the History of Philosophy* 13 (1975), pp. 283–96.

Schroeder, Frederick M., "Conversion and Consciousness in Plotinus, Enneads 5, 1. [10], 7," *Hermes* 114 (1986), pp. 186–95.

———, "Synousia, Synaisthaesis and Synesis: Presence and Dependence in the Plotinian Philosophy of Consciousness," *Aufstieg und Niedergang der römischen Welt* 36, no. 1 (1987), pp. 677–99.

Schumann, Robert, *Kreisleriana: Opus 16*, ed. Ernst Herttrich (Munich: Henle, 2004).

Schwyzer, Hans-Rudolf, "'Bewusst' und 'Unbewusst' bei Plotin," in E.R. Dodds (ed.), *Les sources de Plotin* (Geneva: Fondation Hardt, 1960), pp. 343–90.

Seel, O., "Zur Vorgeschichte des Gewissens-Begriffes im altgriechischen Denken," in Séglas, Jules, "Mélancolie anxieuse avec délire des négations," *Le progrés médical* (1887), pp. 417–19. Horst Kuch (ed.), *Festschrift Franz Dornseiff Zum 65 Geburtststag* (Leipzig: Bibliographisches Institut, 1953), pp. 291–319.

Seneca, Lucius Annaeus, *Lettere a Lucilio*, 2 vols., ed. and trans. Caterina Barone (Milan: Garzanti, 1989).

Sextus Empiricus, *Outlines of Pyrrhonism*, trans. R.G. Bury (Cambridge, MA: Harvard University Press, 1933).

Sharples, Robert W., "Alexander of Aphrodisias: Scholasticism and Innovation," *Aufstieg und Niedergang der römischen Welt* 36, no. 2 (1987), pp. 1177–1243.

Sherrington, Charles Scott, *The Integrative Action of the Nervous System*, 2nd ed. (New Haven, CT: Yale University Press, 1947).

——, *Man on His Nature* (New York: Macmillan, 1941).

Siebeck, H., "Der Begriff des Bewusstseins in der alten Philosophie," *Zeitschrift für Philosophie und philosophische Kritik* 80 (1882), pp. 213–39.

Sierra, Mauricio, and German E. Berrios, "Depersonalization: A Conceptual History," *History of Psychiatry* 8 (1997), pp. 213–29.

——, "The Phenomenological Stability of Depersonalization: Comparing the Old with the New," *Journal of Nervous and Mental Disease* 189, no. 9 (2001), pp. 629–36.

Simmons, Alison, "Changing the Cartesian Mind: Leibniz on Sensation, Representation and Consciousness," *Philosophical Review* 110, no. 1 (2001), pp. 31–75.

Simplicius of Cilicia, *Simplicii in libros Aristotelis De anima commentaria*, ed. Michael Hayduck (Berlin: Reimer, 1882).

Smith, Andrew, "Unconsciousness and Quasiconsciousness in Plotinus," *Phronesis* 23, no. 3 (1978), pp. 292–301.

Snell, Bruno, review of *Syneidesis-Conscientia* by Friedrich Zucker, *Gnomon* 6 (1930), pp. 21–30, rpt. in *Gesammelte Schriften* (Göttingen: Vandenhoek & Ruprecht, 1966), pp. 9–17.

Solmsen, Friedrich, "αἴσθησις in Aristotelian and Epicurean Thought," *Kleine Schriften*, vol. 1 (Hildesheim: Olms, 1968), pp. 612–33.

Sorabji, Richard, *Animal Minds and Human Morals: The Origins of the Western Debate* (Ithaca, NY: Cornell University Press, 1993).

——, "Aristotle on Demarcating the Five Senses," in Jonathan Barnes, Malcolm Schofield, and Richard Sorabji (eds), *Articles on Aristotle*, vol. 4, *Psychology and Aesthetics* (London: Duckworth, 1979), pp. 77–92.

——, "Body and Soul in Aristotle," *Philosophy* 49 (1947), pp. 63–89.

——, *The Philosophy of the Commentators, 200–600 AD: A Sourcebook*, vol. 1, *Psychology* (London: Duckworth, 2004).

Starobinski, Jean, "Brève histoire de la conscience du corps," in Robert Ellrodt (ed.), *Genèse de la conscience moderne: Études sur le développement de la conscience de soi dans les littératures du monde occidental* (Paris: Presses Universitaires de France, 1983), pp. 215–29.

———, "Le concept de cénesthésie et les idées neuropsychologiques de Moritz Schiff," *Gesnerus* 34, no. 1/2 (1977), pp. 2–20.

———, *Jean-Jacques Rousseau: La transparence et l'obstacle* (Paris: Gallimard, 1971).

Sticker, Anton, *Die Leibnizschen Begriffe der Perception und Apperception* (Bonn: Cohen, 1900).

Striker, Gisela, "The Role of *Oikeiosis* in Stoic Ethics," *Oxford Studies in Ancient Philosophy* 1 (1983), pp. 145–67.

Strohmaier, Gotthard, "Avicennas Lehre von den 'inneren Sinnen' und ihre Voraussetzungen bei Galen," in Paola Manuli and Mario Vegetti (eds.), *Le opere psicologiche di Galeno: Atti del terzo colloquio galenico internazionale*, Pavia, 10–12 September, 1986 (Pavia: Bibliopolis, 1986), pp. 231–42.

Sully, James, *Illusions: A Psychological Study* (New York: Appleton, 1893).

Taine, Hippolyte, *De l'intelligence*, 2 vols., 6th ed. (Paris: Hachette, 1892).

Telesio, Bernardino, *De rerum natura*, 3 vols., ed. Luigi De Franco (Cosenza: Nuova Italia 1965–).

Themistius, *Commentaire sur le traité De l'âme d'Aristote*, ed. Gérard Verbeke (Louvain: Publications Universitaires de Louvain, 1957).

———, *On Aristotle On the Soul*, ed. and trans. Robert B. Todd (London: Duckworth, 1996).

———, *Themistii in libros Aristotelis De Anima paraphrasis*, ed. Richard Heinze (Berlin: Reimer, 1899).

Theophrastus, *Theophrastus of Eresus: Sources for His Life, Writings, Thought, and Influence*, 4 vols., ed. William Wall Fortenbaugh and Andrew Barker (Leiden: Brill, 1993).

Thomas Aquinas, *Commentaria in Aristotelem et alios*, ed. Roberto Busa (Stuttgart: Fromann-Holzboog, 1980).

———, *Commentary on Aristotle's De Anima*, trans. Kenelm Foster and Silvester Humphries (1951; Notre Dame, IN: Dumb Ox Books, 1994).

———, *In Aristotelis librum De anima commentarium*, ed. Angelo Maria Pirotta, 4th ed. (Turin: Marietti, 1959).

———, *Opera Omnia: Iussu impensaque, Leonis XIII P.M. Edita* (Rome: Ex Typographia Polyglotta, 1882–).

Thompson, D'Arcy Wentworth, *A Glossary of Greek Fishes* (London: Oxford University Press, 1947).

Tilliette, Xavier, "Nouvelles réflexions sur le cogito biranien," *Revue de métaphysique et de morale* 4 (1983), pp. 436–46.

Turgot, Anne-Robert-Jacques, "Existence," in Denis Diderot (ed.), *Encyclopédie: Dictionnaire raisonnée des sciences, des arts et des métiers* (Paris: Briasson, 1756), vol. 6, pp. 260–67.

Valéry, Paul, *Cahiers*, 29 vols. (Paris: Centre National de Recherches Scientifiques, 1957).

————, *Cahiers*, 2 vols., ed. Judith Robinson, 2nd ed. (Paris: Gallimard, 1974).

Vancourt, Raymond, *La théorie de la connaissance chez Maine de Biran: Réalisme biranien et idéalisme*, 2nd ed. (Paris: Montaigne, 1944).

Vasiliu, Anca, *Du Diaphane: Image, milieu, lumière dans la pensée antique et médiévale* (Paris: Vrin, 1987).

Weber, Ernst Heinrich, *E.H. Weber on the Tactile Senses*, ed. and trans. Helen E. Ross and David J. Murray, 2nd ed. (Erlbaum, UK: Taylor and Francis, 1996).

————, *Tastsinn und Gemeingefühl*, ed. Ewald Hering (Leipzig: Engelmann, 1905).

Weckowicz, Thaddeus, "Depersonalization," in Charles G. Costello (ed.), *Symptoms of Psychopathology: A Handbook* (New York: Wiley, 1970), pp. 152–66.

Weir Mitchell, Silas. "The Case of George Dedlow," *Atlantic Monthly* 18, no. 150 (1866), pp. 1–11.

————, *Injuries of Nerves and Their Consequences* (New York: Dover, 1965).

————, "Phantom Limbs," *Lippincott's Magazine* 8 (1871), pp. 563–69.

Wiesner, Jürgen, "The Unity of the Treatise *De Somno* and the Physiological Explanation of Sleep in Aristotle," in G.E.R. Lloyd and G.E.L. Owen (eds.), *Aristotle on Mind and the Senses: Proceedings of the Seventh Symposium Aristotelicum* (Cambridge: Cambridge University Press, 1978), pp. 243–80.

Wolff, Christian Freiherr von, *Psychologia empirica* (Hildesheim: Olms, 1738).

Wolfson, Harry Austryn, "The Internal Senses in Latin, Arabic, and Hebrew Philosophic Texts," *Harvard Theological Review* 28, no. 2 (1935), pp. 69–133, rpt. in *Studies in the History of Philosophy and Religion*, vol. 1 (Cambridge, MA: Harvard University Press, 1973), pp. 250–314.

Zeller, A., "Über einige Hauptpunkte in der Erforschung und Heilung der Seelenstörungen," *Zeitschrift für die Beurtheilung und Heilung der krankhaften Seelenzustände* 1 (1838), pp. 515–69.

Zone Books series design by Bruce Mau
Typesetting by Archetype
Image placement and production by Julie Fry
Printed and bound by Maple-Vail